THE SCIENCE AND TECHNOLOGY OF FOODS

FOODS

FOURTH EDITION

ONE WEEK LOAN

THE SCIENCE AND TECHNOLOGY OF
FOODS
FOURTH EDITION

written by
R K PROUDLOVE

with contributions from
SUZAN GREEN

FORBES PUBLICATIONS

The Science and Technology of Foods Fourth Edition
(Revised and Enlarged for the GCE A/S and A-Level Examination)

written by R K Proudlove
with contributions from Suzan Green

© Forbes Publications 2001
Abbott House
1-2 Hanover Street
London
W1S 1YZ

ISBN 1 899527 20 6

Printed in Great Britain by Bell and Bain Ltd,
Glasgow

Acknowledgement

My thanks to Susan Green BSc MSc, Senior Lecturer in Consumer
Behaviour, Centre for Food, Sheffield Hallam University UK, for her
valuable contributions in Consumer Product Management.

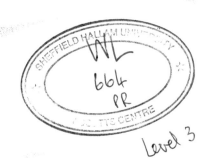

CONTENTS

Preface

Today's food industry produces a vast range of products. New product development is a continuous process and the life-span of new food products today can be relatively short. Consumers demand choice, variety, convenience and, above all, safety. To achieve these objectives the food industry makes use of food technology and all its constituent disciplines and related areas.

For the 21st century food technology is, and will increasingly become, a vital subject area.

Changes in demands for subject knowledge means that the teaching of food-related topics is beginning, increasingly, with younger and younger age groups so that children can acquire the learning to enable more effective consumer understanding.

By using aspects of food technology, the food industry is able to deal with the variety of threats and problems, which arise periodically and, frequently, unpredictably. For example, the emergence of new pathogens gaining access to food products is a major issue. Problems have emerged associated with *E. coli* but others are appearing, such as a very resistant organism *Salmonella typhimurium DT104.*

The topic of food features more and more frequently in newspaper headlines, and the demand for food technology skills grows.

Food technology is an exciting subject with numerous interesting areas, challenges and variety. When I first started writing about the science and technology of foods I could not have foreseen the rapid developments which have lead to the creation of the many worthwhile and awarding careers offered within the food industry today.

Many thanks to my colleague, Suzan Green, for her contribution to the material on consumer product management, which meets new developing subject requirements. Whether you are learning about the science and technology of foods as a dedicated subject choice or because of its relevance to many other subjects, I welcome all readers to the fascinating and fast changing world of food technology.

R.K Proudlove

Section 1
THE COMPOSITION OF FOODS

The majority of foods are complex mixtures of a large number of different compounds. However, these mixtures are rarely constant. The chemical composition of a fruit, for example, will vary according to variety, stage of ripeness, climate, growing conditions, position on the tree and even in some cases atmospheric pressure. Similarly, the composition of cows' milk varies according to breed, stage of lactation, diet and time of year. Figures quoted for levels of a component in a food are often only average figures and an analysis of the food may give a somewhat different figure.

The general composition of foods is summarized in Figure 1, and, with the exception of dried and concentrated foods, water is always the main component, often 80-90% by weight of the food.

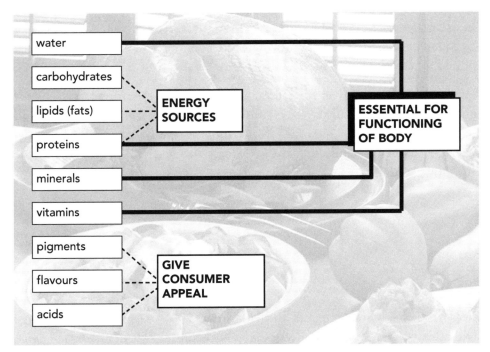

Figure 1
The composition of foods

In addition to the components listed in Figure 1, most manufactured or processed foods contain a number of additives to fulfil various functions.

A particular food component, itself, may be made up of a large number of smaller components; for example a fruit flavour may have over 100 different constituents.

Chapter 1

Water

PREVIEW

- Structure of the water molecule

- Hydrogen bonding

- Linking of the polymers by hydrogen bonds

Although water is the main component of most foods, surprisingly many other food components, *eg* fats, proteins, some vitamins and pigments are unable to dissolve in it. As well as being essential to life, water plays a very important role in the behaviour of foods, particularly during cooking and processing.

In order to understand why water is important in food in this way let us first consider its structure. The water molecule contains two atoms of hydrogen bound to one atom of oxygen by the sharing of electrons.

However, the oxygen atom has the ability to attract electrons towards itself and so the sharing of the electrons is uneven between the oxygen and hydrogen atoms. This has the effect of giving the oxygen atom a partial negative charge (δ-) and the hydrogen atoms a corresponding positive charge (δ+) to balance this.

Figure 1.1

Structure of a water molecule

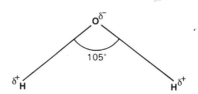

A 'North Pole' of a magnet will attract a 'South Pole' and similarly a d- charge will attract a δ+. This weak electrostatic attraction is called a *hydrogen bond*, and is usually represented by three dashes in line, as shown in Figure 1.2.

Figure 1.2

Hydrogen bond

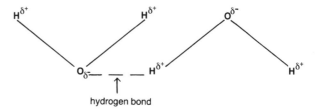

In water, hydrogen bonds are constantly being formed and then broken. If the temperature rises, molecular movement increases and so hydrogen bonds decrease. Conversely, as the temperature falls water molecules move less so more hydrogen bonds form until finally so many exist that water solidifies into ice.

Hydrogen bonding occurs widely in foods and is responsible for some very important phenomena. For example, hydrogen bonds are involved in the gelatinisation of starch, the setting of jams and the tenderness of steak. Although these bonds are very weak they often occur in considerable numbers and therefore can have a combined effect in a food. A common example found in many food products is the linking together of long polymer chains such as polysaccharides. The hydrogen bonding may link directly from one chain to the next by the means of hydroxyl groups (OH) or may involve a water molecule as a bridge.

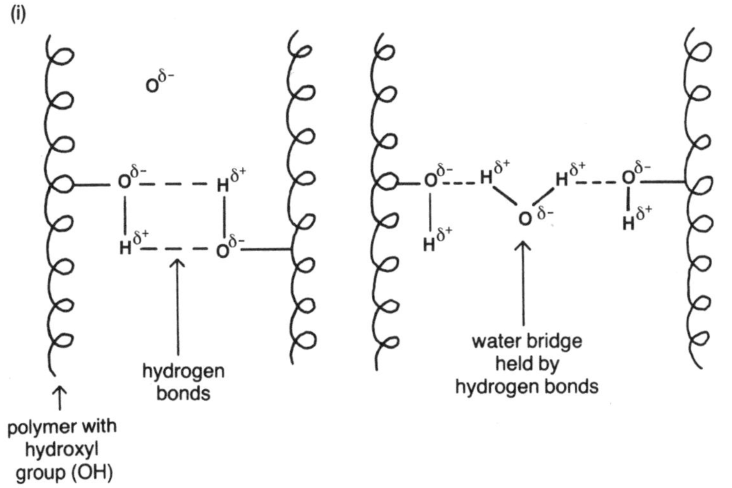

Figure 1.3
Linking of polymers by hydrogen bonds

(Please see sections on the gelatinisation of starch and the gelling of pectin.)

Chapter 2
Carbohydrates

PREVIEW

- Carbohydrates – $C_x(H_2O)y$

- Sugars – monosaccharides – glucose, fructose
  – disaccharides – maltose, sucrose, lactose

- Non-sugars – simple polysaccharides – starch, cellulose, glycogen
  – complex polysaccharides – pectin, gums

- A reducing sugar, *eg* glucose, breaks down Fehling's solution to give red precipitate

- Sucrose – non-reducing sugar

- Optical activity – dextrorotatory, glucose (+)   – hence dextrose (+)
  – laevorotatory, fructose (-)   – hence laevulose (-)

- Inversion of sucrose – sucrose→glucose+fructose

- Invert sugar = glucose + fructose

- Maltose = glucose+glucose, combined by α, 1-4 glycosidic link

- Lactose = galactose+glucose, combined by β, 1-4 glycosidic link

- Sucrose = glucose+fructose, combined by α, 1-2 glycosidic link

- Starch – chains of α–glucose

- Starch – two types – amylose – straight chains but in form of coil
  – amylopectin – highly branched 'like a tree'

- Diastase = α–amylase + β–amylase

- Breakdown starch to dextrins and maltose

- Starch gelatinisation – faster with larger starch granules, easier with amylose

- Hydrogen bonding of water important in gelatinisation

- Retrogradation opposite of gelatinisation, water loss from gel known as syneresis

- Cellulose   – chains of β–glucose joined by β, 1-4 glycosidic links

- Glycogen   – chains of α–glucose similar to amylopectin

- Pectin – complex polysaccharide – chains of galacturonic acid in various combinations with methyl-galacturonate

- Pectin gels to form jelly, jams and preserves – depends on: amounts of sugar and pectin, molecular weight of pectin, number of methyl groups, pH

Over half the organic matter on the earth is carbohydrate in one form or another. The most widespread is cellulose. Although cellulose is not digested by humans it is nevertheless important in the diet as a main contributor of dietary fibre. Starch is the most common carbohydrate in human food.

The process of photosynthesis is responsible for producing carbohydrates in plants and is generally represented by a simplified equation:

$$6CO_2 + 12H_2O \xrightarrow[\text{chlorophyll}]{\text{sunlight}} C_6H_{12}O_6 + 6O_2 + 6H_2O$$

In reality a complex series of chemical changes occurs and may continue to produce a whole range of carbohydrates.

In general carbohydrates may be represented as: $Cx(H_2O)_y$. Hence, the name 'hydrates of carbon' or carbohydrates.

There are a number of different types of carbohydrates and the most common ones found in food are given in Table 1.1.

Sugars (sweet)	Monosaccharides	Glucose
		Fructose
	Disaccharides	Maltose
		Sucrose
		Lactose
Non-sugars (not sweet)	Simple Polysaccharides	Starch
		Cellulose
		Glycogen
	Complex Polysaccharides	Pectin
		Gums

Table 1.1

Classification of commonly occurring carbohydrates

SUGARS

MONOSACCHARIDES

These sugars contain from two to seven carbon atoms, but the most common ones in foods contain six (hexoses) and occasionally five carbon atoms (pentoses). The formula: $C_6H_{12}O_6$ refers to any monosaccharide with six carbon atoms and not just to the most common monosaccharide, glucose.

Glucose
Glucose or dextrose occurs widely in fruits, onions, potatoes and is used in many manufactured foods.

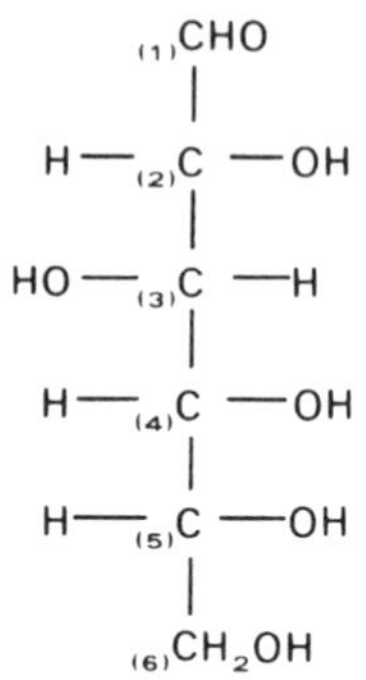

As pointed out above, like all hexoses, the formula of glucose is $C_6H_{12}O_6$ but this conveys very little. Written as a structural formula it can be represented as shown in Figure 1.4.

In reality this straight chain form does not exist, but glucose normally takes the form of a six-sided structure.

Figure 1.4 (above)

Structural formula of glucose

Figure 1.5 (right)

α-glucose and β-glucose

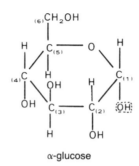

α-glucose

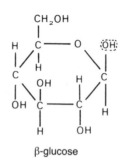

β-glucose

(NB When writing these formulae always check that they add up to $C_6H_{12}O_6$)

There are two forms of glucose shown above: α–glucose with the hydroxyl group (OH) on carbon atom 1 at the bottom, β–glucose with the hydroxyl group at the top. It is important to remember that this is the only difference between the two glucoses shown.

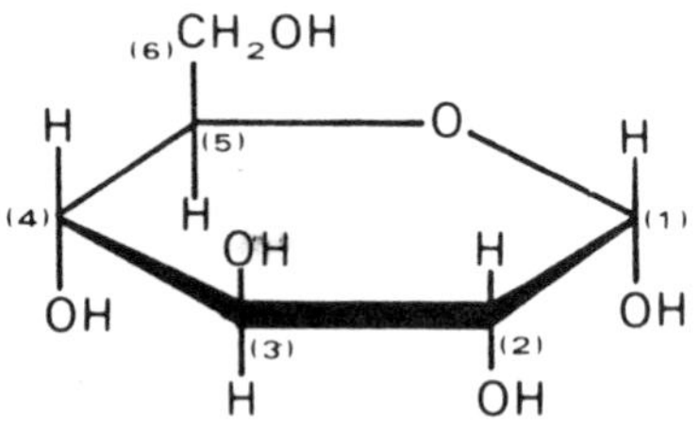

In the ring structure the six-sided figure is represented as a plane at right angles to the paper and the groups of –H and –OH are above or below this plane. It is conventional to miss out the carbon atoms in such a structure and a bend in the ring indicates the presence of a carbon atom as shown in Figure 1.6.

(NB The thick part of the ring is effectively the closest part of the plane to you. This ring structure is called the configuration of glucose)

More recent work has shown that the plane is not flat but has a certain shape and in most cases this shape is said to resemble a 'chair'.

Glucose is a *reducing sugar*. This means it has the ability to break down Fehling's solutions to form a brick red coloured precipitate.

Fehling's solution is, in fact, a mixture of two solutions which have to be mixed at the time of carrying out the test for a reducing sugar:

Fehling's 1(orA) –   copper sulphate solution

Fehling's 2(orB) –   a mixture in solution of sodium hydroxide and
                       Rochelle salt (sodium potassium tartrate).

After mixing equal amounts of the two solutions the sugar is added and boiled. A brick red precipitate of copper I oxide (cuprous oxide) is formed if the sugar is a reducing sugar.

'*Glucose sugar*' is often used in the food industry, particularly in confectionery manufacture. It is never pure glucose but a mixture of glucose, maltose and other carbohydrates of higher molecular weight called dextrins. The terms

(1)–(6) = carbon atoms

Figure 1.6

Ring structure of glucose

dextrose equivalent (DE) is used to indicate the level of glucose and maltose in the syrup. A low DE syrup is less sweet than a high DE syrup, as the latter contains more glucose.

Fructose

Fructose or laevulose is about one and half times sweeter than glucose, but it is often found with glucose in many foods, particularly fruits. It is a reducing sugar and because of its sweetness it is of importance in confectionery manufacture. Both fructose and glucose show *optical activity* in solution. If a plane of polarised light, *ie* light with wave motion in one plane only, is passed through a solution of the sugar, the plane is rotated in one direction. This can be seen using a polarimeter.

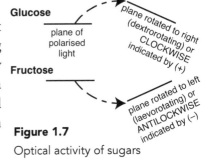

Figure 1.7
Optical activity of sugars

As glucose is dextrorotatory it has the alternate name of dextrose, and similarly the laevorotatory fructose can be called laevulose.

A mixture of equal amounts of glucose and fructose is known as *invert sugar*. Invert sugar occurs naturally in honey and is produced in jams during the boiling of the fruit with sugar. Invert sugar is always produced by the splitting of sucrose (sugar) into equal amounts of fructose and glucose. Bees produce the invert sugar in honey when collecting nectar, which is mainly sucrose, by the action of enzymes in their bodies. Acid in fruit will similarly split sucrose, and the process is called *inversion*.

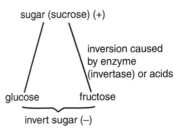

Figure 1.8
Inversion of sucrose

Sugar in solution is dextrorotatory (+). Fructose is more strongly laevorotatory than glucose is dextrorotatory, and therefore sucrose (+)

Fructose is converted or 'inverted' to (-) invert sugar. Hence the term *inversion* is related to the change from (+) to (-) in optical rotation.

Fructose has a difficult structure to remember and this is further complicated by the fact that in the free state fructose is similar to glucose in having a six-sided structure. However, when combined with other sugars, for example with glucose to form sucrose, fructose exists as a five-sided structure.

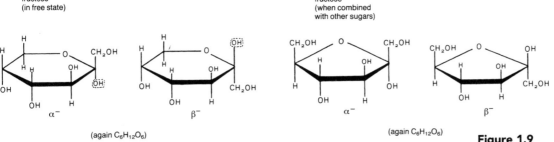

Figure 1.9
Structure of fructose

DISACCHARIDES

Disaccharides are formed from two monosaccharides which may be the same or different. In nature this combination is easily carried out under the control of enzymes, but it is impossible to achieve in the test-tube. Two monosaccharides condense together and eliminate water:

$$C_6H_{12}O_6 + C_6H_{12}O_6 \rightarrow C_{12}H_{22}O_{11} + H_2O$$

Thus, the general formula for all disaccharides, *ie* disaccharides made up of two hexoses (six carbon atoms), is $C_{12}H_{22}O_{11}$. In foods, of the many known disaccharides only three are of importance. These are maltose, lactose and sucrose.

Maltose

Maltose or malt sugar is a simple disaccharide made from two glucose units. The two glucose units are linked across carbon atom (1) on the left-hand glucose to carbon atom (4) on the right-hand glucose.

(NB A β-maltose does exist but is less common; its structure is the same except the OH on the carbon atom on the right-hand side is at the top)

Figure 1.10

Structure of maltose

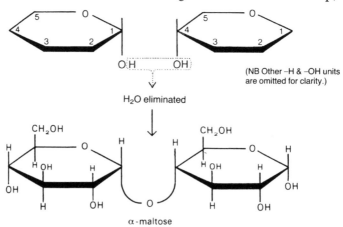

α-maltose

When the two glucoses condense together water is eliminated and the remaining oxygen atom forms a bridge between the two glucoses. This bridge is called a *glycosidic link*. In this case the glycosidic link is called an α, 1-4 link, because the left-hand sugar is an α–form and the link is between carbon atoms 1 and 4 of the two sugars joined.

Figure 1.11

α, 1-4 glycosidic link

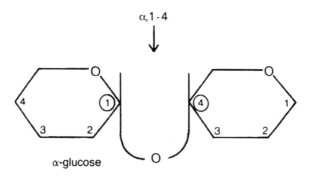

α-glucose

Maltose is a reducing sugar and is produced when starch is broken down by the action of enzymes (amylases), particularly in the malting process of barley for beer making. (See section on starch).

Lactose

This disaccharide is only found in milk. Lactose occurs in different amounts in cows' milk (4-5%), compared with human milk (6-8%). This fact has to be taken into account when manufacturing baby food from cows' milk. Lactose, in its pure state, is a white crystalline solid. Crystals of lactose can sometimes be found in cans of sweetened condensed milk.

After concentrating milk by evaporating some of the water it contains, a large amount of sugar (sucrose) is added to preserve the product. Sucrose is more soluble than lactose in water, and as there is limited water available, the lactose is forced out of the solution. If the lactose crystallises slowly it may form crystals as big as marbles. However, it is usual to seed the sweetened condensed milk with very small crystals of lactose which causes the lactose to crystallize out quickly and thus only form very small crystals which can hardly be noticed.

Lactose is reducing sugar and is composed of the two monosaccharides, galactose and glucose. The galactose is in the β–form combined with α–glucose to form α–lactose or with β–glucose to form β–lactose.

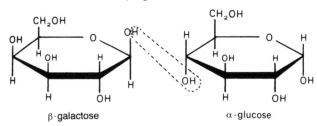

β·galactose

α·glucose

(note the only difference with β-glucose is on carbon atom 4)

α·lactose

In the case of lactose the glycosidic link is a β, 1–4 link as the galactose on the left is in the β-form

etc

β·lactose

Figure 1.12

Structure of lactose

Sucrose

Ordinary sugar is almost pure sucrose. Less refined sugar, found sometimes in overseas countries, is sweeter because it contains some invert sugar. Sucrose produced from sugar beet or from sugar cane, after refining, is exactly the same product. Most sugar in this country is now produced from beet, which needs over twice the land area to produce the same amount of sugar as cane. The consumption of sugar, although less in recent years, is still at too high a level. Everyone is aware that too many sweets and too much sugar lead to tooth decay, but there may be more serious consequences of high sugar intake. It was thought that there was a direct correlation between sucrose intake and coronary heart disease, but this is now disputed. However, sucrose does cause an increase in blood fatty acids and high levels of these have been implicated in heart disease.

Figure 1.13

Structure of Sucrose

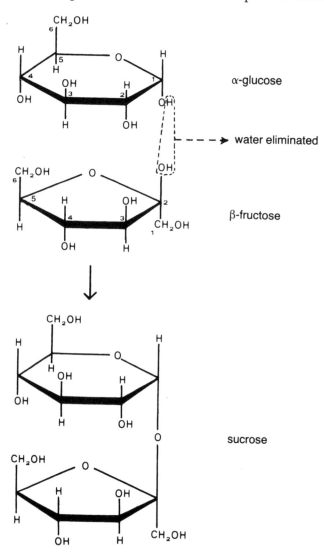

Sucrose is **not** a reducing sugar. Its structure is built from α–glucose and β–fructose and there is only one sucrose because of the unusual linking of the two monosaccharides. In this combination the fructose has a five-sided structure. (The formula is difficult to remember, but it is easier to show the structure by placing the structure of glucose above that of fructose.)

The glycosidic link is an α, 1-2 link, which is unusual. Sucrose is the basis of a very large confectionery industry. Most types of confectionery are made from sugar which has been crystallised in a controlled manner from boiled syrup.

NON-SUGARS

SIMPLE POLYSACCHARIDES

Simple polysaccharides are long chains of one type of monosaccharide joined together. They are, therefore, big molecules and consequently insoluble in water. Usually these polysaccharides exist as long chains with their component monosaccharide units joined together with 1-4 glycosidic links (as we saw in the case of maltose). Occasionally there may be branches in the chains formed by 1-6 glycosidic links, and very occasionally by 1-2 or 1-3 links.

The general formula of the main simple polysaccharides in foods is $(C_6H_{10}O_5)n$ where n can be many thousands of monosaccharide units. There are three polysaccharides of importance in this group; starch, cellulose and glycogen.

Starch

Starch is the energy reserve of plants. It is converted, when required, into sugars, particularly maltose and glucose. All plant storage organs are rich in starch, particularly seeds, tubers and unripe fruits. Starch is always accompanied by enzymes which can readily break it down and these can cause problems in food manufacture.

Starch exists in granules which are unique, in shape and size, to a particular plant source. It is possible by using a low power microscope to identify a particular type of starch by its shape and size. Some granules such as rice are small and angular whereas potato granules are large and more spherical.

Starch exists in two structural forms. The simplest form is amylose which is straight chain of α–glucose units. Amylopectin (not to be confused with pectin) is composed of many shorter chains of α–glucose with many branches.

In many plants there are about four times as much amylopectin as amylose. However, the higher the amylose level the easier it is for a starch gel, which is an important property of starch in cooking and food processing.

Amylose is made up of about 300 glucose units joined together, but the number of units varies enormously. The α–glucose units are joined by α, 1-4 glycosidic links to make a chain, but very occasionally a branch may be formed particularly by an α, 1-6 link.

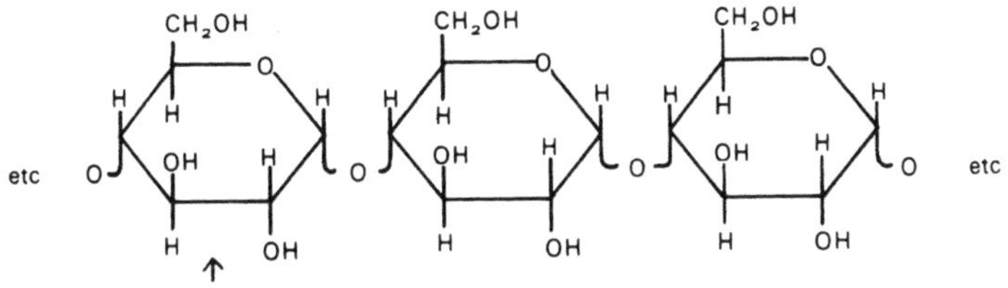

	Amylose content % (by weight)
Waxy mutant maize (corn)	0–6
Rice	16
Tapioca	18
Sweet potato	18-20
Potato	20–23
Wheat	22-25
'Steadfast' pea	65
Sugary mutant maize (corn)	60–70

Table 1.2

Amylose levels in some starches

Figure 1.14

Structure of amylose

Remember that the glucose ring is in reality in the form of a 'chair'. This chair formation tends to cause the chain of glucose units to spiral and there are six glucose units per turn of the spiral.

Amylopectin is a more complex structure and is much larger than amylose, often having several thousand glucose unit components. The glucose units are linked to form short branching chains which again are in spiral form. This tends to give amylopectin a tree-like appearance. The branches in the chains are produced by a, 1-6 glycosidic links.

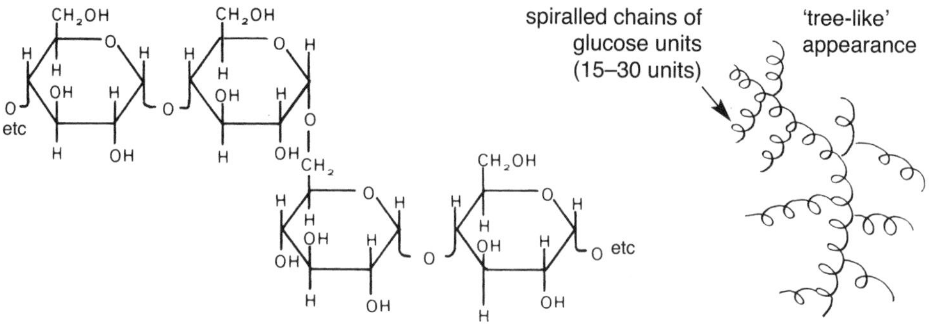

Figure 1.15

Structure of amylopectin

Enzymic breakdown of starch

In plants starch is always accompanied by $\alpha-$ and $\beta-$amylases, known collectively as *diastase*. The two enzyme systems work together rapidly to break down starch to maltose and some dextrins. Although the enzymes work together it is easier to consider their actions separately. $\alpha-$Amylase is also known as liquefying or dextrinogenic amylase. This enzyme rapidly increases its activity during the germination of seeds. In malting of barley germination is encouraged for this reason. This amylase can split a, 1-4 links between the glucose units at random in the chain, thus breaking the chain down into small lengths known as dextrins (about 6-12 glucose units). The a, 1-6 links of amylopectin are by-passed as shown in Figure 1.16

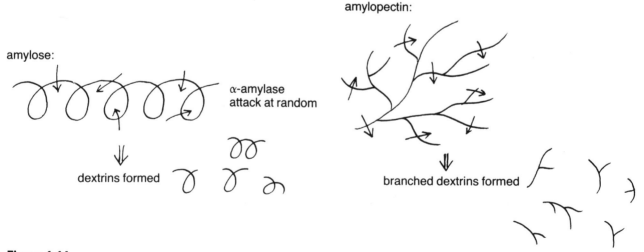

Figure 1.16

Action of α-amylase
(simplified diagram)

If a starch is used, for example, to thicken a soup when manufacturing canned soup it must be heat-treated to ensure no amylase activity is present. If $\alpha-$

amylase is present the starch-thickened soup will suddenly turn back to the viscosity of water as the enzyme breaks down the starch to dextrins.

β-*Amylase* forms maltose from both types of starch. However, the enzyme can only attack starch in an organised manner by removing two glucose units ie maltose, from the free ends of starch molecules. In the case of straight chain amylose molecules the β–amylase will remove maltose units from both ends until all the amylose is converted into maltose. However, in the case of the branched amylopectin, β-amylase is unable to convert completely the starch to maltose because the α, 1-6 links act as a barrier to the action of the enzyme. At each branch, therefore, β-amylase activity is stopped. In the case of amylopectin this will leave a central area in the tree-like molecule untouched by the enzyme. This part of the molecule remaining is called the 'β–limit' dextrin.

In reality, as α- and β-amylase exist together the β–limit dextrin would be attacked by the α–amylase, thus releasing free-ends of the glucose chains for further attack by β-amylase. In this manner the starch will be almost completely broken down to maltose.

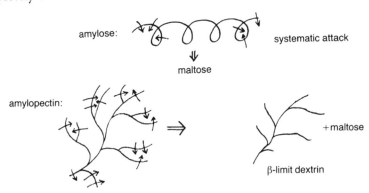

amylose: systematic attack

maltose

amylopectin: +maltose

β-limit dextrin

Figure 1.17

Action of β-amylase

Gelatinisation of starch

A very important property of starch is its ability to form a gel which is able to thicken a large number of foods. Gravies, soups, blancmanges, lemon pie fillings, custards and instant desserts rely on the gelatinisation of starch.

When mixed with cold water starch granules do not dissolve, but just form a suspension. However, when the water is heated the viscosity of the mixture increases, and provided there is enough starch present, a gel is formed. Sometimes a firm gel does not form until the mixture is cooled again.

Starches gel at a certain temperature, called the *temperature of gelatinisation,* but in reality the temperature is a range of temperatures and not usually fixed to a rigid temperature. Large starch granules, e.g. potato, gel more easily and at a lower temperature than small densely packed granules such as those of rice. Amylose gels more easily than amylopectin, and starches rich in amylose consequently gel more easily. Gelatinisation may be divided into three main stages:

Stage 1 – in cold water the starch takes up about 25% (of its own weight) of water.

Stage 2 – occurs about 60 C (depending on starch variety) and the granules swell rapidly, taking up between 3 and 10 times their weight in water.

Stage 3 – so much water has been absorbed (up to 20 times the weight of the granules) that the granules start to split. Starch molecules spill out into the surrounding water and its viscosity increases rapidly. The remaining starch granules stick together to form a three-dimensional network which, on cooling, forms a gel.

Importance of hydrogen bonding

In a starch in water suspension, as in Stage 1, the starch granules are loosely bound together by hydrogen bonds. As the temperature rises molecular movement increases, thus rupturing the weak hydrogen bonds. Water molecules are able to penetrate gradually between the starch molecules. Thus, the starch granules swell, Stage 2, until they burst open, Stage 3. When the temperature falls again water molecules are trapped between the starch molecules. The water molecules effectively help bridge across from one starch chain to another, thus making the three-dimensional gel structure.

If a gel is formed from amylopectin it is done with difficulty because of the tree-like structure of that type of starch. However, gels formed from mainly amylose, on standing show a gradual contraction and the elimination of some of the bound water. This 'weeping' of water from the gel is known as *syneresis* and can sometimes be seen in canned products which have been thickened with starch or flour. The process overall is effectively the reverse of gelatinisation, and is known as *retrogradation*. Starches which are mainly amylopectin are resistant to retrogradation. Starch manufacturers can modify starches rich in amylose by treating them to produce phosphate cross-bonded starches. These starches resemble amylopectin in having the ability to resist retrogradation but gel more easily like amylose.

Figure 1.18

Gelatinisation of starch

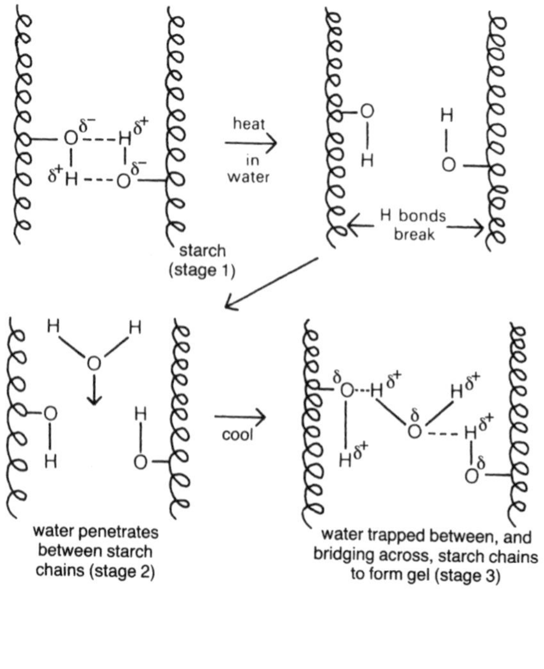

starch
(stage 1)

water penetrates
between starch
chains (stage 2)

water trapped between, and
bridging across, starch chains
to form gel (stage 3)

It is possible for a manufacturer to dry a starch gel to produce what is known as 'pre-gelatinised starch'. On addition of cold water (or milk in some products) the dry powder gelatinises instantly. This is the basis of some instant desserts and quick-cook products, such as some custard mixes.

Cellulose

Cellulose is an important constituent of the diet in supplying roughage or fibre. It has the ability to hold water and thus in the large intestine facilitates the muscular movement of the gut. Highly refined food is low in fibre, whereas 'primitive' foods which tend to be rich in fibre protect against the 'diseases of civilisation' such as obesity, diabetes, diverticular disease and cancer of the colon. There is also evidence that high fibre beneficially affects absorption of nutrients from the gut into the body and may help control blood cholesterol levels. Cellulose is only part of the fibre story; a number of other substances such as hemicelluloses, pectins and gums are involved.

Cellulose gives strength to plants in the form of long fibres. These fibres run in certain directions, particularly in stems, to resist wind, for example. There is another type of cellulose which is amorphous and tends to absorb large amounts of water. This latter fact has been made use of in slimming foods. The cellulose swells in the stomach to give a 'full-feeling', but is not digested.

Cellulose is a very large molecule, often made up of several thousands of monosaccharide units. The monosaccharide unit in cellulose is β–glucose. It is important to notice the difference: starch is composed of α–glucose, cellulose is composed of β–glucose.

The β–glucose units are joined together by β, 1-4 glycosidic links. In cooking and heat processing the rigidity shown by cellulose in plant tissues may be reduced, but cellulose is not generally affected, as for example starch is during its gelatinisation.

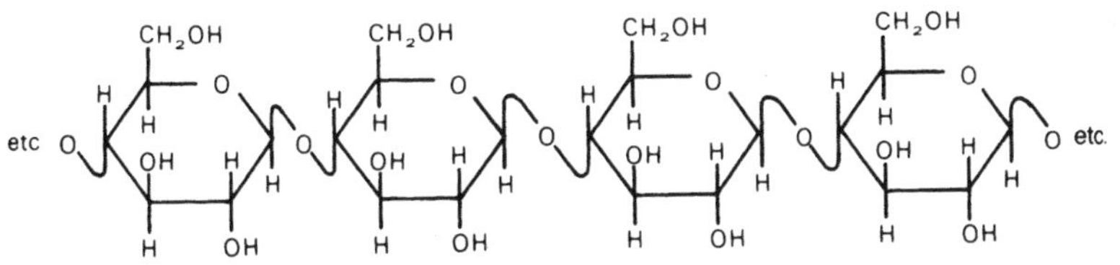

Figure 1.19
Structure of cellulose

Hemicelluloses are complex mixtures of substances which do not form fibres and are found in plants between their cells. They are often polymers of pentoses (5 carbon atoms) such as xylose.

Glycogen

Glycogen, like starch, is a reserve carbohydrate, but is found in animals. It is readily broken down to maltose and α–glucose, which is used up rapidly during muscular activity. Glycogen levels are important in muscle at the time of the animal's slaughter. Insufficient glycogen will produce meat of low acidity which leads to poor colour, poor texture and inferior keeping quality. (See section on conversion of muscle into meat in Commodities and Raw Materials)

Glycogen is a large molecule closely resembling amylopectin, but with very short branched chains of about half the length of those found in amylopectin.

COMPLEX POLYSACCHARIDES

Complex polysaccharides are long chains, sometimes branched with more than one type of monosaccharide joined together. Often these polysaccharides are built up of various derivatives of carbohydrates, particularly uronic acids.

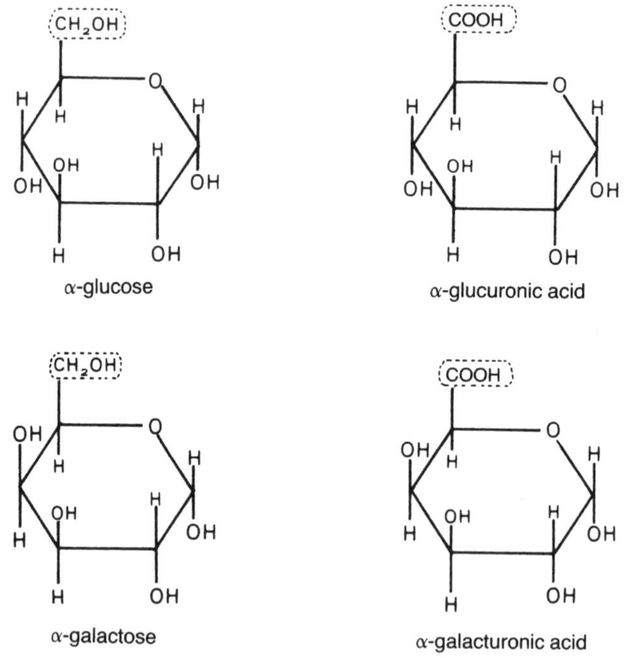

Figure 1.20

Uronic acids and corresponding monosaccharide bases

α-glucose

α-glucuronic acid

α-galactose

α-galacturonic acid

Pectin

Pectin is the most common example of a group of complex polysaccharides. Pectins are essential in jam making, but are also important in many other foods and for various functions. They occur naturally in the middle lamella between plant cells and also in cell walls. They are polysaccharides composed of α–galacturonic acid and its derivate methyl-galacturonate.

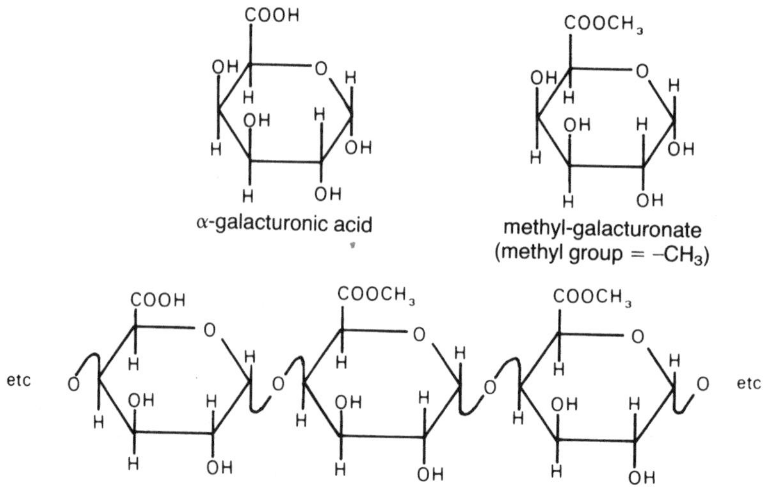

Figure 1.21

Structure of pectin

α-galacturonic acid

methyl-galacturonate
(methyl group = $-CH_3$)

etc   etc

The glycosidic link between the derivatives α–galacturonic acid and methyl-galacturonate is an a, 1-4 link. Note the link is different from that in starch as the right – OH group is at the top.

Pectins are very variable in their composition. Chain lengths are variable and there is an infinite variation in the combination and order of each of the monosaccharide derivative units. Thus, it is impossible to obtain two pectins which are exactly the same.

There are several different types of pectins and their names are somewhat confusing. 'Pectin' and 'Pectic substance' are general names for the whole group. 'Protopectin' is thought to be a parent pectic substance in plants from which other pectic substances are produced. *Pectinic acid* is pectin which contains a considerable number of the methyl-galacturonate units and is the pectin which forms a gel with sugar and acid in jams and other preserves. *Pectic acid* is made up of just α–galacturonic acids with few methyl galacturonates and it is incapable of gelling with sugar and acid. Unripe fruit is rich in pectin and on ripening the protopectin is broken down by enzymes to pectinic acids, then pectic acids, and the chains of units broken. Thus a firm and crisp fruit becomes soft and juicy in its ripe form.

Pectic substances under the right conditions form gels, *ie* jams, jellies (not table jelly which is gelatine based) and preserves. Pectins derived from different sources vary widely in their jelly (gel) forming properties due to the different length of their chains and to the different numbers of methyl groups in their structures. A firm gel depends on:

(1) Amount of sugar   (4) Number of methyl groups
(2) Amount of pectin   (5) pH
(3) Molecular weight of pectin

A good gel is formed when there is sufficient sugar (about 65-68%). The sugar is thought to act as a dehydrating and orientating agent in bringing the pectin chains together and binding up water so that a three-dimensional gel structure can develop.

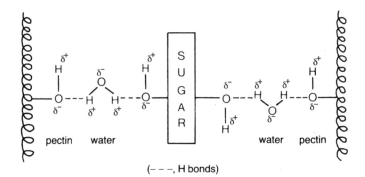

Figure 1.22
Gel structure of jam

Again the importance of hydrogen bonding is seen in building up the gel structure. Some of the sugar is inverted by the natural acid of the fruit, usually under-ripe fruit, to invert sugar. Not only is invert sugar very sweet but it is very soluble in water. Any water will be dissolved in by invert sugar, thus making it unavailable as water-of-crystallisation for the sucrose. Thus the high amount of sucrose does not crystallise out on standing but the jam stays as smooth gel. Obviously, the pectin chains must be long enough to make a three-dimensional network possible. If there are not enough methyl-galacturonate units present then there must be too many α–galacturonic acids which prevent the jam setting. This can occur when using ripe fruit. If the pH of the jam is not around pH3.5, these α–galacturonic acids may ionise, thus:

$$- COOH \rightarrow etc - COO^- + H^+$$

The charged carboxyl units -COO will tend to force the pectin chains apart, preventing gel formation. (Remember like charges repel each other.)

Boiling is carried out in jam making to bring the total dissolved solids, mainly sugar, to be about 68%. Over-boiling will break down the pectin chains and effectively reduce their molecular weights. Low molecular weight pectins will not gel properly.

Some fruits, such as strawberries, are deficient in pectin, so a commercial pectin preparation is added. These are usually prepared from apple residues left from cider making. Some pectins, gel very rapidly and are useful for jams where it is desirable to suspend whole fruits or pieces of fruit in the jam.

Pectin is not always useful; for example, in some wines it may form a permanent haze. In some soft drinks, such as bitter orange, pectin helps to support pieces in the drink and strengthen the 'permanent cloud stability' of the drink.

Gums

Gums are a very diverse group of polysaccharides which have the ability to absorb large quantities of water and form firm gels under the right conditions. Used in foods in small amounts they often act as thickeners, stabilisers and emulsifiers.

Some plants produce gums on their stems or fruit when they are injured. Many of these gums are dried and sold commercially for use as thickeners and adhesives. Common examples of these are gum tragacanth, gum arabic, gum karaya and gum ghatti.

A number of important gums are produced from various seaweeds. Alginic acid, or its more common form sodium alginate, is produced from giant kelp. Another, similar gum is carageenan produced from Irish moss. Both of these gums are used widely as stabilisers in food products such as ice-cream, syrups, processed cheese and salad dressing. Agar, produced from red seaweed, has the ability to absorb enormous amounts of water and to form gels at very low concentrations. Although used as a stabiliser, and to replace gelatine in some confectionery, its main use is in the production of media for the cultivation of micro-organisms.

PRACTICAL EXERCISES: *carbohydrates*

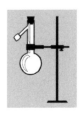

SAFETY – All experiments require care and some involve particular hazards. All chemicals, particularly acids and alkalis, should be handled carefully, and ideally plastic gloves and safety glasses should be worn. The experiments are designed for simple laboratories or test kitchens with a minimum of specialised equipment.

1. Comparison of sweetness

Take sucrose as the standard at a value of 100 and compare the sweetness of a range of sugars, particularly glucose, fructose, lactose and maltose, giving a value to each.

2. Test for all carbohydrates – Molisch reagent

To a solution of a sugar in a test tube add a few drops of Molisch reagent (alpha naphthol in alcohol) and shake well. **Carefully** pour a little concentrated sulphuric acid down the inside of the tube and form a layer under the sugar solution. After standing a purple ring forms between the two layers for all carbohydrates.

3. Test for reducing sugars – Fehling's Test

Mix small but equal amounts of Fehling's 1 and 2 and add small amount of sugar solution. Boil in a water bath for two minutes. *Warning:* Do not boil in a naked flame. A brick-red precipitate is formed, indicating a reducing sugar.

4 Test for monosaccharide – Barfoed's Test

To a solution of a sugar (known reducing sugar) add excess of Barfoed's reagent. Mix and boil in a water-bath for three minutes. A monosaccharide produces a red precipitate and colouration.

5. Test for starch

Disperse some of the sample of starch in water and add a few drops of iodine solution. A dark blue/black colour indicates the presence of starch, but a lighter blue colour indicates a higher concentration of amylose and a brown/black colour the presence of higher amounts of amylopectin.

6. Microscopic examination of starch

Take a small amount of starch (maize, rice, potato, wheat and as available) on the point of a knife, moisten with a drop of alcohol and then add a drop of water, stir and apply a drop to a microscope slide. Cover the drop with a cover-slip and press to ensure a thin layer of starch. A drop of iodine may be added to aid identification of the starch. Compare the different starch granules for shape, size and striations.

7. Gelatinisation of starch

Make a mixture of starch in water (20% by weight). Heat the mixture and note the temperature. Continue to heat until the suspension thickens, record the temperature of gelatinisation. Allow to cool. Note any increase in viscosity of the starch gel.

8. Pectin gels

Warning: during boiling splashing may occur, which could result in painful burns.

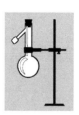

Special requirements:

commercial preparations of pectin, buffer solutions from pH 2.5 to 4.0

Preparation of pectin gel:

Sugar 68g

Buffer solution 150 cm^3

Pectin 0.8g

Add the pectin to the buffer solution, stir well to dissolve. Gradually add sugar with stirring and heating. Boil for about 10 minutes (ideally to reach 68.5% total solids measured with a refractometer)

Variables:

1. Sugar total solids) – vary the sugar content, eg 50, 55, 60, 65g. (Note the effect on gel strength.)
2. pH – vary the pH by using different buffers from pH 2.5 to 4.0
   which pH gives the strongest gel?
3. Pectin quantity – vary the amount of pectin, eg 2, 4, 6 and 8g

Chapter 3
Lipids (fats)

PREVIEW

- Lipids: Simple lipids, eg natural fats, waxes
  Complex lipids eg phospholipids
  Lipoids, eg steroids

- Natural fats – mixtures of mixed triglycerides

- Mixed triglycerides → glycerol + 3 different fatty acids

- Glycerol – structure similar to 'bent tuning fork'

- Saturated fatty acids – acid group (-COOH) plus carbon and hydrogen sometimes in long chains

- Unsaturated fatty acids – contain at least one double bond between two adjacent carbon atoms

- Common saturated fatty acids include stearic, palmitic and myristic

- Most common unsaturated fatty acid is oleic

- Essential fatty acids are linolenic and arachidonic

- Iodine value – measure of unsaturation, ie number of double bonds in fat

- Hydrogenation – eliminates double bonds by adding hydrogen, this hardens a fat or oil

- Interesterification – technique to rearrange fatty acids attached to glycerol

- Monoglyceride = glycerol + one fatty acid
  = glycerol + two fatty acids
  – acts as emulsifying agents eg glyceryl monostearate

- Waxes – esters of long chain alcohols and fatty acids

- Phosphilipids – eg lecithin = glycerol + two fatty acids + phosphoric acid + base eg choline, acts as naturally occurring emulsifying agent

- Lipoids – eg steroids, such as cholesterol

- Body produces about twice its requirement of cholesterol

- Accumulation of cholesterol in blood vessels not necessarily connected with diet

- Rancidity – hydrolytic – caused by enzymes
  oxidative – caused by presence of oxygen, metals eg copper, UV light and heat. Requires unsaturated fatty acids

- Antioxidants – absorb oxygen or stop complex reactions in oxidative rancidity

Lipids form a very large group of vaguely connected compounds. The true fats are the largest sub-group of lipids and are the best source of energy in the diet. Lipids also include compounds, which are vitamins, emulsifying agents, waxes, pigments and antioxidants. All lipids are soluble in organic solvents such as petroleum ether, chloroform or ethyl ether.

Lipids are very widely distributed in foods, even in food not considered to be 'fatty'. Even fruits contain some lipid, in the form of 'cutin', for example, which gives the shine to apples. Nuts are a particularly good source of lipid, for example pecans, groundnuts, and walnuts can contain between 55 and 75% of lipid.

In addition to the naturally occurring lipid in a food, fat is often added during the cooking or preparation of the food. Not only do fats add flavour, carry flavour and add richness but they are a good means of transferring heat in the cooking process.

There are a number of ways of classifying lipids, a simplified classification is given in Table 1.3. It is important to remember that oils and fats are chemically similar. However, oils are liquid at room temperature, whereas fats are solids. In hotter countries some fats will become oils and conversely some oils will be fats in colder countries.

Type	Examples
Simple lipids	Natural fats
	Waxes
Complex lipids	Phospholipids
Lipoids	Steroids

Table 1.3

Classification of lipids

SIMPLE LIPIDS

NATURAL FATS

Fats are chemically placed in a class of substances known as *esters*. Esters are formed by the reaction of an alcohol and an organic acid. In natural fats the alcohol involved is always glycerol (glycerine). Glycerol is a more complex alcohol, compared with ethyl alcohol, in that it has three hydroxyl groups.

In reality glycerol takes the form of a 'bent tuning-fork' as shown in Figure 1.23(b).

Figure 1.23

Structure of glycerol

The acids which react with glycerol can be represented as R-COOH, where –COOH is the acidic carboxyl group. The H of the –COOH will be removed, in effect, and combined with one –OH group from glycerol to form water. The rest of the acid will become attached to the glycerol structure as shown in Figure 1.24.

The resulting ester formed in this reaction is called a triglyceride. If all three fatty acids are the same the triglyceride is called a *simple triglyceride*. Simple

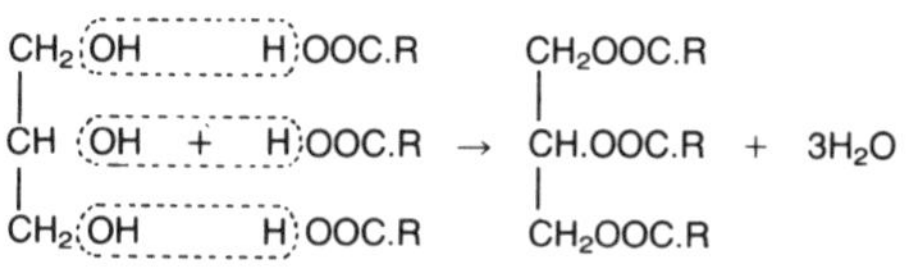

$$
\begin{array}{ccc}
\begin{array}{l}
CH_2\text{-OH} \quad\quad H\text{-OOC.R} \\
CH\text{-OH} + H\text{-OOC.R} \\
CH_2\text{-OH} \quad\quad H\text{-OOC.R}
\end{array}
&\rightarrow&
\begin{array}{l}
CH_2OOC.R \\
CH.OOC.R + 3H_2O \\
CH_2OOC.R
\end{array}
\end{array}
$$

$$
\begin{array}{ccc}
\begin{array}{l}
CH_2\text{-OH} \quad\quad H\text{-OOC.R}^1 \\
CH\text{-OH} + H\text{-OOC.R}^2 \\
CH_2\text{-OH} \quad\quad H\text{-OOC.R}^3
\end{array}
&\rightarrow&
\begin{array}{l}
CH_2OOC.R^1 \\
CHOOC.R^2 + 3H_2O \\
CH_2OOC.R^3
\end{array}
\end{array}
$$

mixed triglyceride

Figure 1.24 (left)

Formation of a simple triglyceride

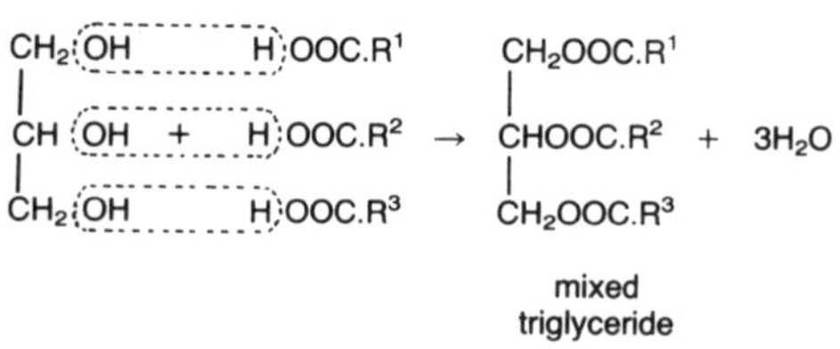

Figure 1.25 (right)

Formation of a mixed triglyceride

triglycerides usually do not occur in fats in foods, as the three acids reacting with glycerol normally are different. In this case a *mixed triglyceride* is formed.

These triglyceride molecules are randomly mixed in a fat, but sometimes they occur in a more organised manner. In chocolate, for example, the triglycerides fit together to form stable fat 'crystal'. If the chocolate is not made satisfactorily then these triglycerides will rearrange themselves, particularly if the chocolate melts, and may separate out onto the surface to form a white 'bloom'.

All natural fats are *mixtures* of *mixed triglycerides*. Therefore, as glycerol is common to all triglycerides, any differences between natural fats will be due to their different combinations of acids with glycerol. These relatively long chain acids are called *fatty acids*. Most fats contain a variety of fatty acids, but usually two or three dominate, and generally oleic acid is one of the main ones.

Table 1.4

Common fatty acids
(a) Saturated fatty acids

No. of Carbon atoms	Name	Systematic name
4	Butyric	Butanoic
6	Caproic	Hexanoic
8	Caprillic	Octanoic
10	Capric	Decanoic
12	Lauric	Dodecanoic
14	Myristic	Tetradecanoic
16	Palmitic	Hexadecanoic
18	Stearic	Octadecanoic

(b) Unsaturated fatty acids

No. of Carbon atoms	Name	Systematic name	No. of double bonds
18	Oleic	9-octadecanoic	1
18	Oleic	9-octadecenoic	1
18	Linoleic	9,12, 15-octadecatrienoic	3

A list of common fatty acids is given in Table 1.4. Most of the common fatty acids have an even number of carbon atoms, but acids do occur rarely with odd numbers of carbon atoms. Some rarer acids may contain 30 carbon atoms.

A saturated fatty acid has an acid group −COOH and only carbon and hydrogen, with each carbon atom attached by single bonds to the next atom. An unsaturated fatty acid contains at least one double bond between two adjacent carbon atoms. Remember that double bonds are a point of weakness, and not strength, in organic molecules as they can readily be broken by a wide range of substances.

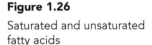

Figure 1.26

Saturated and unsaturated fatty acids

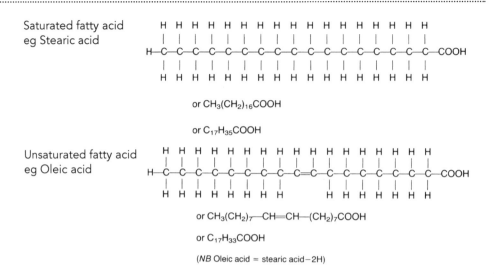

The series of saturated fatty acids is summarised in Table 1.5. Note that the formulae increase by $-(CH_2)_2$ each time.

Fats containing only saturated fatty acids are hard and have melting points about room temperature. Oils contain unsaturated fatty acids and consequently have melting points below room temperature and thus are liquid. However, fats do not melt a fixed temperature but over a range of temperatures. This property gives fats a unique *'plastic'* character. This plasticity results from the fact that fats are a mixture of mixed triglycerides of different melting points. As the temperature rises some triglycerides will melt whereas others remain solid. This allows the solid triglycerides to move within the fat and the fat is 'spreadable'.

Table 1.5

Formulae of saturated fatty acids

No. of Carbon atoms	Name	Formulae
4	Butyric	$CH_3(CH_2)_2COOH$ or C_3H_7COOH
6	Caproic	$CH_3(CH_2)_4COOH$ or $C_5H_{11}COOH$
8	Caprillic	$CH_3(CH_2)_6COOH$ or $C_7H_{15}COOH$
10	Capric	$CH_3(CH_2)_8COOH$ or $C_9H_{19}COOH$
12	Lauric	$CH_3(CH_2)_{10}COOH$ or $C_{11}H_{23}COOH$
14	Myristic	$CH_3(CH_2)_{12}COOH$ or $C_{13}H_{27}COOH$
16	Palmitic	$CH_3(CH_2)_{14}COOH$ or $C_{15}H_{31}COOH$
18	Stearic	$CH_3(CH_2)_{16}COOH$ or $C_{17}H_{35}COOH$

The *Iodine Value* is a measure of the degree of unsaturation, *ie* number of double bonds in a fat. A molecule of iodine will combine with each double bond in a fatty acid. Saturated fats have low iodine values *eg* palm kernel about 15, whereas unsaturated fats have high values *eg* groundnut oil about 90g of iodine per 100g of fat.

Hydrogenation

Some oils are so unsaturated that they are of little use in their natural state. For many years the process of hydrogenation or hardening has been undertaken to remove some of the double bonds in the fatty acids and effectively to make them more saturated. Hydrogenation changes a liquid oil into a solid fat by adding hydrogen across the double bonds in the unsaturated fatty acid molecules. The oil is heated and stirred with a small amount of nickel which acts as a catalyst. The nickel is a surface active catalyst and has 'active sites' where hydrogen atoms are taken up by the unsaturated fatty acids, as shown in Figure 1.27.

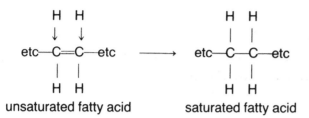

Figure 1.27

Hydrogenation of an unsaturated fatty acid

Oils and fats transfer heat well to foods being cooked, but their usefulness is limited as heat will cause their breakdown. Triglycerides will decompose on heating by a number of methods. Glycerol may be split from the component fatty acids and then be converted to *acrolein*, which may appear as an unpleasant smelling blue smoke. Unsaturated fatty acids are susceptible to oxidation which leads to rancidity (see section on rancidity) The old type of copper pans and utensils greatly accelerated this problem. Recent work has shown that the repeated heating of some vegetable oils may cause the accumulation of carcinogenic substances in the oil. In general, most fats and oils are suitable for frying. In the case of butter and margarine, however, the water present (up to 16%) restricts the rise in temperature during frying. Rapid discolouration and breakdown of the triglycerides occurs, usually accompanied by spluttering.

VEGETABLE OILS

Plants are the major source of oils and fats used in food processing and cooking. Something like 70% of all fat originates in plants. The oils are produced from the seeds of several hundred different varieties of plant. The principal one is soya bean, accounting for nearly 20% of all fat production. Other sources are groundnut (peanut or monkey nut), rapeseed, cottonseed, sunflower, sesame, coconut, palm and palm kernel. These oils are used in margarine, cooking fats and oils, ice-cream and salad dressing. Vegetable oils are usually resistant to rancidity as they contain natural antioxidants.

Soya bean

Although the soya bean has been widely cultivated in the Far East the major producer is the USA, but new varieties are being developed which are capable of growing in colder countries. The soya bean prefers a hot and damp climate. The beans yield between 13 and 20% oil. Soya bean oil is a major component of many margarines and cooking fats.

Groundnut

The ground nut has a number of other names which include peanut, earth-nut and arachis nut. Groundnut oil is often called arachis oil. It is produced in many tropical countries and in sub-tropical areas. The oil content of groundnuts is often as high as 45%. Like soya bean oil, groundnut oil is used in the manufacture of cooking fats, margarine, ice-cream and salad dressings.

Sunflower

The production of sunflower oil is increasing worldwide, particularly in sub-tropical areas. Normally the seed contains between 20 and 30 % of oil, but varieties are yielding up to 40%. It is used in a similar manner to soya and groundnut oil and also, in a less refined form, soaps and paints.

Rapeseed

Rapeseed is the European answer to the American soya bean oil. An alternative source of vegetable oil, which could be grown in Europe, was sought to offset the very large imports of soya bean oil. The heavily subsidised production of rapeseed shows itself in the attractive blocks of yellow fields found in Eastern England and in parts of Europe. Rapeseed yields between 35 and 40% oil. However, early varieties contained a fatty acid known as erucic acid (22 carbon atoms and one double bond) which has been shown to cause heart disease. Varieties have been developed subsequently which are low or free of this fatty acid.

Oil extraction

Two methods of extraction are employed in removing oil from plant sources. The oil is expressed from seeds by physical pressure in some form of press. Instead of this method, or often as well, the oil is extracted by the use of organic solvents. The seed is then broken between heavy rollers and is reduced to a coarse meal. The meal of broken seeds is heated (70-110 C) and stirred in a large vessel. The cells of the seeds burst open and release their oil. The oil is then extracted or expelled from the seed in an expeller or screw press (similar to a mincer). Considerable pressure is exerted, but about 5% of the oil remains in the seed cake and has to be removed by solvent extraction. Petroleum ether is used to wash the oil seed, which is firstly flattened into flakes. Modern continuous solvent extraction systems employ a counter-current method whereby seed moves in one direction and the solvent in the opposite direction. Fresh solvent is used at the end of the process to extract the last traces of oil. Solvent, which has already dissolved some oil, is used initially to remove the easily dissolved oil from seed flakes. The solvent is then distilled off to leave a 'crude' oil which needs refining.

Refining

The oil usually has many impurities such as free fatty acids (odour), pigments, waxes and other material. Refining usually has three stages. Firstly, any free fatty acids must be neutralised. Caustic soda is used which reacts with fatty acids to make a soap. This soap settles to the bottom of the oil which is then washed with warm water several times. The oil is bleached to remove pigments and other colours. Bleaching is carried out by using Fuller's earth or charcoal, which is added to hot oil under vacuum and stirred for about 15 minutes. The Fuller's earth is filtered out to leave a clear oil.

The third process is deodorisation which is carried out by passing steam through the hot oil under high vacuum. Odoriferous substances become volatile and are removed leaving a clear, odour free oil. The oil may be used in this form, but often it is hydrogenated and blended with other fats to make margarine and cooking fats.

ANIMAL FATS

Fat in animals is found mainly in the adipose tissue around organs such as the kidneys and heart, and under the skin. Fat is extracted by the traditional process of rendering which involves gently heating the animal tissue to melt the fat which then easily separates from the protein material. The two principal fats from animals are lard and butterfat. (Please remember that butter itself is not a pure fat, but an emulsion of water in fat.) Both butterfat and butter will be discussed in the section on dairy products (see the dairy products section)

Lard is prepared by rendering fat from pigs. It has declined in popularity because of the growth of hydrogenated vegetable oils and specially prepared fats. It has been used extensively in the past as a shortening agent, but will not cream well. For cake-making good creaming ability is essential. The process of *interesterification* was developed to improve the creaming ability of lard.

Figure 1.28
Interesterification

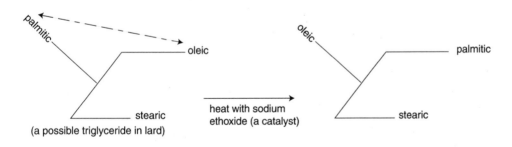

(a possible triglyceride in lard)

The process improves the plasticity of lard and reduces any graininess. Natural lard tends to be made up of large 'crystals' of triglycerides with two saturated fatty acids and one unsaturated fatty acid. These saturated acids are generally stearic and palmitic acids and one is always found in the middle position of the triglyceride molecule. This is the cause of the poor creaming ability of lard. Interesterification causes fatty acids to change their positions and the number of triglycerides with these acids in the centre position is greatly reduced. The lard is heated to about 105 C in the presence of a catalyst (sodium ethoxide) to achieve this change.

The consumption of animal fats has in the last few years declined considerably, and has been matched by an increase in the consumption of vegetable oils and fats.

FISH OILS

Pelagic fish *eg* herring, pilchards, sardines and mackerel, *eg* contain up to about 20% of fat. Spawning reduces this figure dramatically. The fat is not stored in adipose tissue but is distributed throughout the tissues. Fish oils contain a very high percentage of unsaturated fatty acids. Some of these acids may have up to six double bonds. This is reflected in the high iodine value of marine oils, *eg* herring oil has a value of 190-200.The double bonds are readily oxidised which leads to rapid rancidity in this type of oil. Before fish oils can be used they must be processed and hydrogenated. They are usually rich in a number of vitamins particularly A and D. For many years fish oils have been used as vitamin supplements, for example cod-liver oil.

MONOGLYCERIDES AND DIGLYCERIDES

In the natural fats section, the structure of a triglyceride was discussed and involved the esterification of glycerol with three fatty acids. In a similar manner it is possible for glycerol to combine with only one fatty acid. In this case a monoglyceride is formed. A common example of such a monoglyceride is glyceryl monostearate, GMS, which is formed from glycerol and one molecule of stearic acid.

Figure 1.29

Formation of glyceryl monostearate

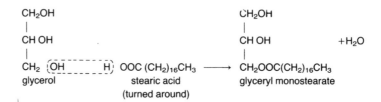

Looking at the structure of GMS it is obvious that the hydroxyl groups (-OH) are not esterified with a fatty acid. Because of this fact, GMS has the useful property of acting as an emulsifying agent. If an oil is mixed with water and stirred it forms a temporary emulsion but then rapidly separates onto the surface of the water. If a very small amount of GMS, or any other emulsifying agent, is added the separation of oil is prevented or considerably retarded. GMS has the ability to surround oil droplets and prevent them coalescing to form larger droplets which rise to the surface ever more rapidly. The hydroxyl groups of the GMS molecule are soluble in water, whereas the stearate part of the molecule is soluble in oil. However, the hydroxyl groups will not dissolve in, and in fact will repel, any fat droplets. In this manner the fat droplets are

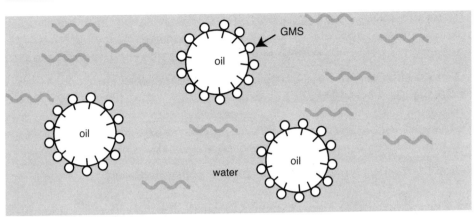

Figure 1.30
Emulsification of oil in water

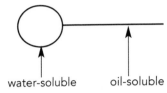

completely surrounded by GMS and cannot combine, and therefore, cannot rise to the surface of the water. The process of emulsification is represented diagrammatically in Figure 1.30. Other emulsifying agents, or emulsifiers, behave in a similar manner and so do soaps and detergents.

Diglycerides are formed in a similar manner to monoglycerides, but obviously two fatty acids combine with glycerol and only one free hydroxyl group remains. Diglycerides also acts as emulsifiers but tend to dissolve more in the fat than water because of the two fatty acids combined with the glycerol. Blends of emulsifiers are used in the food industry in a large range of products where it is necessary to prevent fat separation, for example in margarine, ice-cream, syrups, salad dressing and desserts.

WAXES

Although classified under simple lipids the waxes are complex mixtures of a range of substances. They are usually alcohols which have long chains of 18 to 22 carbon atoms joined to a range of fatty acids such as palmitic, stearic, oleic and linoleic. Waxes line the intercellular air spaces in plant leaves and stems and also are found on the surface of fruits such as apples. This surface wax or 'cutin' limits water loss by transpiration from the fruit and also prevents water entering the fruit. An apple placed under a running tap clearly demonstrates this.

COMPLEX LIPIDS

A large group of naturally occurring substances are formed from glycerol, and other alcohols or sugars, combined with phosphoric acid and a range of alkaline or basic substances. The most important group is the *phospholipids* of which the *lecithins* are very significant in foods. The general structure of a lecithin is given in Figure 1.31. Like the monoglycerides and diglycerides, lecithin acts as emulsifiers because they have fat-soluble and water-soluble parts to their structures.

Lecithins are thus important natural emulsifying agents found in many foods

Figure 1.31

Lecithin

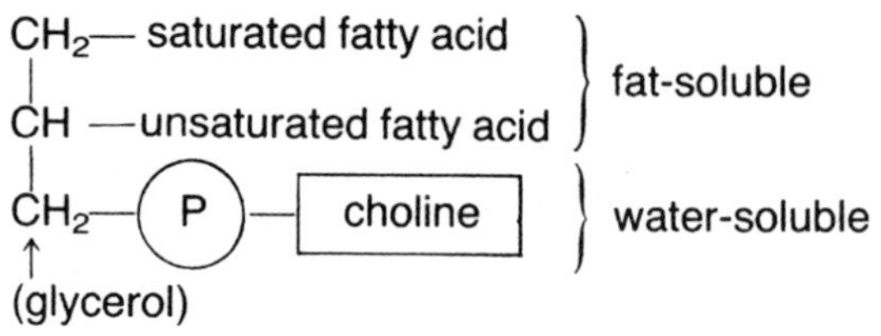

$$\left.\begin{array}{l} CH_2\text{— saturated fatty acid} \\ CH\text{ —unsaturated fatty acid} \end{array}\right\} \text{fat-soluble}$$

$$\left.\begin{array}{l} CH_2\text{—}\boxed{P}\text{—}\boxed{\text{choline}} \\ \uparrow \\ \text{(glycerol)} \end{array}\right\} \text{water-soluble}$$

$$\boxed{P} = \text{phosphoric acid } (H_3PO_4)$$
$$+$$
$$\text{choline} = HO-CH_2-CH_2N\equiv(CH_3)_3$$

such as milk, egg yolk and vegetable oils. The best commercial source is from the soya bean.

LIPOIDS

The group of substances known as *steroids* are classified as lipids, or lipid-like, hence *lipoid*. The lipoids could also include the carotenoids and tocopherols, but these are dealt with in Sections 1.6.2.1, 1.6.2.3 and 1.7.1.1. The steroids are not fatty acid derivatives and include *cholesterol*, vitamin D and some bile acids.

Cholesterol occurs widely in animal fats, and the human body produces up to twice its own requirement for use in manufacture of vitamin D_2 and a number of hormones. However, up to about 25% of blood cholesterol comes from the diet. Butter contains about 250mg/100g whereas egg yolk solids are as high as 3-5% cholesterol. During the refining of oils steroids are often removed during the treatment with caustic soda. However, many vegetable oils contain some steroid generally known as *phytosterol*. The structure of cholesterol is given in Figure 1.32 and it can clearly be seen to be totally different from other lipid structures.

Figure 1.32

Cholesterol

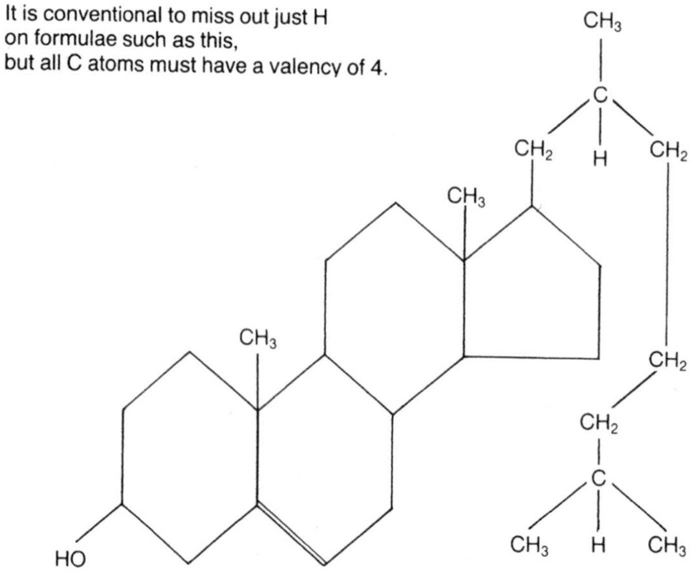

It is conventional to miss out just H on formulae such as this, but all C atoms must have a valency of 4.

RANCIDITY

The flavour of rancid fat is well known to everyone, but some people, particularly from hotter countries, have grown to prefer some degree of rancidity in their fatty foods. Two types of rancidity occur in fats and these are termed *hydrolytic* and *oxidative rancidity*.

Hydrolytic rancidity is the less common of the two overall but is quite common in emulsion systems such as butter, margarine and cream; it also occurs in nuts and some biscuits. Water must be present for hydrolysed rancidity to occur as, in effect, it is the reverse process of the esterification of glycerol with three fatty acids. The triglycerides are hydrolysed and the three fatty acids are set free. In the presence of water alone, the process is very slow but certain enzymes generally called lipases or lipolytic enzymes (split fat) greatly accelerate the process. Some bacteria produce these enzymes and so will cause this type of rancidity if they contaminate a certain fat or food. The free fatty acids produced by this hydrolysis often have unpleasant flavours. This is particularly so with the short chain fatty acids, but flavour disappears above about 14 carbon atoms. Hydrolytic rancidity in butter yields the dreadfully rancid smelling butyric (butanoic) acid. However this rancidity is actually desirable in the production of certain cheeses, particularly blue cheese, as without the release of free fatty acids the cheese does not develop its full flavour. Fats should be heat treated to kill any micro-organisms and inactivate any enzymes present.

In food, *oxidative rancidity* or *autoxidation* is by far the most important type of fat deterioration. Fats, and oils particularly, slowly take up oxygen over a period of time and then the flavour of rancidity is eventually detected. At this stage rancidity is well advanced and cannot be reserved. This uptake of oxygen, and the chain of events which it starts, is related to the unsaturation of the fat, *ie* the number of double bonds in the constituent fatty acids. Hard fats are resistant to this oxidation as they contain fewer double bonds, whereas fish oils being highly unsaturated are very susceptible. The oxidation of fats takes place by means of a chain reaction involving the production of highly reactive particles called *free radicals*. Normally the bonds between carbon and hydrogen atoms are produced by the sharing of electrons (covalent bonds). Some outside energy source, for example, ultra-violet light, splits these shared electrons into single electrons as shown in Figure 1.33.

Initiators

R : H $\longrightarrow$ R · + · H

shared electrons
in fatty acid

free radicals
(R = rest of the fatty acid)

Figure 1.33

Free radical production –
initiation phase

The production of free radicals is initiated by various energy sources such as heat, light, particularly UV light, traces of metals, *eg* copper and iron, and some peroxides. Obviously, to prevent fat becoming rancid these initiators must be kept away from stored fat. Oils should be stored in glass lined containers as iron vessels initiate oxidative rancidity.

Production of free radicals in the fat is called the *initiation phase*. Oxygen is now taken up by the fat as the free radicals combine with the oxygen to make peroxide radicals (ROO·). This second phase is called the *propagation* phase. Peroxide radicals attack other fatty acids and produce yet more free radicals, so the process accelerates.

The hydroperoxides (ROOH) produced are unstable and break down to produce alcohols, aldehydes and ketones. These compounds provide the odour of rancid fat. The process continues at an ever increasing rate until all the fat becomes rancid, or no further oxygen is available, or the free radicals start to react with each other. The last phase is the *termination phase*.

Figure 1.34 (left)

Propagation phase

Figure 1.35 (right)

Termination phase

$$R\cdot + O_2 \longrightarrow ROO\cdot$$

free radical   peroxide radical

then: $RH + ROO\cdot \longrightarrow ROOH + R\cdot$

another fatty   hydro-   a new
acid   peroxides free radical

(interaction of free radicals to make stable products)

$$R\cdot + R\cdot \longrightarrow R:R$$

$$ROO\cdot + R\cdot \longrightarrow ROO:R$$

Oxidative rancidity is an irreversible process of deterioration which can only be retarded and not prevented completely.

Obviously metals and light should be kept away from fat, which must be kept cool and free from oxygen or air. *Antioxidants* can be used which have the ability to absorb oxygen or to prevent the formation of the free radicals by forming stable radicals. The use of the additives is controlled by regulations. Table 1.6

Table 1.6

Permitted antioxidants

Antioxidant	E number	Applications
Form stable free radicals:		
Butylated hydroxyanisole (BHA)	E320	biscuits, stock cakes
Butylated hydroxytoluene (BHT)	E321	chewing gum
Tocopherol extract (Vit. E)	E306	vegetable oils
Synthetic alpha-tocopherol	E307	cereal-based baby foods
Synthetic gamma-tocopherol	E308	" " "
Synthetic delta-tocopherol	E309	" " "
Absorb Oxygen:		
L-ascorbic acid	E300	fruit drinks, dried potatoes
Ascorbyl palmitate	E304	scotch eggs
Sodium L-ascorbate	E301	meat oat, sausages
Calcium L-ascorbate	E302	scotch eggs
Propyl gallate	E310	margarine, vegetable oils
Octyl gallate	E311	" " "
Dodecyl gallate	E312	" " "
Lecithins	E322	low fat spreads (also emulsifier)
Ethoxyquin	No E No.	prevention of 'scald' discolouration in apples and pears

lists antioxidants currently permitted in the European Union. Some foods, particularly vegetable oils and foods containing some spices, *eg* cloves, show marked resistance to rancidity. Salt tends to accelerate rancidity, whereas sugar, in biscuits for example, retards the deterioration.

THE FAT DEBATE

The Western diet is too rich in fats and it is generally agreed that this level of consumption should be significantly reduced. Animal fats, as they are rich in saturated fatty acids and cholesterol, have been heavily criticised over a number of years resulting in declining sales.

Cholesterol and fatty acids form deposits or plaques on arterial walls and obviously this reduces the size of the artery, making it harder for the heart to pump the blood through the blood vessels. At a minimum this leads to higher blood pressure, but often to heart disease and death. However, the connection between high cholesterol foods, such as eggs, and this deposition on the arterial walls is not conclusive. Although it is wise to avoid such foods the deposition may well occur from the cholesterol synthesised in the body. Diets rich in fats have recently been implicated as causative agents of cancer, particularly breast and colon cancers.

In the chapter on carbohydrates it was pointed out that sucrose increases blood fatty acids, whereas high fibre diets decrease them. Modern life styles, involving stress, and the lack of exercise may also increase the problem. However, recent work has shown that a slight to moderate intake of alcohol is beneficial in removing some arterial cholesterol and fatty acids.

Some people are fortunate in having good fat translocation systems in the blood, others have inherited poor systems and are likely to develop problems of this nature.

In the late 1990s, the consumption of antioxidants, particularly vitamins A,C and E, was encouraged to combat the effects of free radicals. Free radicals are thought to damage the special 'bodies' in the blood which move fat around the blood stream. These damaged bodies cannot move fat so easily and so it accumulates in the blood vessels. This is particularly the case with a type of cholesterol known as low-density-lipoprotein- cholesterol (LDL) which readily accumulates. High Density Types (HDL) do not cause the problem to the same degree.

Recent research has shown red wine and tea to have antioxidant properties.

The consumption of polyunsaturated fatty acids, *eg* in soft margarine, has also been shown to lower blood cholesterol levels. Until recently little attention has been paid to what are termed 'essential fatty acids'. The most important of these fatty acids is linoleic acid; linolenic also is essential, but the third essential acid, arachidonic, can be synthesised from the other two in the human body. These essential fatty acids are involved early in the human embryo in the construction of brain and nervous tissue. Deficiency of the acids has been implicated in skin disorders and in the development of multiple sclerosis. However, more recent investigation has shown that they help to reduce heart disease.

Evidence has mounted that the diet of many people in Britain is deficient in essential fatty acids. Fatty fish, such as mackerel, are the only rich source. The Japanese are less vulnerable to heart attacks than Westerners and their diet is rich in fish oils; they and are reputed to suffer very little heart disease.

So, current knowledge suggests that we should consume less fat, but more fish oils at the expense of animal fats, have plenty of exercise and eat plenty of roughage (dietary fibre).

PRACTICAL EXERCISES: *Lipids*

SAFETY – all organic solvents should be treated as highly inflammable and correspondingly should be used away from naked lights and flames.

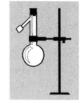

1. Grease-spot test
Take the food sample and wrap a small amount in a filter paper. Allow to dry. A translucent ring on the paper around the food material indicates the presence of lipid.

2. Sudan staining of lipids
The dye Sudan III or IV will stain traces of lipid a red colour. The food material must be broken up in some way; the dye is added to the food. Lipid will absorb the dye and take up the red colour.

3. Solubility of lipids
For safety, work in fume cupboard or in ventilated area. Use a range of organic solvents as available, and also water. Place a small amount of fat in a test tube and add a solvent. Repeat with different solvents and a fresh sample of fat. Observe the solubility of lipid in each solvent.

4. Use of emulsifiers
Stir a sample of oil in water and note the speed of complete separation of the oil. Add a small amount of detergent or soap and note the emulsification of the oil in the water. Repeat using commercial emulsifiers, such as glyceryl monostearate, and lecithin, and also repeat using egg yolk.

5. Acrolein formation

Acrolein is produced by dehydration of glycerol and gives the smell to burnt fat. Heat a few drops of glycerol (glycerine) with a dehydrating agent, eg anhydrous calcium chloride; note the smell of acolein. Repeat with a number of oils and fats.

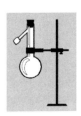

6. Melting point of fats

Take a sample of fat and melt it, then dip the end of a capillary tube into the molten fat. Cool in freezer to solidify the fat; then attach the tube to the bottom of the thermometer. Gently heat the thermometer and tube in a warm bath. Note the temperature at which the fat becomes clear and moves in the tube.

Chapter 4

Proteins

PREVIEW

- Proteins – largest known molecules, built up of amino acids

- Amino acids – always contain an amino group (NH_2) and carboxyl group (COOH)

- Amino acids – Neutral – *eg* glycine, basic – *eg* lysine, acidic – *eg* glutamic acid

- Eight essential amino acids: valine, leucine, isoleucine, phenylalanine, threonline, methionine, tryptophan, lysine. Children also require: histidine and arginine

- Amphoteric – amino acids can act as alkalis or acid

- Iso-electric point – amino group ionised to NH_3^+ (occurs at certain pH) balanced by-COO⁻

- At iso-electric point amino acid called a zwitterion

- Amino acid joined to another by peptide bond

- Primary structure of a protein – sequence of amino acids in the chain

- Secondary structure – definite shape, usually a helix caused by cross-linking by various bonds

- Tertiary structure – secondary structure folded over and held by cross-links to form globule

- Structural proteins – cellular membranes – skin, muscle

- Physiologically active proteins – enzymes, blood proteins

- Nutrient proteins – meat proteins – supply all essential amino acids

- Enzymes – largest group of proteins

- Enzyme name = substrate + ase

- Classification of enzymes by nature of reaction catalysed – *eg* oxidases – perform oxidation, isomerases – rearrange molecules into different structure

- Enzyme action is very specific – compared with a lock and key

- Non-proteins may be needed by enzyme to make reaction possible – known as co-enzymes

- Browning reactions – enzymic – requires polyphenolases + diphenol substrate + oxygen; – non-enzymic – require reducing sugar + amino group (in protein or amino acid)

- Maillard reaction – non-enzymic browning reactions to produce brown melanoidins

- Caramelisation – browning of sugar when heated – not involving an amino group

The molecules of protein are the largest known and are responsible for growth, repair and maintenance of the body. The richer countries of the West, and particularly of the Northern Hemisphere, consume considerably more protein than poorer Third world countries. Protein deficiency diseases are widespread in poor countries. In addition to containing the elements carbon, hydrogen and oxygen, protein also contains nitrogen and occasionally sulphur or phosphorus.

Proteins are large polymers built up of units of *amino acids*. Although over 80 amino acids exist only about 20 are found in food protein. Amino acids always contain an amino group ($-NH_2$) and a carboxyl group ($-COOH$). Some amino acids may contain more than one of these groups and, as we shall see, this will affect their properties.

The general formula of an amino acid is given in Figure 1.36.

The simplest amino acid is when R = H, this acid being amino acetic acid or glycine. In table 1.7 the 20 amino acids are listed with their formulae. If the

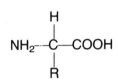

(The R group will vary in each amino acid, see table 1.7)

Figure 1.36 (above)

General formula of an amino acid

Table 1.7

Common amino acids

	R group =
Neutral:	
Glycine	H-
Alanine	CH_3-
Valine	$(CH_3)_2CH-$
Leucine	$(CH_3)_2CH\ CH_2-$
Isoleucine	$CH_3CH_2\ CH(CH_3)-$
Norleucine	$CH_3(CH_2)_3-$
Phenylalanine	$C_6H_5CH_2-$
Tyrosine	$C_6H_5(CH)CH_2-$
Serine	$HOCH_2-$
Threonine	$CH_3CH\ (OH)-$
Cysteine	$HSCH_2-$
Cystine	$HOOCCH(NH_2)\ CH_2\ S_2\ CH_2-$
Methionine	$CH_3SCH_2CH_2-$
Tryptophan	
Basic (2–NH_2 groups)	
Ornithine	$H_2N\ (CH_2)_3-$
Arginine	NH_2
	$HN=C-NH\ (CH_2)_3-$
Lysine	$H_2N(CH_2)_4-$
Histidine	
Acidic (2–COOH groups)	
Aspartic acid	$HOOC\ CH_2-$
Glutamic acid	$HOOC\ (CH_2)_2-$

amino acid contains one amino group (alkaline) and one carboxyl group (acid) then it is neutral. More than one amino group gives the amino acid an alkaline or basic character; similarly, more than one carboxyl group makes the amino acid more acidic. The amino acids have been sub-divided according to these features in the table.

Amino acids can be further sub-divided into essential amino acids (indispensable in the diet) or non-essential amino acids (which the body can synthesise sufficiently). There are eight essential amino acids. These are:

Valine	Threonine
Leucine	Methionine
Isoleucine	Tryptophan
Phenylalanine	Lysine

Children also require histidine during rapid growth. Arginine may also be considered as essential as it is only synthesised slowly in the body.

Proteins in food may be classified on their amino acid content. Proteins that contain all the essential amino acids, for example meat proteins, in proportions capable of promoting growth are described as *complete proteins* or proteins of *high biological value*. These proteins used to be called *first class proteins* and proteins deficient in one or amino acids were *second class* eg plant proteins. However, as any vegetarian will quickly point out, it is very simple to mix foods of plant origin to ensure that the meal contains all the essential amino acids.

As a direct consequence of their dual basic-acidic nature, amino acids can react with both acids and alkalis. Such behaviour is termed *amphoteric*. At a certain pH the amino acid will be ionised with a negative carboxyl group (-COO⁻) balanced by a basic amino group (-NH$_3$+). This pH is called *isoelectric point* and the amino acid is called a *zwitterion*. If acid is added and the pH falls below the iso-electric point the amino acid becomes positively charged, and conversely becomes negatively charged as the pH is raised.

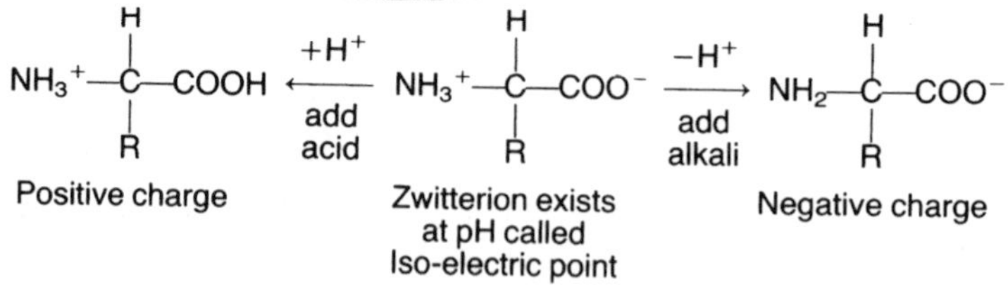

Figure 1.37

Iso-electric point of an amino acid

$$NH_3{}^+—\overset{\overset{H}{|}}{\underset{\underset{R}{|}}{C}}—COOH \quad \xleftarrow[\text{add acid}]{+H^+} \quad NH_3{}^+—\overset{\overset{H}{|}}{\underset{\underset{R}{|}}{C}}—COO^- \quad \xrightarrow[\text{add alkali}]{-H^+} \quad NH_2—\overset{\overset{H}{|}}{\underset{\underset{R}{|}}{C}}—COO^-$$

Positive charge   Zwitterion exists   Negative charge
                              at pH called
                              Iso-electric point

The phenomenon can be useful if the amino acids are placed in an electric field as positive amino acids will migrate towards a negative electrode and negative amino acids towards a positive electrode. This is the process of *electrophoresis* which is used to separate amino acids or proteins.

Amino acids can combine through their amino and carboxyl groups. When two amino acids condense together in this way a *dipeptide* is formed and where many combine a *polypeptide* if formed and finally a protein. The link is called a *peptide bond* and is shown in Figure 1.38. protein.

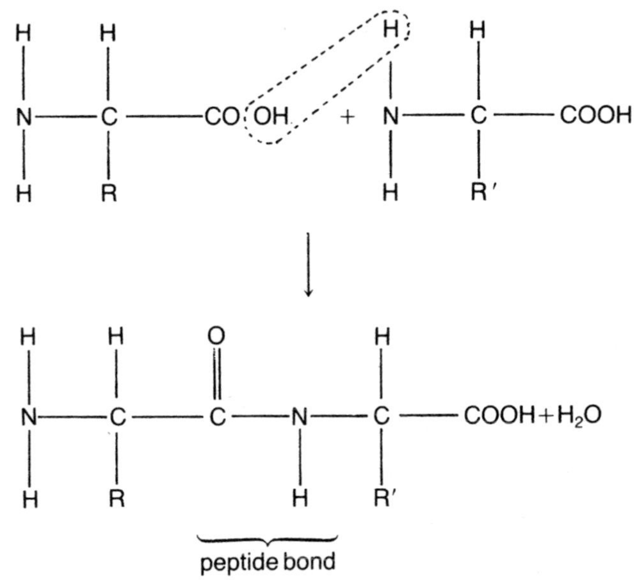

Figure 1.38
Peptide bond

Each amino acid is linked to the next by peptide bonds to build up a chain of hundreds or even thousands of amino acids. As only about 20 amino acids are involved they are linked in an infinite variety of combinations to make an enormous number of different proteins.

THE STRUCTURE OF PROTEINS

The structure of proteins is different from that of other food components in that several orders of complexity have been recognised. Firstly, there is the *primary structure* which is the sequence of amino acids in the protein chain. In the *secondary structure* the amino acids are further linked by various bonds to give the protein a definite shape which is often in the form of a spiral. The most important group involved in cross linking is the –SH group found in the amino acid cysteine. This forms a *disulphide* bridge. This bridge is important in breadmaking as it gives elasticity and extensibility to the dough.

Other links are formed between the amino acids which contribute to the coiling of the chain of acids. These include the ubiquitous hydrogen bonds and the electrostatic attraction between positively charged amino groups (NH_3^+) and negatively charged carboxyl groups (COO^-).

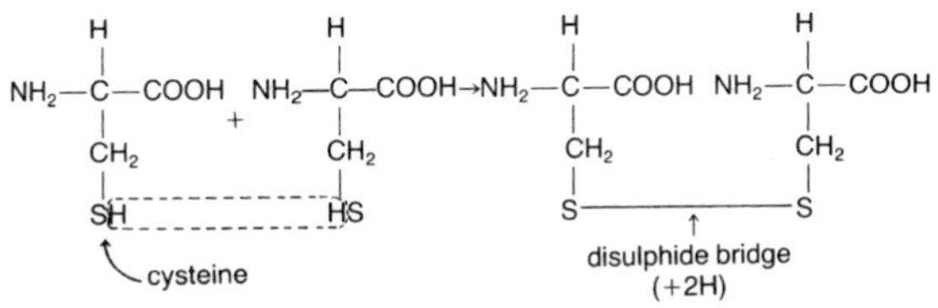

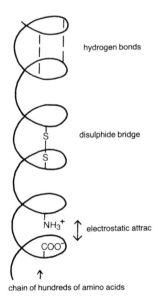

hydrogen bonds

disulphide bridge

electrostatic attrac

chain of hundreds of amino acids

Figure 1.39 (left)
Disulphide bridge

Figure 1.40 (above)
Secondary protein structure (diagrammatic representation showing cross links

The spiral or helix of the secondary structure may be folded over and held firmly by crosslinks to form a globule; this is the *tertiary* structure. There are even further protein structures such as fibres. Water plays an important role in these structures as without it they uncoil and lose that particular structure to varying degrees.

The structure of a protein may be readily changed by a number of agents causing molecules to aggregate and precipitate. This process is known as *denaturation*, and although usually it is irreversible, it can on occasions be reversible. Denaturation can be caused by heat, acids, alkalis, heavy metals, salt and ethanol. Violent agitation can also cause denaturation.

Reversible denaturation of a protein is slight unwinding of the polypeptide chain caused by mild denaturing conditions. If the protein is removed from the conditions it can regain its original structure and properties. This has been found recently in enzymes (see Section 1.4.2.2) which are sometimes only reversibly denatured in blanching and reactivate themselves during storage of the food.

Unfolding of a molecule occurs in *irreversible denaturation* leading to loss of some properties of the protein, but often making it more digestible. This is the reason for cooking of meat and many protein foods. The cooking of egg illustrates the irreversible changes which occur in a protein when it is denatured. Solubility of the protein is lost; viscosity increases enormously; the egg becomes opaque; but digestibility is improved.

CLASSIFICATION OF PROTEINS

The simplest way of classifying proteins is by their function. There are three main features for proteins – structural, physiologically active and nutrient.

Table 1.8

Classification of proteins by function

Function	Examples
Structural	cellular membranes
	muscle
	skin
Physiologically active	enzymes
	hormones (not all)
	blood proteins
	nucleoproteins
Nutrient	meat proteins –
	supply all essential amino acids

STRUCTURAL PROTEINS

Structural proteins posses mechanical strength, which is due to an organised arrangement of their component amino acid and polypeptide chains. Some structural proteins are quite rigid whereas others are elastic. The inelastic or rigid proteins have polypeptide chains packed closely together and cross linked with hydrogen bonds. This tends to make 'sheets' of protein much like a sheet of silk.

Elastic and extensible proteins are in the form of coils, or 'spring-like' as they will stretch but then revert to their original shape.

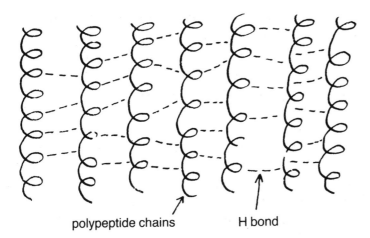

polypeptide chains   H bond

Figure 1.41
Sheet structure of a protein

The coils are held together by hydrogen bonds and by disulphide bridges (-S-S-). In wheat gluten there is an equilibrium between the –SH groups and the disulphide bridges thus: -SH + HS- → -S-S- + 2H. As fermentation proceeds by the yeast in bread making the disulphide bridges split to sulphydryl groups (-SH) but then reform to make disulphide bridges. Thus the dough is extensible but retains its elastic properties due to the disulphide bridges. Muscle myosin, skin, epidermis and blood fibrinogen are similar elastic proteins.

PHYSIOLOGICALLY ACTIVE PROTEINS

Enzymes

Enzymes are the largest single group of proteins and are often referred to as organic catalysts. In fact without enzymes no biological process could take place and life would be impossible.

Enzymes are very specific, some acting on one particular bond in one organic substance. The substance upon which an enzyme acts is called the *substrate*. Usually enzymes are named after the substrate upon which they act:

Enzyme names   = substrate + ase

eg maltase   = malt (ose) + ase

eg pectinase* = pectin + ase

(a general name for a group of enzymes)

Like protein, enzymes can be classified in a number of ways, but the most common method is now by the type of reaction they catalyse.

Table 1.9

Types of enzymes

Enzyme	Reaction performed
Oxidases	Oxidation – add oxygen or remove hydrogen
Reductases	Reduction – add hydrogen or remove oxygen
Transferases	Transfer groups between molecules
Isomerases	Rearrange molecules into different structures
Synthetases	Build up more complex molecules from simpler ones
Hydrolases	Hydrolysis – adding water

Enzymes have the effect of reducing a single-step, high-energy reaction into a multi-stage process involving a small amount of energy. They are highly selective and the reaction between an enzyme and its substrate has been likened to a lock and key. Figure 1.42 shows diagrammatically what is thought to happen in a enzyme catalysed reaction involving splitting a substance into two smaller units.

Figure 1.42

Enzyme action

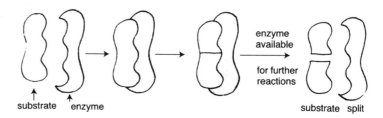

Enzymes are surface catalysts and are therefore readily blocked by a large variety of substances which can adhere to their surface. Enzymes often need the help of another non-protein substance called a *co-enzyme* to make a reaction possible. Often these co-enzymes are vitamins or derived from vitamins. In a similar manner enzymes sometimes need *activators* which are normally metals such as magnesium and occasionally non-metals such as chlorine (as chloride).

Enzymes prepared from a wide range of sources have many uses in food manufacture. Invertase is used extensively in confectionery to produce invert sugar in a wide range of products. Meat has been tenderised by enzymes such as papain from paw-paw or papaya, bromelin from pineapples or ficin from figs. Pectinases from fungal sources have been used to remove pectin hazes from wines. In foods which have not been heat-treated, enzymes may be active during storage and cause significant deterioration. Even at frozen temperature some enzymes may be active and produce flavour, colour or texture changes in the product. Before canning, drying or freezing a number of foods, particularly vegetables, the product is *blanched* to inactivate the enzymes. The enzyme peroxidase is one of the most heat-resistant enzymes and it is assumed that testing for the absence of peroxidase after blanching will indicate the inactivation of all enzymes present in the food. However, recent work has shown that although there are some more heat-resistant enzymes, a number of enzymes can actually reactivate themselves during storage and damage the product. Blanching involves a short heat treatment of one or two minutes with boiling water or steam and some recent developments use microwaves.

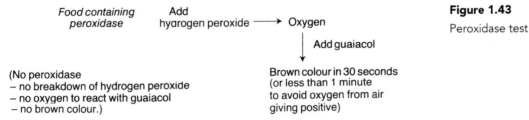

Figure 1.43

Peroxidase test

Some *hormones* are also proteins and hold key positions in many metabolic processes. *Nucleoproteins* are important physiologically active proteins found in food, particularly in meat. They are conjugates of nucleic acid and protein. There are two classes of these proteins: deoxyribonucleic acid (DNA) proteins and ribonucleic acid (RNA) proteins. There are a number of different blood proteins, but haemoglobin is important because of its function as an oxygen carrier.

The red colour of meat is mostly due to the pigment myoglobin which has a structure similar to that of haemoglobin. Haemoglobin is lost from meat when the blood is drained from the carcass after slaughter and so does not contribute to the colour of meat significantly (see section on meat).

Nutrient proteins

As the body is unable to synthesise the essential amino acids it is necessary for certain nutrient proteins to be taken in the diet. Animal proteins are the obvious main individual nutrient proteins but plant proteins are now consumed in greater quantities. The high cost of animal proteins has led to the development of a wide range of *novel proteins* or *meat substitutes*.

NOVEL PROTEINS (meat substitutes or analogues)

New types of proteins have been developed because of the high cost and inefficient production of protein in animals. Many parts of the world are suffering from protein malnutrition or 'kwashiorkor'. It is hoped that new proteins will help to reduce this problem.

Novel proteins can be manufactured to have a protein quality of high biological value, similar to meat, or they can enrich poor diets based on cereals or crops such as cassava.

Two general types of novel proteins are being produced and new ones are being developed, based on naturally occurring proteins such as soya protein, or biosynthesised protein produced by fermentation of various substrates such as waste carbohydrate, *eg* Quorn.

Soya protein

Yet again we come across the useful soya bean plant. It is used to make *textured vegetable protein* or TVP. Soya bean meal is defatted and then mixed with water.

The dough-like mass is then extruded and at the same time heated under pressure. It dries into a mass of spongy-like consistency, which can be cut into chunks, or ground into granules. Before the extrusion stage, colour, flavouring and salt are often added. The dried pieces of TVP are usually referred to in 'meat terms' such as mince, and chunks. This product probably would have been more successful if this obvious comparison with meat had not been made, as TVP invariably loses in any such comparison. The dried TVP pieces must be reconstituted in water before use or in a suitably flavoured sauce.

Spun soya is an improvement of TVP as it tends to duplicate the more fibrous texture of meat products. Soya proteins do have some disadvantages. Soya proteins are deficient in the essential amino acid methionine and therefore need fortification with this if used as primary protein sources. Some people have difficulty in completely digesting soya protein and others are affected by carbohydrates present, such as raffinose, which cause excessive flatulence because they are fermented by bacteria in the colon.

Biosynthesised proteins (or single cell proteins)
These proteins are produced by bacteria or fungi growing on suitable substrates usually by a continuous fermentation method. Waste carbohydrate material can be converted by some fungi to proteins; this protein is then extracted and used as food supplement. The proteins, themselves, taste like mushrooms and are generally in a powder form after extraction, and are suitable for addition to other foods.

Toxicological studies have to be carefully carried out and nutrition trials have to be extensive. Starving people surprisingly often show considerable resistance to new products of this nature. This type of product is increasing in popularity in a wide range of recipe dishes as a substitute for meat dishes.

BROWNING REACTIONS

There are many occasions when it is desirable to have browning of foods particularly in cooking by roasting, baking and grilling. There are equally numerous occasions when a brown product indicates deterioration and loss of nutritive value. There are two main groups of browning reactions, those involving enzymes and those occurring between proteins and carbohydrates.

Enzymic browning

When many varieties of apple are eaten or peeled they rapidly start to develop a brown colouration. Many other fruits and vegetables show this browning, particularly potatoes, pears, avocados and bananas. Browning occurs when the tissue is physically damaged or is diseased.

The enzymes which cause this browning are called *polyphenolases* or polyphenol oxidases. The substrates for the enzymes are phenolic compounds, particularly diphenols such as catechol (in apples).

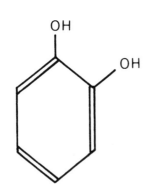

Figure 1.44

Catechol
NB The best substrates for the polyphenolases must have two adjacent-OH groups on a benzene ring

Monophenols can also act as substrates but are much slower in their reaction. Some fruit and vegetables possess the enzymes and not the substrates, and therefore do not brown, *eg* citrus fruits. The third requirement for a fruit to brown is oxygen or air. A series of reactions occurs after the initial action of the enzyme on the substrate eventually to produce brown pigments or *melanoidins*.

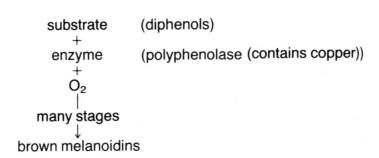

Figure 1.45

Enzymic browning

This browning reaction is undesirable and unsightly, particularly in fruit salads, peeled apples and potatoes. Cider is a golden brown colour because of this reaction and so is the colour of tea.

There are many methods of preventing the reaction, but only a few are used. The enzymes can be destroyed by heat or inactivated with sulphites or sulphur dioxide. Oxygen can easily be excluded from the food, for example peeled potatoes are immersed in water. The water should be boiled, to drive out any dissolved oxygen, and then cooled before use. Addition of a little salt will help. Acids will prevent the action of the enzymes and lemon juice is often used in cookery for this purpose.

Non-enzymic browning

When foods are roasted, baked or grilled, non-enzymic browning occurs and is considered desirable because of the appetising colour, odour and flavour it produces. Sometimes, however, it is undesirable and indicates deterioration in a food; for example, the gradual browning of dried milk powder.

Maillard in 1912 noticed that brown colouration was produced when a solution of glucose was heated with the amino acid glycine. This reaction between the amino group (NH_2) of a protein or amino acid and the (potential) aldehyde group of a reducing sugar is called the *Maillard reaction*.

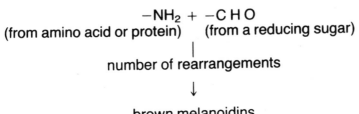

Figure 1.46

Maillard reaction

NB The reacting groups are attached to their relevant molecules and, in some cases, large proteins are involved

There will be some loss in nutritive value of proteins involved in non-enzymic browning. Amino acids containing extra amino groups, for example lysine, are obviously more susceptible. The complexity of foods poses many problems for controlling this type of browning. Products which brown slowly during storage should be kept at a lower temperature. The moisture content of a dried product is critical. Skimmed milk powder requires about 5% moisture before browning can proceed. The Maillard reaction proceeds more rapidly under alkaline conditions and therefore addition of an edible acid such as citric acid will slow down the reaction. Some foods can be treated with enzymes to remove either the protein or the sugar, *eg* in egg white, glucose is removed by yeast fermentation before drying.

Sugar can undergo browning in the absence of an amino group and this is *caramelisation* (often confused with the Maillard reaction). Caramelisation occurs when sugars are heated above their melting points to produce a range of brown substances collectively known as caramel. Ascorbic acid, vitamin C, can undergo a form of non-enzymic browning in fruit juices, particularly in grapefruit, when it is oxidised and eventually forms brown pigments.

PRACTICAL EXERCISES PROTEINS AND BROWNING REACTIONS

Try the following tests on dried egg, dried milk and gelatine.

1. Test for all proteins – Biuret test

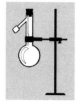

Take a test tube about 1/8th full of protein solution (or suspension) and add an equal quantity of sodium hydroxide solution. Add one drop of copper sulphate solution. A violet colour is obtained for all proteins.

2. Heating proteins

Take a sample of protein and strongly heat in a tube (ignition tube). Test the end of the tube with moist red litmus paper. A blue colour is produced as fumes of ammonia are given off because of the nitrogen content of the protein.

3. Protein denaturation

Add some egg albumin to water in a test tube and pour a few cm in other tubes for the following tests:-
(a) heat gently, then boil
(b) add a few drops of hydrochloric acid
(c) add a few drops of sodium hydroxide
(d) add a few drops of mercuric chloride solution (poison)
Observe the effects on the protein solution.

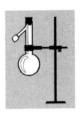

4. Millon's test – for tyrosine

Take about 1/8th of a test tube of protein solution and add a similar amount of Millon's reagent (mercurous and mercuric nitrates in nitric acid – **poisonous**). A white precipitate is formed which becomes brick-red when heated in a water-bath.

5. Sakaguchi's test – for arginine

To a small quantity of protein solution add a few cm³ of sodium hydroxide solution. Add about four drops of 2% solution of a-naphthol (in alcohol), a drop of sodium hypochlorite solution (or bleaching powder). Arginine causes the production of a carmine colour.

6. Xanthoproteic test – for amino acids with a phenyl group

To a small quantity of protein solution add a few drops of concentrated nitric acid. Take care! Boil in water bath. Cool under a running tap and add ammonium hydroxide to make it alkaline. An orange colour is produced by phenylalanine, tyrosine and tryptophan.

7. Enzymic browning reactions

Slice an apple into a number of thin slices and carry out the following:
(a) break one slice
(b) crush one slice
(c) immerse one slice in water
(d) immerse one slice in water which has been boiled then cooled
(e) immerse one slice in dilute acid solution (eg citric acid solution)
(f) immerse one slice in 5% salt solution

Repeat for potato, and observe for any browning produced. If available, treat slices with catechol, resoricinol and tyrosine.

8. Non-enzymic browning – the Maillard reaction

Make a solution of glucose (about 10%), add some protein or amino acid, as available. Boil in water bath and note any browning. Repeat but:
(a) add a few drops of acid
(b) add a few drops of sodium hydroxide
(c) add a few drops of a sulphite solution

Chapter 5

Minerals

PREVIEW

- Calcium most abundant mineral in body, followed by phosphorus

- Calcium – from dairy products and some vegetables
  – bound by phytic or oxalic acid

- Phosphorus – occurs in all cells – readily found, therefore, in foods

- Iron – essential for haemoglobin
  – must be absorbed in iron II or ferrous form

- Iron used in haemoglobin can be recycled in body

- Potassium and sodium involved in electrolyte balance in body and control of cosmotic pressure within cells

- Excess salt consumption may cause high blood pressure and fluid retention in the body of susceptible individuals

- Trace elements – very small amounts required generally by enzyme system

- Lack of iodine causes goitre – 'Derbyshire neck'

- Higher amounts of trace elements are toxic

The human body requires a range of mineral substances which can be absorbed from food. Unfortunately in many cases food processing and cooking techniques reduce the level of available minerals in foods. This is sometimes offset by the enrichment of foods, for example, breakfast cereals, with a number of minerals particularly iron. Some of the minerals are only required in trace amounts and excessive intake of them may cause poisoning.

Calcium and phosphorus

These two elements will be considered together as they exist in the body as calcium phosphate which makes up the structure of bones and teeth. There is about 1-1.5 kg of calcium and 0.75 – 0.1 kg of phosphorous in the body. Fortunately phosphorus is a natural constituent of plant and animal cells and, therefore is readily obtained from food. Shortage of calcium in the diet, however, affects the bones and teeth which can become weakened and soft. Only about 40% of calcium in food is absorbed by the body, so for some people there is a risk of calcium deficiency. This deficiency leads to the disease of osteoporosis. The main sources of calcium are dairy products, especially cheese, bread and some vegetables. Some vegetables and wholemeal flour contain a substance called *phytic acid* which can combine with calcium and make it unavailable to the body. Similarly *oxalic acid*, poisonous in higher quantities, will form calcium oxalate which is unavailable to the body. This occurs in spinach, for example.

Iron

Iron is an essential constituent of the blood pigment, haemoglobin, and is involved in transport of oxygen around the body. Anaemia is a clinical condition associated with iron abnormalities in metabolism. However, deficiency of nutrients other than iron may be the true cause. The daily intake for an adult male should be about 10mg; females require slightly more, particularly during menstruation, pregnancy and lactation.

Fortunately, the iron used in haemoglobin is re-cycled when red blood compounds are broken down in the body after their usefulness has ended. A wide range of foodstuffs contain nut particularly liver, some fish, kidney, eggs, brown bread and flour. A number of foodstuffs are enriched with iron, for example, breakfast cereals have iron added at the rate of 6-10mg/100g.

There is evidence that some forms of iron used for food enrichment purposes are poorly utilised by the body. Iron must be in the iron II or ferrous form to be utilised. The oxidised iron III or ferric form is, in fact, more common in foods than the reduced iron II form, and must be reduced to iron II in the body. The absence of oxygen, or reducing conditions, will ensure that the iron II form is taken into the body. Ascorbic acid or vitamin C is a reducing agent and will aid the intake of iron in this manner. A glass of orange juice, particularly a formulated juice with added ascorbic acid, will ensure the utilisation of iron from an enriched breakfast cereal which is eaten after the juice.

In food processing loss of iron occurs as it dissolves into processing water which may be discarded. Finely chopped or diced vegetables present a large surface area to water and therefore many substances including iron readily dissolve in the water. In certain vegetables iron accumulates near the peel and therefore, peeling will usually remove the iron.

Potassium and sodium

Both these elements are important in cell and body fluids. Potassium is used in soft tissues and helps to control pH and osmotic pressure within the cell. Sodium and potassium usually occur with chlorine and are taken into the body from a wide range of foods and chlorides. Sodium and potassium are involved in maintaining an electrolyte balance in the body. Excessive amounts are excreted by the kidneys so that a balance particularly between the concentration of sodium and chloride is maintained.

There is growing evidence that many people eat too much salt (sodium chloride) with their food. Not only is salt used in cooking but it is liberally added to the food during the meal. This excess consumption of salt leads to excess sodium in the body and the electrolytic balance is upset. Excessive salt has been shown to lead to high blood pressure, some stress and nervous symptoms and possibly to kidney disease in susceptible individuals. People suffering from high blood pressure are usually put on a salt-free diet and are recommended salt substitutes, particularly potassium chloride. High salt intake also causes the retention of body fluid, which obviously causes weight increase and has been implicated with the symptoms of pre-menstrual tension in some women.

The body can obtain enough sodium from a normal diet without the unnecessary additions in the food factory or kitchen. The current theory is that salt will only cause high blood pressure in those with a family history of such problems.

Trace elements

Very small amounts of some minerals are needed in the body. The essential trace elements are; chromium, cobalt, copper, fluorine, iodine, manganese, molybdenum, nickel, selenium, silicon, tin, vanadium and zinc. Many of these substances are essential constituents of enzyme systems but some are involved in other functions. For example, iodine is essential for the thyroid gland to produce the hormone thyroxine. The body requires about 20 – 40mg of iodine daily and normally this is available from fish, other seafoods and vegetables. Shortage of iodine can cause goitre, which is an enormous enlargement of the thyroid gland (known as 'Derbyshire neck') Salt is 'iodised' with potassium iodide to supplement the iodine from food. However, certain processes lower iodide levels in food and supplementation of salt may be insufficient particularly for people on low salt diets.

PRACTICAL EXERCISES: *MINERALS*

A food sample should be converted into ash before the following tests are performed. The sample is placed in a crucible is then heated in a muffle furnace for two or three hours to ash the sample If a furnace is not available, heat for a longer period with a bunsen, which for some products might be sufficient.

To a few drops of a solution of the ash carry out the following:-

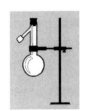

1. Chloride –

Add a few drops of silver nitrate solution, which gives a white precipitate with chloride.

2. Sulphate –

Add a few drops of barium chloride solution. A white precipitate, which does not dissolve on adding hydrochloric acid, indicated the presence of sulphate.

3. Carbonate –

Add a few drops of dilute sulphuric or hydrochloric acid. Effervescence will occur if a carbonate is present. Also test the dry ash with acid.

4. Phosphate –

Add concentrated nitric acid. Take care! Then add ammonium molybdate solution (10%). Heat in boiling water and look for the formation of a yellow colour or precipitate.

5. Flame test for metals –

Use a special wire loop and dip into the ash solution. Place the loop in a bunsen flame and note the colour;

    Potassium – lilac

    Calcium – red

    Copper – green

    Sodium – yellow

6. Test for iron (Iron III or ferric compounds)

To a few drops of the ash solution add hydrochloric acid and the ammonium thiocyanate solution (10%). A red colour indicates the presence of ferric (iron III). Iron II or ferrous compounds can be detected by treating the sample with hydrogen peroxide and gently heating. This converts iron II to iron III, which is then detected as above.

Chapter 6

Vitamins

PREVEIW

- **Vitamins** – organic substances required in very small amounts
- **Water-soluble vitamins:**
  Ascorbic acid (C)
  'B' complex
- **Fat-soluble vitamins:**
  Retinol (A)
  Calciferols (D)
  Tocopherols (E)
  Naphthoquinones (K)
- **Ascorbic acid (C):**
  deficiency causes 'scurvy'
  destroyed by heat, leached by water, oxidised readily, stable in acid
  natural reducing agent
  considerable losses in cooking and processing
- **Thiamin (B_1)**
  deficiency causes 'beri-beri'
  destroyed by heat, leached by water, sulphur compounds cause breakdown
  lost in cooking and processing, particularly in milling cereals, eg rice
- **Riboflavin (B_2)**
  deficiency causes skin problems – but rare
  heat-stable but destroyed in alkali
  useful yellow colour
- **Pyridoxine**
  deficiency rare
  lost in milling cereals
  destroyed by heat, particularly in alkali
  susceptible to light
- **Cyanocobalamin (B_{12})**
  deficiency causes pernicious anaemia
  found in animal products only
  heat-stable, not lost in cooking or processing
- **Nicotinic acid (niacin)**
  deficiency causes pellagra
  soluble in water but usually unaffected by cooking or processing
  often unavailable in a food eg in cereals
- **Pantothenic acid**
  deficiency rare
  destroyed by dry heat, acids and alkalis

- **Biotin**

  deficiency rare

  unaffected by cooking or processing

  bound by egg protein – avidin

- **Folic acid**

  deficiency causes anaemia

  may be deficient in some UK diets

  destroyed by heat processing, particularly in presence of air

- **Retinol (vitamin A)**

  deficiency causes 'night blindness'

  excessive amounts cause poisoning

  carotenoids converted to retinol but require β–ionone ring in their structure

  stable in cooking and processing, but oxidised in dried products easily

- **Calciferols (vitamin D)**

  deficiency causes 'rickets'

  synthesised by action of sunlight on skin or from fish liver oils

  related to cholesterol

  unaffected by cooking and processing

  excessive intake causes poisoning

- **Tocopherols (vitamin E)**

  deficiency rare in humans

  sterility in rats

  natural antioxidant

  extravagant health claims

  lost in processing by oxidation

- **Naphthoquinones (vitamin K)**

  deficiency – uncontrolled bleeding

  one form produced in gut by bacteria

  little loss in cooking or processing

Vitamins are organic substances, which are required in small quantities but cannot be synthesised by the body. A substance which acts as a vitamin for one animal may not always be required by others, for example, many animals synthesise their own vitamin C. Low levels in the diet of a vitamin will cause a *vitamin deficiency disease,* which may be fatal if not remedied. However, although figures may be quoted for the vitamin content of particular food there is no guarantee that the vitamin can be absorbed from the food into the body during digestion. Many vitamins can be bound with other substances in the food. A balanced diet will ensure that the body receives at least its minimum requirement of vitamins. High levels of certain vitamins have been advocated by some experts, and some fanatics, to cure all manner of illnesses. The body can become adjusted to higher levels of vitamins and can develop deficiency diseases when the level of vitamin intake is lowered to a normal level.

An argument often made against processed foods is that they contained fewer or lower concentrations of vitamins or even none at all. Certainly processing reduces the level of many vitamins, but equally bad storage and poor cooking techniques take their toll of vitamins in the diet. Often the food manufacturer has the opportunity of adding vitamins to a food product, thus making it a better source than the original 'fresh' product. Margarine, by law, must contain 900mg/100g of vitamin A and 8mg/100g of vitamin D, which is similar to the vitamin level of summer butter. However, most butter often falls below these levels!

It is normal to divide the vitamins into two groups; water-soluble and fat-soluble vitamins. There has been some confusion over the naming of vitamins and the letter each one was assigned. Groups of vitamins, for example the B group, have similar structures and, therefore, have been given the same letter but with a number postscript. To avoid difficulties it is better to remember the names of the vitamins in common usage. The vitamins are listed in Table 1.10 with their main sources and uses in the body.

Table 1.10

Vitamins

Name	Letter	Source	Use in body
Water-soluble			
Ascorbic acid	C	Potatoes, fruit, rose hips	Proper formation of teeth, gums, blood vessels
'B complex':– Thiamin	B_1	Wheatgerm, yeast	Co-enzymes in many reactions
Riboflavin	B_2	Kidney, liver, cheese	
Pyridoxine	B_6	Yeast, liver, grain	
Cyanocobalamin	B_{12}	Liver, fatty fish	
Nicotinic acid	–	Yeast, meat, liver	
Pantothenic acid	–	Many foods	
Biotin	–	Liver, yeast	
Folicacid	–	Broccoli, waterrcress, liver	
Fat-soluble			
Retinol	A	Fish oils,milk, green vegetables	Necessary for skin, normal growth and eyesight
Calciferols	D	Butter, margarine, fish oils, fatty fish	Necessary for calcium absorption in formation of bones and teeth
Tocopherols	E	Wheatgerm, vegetable oils	Important in cell metabolism
Naphthoquinones	K	Spinach, kale, cauliflower	Involved in blood clotting

WATER-SOLUBLE VITAMINS

ASCORBIC ACID (Vitamin C)

More has been written about this vitamin than any other and probably more has been claimed for its benefits. There is some evidence that it helps to speed up the curing of a common cold and it may also help to alleviate the symptoms of a number of other illnesses; some believe it helps prevent cancer. This is based on the evidence that animals which synthesise their own vitamin C suffer such diseases less often. The function of ascorbic acid in the body is still not fully understood, but it is involved in the formation of hydroxproline which is a key constituent of collagen. Deficiency of vitamin C leads to the disease of scurvy which used to be the cause of misery and finally death for sailors on long voyages up to the last century. Symptoms of the disease include lassitude, swelling and bleeding of gums, loosening of teeth, bruising, internal bleeding and finally death. Fresh fruit from any source quickly cured the disease. British sailing ships during the 19th century put into ports of the West Indies to take on board lime juice which was known to cure the sickness, hence the term for British sailors 'Limies'.

Vitamin C is ascorbic acid in either the oxidised or reduced form. The latter is a powerful reducing agent and use can be made of this property in food processing, as an antioxidant.

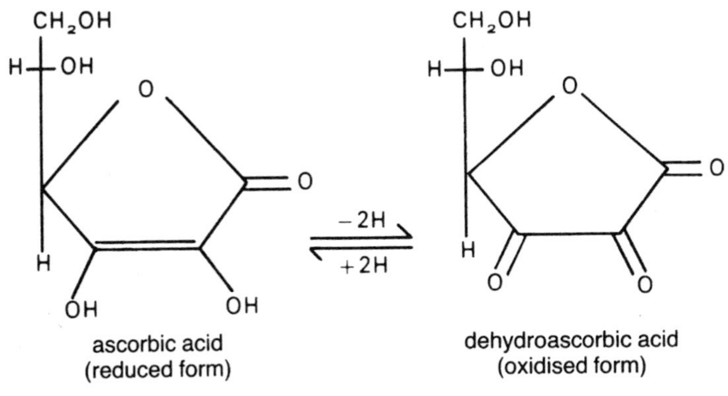

ascorbic acid
(reduced form)

dehydroascorbic acid
(oxidised form)

Figure 1.47
Vitamin C

Some fruits, particularly berries, are rich in vitamin C, for example blackcurrants can contain 200mg/100g, rose hips 175mg/100g and strawberries 60mg/100g. Oranges, considered by many a good source, contain 50mg/100g .Tropical fruits often contain considerable amounts of the vitamin and similarly fruit exposed to the sun usually contains more than fruit in the shade. Outer layers of many fruits contain more than inner layers. New potatoes contain perhaps 30mg/100g which falls to as little as 8mg/100g after six months storage.

Although figures are quoted for levels of the vitamin in a certain food these levels are frequently much lower as the vitamin is easily destroyed by oxidation, heat and water extraction. When a foodstuff is processed it is often cut, diced or chopped and because of this enzymes are released which catalyse the oxidation of ascorbic acid. Acid will greatly retard the loss due to oxidation, as oxidation is most rapid under alkaline conditions, and in the presence of small amounts of copper, such as copper pans.

When cooking some vegetables, such as runner beans, it is a common practice to add a small amount of bicarbonate of soda (sodium hydrogen carbonate) in order to prevent chlorophyll loss, thus keeping the bright green colour of the fresh vegetable. Chlorophyll is stable under alkaline conditions which is directly opposite to ascorbic acid. Thus the addition of bicarbonate of soda, making the vegetable slightly alkaline, will cause the loss of vitamin C. However, does this matter in a balanced diet? Most people do not rely on runner beans as a source of vitamin C and the benefits of cooking an attractive product instead of a muddy-grey one far outweighs this slight loss of vitamin C in the diet.

During cooking and processing, losses of up to 75% of ascorbic acid may occur. Short processes involving small volumes of water incur the smallest losses. However, most processes cause significant losses particularly dehydration, canning and freezing. Fortunately, if blanching is required, as for example before canning or freezing, ascorbic acid may be added to the blanching water. This not only increases the vitamin C level of the product but often produces colour and flavour improvements.

There is still a debate as to what the daily intake of vitamin C should be. In 1969 the DHSS recommended 30mg per day; in 1973 the US Food and Drug Administration recommended 60mg; and now some authorities say the figure should be as high as 100mg. However, an intake of as little as 10mg will prevent the symptoms of scurvy.

THE VITAMIN B COMPLEX

Often vitamins of this group are found associated with protein, for example in liver, kidney, cheese and yeast. Many of the vitamins in the group act as co-enzymes and therefore deficiency in the diet may interfere with vital enzyme controlled reactions in the body.

Thiamin (Vitamin B_1)

This vitamin follows closely the behaviour of ascorbic acid in foods, although normally it is not found with ascorbic acid. It is readily soluble in water and is rapidly destroyed by heat in neutral or alkaline solutions but is relatively stable in acid conditions. The vitamin will leach out of a food in proportion to the amount of water in contact with it, the surface area of the food exposed and the degree of agitation of the food in the water. Any process that minimises the length of time a food is subjected to these three factors, the less will be the vitamin loss. In cooking, thiamin loss may vary from 15 – 60% depending on the amount of water used and the temperature of cooking.

Serious losses of thiamin occur when sulphur dioxide or sulphites, such as sodium metabisulphite, are used as preservatives. These sulphur compounds are also used to inhibit browning, for example in frozen chipped potatoes. In such products thiamin is readily lost.

The disease known as beri-beri, in any of three different forms, occurs when the diet is deficient in the vitamin. In the Far East polishing of rice, by removing the outer layer of the grain, caused widespread outbreaks of the disease. If the rice is parboiled before milling, then dried, the vitamin migrates from the outer layers of the rice grain into the centre and is therefore not lost during milling. The disease can show a range of symptoms developing through loss of appetite, muscular weakness, palpitations, fever and sudden heart failure. Treatment with thiamin causes rapid recovery. In Western diets the disease is rare but has been found in people suffering from anorexia and alcoholism. An average man requires about 1 – 5mg per day of thiamin.

Riboflavin (Vitamin B_2)

Although classed as a water-soluble vitamin it is not as soluble as others in the group. In most foods the vitamin is heat-stable and can withstand boiling in acid conditions. However, like ascorbic acid and thiamin it is decomposed by heat under alkaline conditions, which fortunately rarely occur in foods. Again the best sources of vitamin are liver, yeast and dairy products, but it is fairly common in most foods. Deficiency of the vitamin shows itself in skin problems, particularly cracking of the skin around the mouth. About 2mg per day is needed in the diet. Riboflavin and its derivative riboflavin phosphate are useful food colours giving attractive yellow shades.

Pyridoxine (Vitamin B_6)

Deficiency of this vitamin is rare as it occurs in a fairly wide range of foods. Like thiamin, however, it can be lost during the milling of grain. It can be destroyed by heat, particularly under alkaline conditions, and is susceptible to light. Dermatitis, nervous problems and some types of fits may be caused by deficiency of the vitamin. About 1 – 2mg per day is sufficient for most adults.

Cyanocobalamin (Vitamin B_{12})

This vitamin, which has an extremely complex structure, is not found in fruit or vegetables. The main source is animal food, but it sometimes occurs in seaweed products and fungi. Pernicious anaemia results if the diet is deficient in the vitamin and usually strict vegetarians (vegans), who eat no animal food, are the only people susceptible. The recommended daily amount required in the diet is only 3mg (ie 0.000003g). The vitamin is heat-stable and is not usually lost in processing.

Nicotinic acid (niacin)

The related compound nicotinamide has a similar biological function as a co-enzyme involved in the metabolism of carbohydrates. Readily soluble in water, this vitamin is unaffected, however, by most cooking and processing operations. Although found with other B vitamins in liver, yeast and meat, it can also be synthesised to a limited amount from the amino acid tryptophan. Deficiency disease takes the form of diarrhoea, mental problems and skin disorders, and is generally known as *pellagra*. This is an example of a vitamin which is often not available in a food as it is bound to be some other substances and cannot be released by enzymes found in the human digestive system. This occurs particularly in cereals, and people living for example on maize, may develop symptoms of pellagra. The normal dietary requirement is about 18mg per day.

Pantothenic acid

This vitamin, although present in most foods, is destroyed by the dry heat, acids and alkalis. It forms part of the co-enzyme known as co-enzyme A, which is involved in metabolism of lipids and carbohydrates. Daily requirements are about 6mg, but deficiency disease is highly unlikely to occur.

Biotin

Biotin is generally unaffected by processing, but a protein called *avidin* in egg white will combine with it, making it unavailable. The bacteria in the human gut synthesise the vitamin so deficiency is very rare.

Folic acid (folacin)

Folic acid is one of the few nutrients which may be deficient in the UK diet, particularly the diet of the elderly and pregnant women. The latter are normally prescribed iron tablets supplemented with vitamins, which include folic acid for this reason. Liver, broccoli and watercress are food sources, but some may be produced by intestinal bacteria.

Folic acid deficiency causes a type of anaemia in which red blood cells become enlarged (megalobastic anaemia). People, particularly pregnant women, living on poor diets, such as those based on cassava, rice or wheat, have shown the symptoms. The vitamin is involved in the synthesis of a number of compounds in the body including some amino acids. Heat processing can destroy the vitamin particularly in the presence of oxygen or air. About 0.4mg per day is needed by an adult.

FAT-SOLUBLE VITAMINS

RETINOL (VITAMIN A)

This was the first fat-soluble vitamin to be discovered and it occurs only in animal products such as fish oils, dairy products and liver. However, many green vegetables and carrots contain carotenoid substances (see sections 1.7.1 and 1.7.1.1) which can be converted partially or completely into retinol. The carotenes (a, b & g) show vitamin A activity, which is often called *pro-vitamin* A.

In figure 1.48 the ring at the left of the structure is known as β–*ionone* ring. Caroteniods must have this ring in their structures in order to act as a pro-vitamin A. Lycopene, the red pigment of tomatoes, has open rings at both ends of its structure and therefore shows no vitamin A activity. It is obvious, therefore, that β–ionone rings can be converted into two molecules of retinol and therefore has double the pro-vitamin A activity compared with α– and γ–carotenes which have only one β–ionone ring. Unfortunately, carotenoids are not easily absorbed from the gut.'

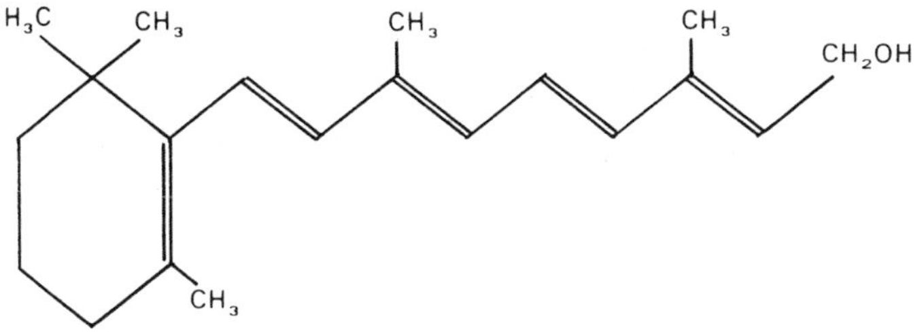

Figure 1.48
Structure of retinol

Vitamin A deficiency will cause a general deterioration in health and maintenance of skin. Colour and 'night blindness' are usually the first symptoms of a deficiency. Pilots flying night missions in the War were encouraged to eat plenty of carrots to help them see in the dark. Dairy products and fish liver oils, particularly, would have been a better recommendation!

It is possible to be poisoned by excessive intake of vitamin A which can cause drowsiness, skin and bone disease and liver enlargement. Retinol is fairly stable during cooking but may be destroyed by oxidative rancidity. Dehydrated products, such as dried diced carrot, can quickly lose their colour (carotenoids) and the pro-vitamin A activity, if exposed to air or oxygen.

CALCIFEROLS (VITAMIN D)

Vitamin D, not only occurs in fish liver oil and dairy products, but can be synthesised in the body by exposure to sunlight (UV light). By our definition of a vitamin, therefore, vitamin D should not be included. However, as we know, only too well, sunlight is often absent in the UK and people could show deficiency of the vitamin leading to the disease known as *rickets*. As calcium absorption and bone formation is impaired, particularly in children, the disease shows itself in the bending of bones in the legs and other deformities. Cod liver oil contains vitamin D type compounds and it is therefore a traditional remedy for rickets. Rickets has largely been eliminated with perhaps the exception of some immigrant communities. Some darker skinned immigrants, not eating foods containing sufficient calciferols, have shown symptoms of rickets. Ultra violet light is not absorbed as much by a darker skin and therefore there is insufficient synthesis of the vitamin in the body.

Vitamin D is related structurally to cholesterol and is derived from this steroid in the skin.

Figure 1.49

Structure of calciferol

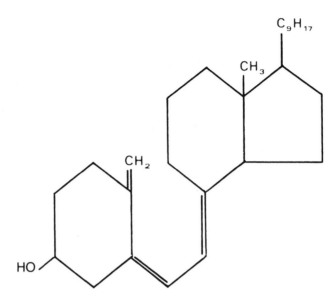

There are two calciferols which differ slightly. Cholecalciferol (vitamin D_3) is formed in the skin and ergocalciferol (vitamin D_2) can be prepared from yeast.

Vitamin D is unaffected by cooking processes and is resistant to heat. About 2.5mg is sufficient for adults. Excessive intake can cause poisoning which damages the kidneys and may be fatal.

TOCOPHEROLS (VITAMIN E)

There are eight different, but related, substances, which show vitamin E activity. They occur particularly in wheat germ and in a number of vegetable oils, but are widely distributed in small amounts. α–Tocopherol is the most common form. Original research on the vitamin showed that deficiency produced sterility in rats. However, in humans, dietary deficiency is unusual but may occur in babies, leading to anaemia and possibly blindness.

The role of vitamin E in human metabolism is still obscure but it may be involved in certain cell metabolic reactions. Many claims have been made for health giving properties of vitamin E and its curing of diseases such as diabetes or heart disease. Large doses are said to have cosmetic uses and possible 'anti – ageing' effects. None of these claims have been validated.

However, vitamin E is a widespread naturally occurring antioxidant. It has clearly been shown to retard oxidative rancidity of lipids, particularly in vegetable oils. This antioxidant property will also be of value in protecting other vitamins, such as retinol, which are susceptible to oxidation in certain food products.

As tocopherols can be oxidised easily they are often lost in processing; for example, the vitamin E activity of wheatgerm is lost completely during the wheat milling process. Excessive intake of the vitamin is not toxic and therefore use could be made of added vitamin E to certain foods to protect against oxidative rancidity.

NAPHTHOQUINONES (VITAMIN K)

This fat-soluble vitamin is found in two forms; vitamin K1 found in green vegetables and vitamin K2 which is produced by bacterial decomposition of protein in the gut. Biochemists have produced a water-soluble version, K3, which can be used to treat deficiency symptoms. The main function of the vitamin is in blood clotting; a symptom of deficiency is uncontrolled bleeding after even a slight injury. Fat absorption in babies may be impaired by insufficient vitamin K in the diet.

As with most of the fat-soluble vitamins, losses during cooking and processing are very low.

PRACTICAL EXERCISE: *VITAMINS*

It is only possible to carry out simple experiments on ascorbic acid, which is readily available.

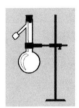

Determination of Vitamin C

The dye 2 : 6 dichlorophenol indophenol (DCPIP) is discolourised by ascorbic acid (and other reducing agents). The dye is available in special tablets, and usually one tablet, when made into solution is decolourised by 1mg of ascorbic acid.

Ascorbic acid can be determined in fruit juices, natural fruits and other fruit products.

Use a pipette and put 10cm3 of juices into a standard 100cm3 flask; add about 50cm^3 of acetic acid and make up to volume with distilled water. Make up a dye solution as per label instructions and fill into a burette.

Pipette 10cm3 of prepared juices into a flask and add a few drops of acetone (this is to remove sulphur dioxide, which interfaces with the titration). Titrate the dye, which is discolourised, until all the ascorbic acid in the juice is used up, and the end-point is when a faint pink colour persists. Calculate the ascorbic acid content of the juice.

Chapter 7

Pigments

PREVIEW

- **Colour** good indicator of the freshness of food
- **Pigments naturally occurring**
  Isoprenoid derivatives
  Tetrapyrrole derivatives
  Benzopyran derivatives
- **Isoprenoid derivatives**
  carotenoids – contain 40 carbon atoms
  yellow/ orange/ red
  require complete β–ionone ring to have pro-vitamin A activity
  most common β–carotene
  stable to heat but can be oxidised
  if contain hydroxyl group (OH) known as *xanthophylls*
- **Tetrapyrrole derivatives**
  chlorophylls
  4 pyrrole rings held together by methene (-CH=) bridges
  atom of magnesium held in centre of structure
  very unstable, readily destroyed in cooking
  susceptible to acids but stable in alkalis
  pheophytin, grey/ brown formed when magnesium is replaced by hydrogen due to acids in cooking
- **Haemoglobin**
  red pigment of blood
  similarly myoglobin – red pigment of muscle
  similar structure to chlorophyll but different side chains and iron II in centre of structure
  oxyhaemoglobin and oxymyoglobin bright red, if lose oxygen become dull red or purple haemoglobin or myoglobin
  pink colour in cured meats due to nitrosomyglobin
- **Benzopyran derivatives**
  anthocyanins
  red to purple water soluble pigments found in flowers and many fruit
  anthocyanin = anthocyanidin + sugar(s)
  anthocyanidins, named after flowers, *eg* peonidin – deep red
  anthocyanins red in acid, blue in alkali
  react with metals to form grey compounds
- **Colours as food additives**
  most derived from coal tar
  permitted list only may be used in foods
  very stable, known colour intensity and cheaper than natural colours

The attractive and often unique colours of a particular food are due to the presence of small amounts of pigment molecules. The colour plays an important role in the appeal of a food and is of equal consequence in manufactured foods, such as convenience products, as in natural foods. Colour plays a part, with other factors, in the overall organoleptic assessment of the food. If, for example, a strawberry flavoured ice-cream is coloured green it will confuse many tasters. Colour is a good indicator of the freshness of foods as microbial deterioration or other spoilage is always accompanied by a change in colour. Fruit and vegetables indicate their ripeness by a change in colour.

Food colours are usually divided into those which occur naturally and those which are synthetic. However, this is a little confusing as some natural food colours can be readily synthesised and the natural and synthetic colours are indistinguishable. Synthetic or manufactured colours grew out of the dye industry, initially developed for textiles. Colours were selected for foods because they were low in perhaps lead or arsenic. Legislation has subsequently demanded very high levels of purity and high colour potential. Much criticism is levelled at these colours by those opposed to additives. However, the main synthetic food colours have been subjected to extensive toxicological testing and are only approved when known to be safe. These colours offer advantages to the food manufacturer which include: lower price, consistency and strength of colour, known performance during food processing and, usually, readily availability.

COLOURS NATURALLY PRESENT IN FOODS

Colour compounds are often complex structures. Pigments occurring naturally in foods are often blends of a number of different pigments and a food sometimes has different pigments at different stages of its existence in the 'unharvested state'. For example, a tomato is coloured green with chlorophyll when unripe; this green colour, and chlorophyll, gradually disappears on ripening whilst the red carotenoid, lycopene, is synthesised. As animals age their fat becomes more yellow as carotenoids become dissolved in the fat over a long period of time.

Table 1.11 shows naturally occurring pigments, with the main examples of each and where they can be found. (Please remember that these compounds can be extracted or synthesised in some cases and added to the foodstuffs, but it is convenient to classify them as naturally occurring.)

ISOPRENOID DERIVATIVES – CAROTENOIDS

These compounds are derived from isoprene (C_5H_8) and all true carotenoids have 40 carbon atoms, *ie* eight isoprene units. These pigments vary from yellow to red and are mainly fat-soluble. The pigments are structurally related to retinol, vitamin A.

Table 1.11

Naturally occurring colours

Main group	Examples	Colours	Occurrence
Isoprenoid derivatives	Carotenoids:		
	carotenes	orange	carrots, apricot, fish oil
	lycopene	red	tomatoes, water melon
	xanthophylls	yellow	citrus juice
Tetrapyrrole derivatives	Chlorophylls	green	vegetables, unripe fruit
	Pheophytin	grey/brown is heated	produced when chlorophyll
	Haemoglobin	dull red	blood (no oxygen)
	oxyhaemoglobin	bright red	blood (with oxygen)
	Myoglobin	purple/red	muscle/meat
	Oxymyoglobin	bright red	muscle (with oxygen)
Benzopyran derivatives	Anthocyanins	red/blue/ purple	blackcurrants, flowers, cherries
	Flavones	white/yellow	potato, apples
	Tannins	brown	tea

Carotenoids must have a β–ionone ring to have pro-vitamin A activity, (see Section 1.6.2.1). In Figures 1.50 and 1.51 are the structures of the most common carotenoid, β–carotene, showing two β–ionone rings, and carotene is always accompanied by other carotenoids, for example in carrots by α– and γ–carotene.

The carotenoids are generally stable to heat during processing and cooking but can be readily oxidised in dehydrated foods to form colourless compounds. The alternating double-single bonds, conjugated double bond system, explains the intense colour of these compounds and their stability in most situations.

Figure 1.50

Structure of b-carotene

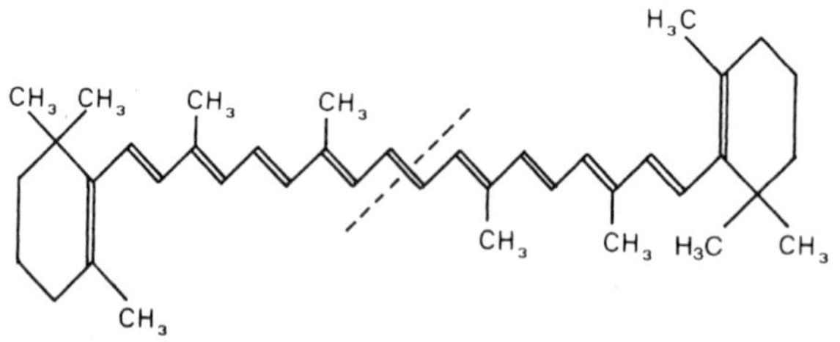

Figure 1.51

Structure of lycopene

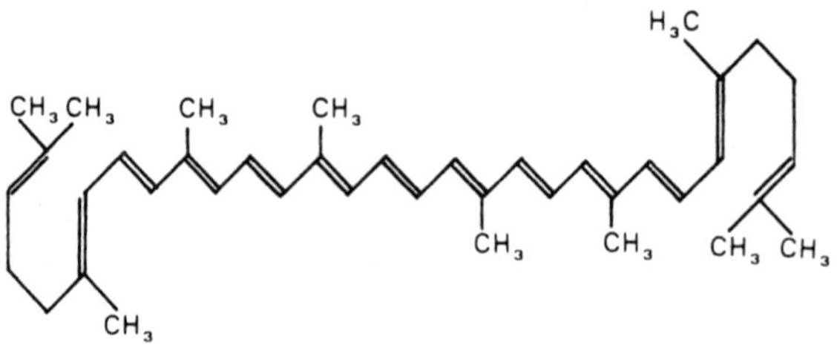

Carotenoids can readily be seen as the dominant colour of tomatoes, water melons, peaches, peppers, carrots, apricots and spices such as saffron. However, one cannot assume that a yellow, orange or red colour is a carotenoid as a number of the more reddy pigments can easily look like some anthocyanins. The carotenoids are often masked by other pigments, particularly by chlorophyll. When a fruit ripens chlorophyll is broken down and the yellow/red carotenoid is exposed to give the ripe appearance of the fruit. Lycopene is an exception as it is synthesised by tomatoes as chlorophyll is broken down during ripening.

Considerable quantities of carotenoids are extracted and used as colours for manufactured foods. However, as the carotenoids are insoluble in water they are often converted into emulsions in water before mixing with a food. The most important applications of carotenoids are in colouring soft drinks, jellies, boiled sweets, desserts and yogurts. Carotene as a suspension in oil can be used to colour margarine, with the advantage that it adds pro-vitamin A activity to the product.

Carotenoids which contain hydroxyl groups (-OH) are called *xanthophylls*. They are often mixed with carotenes in food pigments and tend to have a light yellow colour. A typical example is cryptoxanthin which, in effect, is β–carotene with one hydroxyl group (OH) attached to the second β–ionone ring on carbon atom 3. Cryptoxanthin is the chief pigment of maize, paprika and mandarin orange.

In Table 1.12 a summary is given of some of the combinations of carotenoids to give the colour of a particular food product.

Food	Carotenoids
Orange	β-carotene, lycopene, cryptoxanthin, xanthophyll, violaxanthin
Red pepper (Chilli)	α-carotene, β-carotene, capxanthin
Carrot	α-carotene, β-carotene, γ-carotene, xanthophyll
Maize	α, β, γ-carotenes, zeaxanthin, crytoxanthin, xanthophyll and several others
Peach	β-carotene, crytoxanthin, xanthophyll, zeaxanthin

Table 1.12

Combinations of carotenoids in foods

TETRAPYRROLE DERIVATIVES

Chlorophylls

Chlorophylls are the most common pigments found in foods as they occur in leaves, unripe fruit and many vegetables. Chlorophylls occur within the cells in small bodies, the chloroplasts, and usually there is three times as much a as b. Chlorophylls are large molecules composed of four pyrrole rings (hence tetrapyrrole) held together by methene bridges (-CH=). In the simplified structure of a chlorophyll given in Figure 1.52, the four pyrrole rings can be seen and in the centre an atom of magnesium is held. Around the outside of the structure in positions 1 to 8 there are different groups such as methyl, ethyl, vinyl, and a specific alcohol is attached at position 7 called phytol.

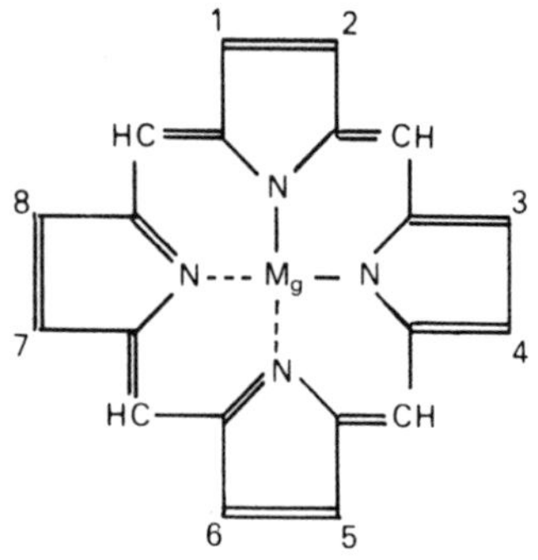

Figure 1.52

Structure of chlorophyll (simplified)

Chlorophyll (b) differs from (a) in that it has an aldehyde group (CHO) in position 3 instead of the methyl group (CH$_3$).

The chlorophylls are very unstable molecules when the living plant cell is killed during cooking or processing. Thus the green colour of chlorophylls is readily lost during heat processing. As the chlorophylls exist as protein complexes in the living cell, when the cell is killed by cooking or processing the protein is denatured and the chlorophyll released. Acids present in the food, or produced by heat, are able to substitute two atoms of hydrogen for the magnesium in the centre of the chlorophyll. The chlorophyll changes to an olive green colour or even to brown as the substitution of magnesium by hydrogen produces a substance called pheophytin. Pheophytin has the same tetrapyrrole structure as chlorophyll but contains hydrogen and not magnesium in the centre of the structure.

Obviously, in the absence of acid this reaction will not occur, or only slightly. Sodium hydrogen carbonate (bicarbonate of soda) can be added to vegetables to make them slightly alkaline and thus reduce chlorophyll decomposition, keeping the bright green colour. However, as pointed out in Section 1.6, a number of vitamins, particularly C and B$_1$, are easily destroyed under alkaline conditions.

A number of vegetables such as peas, spinach, sprouts and cabbage, produce a number of acids during heat processing, such that the pH may fall from about 6.6 to 6.1. These acids will accelerate the decomposition of chlorophyll unless the acidity is decreased by the addition of bicarbonate.

Some metals react with chlorophylls to form bright green compounds. Iron III, zinc and copper II ions will replace the magnesium in chlorophyll to produce stable green products. Unscrupulous manufacturers in the past have added copper salts to canned vegetables to improve their colour. Obviously this practice could lead to poisoning.

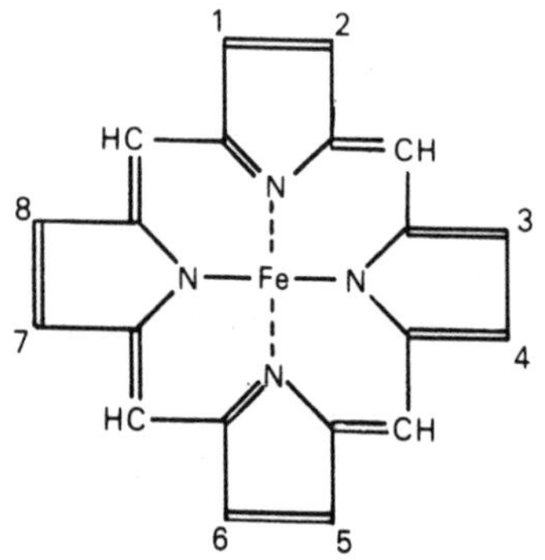

Haemoglobin and myoglobin

A remarkable coincidence of nature is that the red pigment of many animals, haemoglobin, is structurally very similar to the green pigment, chlorophyll, of plants. Haemoglobin, however, contains a tetrapyrrole derivative, called haem, with iron II and not Mg in the centre of the structure. In blood, haemoglobin exists as four haem units, joined to one molecule of protein.

Figure 1.53

Structure of haem

The groups attached at positions 1 to 8 are methyl, vinyl, methyl, vinyl, methyl, propanoic acid, propanoic acid and methyl, in that order.

Myoglobin is the principal pigment present in muscle, and it is composed of only one haem unit and one protein molecule.

The unique property of haemoglobin and myoglobin is the capacity to bid a molecule of oxygen but without oxidising the iron II (ferrous) to iron III (ferric) in the centre of the structure. The reaction is readily reversible and is the life-giving system which transfers oxygen from the lungs to the tissues.

Haemoglobin and myoglobin are a dull purple/red colour but change to a bright red colour when combined with oxygen to form oxyhaemoglobin and oxymyoglobin respectively. This can be seen readily in a joint of beef, the side exposed to the air is bright red but the side next to the plate or packing tray is starved of oxygen and therefore dull red.

If the haem units become detached from the proteins in either myoglobin or haemoglobin they are susceptible to irreversible changes. In this situation, perhaps caused by heat, acids or oxidising agents, the iron is converted from iron II to iron III and the pigment becomes a brown colour due to the formation of methaemoglobin or metmyoglobin. This is readily shown when cooking meat. Heat denatures the protein and allows the haem to disengage itself from the protein, and thus the iron in the haem contains is readily oxidised to the iron III form. Sometimes slight changes occur in the haem structure which result in the formation of green pigments. This can sometimes be seen at the edge of slices of cooked meat.

In cured meat a pink colour is produced as nitrosomyoglobin produced by nitrogen II oxide (nitric oxide (NO)) replacing oxygen held by iron in the structure. The nitrogen II oxide is produced from nitrates and nitrites used in the curing operation.

BENZOPYRAN DERIVATIVES

Anthocyanins

These water-soluble pigments are responsible for many of the bright colours of flowers and many fruits. Unlike many other pigments, the anthocyanins change their colours under various conditions particularly changing pH. Colours range from red to blue and purple.

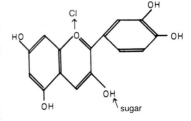

Figure 1.54
Structure of an anthocyanidin

Anthocyanins are made up of a complex ring structure (see figure 1.54) and attached to this is a sugar or a number of sugars. The ring structure is called an *anthocyanidin*.

An anthocyanin = anthocyanidin + sugar(s).

If the number of hydroxyl groups (OH) is greater in the anthocyanidin the resulting anthocyanin is more blue in colour. If the number of methoxyl groups (OCH$_3$) is increased the colour becomes more red. The anthocyanidins have interesting names based on flowers, for example, peonidin produces a red anthocyanin and delphinidin a blue one.

The anthocyanins are good pH indicators as they are red at low pH (acid) and blue at high pH (alkaline). The colour can be lost if sulphur dioxide or sulphites are used to preserve a product as, for example fruit pulp, where the pigments are decolourised.

The pigments can combine with metal particularly iron, tin and aluminium. Some fruits canned in unlacquered cans produce a greyish sludge of anthocyanin which has combined with the metal of the can.

Anthocyanins are very stable in acid conditions and therefore can be extracted and used in acid foods to achieve strong red colours. Canned strawberries can have citric acid added to lower the pH to almost 3 so that an excellent red colour is obtained. Anthocyanins can be added to soft drinks, confectionery, jellies, yogurts and desserts.

There are a number of *flavone* derivatives which have a similar structure to that of anthocyanidins but are usually colourless, yellow or orange pigments. (NB most bright yellow and orange fruits are coloured by carotenoids.) An example of this type of pigment is quercetin which is found in onion skins, hops and tea.

The tannins are another similar group of pigments which are complicated mixtures giving red or brown colour. The significance of tannins in a number of foods is due to the astringency which can readily be appreciated when drinking strong tea. Tannins give body, fullness of flavour and help preserve some red wines, particularly wines from the Bordeaux region, such as clarets, famed for their longevity.

COLOURS AS FOOD ADDITIVES

Food dyes (or synthetic colours) are used throughout the world, although the USA and Europe are the main centres for toxicological tests. In the EU there is a special Food Colourants Working Party which submits detailed suggestions on behalf of food manufacturers; and a list of permitted colours is published and reviewed by the EU at regular intervals. Many of the colours have been known for many years; and the colour industry is an established one aware of consumer reactions and market requirements. Most of the compounds are complex nitrogen-containing structures derived from coal-tar. It cannot be denied that a colourful product is attractive and so there will always be a demand for such colours, particularly as natural colours may be limited, expensive or unavailable.

Currently approved permitted food colours in the EU are split into the naturally occurring and those of dye origin.

Tartrazine has been implicated in an allergic reaction of some people to coloured soft drinks, such as orange squash. The allergy show itself in coughing and itching about the neck. It has also been implicated as a cause of hyperactivity in children.

Many colours have been withdrawn from use over the last few years and it can be assumed that any suspected or implicated in any toxicological disease will be withdrawn.

PRACTICAL EXERCISE: PIGMENTS

Use a range of fruits and vegetables to test the following pigments. Note colour changes produced.

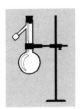

1. Chlorophylls
Boil samples of green vegetables in the following:
(a)   distilled water
(b)   dilute alkali
(c)   dilute acid
(d)   dilute copper sulphate solution

2. Carotenoids (eg in carrots)
(a)   Dice the carrots and boil for 10, 20 and 30 minutes
(b)   Pressure cook samples at various pressures and for various times
(c)   Compare colours of diced carrots after each process

3. Anthocyanins (eg in red fruits: strawberries, plum, raspberry)
Repeat (a), (b) and (c) above (exercise 1)
(d)   add a few drops of a 5% stannous solution (tin 1)
(e)   add a few drops of a 5% ferric (iron III) chloride solution

Chapter 8
Flavours

PREVIEW

- Taste   – Four tastes – salt, sweet, sour, bitter

  Sweet   – detected on tip of tongue

  Sour   – detected on sides of tongue

  Salt   – detected on sides and tip of tongue

  Bitter   – detected on back of tongue
- Saltiness property of electrolytes, eg sodium chloride
- Salt-substitutes – potassium based, eg potassium chloride
- Sweetness   – saccharin   – bitter after taste

                                 – up to 500 times as sweet as sucrose

                – aspartame   – sweetener, 200 times as sweet as sucrose

                                 – made from phenylalanine and aspartic acid
- Sourness   – due to acid

              – essential for some products eg citrus fruits
- Bitterness – due to alkaloids eg quinine
- Odour   – large number of compounds give characteristic flavour of foods
- Essential oils – blends of many flavour compounds, naturally occurring
- Oleoresins   – extracted by solvents from spices and other products
- Terpenoids   – large group of flavour compounds

                  – monoterpenes – because of volatility, are most
                     common flavours
- Monoterpenes – acyclic, eg citral

                – monocyclic, eg limonene

                – bicyclic, eg pinene
- Some non-terpenoid flavour compounds – esters, eg amyl acetate in bananas, diacetyl in butter
- Vegetables   – limited range of odourous compounds

               – sulphur compounds released on cooking
- Flavour   – modifiers

               – monosodium glutamate (MSG) and ribonucleotides

               – enhance meat and vegetable flavours, suppress harsh flavours, eg onion
- Taste panels – comparison and difference tests

                – triangle test

                – ranking

                – flavour profile

The flavour of foods is one of the delights of eating. Food without a certain flavour level is usually considered dull and unappetising and restaurants producing such dishes quickly lose their clientele. Flavour is a combination of taste and smell and in many cases is closely linked to 'mouthfeel'.

TASTE

There are only four true tastes and other 'tastes' or flavours are in fact odours. The four tastes – salt, sweet, sour and bitter – are detected by taste buds on the tongue, the pharynx and soft palate. The taste can be detected if the particular substance is in solution in the saliva or in the natural juices of the food. A sweet taste is detected on the tip of the tongue; sour is detected on the sides; salt on the sides and tip; bitter at the back of the tongue and on the pharynx.

The *salt taste* is a property of the electrolytes, *ie* low molecular weight ionised salts, particularly the halides such as sodium chloride. The order of saltiness is as follows: chlorides, bromides, iodides, sulphates and nitrates. Sodium salts are obviously salty whereas potassium salts can be bitter and unpleasant. This is probably why salt-substitutes, *ie* sodium substitutes, for people on salt-free diet, are not considered to be particularly salty and take some time to be accepted.

A *sweet taste* is, of course, typical of the low-molecular carbohydrates such as fructose, glucose and sucrose. Sucrose is an ideal sweetener, with no after-taste and it can add body to soft drinks. However, particularly in confectionery, it is not sweet enough, and it will cause tooth decay and weight increase. Many other substances show a degree of sweetness and some are many times as sweet as sucrose. Saccharin, up to 500 times as sweet, has been used for many years as a sucrose substitute or in sweeter products. Unfortunately it can have a bitter aftertaste and is not particularly stable in heat processed foods.

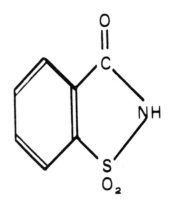

Figure 1.55
Structure of saccharin

Some combinations of amino acids are very sweet. The sweetener, *aspartame*, is made from phenylalanine and aspartic acid. It is nearly 200 times as sweet as sucrose.

Sourness is the taste of acid and is a property of the hydrogen ion (H^+). Food acids are organic acids and are relatively weak or sometimes undissociated (unionised) acids. Some foods require an acid taste to be acceptable, particularly citrus fruits, and to a lesser extent apples and fermented products such as yoghurt.

Bitterness is a property of a number of organic and inorganic compounds, particularly the alkaloids and on occasions substances containing magnesium, calcium and ammonium ions. Some bitter alkaloids include quinine, in tonic water, and caffeine in coffee.

ODOUR

Odours are detected in the nose when compounds in minute quantities come in contact with the olfactory nerve endings. Thousands of different compounds can be detected and they are responsible for giving the characteristic and often subtle 'flavour' of many foods. Food flavour, therefore, is in reality a combination of many odoriferous compounds. The essential requirement for such compounds is that they should be volatile. When a food is eaten the odoriferous compounds change to gases and diffuse through the pharynx up into the nose. We can, of course, smell an odour before eating a food and the memory of this odour, which is always good in most people, stimulates the olfactory senses with a resulting production of saliva, *ie* the mouth 'waters'.

Food flavours are usually complex mixtures of hydrocarbons, alcohols, acids, aldehydes, ketones and esters. The most common types of food flavours, found in fruits and vegetables, are called *essential oils*. This term is somewhat confusing as it is derived from 'essence' and does not mean these oils are essential nutrients for the body. Essential oils occur in most parts of plants and can be readily extracted by pressure or steam distillation. Many of the oils are found in special oil sacs, for example, the skin of oranges contains essential oils which spray from these sacs as the orange is peeled. An enormous industry has developed producing oils, particularly in small island states of the West Indies and Indian Ocean, where they constitute the entire source of foreign exchange. Examples of essential oils include oil of almond, clove, garlic, ginger, lemon, lime, mace, orange and thyme. Less volatile flavour substances can be extracted from plants, particularly spices and herbs, by the use of solvents such as acetone (propanone) and propan -2-ol. These flavour extracts are called *oleoresins*.

The chemical constituents of essential oils are either terpenoids or other compounds.

TERPENOIDS

The terpenoids constitute a very large group of substances which, like the carotenoids, are based on isoprere (C_5H_8). The monoterpenes have two isoprene units (hence their formula of ($C_{10}H_{16}$); the sesquiterpenes have three ($C_{15}H_{24}$); the diterpenes have four units ($C_{20}H_{32}$).

The monoterpenes are the most common group, having the strongest odours. The odour of terpenes is increased if oxygen is included in their structure. As the number of carbon atoms increases, volatility and odour tend to decrease. The monoterpenes can be divided into three main groups; the acyclic, monocyclic and bicyclic monoterpenes.

Acyclic monoterpenes have an open ring structure, but readily close to form a monocyclic monoterpene in certain conditions particularly when heated in the presence of acid, for example in fruit juice. Most of the acyclic monoterpenes have pleasant odours and an oxygenated derivative, citral (actually two similar compounds) gives the flavour to lemon oil.

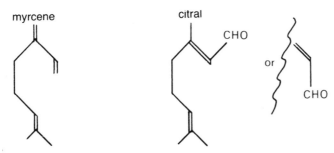

Figure 1.56
Acyclic monoterpenes

Monocyclic monoterpenes represent the most stable form of monoterpenes, and often during storage, processing and extraction of flavours from fruits, other monoterpenes are converted to this group. Lime oil clearly shows the results of such changes as this. Expressed lime oil from the skin of the fruit is similar to lemon oil in odour, but when lime oil is steam-distilled from the fruit pulp and skin, a method commonly used to increase yield, the monoterpenes undergo many changes; for example, citral is partially converted into a monocyclic monoterpene, limonene. Limonene is a common example of this group and is found in many essential oils. A common alcohol, which can be derived from limonene, is α–terpineol, again found in lime oil particularly when it is badly stored or old.

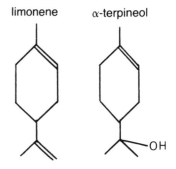

Figure 1.57
Monocyclic monoterpenes

Bicyclic monoterpenes constitute a large group of monoterpenes having an unusual structure of one four-sided ring within a six-sided ring. The pineres have the smell of pine disinfectant but occur in small amounts in many essential oils. There are in this group a number of oxygenated derivatives particularly alcohols.

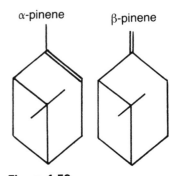

Figure 1.58
Bicyclic monoterpenes

OTHER ODOUR COMPOUNDS

No other single group of compounds in odours of foods is as large as the terpenoids. However, a wide range of substances can be found together with the terpenoids in essential oils and these include hydrocarbons, alcohols, aldehydes, esters, ketones, acids and ethers.

Some flavours, although often very complex mixtures of compounds, depend on one particular substance to give that characteristic flavour. Synthetic flavours used to be made from this particular substance and so were generally poor in comparison with the natural product. Esters are particularly common in fruit flavours and some of the common ones are listed in Table 1.13.

It must be pointed out that to obtain the full characteristic flavour many other substances are needed besides the ones listed in the table and these substances also occur themselves in many other flavours.

Table 1.13

Principal flavouring agents in foods

Food	Flavouring agent	Chemical nature
Almond	benzaldehyde	aldehyde
Banana	amyl acetate	ester
Butter	diacetyl	ketone
Cloves	eugenol	alcohol
Coconut	an aldehyde	aldehyde of 14 C. atoms
Grape	methyl anthranilate	ester
Lemon	citral	aldehyde
Mint	menthol	alcohol
Pear	ethyl acetate	ester
Pineapple	ally caproate	ester
Raspberry	ethyl formate	ester

Vegetables have a limited range of volatile odorous compounds but a number of flavours are developed in cooking. The onion family is rich in sulphur containing compounds, such as alliin, which is converted by enzymes to diallyl thiosulphinate which has the typical strong smell. The cabbage family, similarly, is rich in sulphur – containing compounds which are released on cooking.

MOUTHFEEL

Mouthfeel is often used to indicate the texture of a food when eaten, but it can also be used to indicate sensations such as 'tingling, hot and watery'. The olfactory nerve endings initiate the sensation of smell and the detection of odour, but some nerves in the skin, tongue and cheeks are sensitive to other sensations. Smell ammonia and a 'tingling', quite irritating sensation will be experienced. Many spices and peppers, such as chilli, are described as hot, whereas peppermint may be described as cool.

The texture of food will influence the flavour. Smooth products taste differently from rougher similar products, for example, the sweetness of confectionery may be affected by sucrose crystal size.

FOOD FLAVOURS

Naturally occurring flavours are often extracted from fruit, spices and herbs by the use of solvents or distillation and then used in manufactured food products. Citrus oils can easily be expressed from the peel of the fruit and special machines have been developed for this. A traditional tool in the West Indies, called an écuelle, is used for expressing citrus oils. It is basically a copper funnel to which are attached a number of studs, on which fruit is rubbed. Pieces of peel, some juices and essential oil run down the funnel and are collected. After standing the oil comes to the surface of the mixture and is removed. Steam distillation can be used to increase yield, but as mentioned earlier, in limes, for example, flavour changes will result.

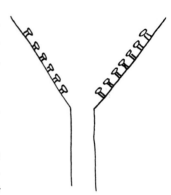

Figure 1.59
An écuelle

Naturally occurring flavours have similar disadvantages to natural colours in being variable, sometimes expensive and often unstable.

Synthetic flavours often meet consumer resistance but have definite advantages for the food processor. Such flavours have been used for many years and are being blended on to sugar, salt, flour or glucose as a means of adding them easily to a dried food product or dissolved in alcohol, *eg* ethanol or propanol, for use in liquid foods. Originally, just esters were used to flavour food products but better analytical techniques have helped to discover a wide range of flavour compounds.

Gas chromatography has probably made the greatest contribution to the study of flavours in being able to separate all the minute components of a flavour which can subsequently be identified by other techniques such as mass spectrometry. A flavour manufacturer cannot analyse a natural flavour then mix all the components, perhaps 100 in all, from various sources to produce an artificial flavour. Normally the main flavouring agents are recognised and these, perhaps with some natural extracts, are blended to make the flavour. In a highly competitive industry the discovery of a particular flavour component is a closely guarded secret on occasions.

Flavours alter in processing and in cooking. A good flavour producer will recognise this and build into his flavour a capacity to change to the desired flavour after processing. A flavour, therefore, might not seem to be correct, but after baking, for example, it may have exactly the right flavour notes. Considerable research is undertaken on flavour precursors for this reason. Intermediate products from the Maillard reaction have, for example, a tendency to develop a 'meaty' flavour.

FLAVOUR MODIFIERS

There are a number of substances used in foods which are capable of enhancing and sometimes reducing the level of a flavour. Salt is a flavour enhancer for some foods and soy sauce has been used for many years in China and Japan. It was found that soy sauce was rich in *monosodium glutamate* (MSG), a derivative of the amino acid glutamic acid, Figure 1.60

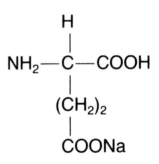

Figure 1.60
Monosodium glutamate

Large quantities of MSG have been used for many years in the food industry and in cooking. Excessive use of MSG can cause dizziness and sickness, first recognised in Chinese cooking and called the 'Chinese Restaurant syndrome'. Food, to which has been added MSG, is often preferred by taste panellists to untreated food. MSG has a 'warm' slightly sweet flavour and it noticeably enhances meat flavours and some vegetable flavours, but generally has no effect on or slightly suppresses sweet flavours. It tends to 'round-off' flavours and will suppress certain strong flavours, such as that of onion. MSG is used in soups, both canned and dried, tinned meats and vegetables.

Ribonucleotides, produced by micro-organisms, have a similar effect to MSG but can be used in very small quantities. Ribonucleotides are now used often as blends with MSG and are formed from ribose, phosphoric acid and a base such as inosine or guanine. They are, of course, naturally occurring particularly in yeast and meat.

TASTE PANELS

No instruments are available which can measure the sensation of flavour.

Although gas chromatographs can separate flavour components, which then can be individually smelt, the overall flavour cannot be measured. Some food industries employ expert tasters with many years of experience, particularly for wine, tea, whisky and some spices. The average food factory has to employ a taste panel to evaluate its products and compare their flavour with those of a competitor. There are a number of standard tasting techniques which can give reliable results if conducted in properly controlled environments where tasters are not influenced by outside factors by each other.

Difference tests are often used with either a pair of unknown food products, or three in a triangle, in which two are identical and the third is to be separated. In *ranking,* a series of samples have to be put in order by the panel according to increasing sweetness, saltiness, flavour or any other characteristic.

A *flavour profile* is an elaborate evaluation of a flavour by a trained panel. The flavour is broken down into its 'components' which are described by any term that accurately describes it, such as mushroom-like, catty, horsey, eggy, and so on. The individual flavour notes are considered; the order of their appearance in the mouth; their strength; the presence of any aftertaste.

Taste panels have many uses but are subject to error and must contain a representative segment of the population to obtain significant results.

PRACTICAL EXERCISE: *FLAVOURS*

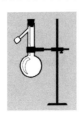

1. Citrus fruits

a) Examine the peel of a citrus fruit with a hand lens and under a low-power microscope. Identify the oil sacs containing the essential oil.

b) Extract oil from oil sacs of a citrus fruit by rubbing the fruit on a grater. Allow to settle and separate the small amount of oil from the skin debris.

c) Crush a fresh lime and note the smell of the essential oil. Gently heat the crushed fruit and note the change in aroma from lemon-like to the typical lime aroma.

2. Taste panels

Set up a taste panel and prepare samples to be tasted by difference (two samples) or by triangle testing (three samples, two identical).

Vary one ingredient in a recipe, for example, salt, sugar, MSG and flavouring. Ask panellists to pick out the one they prefer, or which one is different.

The panel, when experienced, may be able to undertake a 'flavour profile'. Manufactured products may be compared for individual flavour notes; order of their appearance in the mouth; their strength; the presence of aftertastes.

Instant soups are a good starting point.

Chapter 9

Ingredients and Additives

PREVIEW

- **Additives**
  - used to give various functional properties to foods
  - alter either:
    - physical characteristics
    - sensory characteristics
    - storage life
    - nutritional status

- **Starch**
  - modified to improve thickening, binding, stability, mouth feel and to gel
  - cross-linking, main type with phosphate cross-links
  - pre-gelatinised, thicken in cold water.

- **Gums**
  - alginate, celluloses, xanthan, pectins, carageenans and tree gums, *eg* gum arabic
  - all thicken products, many gel or stabilise products.

- **Acidity Control**
  - buffers to control acidity
  - to increase acidity use organic acids e.g. citric acid.

- **Emulsifiers and Stabilisers**
  - emulsifier forms stable emulsion by allowing oil and water to mix
  - stabiliser absorbs large amounts of water
  - emulsifiers also modify starch or protein
  - modify fat crystals.

- **Additives Affect**
  - sensory characteristics of food
  - storage life
  - nutritional status
  - used as manufacturing aids.

- **Additive E Numbers**
  - colours   100–180
  - preservatives   200–290
  - antioxidants   300–321
  - emulsifiers and stabilisers   322–494
  - sweeteners   420–421

- **Other Ingredients**
  - functional proteins; foaming agent
  - sugar syrups; dextrose equivalent concept
  - fat substitutes; protein and carbohydrate based and synthetic.

Most food products are made from a mixture of ingredients and additives. The main food value of the product comes from the ingredients which are helped to achieve their finished product status by the use of additives. The fewer the better now, as additives have received adverse consumer reaction over some time. This has led manufacturers to look for functional properties in the ingredients they use, for example, thickening or emulsifying ability or the opportunity to cross-link with other ingredients to produce a better combined ingredient. This latter synergistic effect is being sought as a property of food ingredients increasingly as new foods with different textures, mouthfeel and behaviour characteristics are constantly being developed.

The main ingredients of food products come under the general headings of carbohydrates, fats and proteins. As well as sources of these, being fruit and vegetable, meat, fish and cereals, increasingly the use of new ingredients from the world of biotechnology will be used. This is already the case with some additives such as xanthan gum.

What are additives?

Additives are chemicals, both synthetic and natural, that are used to give various functional properties to foods. The additives, in the quantities used, are edible but are not foods in their own right. Some additives are very widespread in nature (for example, **pectin, ascorbic acid** (vitamin C)), others come from specific sources, (for example, gums from certain seaweeds). Naturally-occurring additives must be treated and controlled in exactly the same way as synthetic ones.

FUNCTIONAL PROPERTIES OF ADDITIVES

It is possible to divide additives into four main groups according to their functional properties. Additives in a food alter either:

(a) its physical characteristics
(b) its sensory characteristics, such as flavour, texture and colour
(c) its storage life
(d) its nutritional status.

In addition to these four, another group of additives is used by manufacturers as an aid to the production of large quantities of high quality foods. In fact, some additives can fulfil more than one function. For example, thickeners such as starch fall in groups (a) and (b). Vitamin C (ascorbic acid) is an **antioxidant**, therefore belonging to group (c), but is also a vitamin, belonging to group (d).

ADDITIVES AFFECTING THE PHYSICAL CHARACTERISTICS OF A FOOD

A food product may be:

– made thicker and gelled
– made more or less acid

– aerated with gas bubbles
– emulsified.

Thickening or gelling

Hydrocolloids are substances capable of holding, by various means, large quantities of water within their structures, or joined to their large molecules. There are many substances which have this property, including carbohydrates such as starch, pectin, many gums and a few animal products particularly gelatin.

STARCH

Starches come from a variety of sources, but the main ones are from maize or wheat. It is possible to breed different ratios of the two starch components, amylopectin and amylose. This can give a range of starches of varying properties, particularly the speed and extent of their gelatisation. This range can be extended further by chemical or physical modification of the starch granules or molecules.

Why modify starch?

Unmodified starches can be used in cooking, but have limited use in food manufacture. For example, natural waxy starch from maize – this will hydrate and swell rapidly but it loses its viscosity on standing producing a weak bodied paste. Starch is modified to enhance or repress its inherent properties for a particular application, *eg* to provide:

– thickening
– improved binding
– improved mouthfeel

– increased stability
– gelling.

TYPES OF MODIFICATION

Cross-linking (or cross-bonding)

Cross-linking is achieved by a chemical process which places phosphate groups as bridges between starch chains. Thus, starch with a high proportion of amylose takes on the properties of one with a higher amylopectin (highly branched) content. See Figure 1.61

Cross-linking with phosphate can be considered as 'spot-welding' of the starch granules at random spots on the starch chains. This results in a strengthening of tender starches and cooked pastes are more viscous and heavier bodied. Equally of importance is that the modified starch is much less likely to break down due to heating, cook/chill, cook/freeze, increased acidity or agitation.

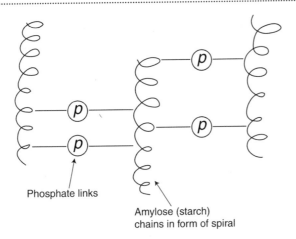

Figure 1.61
Phosphate cross-bonded
starch

Phosphate links

Amylose (starch)
chains in form of spiral

Cross-linking helps to control texture of starch and provides considerable tolerance to the effects of heat, acid and agitation. As a result, it gives better control and improved flexibility in dealing with formulations, processing and shelf-life.

Other ingredients affect the swelling characteristics of starch and the final viscosity of the product being thickened. Acids disrupt the bonding (hydrogen bonding) between starch chains and allow more rapid hydration and thus swelling of the starch. However, unmodified starch will break down at lower pHs, *eg* in pickled products.

Soluble solids, *eg* sugars dissolve in water which would be used to swell the starch, thus reducing the amount of water available and the resulting swelling of the starch. Sugar should be held back in mixing and cooking a product until the starch is completely cooked. Fats and proteins can coat starch granules and delay swelling and lower the final viscosity attained.

Agitation and shearing forces exerted by high-speed mixing, milling, homogenisation or pumping can damage the starch granules.

Cross-linking the starch can build in resistance to shear (agitation) as well as to higher temperatures and acidity.

OTHER STARCH MODIFICATIONS

Stabilisation
Starches can be electrolytically charged with the same electrical charge so that the starch chains repel each other, like two North poles of magnets. This prevents starch from agglomerating and separating out (see: *retrogradation* and *syneresis*).

Acid-modified
The starch is hydrolysed with acid but the granules stay intact, thus producing lower viscosity and clearer starch pastes.

Pre-gelatinised (instant on cold-water swelling starches)

The starch is gelatinised by heating with water in the normal manner, then the mixture is spray-dried. The powder produced will then produce a starch gel more or less instantly on the addition of cold water. This is particularly useful for quick-cook products and instant desserts.

Table 1.14

Uses of modified starches

Starch	Properties	Uses
Acid-modified	Low paste viscosities, low gel strength, clearer	Binder. Fat replacer jelly sweets: imitation cheese spreads
Phosphate cross-linked	High gelatinisation temperature, stable to heat, acid, shear	Canned foods, salad dressing, gravies, HTST* processed foods
Stabilised	Freeze–thaw stability reduced retrogradation, high water-holding capacity	Frozen foods, soups filling aid
Pre-gelatinised (instant or cold-water swelling)	Thickening with cold water, quick hydration	Instant foods, desserts, instant custard, gravies
Corn syrups	(Acid or enzyme hydrolysed starch), sweetening, bulking and thickening control viscosity	Frozen desserts, confectionery, baking products
High fructose corn syrup	High sweetness	Confectionery drinks

(* using plate heat exchangers for rapid heating)

GUMS

A number of gums have useful thickening, gelling and sometimes unusual properties. These gums include alginates, celluloses, xanthan, pectins, carrageenans and tree gums such as gum arabic (acacia), tragacanth and carob bean gum (also known as locust bean gum). All will thicken products, many will gel or stabilise products to prevent oil separation.

Alginates

Alginates are extracted from brown seaweed, where the gum occurs in the cell walls and intercellular spaces. Alginates have many useful properties including the ability to thicken solutions, to form gels and to form thin films. Alginates are complex polysaccharides built up from two main units in random order to make large molecules. The two components are mannuronic and guluronic acids, which are sugar derivatives. The long chains gel with the help of calcium ions (Ca^{++}) which bridge across at special points in the chains called 'action zones'. See Figure 1.62.

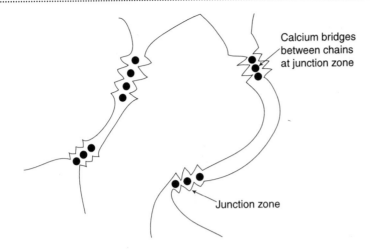

Figure 1.62

'Egg-box' model for alginate gel formation.

Table 1.15

Alginate applications

Main property used	Use	Special reason for use
Thickening	Sauces, syrups cake mixes, pie fillings, soups, canned meat, ice-cream	Thickens batter, moisture retention. Reduces moisture absorption by pastry. Temporary or delay thickening. Checks growth of ice crystals
General colloidal properties	Water ices, whipped cream, imitation cream, stabilise edible emulsions	Checks dripping. Checks separation, gives quick whipping
Drinks		Prevents 'ringing' (colours separate out on standing)
Gel formation	Milk desserts, table jellies, aerated desserts, animal foods	Cold prepared
Film formation		

Xanthan gum

Xanthan gum is a high molecular weight, naturally occurring polysaccharide produced on the outside of the cells (the capsule) of the bacterium *Xanthomonas campestris*. Solutions of xanthan gum are thixotropic, *ie* they become thinner when subjected to agitation or shear, *eg* shaking or stirring, but thicken again on standing. This gives excellent mouthfeel to many products and allows rapid flavour release due to shear-thinning resulting from chewing. Shaking products in bottles also thins the gum allowing easy removal of syrups, toppings and salad dressings.

When xanthan and locust bean gums are mixed at normal temperatures, a greater increase in overall viscosity occurs (synergistic effect). A gel is produced when solutions of the two are heated above 55C and subsequently cooled. A similar synergistic effect occurs with guar gum.

Table 1.16

Xanthan gum – food applications

Bakery fillings	Cold make-up. Filling not absorbed by pastry. Good mouthfeel
Canned foods	Viscosity control-improved ease of pumping and filling due to shear-thinning property. Partial starch replacement permits faster heat penetration
Dry mixes	Rapid/high viscosity build up in cold or hot systems – easy preparation of salad dressings. Milk shakes, sauces, beverages
Frozen foods	Excellent emulsion and suspension stability and viscosity maintenance of dressings, sauces, gravies. Improves freeze–thaw stability of starch-thickened products

CARRAGEENANS

This is a mixed but poorly defined group of polysaccharides also obtained from seaweed. The main use, is gelling, particularly for milk-based desserts. Carrageenan (κ version) reacts with the milk protein (casein) to make a gel, which can be used as the basis of desserts.

CELLULOSES

Cellulose itself will not mix with water and is also indigestible, hence its value as dietary fibre. Cellulose can be modified in a number of ways to make it more soluble or dispersable in water, sometimes with added properties. Methyl cellulose is a derivative which, when mixed with water, on heating becomes thicker but thins again on cooling. This is useful for adding to the tomato filling of pizzas to prevent the filling dripping from the pizza base during cooking. Carboxymethyl cellulose has many uses as a stabiliser to prevent water or oil separation.

Table 1.17

Carboxymethyl cellulose (CMC) applications

Function	**Product**

Stabiliser
Produce: smoothness
          retard ice growth
          resist melting
	Ice-cream
	Ice lollies
	Also milk beverages

Aid to emulsification – stabilise oil emulsion system	Cream substitutes Salad dressings
Inhibit syneresis – repress sugar crystals – improve body	Meringues, fruit cakes, Pie fillings, icings, confectionery
Anti-staling agent – retains moisture	Bread Cakes
Bulking effect	Dietetic foods
Aid to reconstitution	Dried foods

ACIDITY CONTROL

Some products are too acid for most people, whereas many products need to be made more acid to be acceptable. To control the acidity of a product such as sugar confectionery a substance known as a **buffer** may be used. Many types of **acids** are used to increase the acidity of a product, common examples being:

- Sodium lactate *(E325)* – a buffer used in preserves and confectionery
- Calcium citrate *(E333)* – a buffer used in soft drinks, sweets and preserves
- Acetic acid *(E260)*   – vinegar used in pickles, mayonnaise
- Tartaric acid *(E334)* – acid used in desserts and raising agents
- Citric acid *(E330)*   – widely used acid, useful in binding up traces of metals.

The use of raising agents has made possible a vast range of baked products. Sodium hydrogen carbonate (bicarbonate) and an acid such as cream of tartar *(E336)* or calcium hydrogen phosphate *(E341)* make up the raising agents. If the additive has been approved by the EU it has an *E* in front of it. Some additives have a number but no letter *E* as yet. Sodium hydrogen carbonate is an example, surprisingly, with the number *500*.

EMULSIFIERS AND STABILISERS

Emulsifiers and stabilisers play vital roles in many food products; without them the food becomes unstable and separates out into watery and fatty layers. An **emulsifier** allows the dispersion of tiny droplets of oil to be made in water to give a stable emulsion. Examples occur in mayonnaise, sauces, drinks and soups. A **stabiliser** usually works by absorbing large quantities of water and binding them into a stable form. In ice-cream, a stabiliser is added to prevent the formation of large 'crunchy' ice crystals during the freezing process. The ice-cream will thaw gradually with a stabiliser present and not drip over the hand as sometimes happens with home-made products.

Common emulsifiers include:

Monoglycerides of fatty acids *(E471)* – found in frozen desserts. Sucrose esters of fatty acids *(E473)* – used as a wetting agent.

In general, to act as an emulsifier, part of the structure of a substance must be capable of dissolving in water and part in fat **or** oil. In this way the emulsifier arranges itself on the interface between the fat droplets and the water and thus prevents droplets joining together and rising to the surface, as cream rises in milk on standing.

Carbohydrates

Carbohydrates, particularly the starches and gums, can act as stabilisers as they have the ability to absorb water. Some of these substances often act as emulsifiers as well.

Stabilisers and emulsifiers work together in many products. The stabiliser binds up quantities of water and the emulsifier prevents fat droplets joining together and separating out. Figure 1.63 – shows how an oil droplet is emulsified with lecithin (emulsifier) and polysaccharide stabiliser.

Table 1.18
Functions of emulsifiers

Function	Mechanism	Examples
Emulsification	Stabilise oil in water or water in oil emulsions to prevent separation	Mayonnaise, dressings, soups, eg lecithin, glyceryl monostearate (GMS)
Complex formation	Modify starch or protein containing products	Starch – complexing with monoglycerides (GMS) to reduce staling of bread. Protein – complexing with Diacetyl tartaric acid esters of monoglycerides (DATEMs) – lubricate dough in mixing
Fat 'crystal' modification	Modify and stablise fat	Stops fat separating, eg bloom on chocolate, use sorbitan tristearate as emulsifier

Figure 1.63
Emulsification and stabilisation

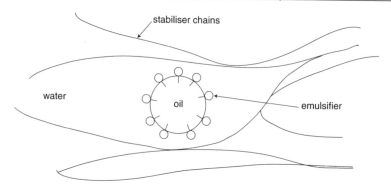

ADDITIVES AFFECTING THE SENSORY CHARACTERISTICS OF A FOOD

A food to be enjoyable must taste, smell and feel right in the mouth. It must also be attractive to the eye. In Britain, until recently, we found coloured foods more attractive. However, there is now a trend towards a preference for non-coloured and naturally-coloured foods.

Food flavourings, although there are about 3,000 of these, are not given *E* numbers. The majority of **flavour** substances used in food are natural and, contrary to public opinion, the number of synthetic flavours is very small. Spices and herbs have been used as flavourings from the earliest times. In fact, so valuable were spices in Roman times that adulteration of a spice carried the death penalty.

As natural flavours are often limited in availability and reliability, there is considerable development taking place in 'nature-identical' flavourings. These are either synthesised or extracted from natural materials and are, in both cases, identical to substances naturally present in food materials. These flavourings are often cheaper, more readily available and behave in a predictable manner during processing and product storage.

Flavours are, in fact, odours and are detected by the nose. We taste only salt, sour, bitter and sweet. Fruit flavours are often termed **essential oils** arising from the word 'essence' and not from being essential to life. Less volatile natural flavourings are extracted by **solvents,** for example, from dried spices. These flavourings may be called **oleoresins.**

A number of substances have been found to have the ability to enhance the flavour of other substances and to modify or mask undesirable flavours. The best known flavour **enhancer** is monosodium glutamate (MSG) *(621)*. It stimulates the taste buds in the mouth. MSG has been used by the Chinese for generations and was found to be the main flavour component of soy sauce. Large amounts have been known to cause sickness or dizziness; the sickness was given the title of Chinese restaurant syndrome! Manufacturers have advertised foods as MSG-free as if this is a particularly harmful additive. However, very many foods contain MSG, an amino acid derivative, as a natural component!

The British have a particularly sweet tooth so sweeteners, particularly sugar, have been used extensively. Sugar usage has decreased and the growth of artificial sweeteners has been considerable. **Saccharin** has been used for many years, but newer sweeter substances are now available. **Aspartame** has in its relatively short life carved out a large niche for itself as a sweetener for soft-drinks, particularly the 'diet' variety. The sweetener is made up of two naturally-occurring amino acids, aspartic acid and phenylalanine. Unfortunately, in acid drinks, over a period of time it breaks down and so products using it must be less acid, with a shorter shelf-life. The sweetener acesulfame is similar in sweetness but more stable.

The visual appearance of a product is a vital selling feature. Colours have been used to modify the appearance of a product to make it more attractive to the consumer. They have been used to colour a food deficient in colour due to certain processing or to ensure a consistent product colour. Recently the consumer has turned against colours more than any other additive, particularly the azo dyes, such as tartrazine *(E102)*. There are 58 permitted colours and **caramel** is the most common. Naturally-occurring colours include a wide range of carotenoids (carrot-like) such as β carotene *(El60a)* and lycopene, *(El60d)* which occurs naturally in tomatoes.

Additives which affect the mouthfeel of a product have been mentioned among group (a). Mouthfeel is a vital characteristic of a product and must be right, whether it be firmness, crispness, smoothness or chewiness. Considerable skill is required in ensuring modern manufactured food products have the desired mouthfeel.

ADDITIVES AFFECTING THE STORAGE LIFE OF A FOOD

One of the major successes of additives such as preservatives is their ability to extend the storage life of a product over a longer period than normal. Preservatives help to reduce or prevent wastage of food through spoilage caused by micro-organisms. They also have the ability to help protect the public from food poisoning caused by certain bacteria. Longer shelf-life enables a greater variety of products to be kept in a store, even by a small corner shop. Similarly, food can be kept in the house for longer periods and sometimes used over a period of time.

Common examples of preservatives include:

- Sorbic acid *(E200)*   – used in soft drinks and processed cheese
- Benzoic acid *(E210)*   – used in soft drinks
- Sulphur dioxide *(E220)* – widely used, often as sulphite *(E221–227)*
- Potassium nitrate *(E252)* – used in curing bacon, ham and other cured meats.

Fats, oils and foods containing them are subject, over a period of time, to the effects of oxygen in turning the product rancid. This type of rancidity is accelerated by light (UV) and by certain metals, particularly copper and iron. Antioxidants are added to foods such as these to slow down or prevent the process of rancidity and thus extend the storage life of the product. Some antioxidants stop the chemical reactions involved in rancidity, whereas others remove oxygen from the product. Another type of rancidity, hydrolytic rancidity, is caused in the presence of water by some enzymes or micro-organisms. This type of rancidity, found in butter, for example, is not prevented by antioxidants.

Common antioxidants include:

- Ascorbic acid *(E300)*   – used in fruit drinks
- Propyl gallate *(E310)*   – used in vegetable oils and chewing gum
- Butylated hydroxyanisole *(E320)* – used in cheese spreads, stock cubes.

Over a period of time some foods deteriorate as certain proteins and amino acids combine with certain sugars to produce brown products. This is called non-enzymic browning and, besides being unattractive, lowers the nutritional value of the food. Sulphur dioxide *(E220)* is used to prevent the browning.

ADDITIVES AFFECTING THE NUTRITIONAL STATUS OF A FOOD

This must surely be the only group of additives never criticised by the anti-additive lobby. The group includes minerals, vitamins and protein supplements. These substances are only legally additives when they fulfil a technological purpose, for example, ascorbic acid (vitamin C) is an antioxidant. Some nutrients must be added to foods by law, for example, vitamins A and D must be added to margarine.

Our diet receives many useful nutrients from this group, particularly in breakfast cereals. A typical flaked breakfast cereal may have the following nutrients added:

- vitamin C   35.0mg/100g
- vitamin B_6 1.8mg/100g
- niacin   16.0mg/100g
- vitaminD   2.8mg/100g

- thiamin (B_1)   1.0mg/100g
- iron   40.0mg/100g
- riboflavin (B_2) 1.5mg/100g

ADDITIVES USED BY MANUFACTURERS DURING PROCESSING

Processing aids are additives that the manufacturer uses to facilitate the production of a foodstuff, usually of higher quality and often more cheaply. **Solvents** are used to extract substances from materials, for example, fruit flavours from peels. **Filter aids** are used to accelerate the filtration of liquid foods in removing suspended particles. **Anti-caking agents** are added to powders to keep them free-flowing, for example, magnesium carbonate *(504)* is added to ensure salt does not cake. These additives, like all additives, would not be used if an alternative method of approach to processing was available.

SUMMARY OF ADDITIVE NUMBERS

When approved, an additive is given a number which is used as part of the ingredient list on a food label. A number without an *E* is controlled by the UK and not as yet by the EU.

Additives	Numbers (in general)
Colours	100—180
Preservatives	200—290
Antioxidants	300—321
Acids, buffers, anti-foaming agents and similar	mainly 300s, from 170 up to 900s
Emulsifiers and stabilisers	322—494
Sweeteners	420—421

OTHER INGREDIENTS

Functional proteins

Proteins are made from a varying number of amino acids which are chemically different and capable of interacting and cross-linking. This can be made use of in foods for a number of functional reasons. Basic (alkaline) proteins can be used in combination with an acidic protein. At the pH of the food the basic protein will have an overall negative electrical charge on its molecule and the acidic protein will be positive. This means the protein chains will be strongly attractive and will readily cross-link. This protein combination will be useful as a foaming agent in foods. A typical foam is produced by whipping egg-white. But this form quickly collapses if there is any fat in contact with it. These functional protein combinations are so strong that they resist the effect of fat and can be whipped up with fat in a formulation such as a creamy dessert.

Sugar syrups

Sugar syrups are produced from starch by controlled acid and/or enzyme hydrolysis. The syrups are colourless, viscous and vary in sweetness according to the level of starch breakdown. The mixture of sugars in the syrup consists of simple sugars like glucose and maltose, with varying amounts of longer chain carbohydrates (dextrins and oligosaccharides).

The degree of breakdown of the starch is expressed as the dextrose equivalent, D.E. A D.E. of 100 indicates total breakdown of the starch into glucose (dextrose).

A D.E. of 65 would mean a syrup of approximately 34% glucose, 33.5% maltose and 32.5% bigger molecules. Higher D.E. syrups are sweeter, lower ones are not as sweet but will thicken and stabilise products.

Table 1.19

The use of sugar syrup

Product	Use of sugar syrup
Bakery products	Help produce brown crust Delay staling by holding water Use about 2 % of high D.E. for colour
Confectionery products	Use in boiled sweets and toffees to prevent sugar (sucrose) crystallisation High D.E. syrups add sweetness and smoothness
Fermented drinks	Add up to almost 10 % of carbohydrate Start to ferment quickly, use high D.E. syrup for cider production

Fat substitutes

There is a large market for fat-free or fat-reduced products. However, consumers still would prefer the mouthfeel associated with a certain level of fat in a product. Unfortunately, lowering fat levels usually lowers flavour levels as many flavours are fat-soluble. Most of the ingredients being used as partial or complete replacements for fat in foods can be classified under three major categories:

- protein-based substitutes
- synthetic compounds
- carbohydrate-based replacements.

All of these produce a sensation in the mouth similar to fat.

Low-calorie protein-based fat substitutes are quite popular in the USA. 'Simplese' is an example of such a product. Being made of protein it cannot be used in cooking, but can be used in frozen desserts, cheese spreads, salad dressings and margarine. Synthetic fat-like substances are resistant to digestive enzymes and, therefore, are low in calorific value. Sucrose derivations such as 'Olestra' are the main types.

Carbohydrate fat replacers mimic the properties of fat as a result of an association of water with the structure of the carbohydrate particles. The ideal carbohydrate fat substitute will possess a structure which strongly binds and orients water in such a way as to provide a sensation identified as the mouthfeel of fat. 'N-oil' is an example of this type of product.

Section 2
COMMODITIES AND RAW MATERIALS

In this section of the book individual food commodities will be discussed and knowledge of individual components from Section 1 will be applied to each food, particularly when discussing chemical composition. Principal methods of processing, handling and technological problems will be reviewed. However, each of the commodities covered is itself a very large subject and therefore only the main areas of interest will be discussed.

Chapter 1

Dairy Products

PREVIEW

- **Milk**
  - produced by mammals after birth of young
  - ideally balanced food for that particular animal's young
  - human milk more lactose but less protein than cows' milk
  - colostrum first secretion after birth, rich in antibodies and vitamins
  - milk vehicle by which disease may be passed from cow; *eg* TB, typhoid, diphtheria and salmonellosis

- **Cows' milk composition**
  - milk legally genuine if at least 3% fat and 8.5% solids-not-fat
  - varies according to breed, age, stage of lactation, season, feed, time and period between milkings
  - Guernsey and Jersey richer in fat
  - lipid content high in saturated short chain fatty acids, *eg* butanoic (butyric) acid
  - caseins – phosphoproteins – about 80% of all milk protein
  - αs- casein sensitive to calcium
  - κ- casein *insensitive* to calcium
  - whey proteins – β-lactoglobulin when denatured gives 'condensed milk' flavour
  - α-lactalbumin

- **Milk processing**
  - pasteurisation 71.1C for 15 seconds (since 1999, some dairies use 71.1C/25 secs to destroy *M. paratuberculosis*
  - to kill pathogens, *eg Mycobacterium tuberculosis* and most spoilage organisms
  - homogenisation breaks down fat globules and prevents cream layer forming
  - sterilisation – 'in-bottle' traditional process, heat to 120C for 15 minutes
  - 'cooked milk' flavour obvious
  - UHT (long life) sterilization for one second
  - no flavour change
  - uperisation, sterilisation by direct steam injection

- **Cream**
  - separated by centrifugal separator
  - single cream – 18% fat
  - double cream – 48% fat
  - whipping cream – 35% fat
  - clotted cream – 55% fat

- **Butter**
  - made by churning cream
  - inversion of colloid as cream
  - oil in water emulsion changed to water in oil emulsion in butter
  - butter 80% fat, maximum water16%
  - starter culture may be used of *Streptococcus lactis* or *cremoris*
  - up to 2% salt may be added

- **Margarine**
  - butter substitute, but now nutritionally superior and less a health risk
  - hard margarines use hydrogenated vegetable fat
  - different blends of oils and fats used to give same product
  - skim milk preparation to give butter flavour blended and emulsified with fat
  - vitamins A and D added by law

- **Skim milk**
  - milk after removing fat
  - no risk from saturated fatty acids
  - more readily available but most dried

- **Dried milks**
  - mostly skim milk, but some whole milk powders
  - fat in whole milk may become rancid – air must be excluded
  - moisture uptake of powder may cause Maillard reaction
  - filled milk – vegetable fat added to skim milk
  - fine particle powders hence poor dispersibility, wettability and hence solubility in water
  - powders re-wetted to form clumps which act as sponges so disperse easily in water
  - most powders spray dried

- **Concentrated milks**
  - evaporated milk – 'cooked milk flavour'
  - salts added, *eg* sodium citrate to improve consistency
  - needs to be heat processed in can
  - condensed milk (sweetened) – large amount of sugar added, no necessity
  - to heat process in can
  - must pasteurise then concentrate by evaporation
  - lactose forced out of solution by sucrose

- **Ice-cream**
  - emulsion of fat in complicated solution
  - very small ice crystals
  - soft ice-cream – milk powder, less fat than hard ice-cream, stabilizer –
  - freeze at – 5C, serve from freezer
  - hard ice-cream – at least 8% fat – sugar not more than 15%
  - freeze and whip in air to give 100% overrun
  - harden at – 40C
  - legally ice-cream must contain at least 5% fat and 7.5% solids-not-fat

- **Cheese**
  - depends on producing lactic acid in milk and coagulating protein with rennet
  - culture of *Lactococcus cremoris* (formerly *Strepotoccus*) and *lactis*
  - culture may be attacked by bacteriophage
  - lactic acid produced to 0.17 – 0.2%
  - rennet attacks κ-casein to make it insoluble
  - calcium can then combine with αs-casein and precipitate it to form curd as basis of cheese
  - ripening of cheese involves:
    (1) hydrolysis of proteins
    (2) hydrolysis of lipids
    (3) conversion of amino acids and fatty acids and fatty acids to flavour compounds

- 'Blue cheeses' – have blue moulds, *eg Penicillium roquefortii* to produce
- colour and flavour
- 'processed cheese'– emulsifying cheese with green cheese, emulsifier and water

- **Fermented milks**
  - yoghurts, two types: set or stirred
  - starter, to produce acid and flavour of *Lactobacillus bulgarius* and
  - *Streptococcus thermophilus*

MILK

A perfectly balanced food, hygienically served, at the right temperature, in the right quantities, would be an ideal food for a developing offspring. Milk is the ideal food but with some limitations. All mammals produce milk from specialized glands to feed their young after birth. Each animal produces its milk of a certain composition to meet the needs of its young and not necessarily those of other animals. Cows' milk contains more protein than human milk but less carbohydrate. In simple terms, to convert cows' milk for human consumption it should be diluted with some sugar added.

Milk is also a vehicle by which antibodies can be passed from the mother to the offspring. *The colostrum* is the first secretion of the mammary glands after birth, containing more vitamins, particularly retinol, riboflavin, thiamin and biotin. Colostrum also contains more globular proteins, to which group of proteins antibodies belong. The mother is able to pass on a certain amount of the immunity she has developed to diseases to her offspring.

Milk is unfortunately also a vehicle by which disease can be passed from an animal to its young or in the case of cows' milk to a large number of people. Before pasteurisation was adopted milk from infected cattle could cause tuberculosis, staphylococcal and salmonella infections, typhoid, paratyphoid, diphtheria and many other diseases.

Table 2.1

Composition of milk

Animal	% Total solid's	% Fat	% Protein	% Casein	% Lactose	% Ash
Human	–	2.0–6.0	0.7–2.0	–	6.0–7.5	–
Cow	12.6	3.8	3.3	2.8	4.7	0.7
Goat	13.2	4.2	3.7	2.8	4.5	0.8
Sheep	17.0	5.3	6.3	4.6	4.6	0.8

Composition of milk

There are over 100 different compounds in milk, which can be considered as a mixture of carbohydrates, proteins, lipids and many inorganic and organic salts dissolved in water. In Table 2.1 a comparison is made of a number of different milks: figures given may vary somewhat for the reasons which will be discussed later.

Cows' milk is the most widespread milk used throughout the world, but it is legally considered to be genuine only if it contains at least 3% fat and 8.5% other solids.

The composition of cows' milk varies according to breed, age, stage of lactation, season, feed, time and period between milkings. The most important single factor governing milk composition is the breed of cow: the principal breeds in Europe are Friesian shorthorn. Ayrshire, Brown Swiss, Jersey and Guernsey. Some of the differences in milk due to breed are given in Table 2.2. In addition to the factors listed above, two other factors will affect milk composition in many cases and these are disease and temperature. In warmer climates, around 28-32C, milk yield falls enormously and its composition may alter.

Breed	% Fat	% Protein	% Lactose
Ayrshire	4.0	3.6	4.7
Friesian	3.9	3.3	5.0
Holstein	3.4	3.3	4.9
Jersey	5.4	3.9	4.9

Table 2.2

Variation in milk composition due to breed

The *lipid content* of milk is mainly fat (butterfat) with small amounts of phospholipids, sterols, carotenoids and vitamins A and D. The fat occurs in globules which are stabilized by the milk fat globule membrane, a complex structure of proteins, phospholipids and enzymes. Any heat processing will damage this stabilization of the milk fat by denaturing the proteins. Fat globules will then coalesce and rise to the surface to produce the 'cream layer'. Fatty acids in the fat are unusual in being mainly saturated with some very short chain acids such as butyric (butanoic), caproic, caprillic and capric. Polyunsaturated acids, particularly linoleic and linolenic acids, are very much in the minority.

Milk proteins are numerous, but are generally classed into two main groups: casein (which is a curd precipitated by acid or the enzyme rennin): and whey proteins.

Casein is a mixture of phosphoproteins (*ie* proteins containing phosphate groups) which comprise about 80% of all the protein in milk and so total 2.5-3.2% of whole milk. The different caseins comprising whole casein have different properties and these include α_s which is coagulated by calcium ions and κ-casein which is insensitive to calcium. In milk the casein exists as colloidally dispersed bodies known as *micelles*. The structure of these micelles is still uncertain but probably the calcium sensitive casein *ie* α_s – is on the inside and is protected by calcium insensitive casein *ie* κ on the outside of the micelle. This protection of the micelle by κ-casein is destroyed by the action of rennin, which then allows calcium to react with the α_s casein, thus causing precipitation and formation of a curd, an essential preliminary in cheese making. The proteins remaining after casein has been precipitated from milk are collectively known as the *whey proteins* and include albumins, globulins, enzymes and protein-*breakdown* products. The most important whey protein is β-lactoglobulin which can be denatured by heat over a period of time.

The protein chains can uncoil during heating and associate with κ-casein, but in so doing expose certain side groups on the chains, particularly those which contain sulphur. This leads to the typical cooked milk flavours of sterilized and evaporated milk. The other main whey protein, α-lactalbumin, is associated and enzymes responsible for *lactose* synthesis.

Milk processing

As we have seen milk is an excellent food, but it is also an excellent growth medium for a vast range of micro-organisms, including a number of pathogenic bacteria. Tuberculosis was widespread until only a few decades age and milk was the main carrier of the disease. Until a few years ago cattle could be infected with *Brucella*, which, although causing contagious abortion in cattle, causes an undulant or repetitive, 'flu'-like disease in humans. Milk can carry this disease and many others have been reported, including typhoid. Bacteria can enter the milk from the udder, operatives during milking, utensils and equipment. Heat treatment of milk is therefore essential to remove harmful bacteria and those which will cause rapid spoilage of the milk.

Pasteurisation, developed by Louis Pasteur whilst working on spoiled wine, consists of heating milk below the boiling point but at a temperature high enough to kill harmful organisms and to reduce spoilage organisms (about 99% are killed). The time and temperature of pasteurisation is fixed to kill the organism *Mycobacterium tuberculosis,* the causative organism of TB. Milk used to be pasteurised in bulk in the 'holder process' when about 300 gallons would be heated and stored for 30 minutes at 62.8 – 65.6C. All batch processes in food production are less efficient, usually demanding more manpower, and less cost-effective than continuous processes. The high temperature short time (HTST) process is a continuous process, which was developed to offset the problems of the holder process. If a high temperature is used for pasteurisation the kill of the bacteria can be achieved in a much shorter time and damage to the flavour and nutritive value of the milk will be less.

A temperature of 71.7C is used for 15 seconds to achieve HTST pasteurisation. Special plate heat exchangers, with milk on one side and steam on the other, are used with a special holding tube through which the milk passes to the cooling section and hence to bottling.

Since 1999 some dairies have pasteurised for 25 seconds to eliminate the more heat- resistant organism *Mycobacterium paratuberculosis. M. paratuberculosis* does not cause TB but has been implicated as a cause of Crohn's disease.

Pasteurisation of milk has very little damaging effect with the exception of the

Figure 2.1

HTST pasteurisation of milk

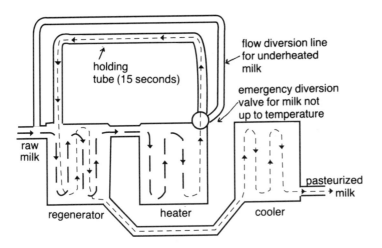

Figure 2.1

HTST pasteurisation of milk

On entering the unit, raw milk is first warmed by already pasteurised milk in the regenerator. It is heated to pasteurisation temperature in the heater and then passes to the holding tube. Insufficiently heated milk is diverted by the thermostatically controlled valves and is reprocessed. After holding for 15 seconds the milk passes to the regenerator to warm incoming milk and then to the cooler. The unit is built up of plate heat exchangers and milk does not come into contact with steam or cooling water.

loss of about half the vitamin C, and about 10% of thiamin and cyanocobalamin (B12) which reacts with breakdown products of vitamin C. Protein of the membrane surrounding the milk fat globules is slightly denatured and this allows fat globules to agglomerate and rise to the surface to form the characteristic cream layer. Leaving bottles of milk out in sunlight does far more damage in causing destruction of all the remaining vitamin C and the production of off flavours.

The process of *homogenisation* is something carried out to prevent the separation of the cream layer and is essential when milk is subject to higher temperatures in sterilization processes. To homogenise milk it must firstly be warmed to about 60C and then forced through a small gap in a pressure homogeniser which reduces the fat droplets to about 1 – 2 mμ (microns, *ie* 0.001–0.002mm). The small fat droplets are very stable and do not separate out into a cream layer.

Sterilization is a much more severe heat process destroying all micro-organisms and most of their spores. Sterilized milk, in its typical crown-capped bottle, was developed in the Midlands so it could be left on the doorstep all day while the family was at work. The strong cooked milk flavour is still preferred by many people. The traditional method of producing sterilized milk is by in-bottle sterilization in which milk is filled and sealed into the bottles, then heated to 120C for 15 minutes. The bottles are cooled by water spray to about 75C, then allowed to cool slowly to room temperature.

The flavour of sterilized milk takes some time to develop, and therefore it is possible to heat milk to high temperature to sterilize it but in a shorter space of time to prevent flavour development. In this way the milk is similar to pasteurised milk. The *UHT (ultra high temperatures) process* was developed for this purpose and involves heating milk in a plate heat-exchange unit at 132C for one second. 'UHT' must be homogenised; it is often packed in cardboard cartons and sold as 'long life milk'.

A more recent method of sterilization, used extensively in Europe, is called *Uperization* and involves injection of steam under pressure into the milk to obtain rapid sterilization. UHT sterilization of milk has little effect on nutritive value, in a similar manner to pasteurisation. However, dissolved oxygen in the milk may cause severe losses in vitamins C, B_{12} and folic acid over a period of time. The injection or uperization method causes removal of dissolved oxygen. In contrast to the UHT method the in-bottle sterilization process causes an overall reduction in the nutritive value of milk. The vitamins are badly affected in that vitamin C content is halved, B_{12} is destroyed and one third of thiamin is lost. The biological value of the proteins is reduced.

CREAM

Cream is milk in which the fat content has been greatly increased by separating out some water. A special cream separator, which is like a centrifugal force as water is heavier than butter fat is used. The separator operates at about 6500rpm.

Figure 2.2

A cream separator

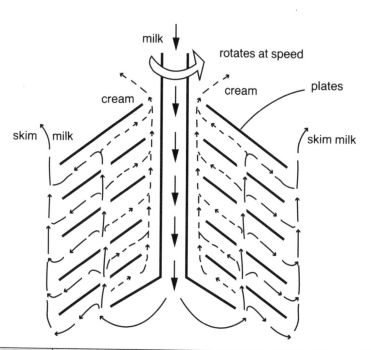

Table 2.3

Types of cream

Type	Fat	Protein	Lactose	Water
Single	18%	3%	4%	74%
Double	48%	15%	2.5%	48%
Whipping	35%	2.2%	3%	59%
Clotted	55%	3%	2.5%	40%

By this method three types of cream are produced, and these are given in Table 2.3, together with clotted cream.

To whip cream into a stable form the fat content must be between about 30 – 38%. A fat content of 36% produces a good foam in which air bubbles are trapped and the cream increases in volume up to three times. The increase in volume is called 'over-run'. *Clotted cream* has the highest fat content and is made by a slow traditional method. Milk is firstly allowed to stand in shallow containers for almost 12 hours at room temperature and then it is heated to about 80C and cooled again slowly for about a day. The cream separates out into a thick layer and is scraped off the top of the milk and packed.

BUTTER

It is appropriate to consider butter after discussing cream, as it is made by churning cream. The churning process causes what is known as an 'inversion of the colloid'. Cream is an emulsion fat in water, whereas butter is an emulsion (or colloid) of water in fat, which is obviously an inversion of the original colloidal state and involves the expulsion of much of the water from the original cream. Thus cream of 35 – 38% fat and 60 – 65% water is converted to butter of 80% fat and 16% water (this being the legal maximum for water content.)

Fresh cream, separated from milk before churning, is used extensively for butter making, but it is also possible to ripen or sour cream to give added flavour. Special cultures of organisms are added to the cream and are allowed to produce about 0.25% lactic acid. Lactic acid producing bacteria are used, such as *Lactococcus lactis* (formerly *Streptococcus*) or *cremoris*. Butter can be salted with up to 2% salt added, but unsalted butter is now more popular.

Before churning the cream is pasteurised and cooled to about 10C at which temperature churning is most efficient. Churning is effected by violent agitation of the cream, which takes about 30 minutes. Small pieces of butter at first appear and then the 'buttermilk' is removed. The butter is washed, salted and 'worked' to obtain the desired consistency with a final water content of up to 16%.

The nutritive value of butter is somewhat variable, as it depends on its fat content and fat-soluble vitamins, mainly retinol (A) and calciferol (D). Carotenoids are the reason for the yellow colour of butter and in summer, because the cow has plenty of green grass, the butterfat is richer in carotenoids and a brighter yellow.

MARGARINE

A substitute for butter which was cheap and readily available was sought in the last century and Napoleon III awarded a prize to Mégès Mouries in 1869 for inventing the first margarine. Margarine, like butter, is an emulsion of an aqueous phase of milk and water dispersed in a fatty phase, usually made of vegetable oils. *Margarine is not a true dairy product.* The original margarine contained beef tallow and now any blend of fat or oil can be used to give the same margarine after processing. Hard margarines use hydrogenated fats but soft-spread margarines use oils which are polyunsaturated and usually low in cholesterol. Examples of three different fat blends used for margarine are given in Table 2.4; however, there are numerous other combinations possible.

The carefully blended oils and fats must be odour-free; have a bland taste and above all have a wide melting range to simulate the sensation of butter melting

Fat	% of fat mixture
1. Coconut oil	55
Hydrogenated vegetable oil	20
Groundnut oil	25
2. Hydrogenated palm kernel oil	70
Coconut oil	20
Palm kernel oil	10
3. Coconut oil Palm kernel oil	40*
Palmoil	7
Hydrogenated groundnut oil	13
Hydrogenated whale oil	20
Groundnut oil	20

*(1939–45)

Table 2.4

Fat blends for margarine

in the mouth. Skimmed milk, to which has been added a starter culture of bacteria, is allowed to sour to produce a butter-type flavour (diacetyl).

Salt, vitamins A and D, colour and sometimes flavour are added to the skimmed milk. The oil blend and the skimmed milk preparation are blended together in the right proportions in a large vessel, which has rotating paddles. An emulsion is gradually formed and is aided by the addition of emulsifying agents such as glyceryl monostearate and lecithin.

The emulsion formed so far in the process is not margarine, as it still does not possess the right texture. The emulsion is passed to a machine called a 'votator' which is in fact a closed cylinder within another cylinder. The inner cylinder is cooled: coming in contact with this the margarine solidifies and is worked into a semi-solid condition which can then be packed.

The greatest challenge facing margarine manufacturers has been to simulate the flavour and mouthfeel of butter. In the past margarine was always inferior to butter. However, the controversy over hard animal fats has resulted in rapid growth of margarine sales, particularly of soft, low in cholesterol, margarines. The vitamin content is controlled by law at 900µg of vitamin A and 8µg of vitamin D per 100g of margarine, thus making it better than most butters as a source of these vitamins. Fortunately for margarine manufacturers, the days of the product being the poor man's butter have passed and we are now in a time of over-production of butter and the accumulation of butter 'mountains'.

SKIM MILK

Milk from which almost all the fat has been removed is known as skim milk. However, a small fraction of the fat, perhaps about 0.1%, is almost impossible to remove by the standard method using a centrifugal separator (Figure 2.2). Removing the fat from milk will also remove the fat-soluble vitamins and so skim milk must not be used to feed babies. Because of the controversy surrounding butterfat and its possible connection with the blocking of arteries, skim milk and semi-skim have become popular and readily available. Most skim milk is solid in powder form.

DRIED MILKS

As milk is about 87% water, in order to transport a large amount of milk great distances it would be advantageous to reduce the bulk of this water or completely remove it. Drying removes most of the water from the milk and also is an excellent means of preservation. The process can produce an excellent product which when reconstituted differs little from fresh milk.

There is little loss of the nutritive value of milk during drying if it is carried out correctly. Overheating during drying will cause significant vitamin losses, protein damage and will encourage browning by the non-enzymic Maillard reaction. The lactose, a reducing sugar, and the amino acid lysine, an essential amino acid, have been implicated in this browning. When dry, milk powders must be kept from contact with moisture and ideally from air. If the moisture levels of the powder are allowed to rise about 5%, the Maillard reaction will slowly take place turning the powder from white, through cream to light brown. This can be observed sometimes in a tin of milk powder which is infrequently used over a long period. The fat in *whole milk powder* is liable to undergo oxidative rancidity fairly rapidly and therefore must be packed in the absence of oxygen. Its shelf-life under ideal conditions is significantly less than skim milk powder. A compromise product, *filled milk,* has been produced for a number of years, particularly in the war and is still popular for the catering trade. Filled milk is skim milk to which is added vegetable oil, it is then homogenised and dried. Various levels of fat in the product are possible and different fats can be used according to specific uses. Filled milk does not offer the possible health risks associated with butterfat and keeps much better than whole milk powders.

Most milk powders are very fine powders which, when added to water, tend to float on the surface, have poor *dispersability* and poor *wettability.* A process of *instantisation* can be used in which the powder is slightly re-wetted so it clumps together. These clumps of powder act like sponges and absorb the water and disperse in it rapidly.

Traditionally, but rarely nowadays, milk powder was made by *roller drying.* The roller drier (see section on drying processes) consists of a hollow drum, internally heated by steam, to which a film of milk adheres and, as the drum rotates, the milk dries to give a flaky powder. The method produces an almost sterile product as the heat treatment during drying is severe, but also the protein may be damaged and will not reconstitute in water easily.

Spray drying has replaced roller drying as it produces a product which is more soluble, of better flavour and colour. Milk is concentrated in an evaporator and then sprayed whilst still hot (80C) into a chamber where the spray meets a blast of hot air (180C) and dries instantly.

CONCENTRATED MILKS

Water can readily be removed from milk by evaporation. Products were made for many years by this method, but all had a marked 'cooked milk flavour'. The advent of the evaporator working under a strong vacuum enabled the concentration to be undertaken at a lower temperature, thus reducing the heat damage, for example at 50C.

Evaporated milk is made by evaporating water from milk to reduce the water content to about 70%. The product sometimes has a poor granular texture, which can be improved by adding either sodium citrate, disodium phosphate or calcium chloride. The product is still highly perishable and has to be homogenised, then sealed into cans and heat processed in retorts at 121C for about 15 minutes, depending on the can size.

Condensed milk is a similar product to evaporated milk, but is sweetened, and in fact depends on its sugar content for preservation. Milk must first be pasteurised, as the product is not heat processed, but it is not cooled as it passes directly to the evaporator. A sugar syrup (60-65% sucrose) is added to the evaporator and the whole milk is concentrated under vacuum at 50-55C. The product is then cooled and agitated at the same time. Often very small crystals of lactose are added to ensure rapid crystallization of the lactose. The addition of the large amount of sucrose forces lactose, less soluble than sucrose, out of solution. If the lactose is allowed to crystallize slowly it produces large crystals, sometimes as big as marbles. Agitation and seeding with small crystals ensures small lactose crystals, which are unnoticed in the product. The product is poured into sterilized cans and sealed without further heat treatment. Condensed milk depends on its high sugar content for its preservation and therefore careful hygiene is needed during this process. Most condensed milk is used in chocolate and confectionery manufacture.

ICE-CREAM

A type of ice-cream originated in Paris in 1774, but frozen desserts of various types have been known since Roman times. Ice-cream is an emulsion of fat in a complicated solution, which is made up of both colloidal and true solutions. Ice-cream contains very small crystals of ice, air sacs, fat globules, colloidal suspensions of casein, stabilizing agents, flavours, colour and sugar solution. Commercially there are two main types: soft ice-cream and hard ice-cream.

Soft ice-cream

This type of ice-cream has grown in popularity over the last few years and tends to be made locally in small batches. The secret in developing an ice-cream mix is to balance the ingredients correctly; too much milk powder, for example, leads to 'sandiness' as lactose may crystallize from the powder. Too little milk powder, which tends to absorb about seven times its own weight of water, will mean too much water, which will form large coarse ice crystals. Stabilizers and emulsifiers are used extensively in ice-cream and these include gelatin, alginates, modified celluloses, carageenans, pectins and various gums such as gum tragacanth. These substances prevent the formation of large ice crystals during the freezing operation and allow only small crystals to form. Stabilizers give body to the product and improve the melting resistance of the ice-cream. The basic principle of operation of a stabilizer is to absorb a large quantity of water; without them ice-cream has poor texture and rapidly melts. A simple formulation for a soft ice-cream is given in Table 2.5.

The ingredients are mixed together and are usually homogenised then pasteurised. Air is whipped into the ice-cream as it is frozen, usually at about -5C. Compared with hard ice-cream there is less air mixed into the product and so it only increases in volume by about 50%, ie an overrun of 50%. The product is usually served directly from the freezer.

Hard ice-cream

For a hard ice-cream at least 8% fat should be used, but in some processes if the figure goes much above 9% the ice-cream may be very heavy, as it will be impossible to mix in enough air to give sufficient overrun. A simplified

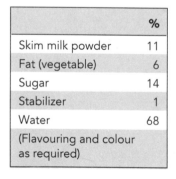

	%
Skim milk powder	11
Fat (vegetable)	6
Sugar	14
Stabilizer	1
Water	68
(Flavouring and colour as required)	

Table 2.5

A soft ice-cream formulation

formulation is given in Table 2.6. In both types of ice-cream the sugar content should not exceed 15%, as it may crystallize out, but small amounts tend to encourage the growth of large ice crystals.

The water used must be warm to aid dissolution and dispersion of the ingredients. The mix is homogenised and pasteurised, then frozen. During the freezing operation the mix is stirred vigorously to incorporate more air then in soft ice-cream, otherwise the mix would freeze to a hard mass. An overrun of about 100% is essential in hard ice-cream. Once frozen the ice-cream may be cut into blocks and wrapped, then hardened at -40C.

Ice-cream has an excellent 'health record', having been involved in few food poisoning outbreaks. It is an energy-supplying food because of its sugar content, but only contains about 3.5% protein.

	%
Skim milk powder	10
Fat (vegetable) (dairy ice-cream – butterfat)	12
Sugar	14
Stabilizer	1
Water	63
(Flavouring and colour as required)	

Table 2.6

A hard ice-cream formulation

NB Legally ice-cream must contain at least 7.5% solid-not-fat and at least 5% fat.

CHEESE

Cheese has been a food from the earliest times and has been made from most milks, particularly goats', sheep's, buffalo's and, of course, cows'. There are several hundred varieties of cheese and it is surprising that a product, depending on complex biological reactions, is extremely consistent in appearance, flavour and nutritional qualities.

Cheese production depends on a number of biological reactions which must occur in the right sequence and which can easily be affected by a number of interfering factors. In 1991 research work indicated that a small amount of cheese in a meal helps repair teeth.

Cheddar cheese manufacture

Pasteurised milk is placed in a large stainless-steel vat equipped with an outer water-jacket. A special culture of lactic acid forming bacteria is added, together with colouring. Usually a culture of *Lactococcus cremoris* and *Lactococcus lactis* is used. Unfortunately, starter cultures can be attacked by viruses known as *bacteriophages* which kill the lactic acid producing bacteria. Special care is always taken to prevent 'phage attack as the starter will be inactivated and a cheese of the right acidity and texture will be impossible to produce. The milk is held at slightly above room temperature (25C) and lactic acid is produced to about 0.17 – 0.2%.

At this stage of acidity the *rennet*, a preparation of the enzyme rennin (or chymosin), is added to coagulate the protein in about 20 minutes. Let us look again at the casein micelle, from the composition of milk, in which the calcium sensitive α_s-casein is protected by the κ-casein, which is insensitive to calcium. The rennet attacks the κ-casein and makes it insoluble.

Thus the α_s-casein is no longer protected from calcium by the κ-casein and so the α_s-fraction combines with calcium and gels to form the *curd*. The curd coagulates into a solid mass which is cut into cubes, either by traditional cutters as shown in Figure 2.3, or by more modern automatic systems.

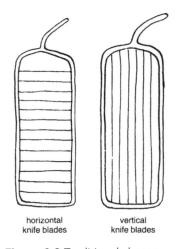

horizontal knife blades   vertical knife blades

Figure 2.3 Traditional cheese cutters

The temperature of the vat is now increased to about 40C to make the curd contract and expel the liquid whey, which is now drained away.

The curd cubes coalesce and settle into a firm mass, which is cut into slabs about 30cm by 60cm. The actual process called 'cheddaring' now begins and involves piling up the slabs of curd and turning them every 15 minutes for about two hours. During this process subtle changes occur in the milk proteins so that the desired firmness and texture of cheese begins to develop.

The slabs are milled into small pieces and the last drops of whey are allowed to escape. Salt is added at this stage at about 0.1 to 0.2% and mixed into the mass of curd-cum-cheese. These pieces are filled into moulds and pressed for about 24–48 hours. The moulded cheeses are covered in cheese-cloth or special plastic coverings. At this stage the cheese is termed a 'green cheese'. The cheese is stored at 10C for about three months to ripen or cure.

Ripening is the period during which the cheese develops its own special character. Enzymes, bacteria and moulds all play a part in ripening the cheese, and the changes which occur are numerous. There are perhaps three general reactions which occur; protein is hydrolysed by proteolytic enzymes; lipids are attacked by lipases; and amino acids and fatty acids form flavour compounds. If most of the proteins are hydrolysed the cheese will become very soft and creamy. Amino acids will be liberated from the protein chains and will contribute to the flavour of the cheese. The breakdown of the lipids, which contains short chain fatty acids, contributes significantly to the flavour of cheese. Effectively the process of hydrolytic rancidity is followed in that free fatty acids, such as butyric (butanoic), are produced and have strong flavours. Amino and fatty acids may also be attacked by enzymes in order to release flavour compounds such as ammonia.

Other cheeses

There are numerous semi-hard and hard cheeses made by modified methods of the Cheddar process, and many are given place names, *eg* Derby, Cheshire and Gloucester. Each variety is produced to give a characteristic level of acidity and moisture which allows the development of the desired flavour and consistency.

Harder cheeses are produced by heating the curd to a higher temperature, cutting the curd finer during milling and by applying a higher pressure during the pressing into moulds.

Blue cheeses are not pressed but gently packed into moulds so that *penicillium* blue mould can grow through the cheese lumps. The most common mould is *P. roquefortii*. The mould produces proteolytic enzymes and often ammonia is released which is a characteristic of the flavour of some of these cheeses.

The *soft cheeses,* such as Camembert and Brie, depend on a different mould *Penicillium camembertii* which produces a white growth. The curd is put into shallow moulds and rubbed with salt which allows the mould to grow. Enzymes from the mould act on the curd to produce the soft and creamy texture of the ripened cheese. Once ripe the shelf-life of the cheese is short.

Processed cheese is a manufactured product from a number of cheeses. It is made by emulsifying the cheese with green cheese in the presence of emulsifying agents and water. The emulsifying agents used are blends of salts, sodium and potassium phosphate and calcium, potassium or sodium citrates.

The cheese is chopped into small pieces, heated and mixed thoroughly with green cheese, water and emulsifier. It is often wrapped in metal foil, and as the heating process kills many organisms it remains moist and keeps for some time.

Cheese *spreads* contain more moisture and often have gums or gelatin to help form a smooth paste.

FERMENTED MILKS

Yoghurt is the best known fermented milk in most Western countries, although it originated from the Balkans and Middle East; but there are a large number of other products such as: cultured buttermilk, ayran, kefir, kumiss an laben.

Yoghurt is milk, often concentrated or with added milk powder, which has developed a characteristic acidity and flavour due to the growth of two micro-organisms. *Lactobacillus delbreukii ssp.bulgaricus* and *Streptococcus thermophilus*. The two organisms must be in equal amounts and one must not outgrow the other or a bitter or too acid a product will result. Yoghurt has long been thought to have therapeutic properties, particularly for convalescents. Most yoghurts do not have such properties, but there are obviously some good nutritional aspects to be considered as yoghurts contain more protein, thiamin and riboflavin than milk, but low fat yoghurts contain less fat-soluble vitamins. However, if the bacterium *Lactobacillus acidophilus* is included in the starter culture then the yoghurt may help patients to recover from gastroenteritis and other gastric disorders.

Yoghurt falls into main types according to its consistency, set and stirred yoghurt. To make *set yoghurt* the fermentation is allowed to take place in the container in which the yoghurt is sold, whereas *stirred yoghurt* is fermented in bulk then packed later.

The ingredients for yoghurt include whole milk, skim milk, evaporated milk, dried milk, stabilizers and thickeners, fruit flavours, colours and sugar. Generally, low fat yoghurts are produced so the fat is separated from the milk using a centrifugal separator. The solids content of the milk is increased by evaporation of some water, addition of evaporated milk or addition of skim milk powder. Ingredients such as sugar, stabilizers, colours and flavours are blended into the milk base. The mix is homogenised then pasteurised at 90C for 30 minutes or by the HTST method, to kill all micro-organisms. The mix is cooled to 44C and inoculated with the starter culture.

To make a *set yoghurt* the mix is incubated at 44C for about $1\frac{1}{2}$ hours, then poured into containers which are kept warm until the yoghurt has fully coagulated. The yoghurt is then cooled to 5-8C and held at this temperature until consumed, ideally within 14 days. Natural yoghurts are usually of the set type.

To make *stirred yoghurt*, which offers advantages in continuous manufacture, incubation is at a slightly lower temperature so that the yoghurt becomes thicker but not coagulated, and continuous stirring ensures that no curd is formed. Fruit and syrup are metered into the containers, followed by the yoghurt mix, which is then cooled and stored as before.

New developments in yoghurts include frozen yoghurt and long life yoghurt where aseptic packaging is used following heat treatment of the yoghurt. 'Bio' yoghurts claim health advantages as they are living cultures including the organism *Bifidobacteruim bifidium* which helps with stomach problems by colonising the gut. The organism also produces acetic acid as a flavouring agent and ferments a milder, creamier product.

PRACTICAL EXERCISES: *DAIRY PRODUCTS*

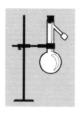

1. Microscopic examination
Using a small quantity, thinly spread out, make slides of milk, homogenised milk, cream and skimmed milk. Observe the fat droplets and compare their size in each product.

2. To test milk for minerals
Warm about 100cm³ of milk to 40C and add several drops of glacial acetic acid. Take care. Stir and continue to add acid until flocculation occurs. Filter, then test the filtrate for chloride, nitrate, sulphate and phosphate (see minerals section for details).

3. Titratable acidity of milk
Pipette 25cm³ of milk into a flask, add phenolphthalein, as an indicator and titrate with 0.1M sodium hydroxide. The end-point is a pale pink colour.
1 cm³ of 0.1 M NaOH is neutralised by 0.009g of lactic acid
∴ g of lactic acid per 100cm³ of milk will be 0.009x titre x (100/25)
(NB: titre = volume of 1.0M NaOH used).

4. Butter manufacture
Allow three pints of milk to stand in a refrigerator for two days. Carefully remove the cream layer from each. Pour the cream into a large stoppered container and shake vigorously for some time. The cream will eventually break and butter will form. Carefully remove the butter milk to leave the butter. A small amount of cold water should be added to wash the butter. Remove surplus water and add a small amount of salt. Taste and compare with commercial butters.

5. Clotting of milk with rennet
Special requirement: commercial preparation of rennet. Keep in a refrigerator.

(a) Effect of rennet concentration:
   To 10 cm³ of milk in each of four test tubes add:
   (i)   0.5cm³ of a 5% solution of rennet in water
   (ii) 1.0cm³ of a 5% solution of rennet in water
   (iii) 2.0cm³ of a 5% solution of rennet in water
Place in a water-bath at 30 – 35C and note the time curd starts to appear in the milk.

(b) The effect of temperature:
   Repeat (a) at temperatures of 20C, 40C and 50C.

(c) The effect of pH:
   To four test-tubes containing 10cm³ of milk each add:
   (i)   0.5cm³ of lactic acid solution (1%)
   (ii) 1.0cm³ of lactic acid solution (1%)
   (iii) 1.0cm³ of 0.1M sodium hydroxide
   (iv) 2.0cm³ of 0.1M sodium hydroxide
Place in a water-bath at 30 – 35C and add 0.5cm³ of a 5% solution of rennet. Note time of clotting of each sample.

6. Preparation of casein from milk
Use a 25cm³ measuring cylinder and 5cm³ of milk and 5cm³ of water; place in a water-bath at about 35C. Add 0.5cm³ of acetic acid (10%) to precipitate the casein. Then add 0.5cm³ of 0.1M sodium acetate to buffer the pH at 4.6. Cool. Allow to stand. Pour off whey proteins and other liquids to leave casein.

7. Yoghurt – to investigate the effect of temperature on yoghurt production.
Heat, but do not boil, about ¾ pint of milk. Cool to 40C. Mix six teaspoonfuls of plain yoghurt (starter culture) with a little of the milk, then add this preparation to the remaining milk. Divide into three samples and seal into suitable containers. Store the containers in a refrigerator, in a room and near a boiler. Note the temperature and examine the samples for curd formation, noting the time when it first appears. Samples of yoghurt produced should not be eaten as there may be a risk of contamination with harmful organisms.

Chapter 2

Meat, Fish, Poultry and Eggs

PREVIEW

- **Meat**
  - muscle, associated connective tissue and adjoining fat
  - number of biochemical changes necessary to form meat
  - good supply of most nutrients
  - connective tissue makes it indigestible

- **Muscle structure**
  - muscle in meat – striated muscle
  - myofibrils make up muscle fibres, held together by sheath, the sarcolemma
  - two proteins in myofibrils – myosin and actin
  - these two proteins responsible for muscle contraction
  - rigor mortis, contraction after death
  - ends of myosin drawn towards the 'Z' line with actin filaments sliding over them

- **Conversion of muscle to meat**
  - high glycogen level important as leads to high lactic acid and final pH of 5.6
  - higher pH leads to poor colour
  - animals must be rested before to slaughter to ensure high glycogen levels in muscles
  - conditioning or ageing after slaughter
  - enzymes breakdown large molecules to smaller molecules, give flavour and tenderness to meat

- **Storage and handling of meat**
  - chill to 5C or less to slow down enzymic changes and microbial growth
  - rapid rigor mortis can cause excessive shrinkage and toughness

- **Meat products**
  - usually comminuted – greater risk of food poisoning
  - 'Wiltshire cure' base of most bacon and ham curing
  - smoking adds flavour and preserves by adding phenolic compounds
  - sausages require preservative usually sodium metabisulphite
  - canned meats require long processing times as the cans are tightly packed
  - 'salami' manufactured in similar manner to cheese

- **Fish**
  - demersal fish – bottom feeders include cod, haddock and flat fish
  - pelagic – middle and surface feeders, generally fatty fish, *eg* herrings and mackerel
  - fish can be 'out of condition' when caught during certain seasons and during –spawning
  - glycogen reserves are low and quickly used up causing rapid rigor mortis
  - final pH not as low as in meat
  - trimethylamine oxide broken down to give trimethylamine – smell of bad fish
  - ammonia also produced in bad fish
  - inosinic acid, partly responsible for fish flavour, broken down to hypoxanthine –contributes to bitter flavour of spoiled fish.

- **Preservation of fish**
  - ice ideal medium for cooling
  - freshwater fish last longer than salt water fish
  - non-fatty fish last longer than fatty fish
  - freezing at sea and storage at –30C extends storage life of fish for several months
  - preservation methods include: salting, marinating, drying, smoking and canning
  - crustaceans undergo rapid enzymic spoilage and microbial attack

- **Poultry and eggs**
  - poultry similar to meat but white breast muscle has little respiratory pigment
  - eggs perform function of reproduction and food for man
  - egg white contains anti-microbial systems in its proteins:
    (1) lysozyme – destroys bacteria
    (2) ovomucoid – inhibits enzyme trypsin
    (3) avidin – binds vitamin, biotin
    (4) conalbumin – binds iron
  - egg yolk good emulsifying properties

MEAT

Meat could be simply defined as the flesh of animals used as food. To be more precise it normally refers to muscle, associated connective tissue and adjoining fat. Offal such as liver, kidneys, heart and brains may also be referred to as meat. However, the flesh of an animal immediately after death is not meat as a considerable number of biochemical changes are necessary to produce meat of the right colour, texture, flavour and cookability.

Meat can supply most of the requirements of man for growth and normal health, as it is a source of all the essential amino acids, many vitamins, essential fatty acids and minerals. Sometimes meat is of poor digestibility as it contains too much connective tissue and this fault is made worse by poor cooking.

Meat is considered to be a main source of protein, but protein can be produced more quickly and much cheaper by other means, for example, low fat soya flour contains 50% whereas lean beef only 25%. Single cell protein from micro-organisms is a very efficient system, but there still remains a problem of acceptability.

The brain disease bovine spongiform encephalopathy (BSE) first indentified in Kent in 1985 has affected meat sales significantly. The Foot and Mouth epidemic of 2001 also had a damaging effect on the meat industry. BSE is declining from 26,682 cases in 1992, 8016 in 1996 and 599 in 1995. Research published in 1996 and onwards indicates that BSE in cattle and new variant CJD (v CJD – Creutzfeldt Jacob disease) in humans carry the same 'fingerprint'. However, both may be triggered by some third unsuggested course. Evidence continues to support the 'prion' theory. Prions are very reactive rogue proteins which appear to be the infective agent.

MUSCLE STRUCTURE

The muscle of animals, which converts to meat, is *striated* or *voluntary muscle,* and consists of long cylindrical cells, *the muscle fibres,* which are parallel to each other. There are striations going across the muscle cells, hence the name *striated muscles.* The muscle fibres are held in bundles by connective tissue, generally small bundles of cells give more tender meat. Each individual muscle fibre is surrounded by a sheath, the *sarcolemma* and within this the fibre is divided into *myofibrils* which are surrounded by fluid. The myofibrils are made from two types of protein: *myosin,* which are thicker filaments: and *actin* which are thinner. These proteins are responsible for the contraction of muscle and for *rigor mortis,* which is the contraction after death. A cross-section of a muscle is given in Figure 2.4 showing the fibre bundles. A longitudinal section of the muscle myofibril shows the light and dark striations and the positions of the proteins, actin and myosin, Figure 2.5.

Figure 2.4

Cross-section of muscle

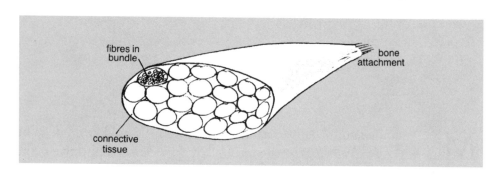

Figure 2.5

Longitudinal section of myofibril

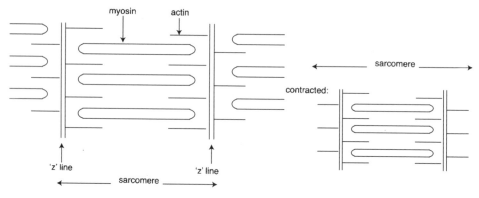

In Figure 2.5 the ends of the myosin filaments are drawn towards the 'Z' lines with the actin filaments sliding over them. There are six actin rods surrounding each myosin filament. This is repeated throughout the length of the myofibril and each muscle, and consequently the whole muscle contracts.

Obviously, energy is required for muscles to contract and this is released from ATP (adenosine triphosphate) which is kept as an energy source in an inactive complex with magnesium. When an electrical nerve impulse is passed to the muscle to stimulate a contraction a change occurs in the fibre sheath, the sarcolemma. Calcium ions are released as a result of this and these split ATP from the magnesium complex and also stimulate an enzyme, myosin ATP-ase, which splits ATP into ADP (adenosine diphosphate) with a release of energy. The magnesium complex of ATP also keeps the proteins myosin and actin apart, but once it is broken down the two proteins link together at their ends. As energy becomes available the actin is dragged along the myosin filaments and contraction occurs. However, there is still much debate on how this actually occurs.

Once the nerve stimulation of the muscle has stopped the system goes into reverse. Calcium ions are removed from the system so that the magnesium – ATP complex reforms and myosin ATP-ase is inhibited. The proteins again become separated. Respiration processes replenish the ATP at the expense of glycogen in the muscle, but if there has been a lot of muscular activity lactic acid is produced in the muscle with a consequent 'oxygen debt'. Panting, involving taking in a large amount of air, resolves the oxygen debt and metabolises the lactic acid. This is a simplified view of a very complex biochemical process which is still being studied and debated.

Conversion of muscle into meat

Although many changes occur in muscle post mortem, the final quality of meat is influenced by a number of factors pre-slaughter.

Before slaughter, animals may lose weight, or become infected with disease from other animals in the abattoir. This loss in weight may cause loss of moisture from the muscle, ultimately leading to tougher or stringy meat, and the reduction of glycogen in the muscle, which as we shall see, can affect meat in a number of ways.

When an animal is killed, or dies naturally, after a period of time the muscles throughout the carcase stiffen in *rigor mortis,* remaining in this condition for some time, after which they soften again. If muscle is cooked while still in rigor it will be tougher and of a darker colour than if it is allowed to pass though rigor before cooking. Meat cooked before rigor, however, is always tender, but commercial distribution systems for meat do not generally allow this to happen.

ATP is replenished after contraction of the muscle by using up the store of glycogen. When an animal is killed the circulation of blood ceases, but the muscle's biochemical processes try to carry on as usual. Glycogen is broken down in the production of ATP as before, but because there is no oxygen available, anaerobic glycolysis occurs and lactic acid is produced. As a result of this lactic acid, the pH of the muscle falls, and enzymes become inhibited as the enzymes involved are inactivated. The ATP becomes gradually depleted in other reactions and as a result the actin and myosin combine and the muscle contracts, but is unable to relax again – the state of rigor mortis. The ultimate pH in the muscle is important, and is generally about pH 5.6. At a higher pH the meat will not keep well, being subject to microbial attack and having poor colour and water-holding capacity. The more glycogen in the muscle before slaughter the more lactic acid is produced and the ultimate pH is lower.

There are a number of factors that affect glycogen levels in muscle. Only well-fed animals have muscles with the maximum glycogen, and this is readily depleted, particularly in pigs, if the animal is chased excited or is subject to any stress. Animals kept in pens often fight; this leads to depletion of glycogen when the animals were thought to be resting before slaughter. Sugar feeding before death helps to replenish depleted glycogen reserves.

After a few hours rigor mortis disappears and the carcase becomes soft and pliable and the meat is tender, juicier, with more flavour. This period post-rigor is the *ageing* or *conditioning* period of meat and can be an important factor in producing high quality meat. During the ageing process numerous enzyme systems are active that break down large molecules, particularly proteins to release amino acids and lipids to release fatty acids. The actin filaments are thought to become detached from the Z-line and this leads to increased tenderness in the meat. Connective tissue is not broken down during this ageing period and therefore will still cause meat to be stringy. The release of amino acids, and other nitrogen containing substances and some free fatty acids leads to the development of the typical meat flavour, which becomes a main attraction when meat is cooked.

Storage and handling of meat

The processes outlined above can continue, leading eventually to deterioration of the meat. Game animals because of their tougher muscle structure need a much longer period of conditioning and are therefore 'hung' for longer periods than other animals and usually at room temperature. Meat must be stored at chill temperatures to slow down the enzyme changes after conditioning and minimise microbial growth. Usually temperatures of 5C or less are used, but lower temperatures approaching freezing will greatly extend storage life. Similarly the addition of 10% of carbon dioxide to a chill store will extend storage life but may cause some darkening of the meat. Micro-organisms rapidly contaminate the previously sterile muscles of animals after slaughter. The micro-organisms come from many sources in the abattoir, including personnel, knives, floors, the hide and hooves of the animal, excreta and the air. Some organisms will grow on the surface of the meat and some will penetrate it, ultimately to cause putrefaction. Chilling meat slows down the growth of these organisms but a number can grow at refrigeration temperatures.

The butcher prepares cuts of meat often in a traditional manner and produces a range of meat products. In Figure 2.6 are shown the traditional meat cuts, but these are only a guide as they vary enormously throughout the country.

There is a growing tendency to sell meat by its end-use, *eg* stewing, braising and frying steak and traditional joints are preferred with less fat. The butcher has to suffer many complaints about his products, the reasons for which are often beyond his control, and often include bad cooking.

Toughness is probably the most common complaint, as has been mentioned previously, but rapid rigor mortis can lead to excessive shrinkage and toughness

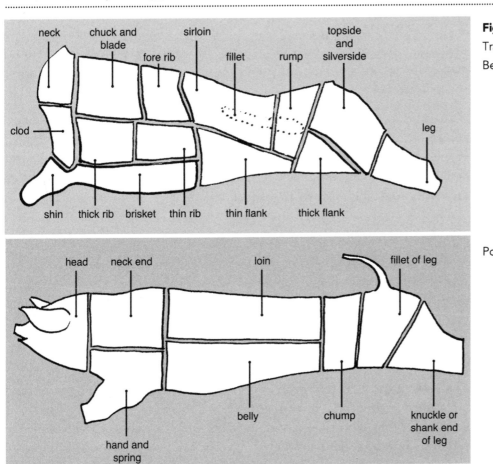

Figure 2.6

Traditional meat cuts

Beef

Pork

Lamb

of the meat and is one of the more common reasons for this complaint. Holding muscle at too high a temperature after slaughter causes this.

In pork a condition known as PSE of muscle, *ie* pale soft exudate, results if the pH falls too rapidly. This is often a hereditary condition. The proteins denature and lose some of their water-holding capacity causing fluid to exude. In beef, if glycogen is depleted before slaughter, the pH remains too high. Too high a pH causes the muscle to have too great a water-holding capacity. As a result of this oxygen cannot penetrate the meat and combine with myoglobin to give bright red oxymyoglobin which gives the attractive bright red colour of meat. The meat, therefore, remains dark red and tends to be somewhat dry to the palate. The condition produces what is known as 'dark-cutting' beef.

MEAT PRODUCTS

There are numerous products throughout the world and there is an enormous market for manufactured meat products such as sausages, pies, canned meat and delicatessen products.

Meat products, usually comminuted in some form or other, are extremely vulnerable to microbial contamination and have been implicated in a number of food-poisoning outbreaks. The work area must be hygienic and care must be take to avoid contamination from operators in the factory who might be carriers of some pathogens, *eg Salmonellae*.

Curing

A wide range of products, particularly pork derivatives, are cured by the process which started thousands of years ago, salting. Heavy salting of products is not now carried out as the characteristic flavours of cured hams, bacons and smoked meat are preferred.

Bacon

The basis of most current procedures is the 'Wiltshire cure'. The pig carcases are scalded at about 62C to remove the hair and any coarse hair is singed. The carcases are then cleaned and split into sides which are cooled and trimmed to remove some bone and unwanted muscle. The temperature is reduced to about 5C when curing is started, by pumping brine into the sides. This brine varies in composition but is generally about 25-30% salt and 2.5-4% potassium nitrate. The sides are stacked in tanks, perhaps as many as twelve deep, and are covered in brine for about five days. Usually the brine is inoculated with salt-tolerant bacteria (halophilic) which are encouraged to grow by the addition of some sugar and by protein leaching from the pork muscle. The bacteria convert the potassium nitrate to nitrite, which is broken down to release nitrogen II oxide (nitric oxide) which combines with myoglobin to give the characteristic pink colour of cured meat. The sides of pork are removed from the tanks and matured for about two weeks during which time the typical flavour develops. This 'green' bacon may be consumed or may be smoked. Smoke not only adds flavour but adds phenolic substances which act as preservatives. Liquid smoke flavours are being used in increasing amounts, as they are easy and convenient to use. It is possible to charge the bacon slices electrostatically so that when the smoke liquid droplets are sprayed they cling all over the surface ensuring an even 'smoke'. A growing technique is in the preparation of bacon by slice curing in which individual slices are passed for up to 15 minutes through a weaker brine (10% salt and 0.02%) sodium nitrite). The overall process is rapid and maturation is complete in a few hours. A good uniform product is produced in a manner which can easily be automated.

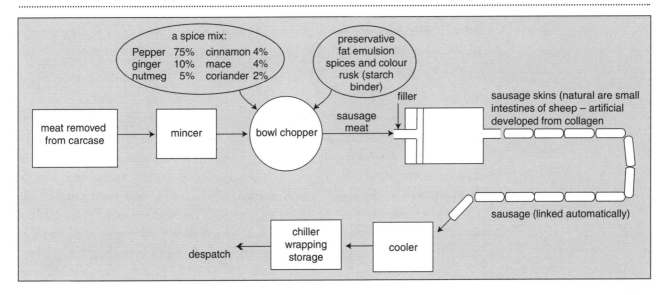

Figure 2.7

A sausage production line

Sausage manufacture

Meat included in sausages may come from a number of different parts of the pig's carcase but this meat is always chopped or minced during manufacture. This **comminution** process causes an enormous increases in the surface area available to micro-organisms and the process also distributes these microbes throughout the bulk of the meat, where moist conditions and ample food materials enable rapid growth. The use of chemical preservatives in sausages thus increases what would be a very short shelf-life.

Normally the preservative used is sulphur dioxide (not exceeding 450ppm): but obviously this cannot be added to sausages as a gas but has to be available from a solid sulphite, normally sodium metabisulphite. Fortunately, not only is this preservative active against spoilage organisms which prefer to grow at room temperature, but it is also active against some food poisoning bacteria, particularly *Salmonella*. However, some spoilage organisms are less affected by sulphites and cause sourness to develop in the sausage, thus making them unpalatable, before pathogenic organisms can multiply to any extent.

Many types of sausage are available, but in Germany particularly, the number of types is much greater. Some sausages such as bologna and frankfurters are cured then cooked and consequently have a much longer shelf-life even at room temperature. Many products are smoked which lengthens their lives even further.

Canned meats

When meat is sealed into a can and heat-processed in order to sterilize the product the manufacturer is faced with the problem that heat penetration is slow and the process takes a long time. This long period of heat-sterilization affects the eating quality of the meat and any reduction in the process would improve the organoleptic properties of the meat, but, of course, would present possible risks of spoilage and food poisoning. A large piece of meat such as a ham is very difficult to process and is normally only pasteurized. The product must, therefore, be stored under refrigeration to prevent spoilage. Nevertheless there is a wide range of canned meats available which include beef, pork and poultry products.

Salami

The production of salami and similar fermented sausages follows to some extent the manufacture of cheese. As with cheese, preservation depends on a fermentation producing lactic acid by bacteria, which also produce desirable flavour compounds. Starter cultures are used to bring about rapid lactic fermentation in the meat, which is often held at 30 C and high humidity to effect what is known as the 'sweating process'. The drop in pH causes a fall in the water-holding capacity of the meat, which allows the product to be dried easily. The product is smoked and air dried and so has a long shelf-life.

FISH

Unlike most meat producing animals, fish have to be caught; for many developing countries they are their only source of animal protein and therefore are very valuable foods. Fish farming is increasingly becoming popular as suitable species become available and economic and disease problems are overcome.

There are many hundreds of fish species used as food and each has its own composition, properties and processing behaviour. The *demersal* fish are bottom feeders and include 'round fish' such as cod and haddock and the 'flat fish' such as plaice and soles. The *pelagic fish* live in the middle and upper layers of the sea and are generally fatty fish such as herrings and mackerel, containing an average 20% lipid. A number of fresh water fish are eaten and besides the more expensive salmon and trout species certain types of carp, perch and pike are popular in some regions. In addition to the fin-fish, there are numerous shellfish, such as mussels, cockles and oysters, and a range of crustaceans particularly the shrimps, craps and lobsters.

FISH QUALITY

The most important factor in handling fish is that it is highly perishable and quickly deteriorates. However, there are a number of factors which affect the initial fish quality, particularly the time and place of capture. Some fishing grounds may be low on food, but there is generally a seasonal cycle of feeding with fish moving from one area to another. Spawning occurs at certain times and in certain areas. Fish caught in any of these situations will be 'out of condition', which will be shown in reduced fat content in pelagic species, high water levels and lower protein contents. Fish muscle contains glycogen and the process of rigor mortis also occurs as in meat. However, glycogen reserves may be low in poor quality fish, little lactic acid is produced after death, and the ultimate pH is high giving soft flesh in the fish. Fish obviously cannot be rested before death and in fact some fish 'fight' during capture, in the case of game fish for some time, and also flap or jump about on board after capture. As a result there is significantly less glycogen in fish than in meat and the pH is only about 6.5 compared with 5.6 or less in meat.

Fish rapidly pass into rigor and start to undergo bacterial deterioration immediately afterwards. Most fish are put in ice or frozen to arrest bacterial growth, and this is particularly effective with tropical fish as their inherent bacteria are used to ambient temperatures of 25C. Fish flesh has a nitrogen-containing compound, trimethylamine oxide which is broken down by bacteria into trimethylamine, which has the characteristic smell of bad fish. Although this substance can be easily detected, it can be determined chemically as an indicator of fish quality.

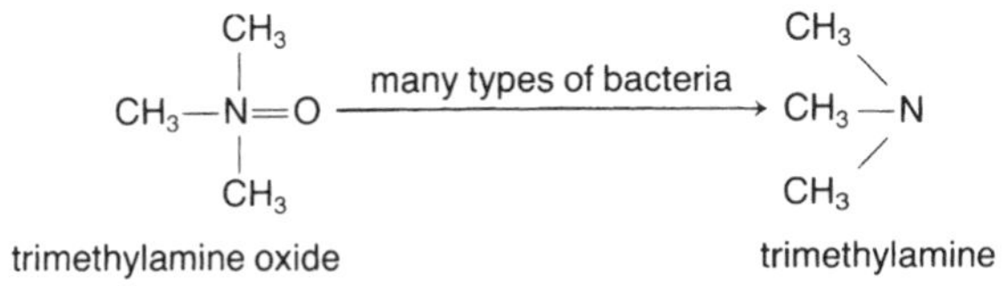

$$CH_3-N=O \xrightarrow{\text{many types of bacteria}} CH_3-N$$

trimethylamine oxide   trimethylamine

Figure 2.8

Production of trimethylamine in fish

Ammonia is often produced by bacteria when they attack the protein of fish muscle, again this adds to the smell of bad fish. Any lipid material in fish is usually highly unsaturated, particularly oils in fatty fish, and is therefore susceptible to oxidative rancidity, which again is an indication of poor quality fish.

The typical, but slight, flavour of fresh fish is due in part to inosinic acid. When the fish starts to deteriorate this substance is broken down to hypoxanthine which contributes to the bitter flavour of spoiled fish. The measurement of hypoxanthine levels in fish is an indicator of freshness.

PRESERVATION OF FISH

The lower the temperature the slower the bacterial and enzyme activity in fish and, consequently, the longer the 'shelf-life'. Fish can, therefore, be chilled or frozen.

Chilling (icing)

Ice is an ideal medium for chilling fish and some species may be stored for periods of up to a month. Ice has a relatively large cooling capacity; for good chilling of the fish the ice must be melting which has the added advantage of washing the fish and keeping it moist. Freshwater fish last longer in ice than saltwater species, and similarly non-fatty fish have a longer shelf-life than fatty fish. Tropical fish, as they are acclimatized to high ambient temperatures, last longer than cold water species when stored in ice.

In some parts of the world it is not practical to produce and store ice, and an alternative, which is gaining popularity, is the production of chilled sea water, CSW, or refrigerated sea water, RSW. In the former method, sea water is chilled by mixing in ice and then the fish are kept fresh in this mixture. To produce RSW a refrigeration plant is necessary to reduce the temperature of seawater to about –1C.

Freezing

Freezing fish, after preparation at sea, and storing at about –30C can extend the shelf-life of most fish to several months or even a year. Enzymic and bacterial action is almost completely stopped at this temperature and water, required for bacterial growth and enzymic activity, is effectively removed and locked away as ice. The freezing operation may reduce the number of micro-organisms in frozen fish, but on thawing the numbers will more than make up for this decrease. The poorer the quality of the fish, it will be even poorer after freezing and frozen storage. Only the freshest raw fish should be frozen. Often fish are *glazed* after freezing by dipping them into water so that a film of ice forms on the surface of the fish. This glazing prevents 'freezer burn' which in fact is dehydration caused by loss of water (ice) from the surface of the fish. Also the technique prevents oxidation of any fat in the fish by acting as a barrier against air.

Salting

This is a traditional method of processing fish throughout the world, either using salt brines or dry salt. Often the technique is used in conjunction with drying or smoking. Sufficient quantities of salt, through the osmotic effect, prevent the growth of spoilage organisms. Generally a concentration of 6 to 10% of salt in the fish tissues is required.

Fatty fish are slower to salt than non-fatty fish and thicker, fresher fish are similarly slower to salt.

In brine salting the fish are immersed in a salt solution, whereas in dry salting salt is actually rubbed into the surface of the fish. If salt levels are not high enough some bacterial growth may occur producing putrefaction.

Marinades

In addition to salt, acetic acid (vinegar) is used to produce marinated fish. Fatty fish are often preserved in this manner, eg marinated herrings, and have a good shelf-life.

Drying

Sun-drying of fish is an ancient method of preservation which is still used in many warmer areas. The quality of the product is very variable and, of course, cannot be controlled. Infestation of dried fish by flies is common in many tropical areas. Tunnel driers produce a better quality product but the highest quality of all is produced by freeze-drying.

Smoking

Smoking fish is another well tried technique of preservation; not only does smoke give flavour to fish but it has a preservation effect due to phenolic compounds. In addition the heat from the fire will dry the product and cook it. The long storage life of some smoked fish is due to the drying and cooking. This type of smoking is called *hot smoking,* but in *cold smoking* the temperature is kept low to avoid cooking and the product must be stored at refrigeration temperatures, *eg* Finnan haddock.

Canning

Fish for canning must be carefully selected for shape and size and generally must be packed by hand into the cans. The fish must be gutted, cleaned and trimmed, and may be smoked, salted or partially dried before canning. In a similar manner to canning meat, the fish is tightly packed into the can and so heat penetration and hence the sterilisation process can be very slow. Some fish, *eg* anchovies, are so heavily salted that no heat-processing is necessary. Fatty fish withstand the heat process much better than white fish, which tend to suffer considerable protein damage.

Fish proteins often contain amino acids with sulphur groups, which on heating release hydrogen sulphide. This gas can combine with iron of the can to produce unsightly black stains, and for this reason special lacquered cans must be used. Generally the lacquers contain zinc oxide which produces white zinc sulphide which is not noticed.

CRUSTACEANS

This large group of generally expensive sea-foods is characterised by being animals with external skeletons or shells of *chitin.* Most edible crustaceans are ten-legged.

Crabs

As all crabs spoil rapidly, through enzyme activity, when they are dead, it is usual to keep them alive as long as possible. Boiling will inactivate enzymes, particularly if the crabs are boiled in salt water and then they should be chilled. After boiling, crabs or crabmeat may be frozen or canned. Generally only the white crab meat is canned.

Prawns and shrimps

These crustaceans are very readily spoiled by their enzyme systems when they are dead; it is therefore customary to boil them immediately in seawater after catching. They are also found to contain large numbers of micro-organisms which again effect rapid spoilage. An alternative is to remove the heads, which contain most of the digestive enzymes, and chill the tails in ice. Most prawns can be frozen into blocks.

Molluscs

Molluscs can be dried, smoked, canned or frozen, but many are eaten fresh. Mussels and oysters are often marinated in vinegar or bottled.

POULTRY AND EGGS

In the muscle of poultry lactic acid is produced after death, and the bird passes through rigor mortis in much the same way as meat and fish. In chicken particularly the breast muscles are little used and so they only need a small amount of haemoglobin and myoglobin. In consequence the breast muscle is white whereas the leg muscle produces dark meat.

Nutritionally chicken and beef muscle are similar, but as a source of protein chicken protein is produced more quickly and more cheaply.

PROCESSING

The poultry-processing industry is one that has become rapidly mechanised with a demand for large numbers of young, uniform chickens. Automated processes are used for rapid killing, dressing and chilling of the carcases. Rapid production and quick freezing minimise problems of infection by micro-organisms.

Birds are generally not fed for several hours and are initially electrically stunned, followed by cutting the head to sever the main blood vessels. Blood is drained away and the birds are scalded with boiling water. The feathers are plucked and this can be mechanised but requires subsequent visual inspection. Feet, heads and viscera are removed. The carcases are often cooled in iced water to reduce enzyme action and colour changes. The chickens are then dried, trussed and packed into polythene bags before to freezing in a blast freezer.

EGGS

The hen's egg performs two important purposes, that of serving as a means of reproduction for the species and, secondly, providing a nutritious, convenient and cheap food. The egg is equipped with means of defending the embryo chick against micro-organisms during its development, but some of the systems may affect the nutritional aspects of the egg for man.

Structure of the egg

The outer shell of an egg is composed mainly of calcium carbonate, lined with membranes and having a number of pores for gas exchange. These pores are covered by a wax-like layer, known as the *cuticle*. This cuticle protects, in part, against microbial invasion and controls water-loss. The structure of an egg is given in Figure 2.9.

The egg white is divided into a thick layer around the yolk and a thinner layer

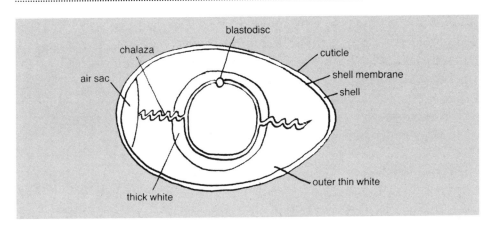

Figure 2.9
Structure of the hen's egg

next to the shell. This thick layer anchors the yolk, together with the chalazae, in the middle of the egg where it is less vulnerable to microbial attack. Egg whites foam readily and are therefore useful for making souffles and meringues. However, in the egg the white has an important function as it possesses special antibacterial properties, which, under normal circumstances, prevent the growth and multiplication of micro-organisms which have penetrated the shell. The enzyme, *lysozyme*, actually destroys bacteria by lysis (splitting) of their cell walls. The *ovomucoid* is a protein in the white, which inhibits the enzyme *trypsin* and the protein *avidin* binds up the vitamin biotin. *Conalbumin* acts as a sequestrant and binds up iron and copper. Fortunately, cooking an egg destroys the properties of ovomucoid and avidin. The pH of eggs is unusual in being alkaline, often as high as 9.0, again an anti-microbial property. The yolk is rich in nutrients and is the most vulnerable part of the egg to micro-organisms. The yolk has good emulsifying properties, and so is used in the preparation of mayonnaise, salad dressings and cakes.

Quality of eggs
Biological changes gradually take place inside the egg and unless these can be controlled, loss in quality results. The thick white of the egg generally becomes thinner and membranes around the yolk weaken. Loss of water during storage causes an enlarged air sac, which can be reduced by humidification of the store.

Candling of eggs is a method which is used for checking the quality of eggs. The egg is illuminated with a light so the following flaws can be seen: the yolk position and size; the size of air sac; the presence of blood or 'meat' spots.

The yolk index is another method of determining quality. The height of the yolk is measured with a special tripod micrometer, and its width is measured with calipers. The index is calculated thus:

$$\frac{\text{Height of yolk}}{\text{Width of yolk}} = \text{yolk index}$$

A fresh egg usually has an index of about 0.45 and this gradually falls on ageing as freshness decreases.

In 1988 the problem of Salmonella (*S enteritidis*) in egg yolks was first recognised: this has now been brought under control. The organism entered the yolk of the egg during its formation in the ovaries of the chicken. The normal defence systems of the egg were, therefore, avoided by the bacteria. There was a potential health risk for any product using raw eggs such as mousse and cheesecake.

Egg processing
Frozen whole egg is produced in large quantities for use in food manufacture. Eggs are washed and any bacteria on the surface are destroyed by chlorine in the wash water. The eggs are broken mechanically and mixed to an homogeneous product which is pasteurized at 63C for 60 seconds. Any shell pieces are filtered out and the liquid egg is filled into cans and frozen in a blast freezer.

Dried egg is an alternative to frozen egg and is usually made by spray-drying, although freeze-drying produces an excellent but expensive product. Eggs are prepared as above and spray-dried in a drier, which can be used for milk powder.

PRACTICAL EXERCISES: MEAT, FISH AND EGGS

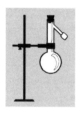

1. Microscope examination of meat and fish muscle
Place a small amount of tissue on a slide, add a drop of water and attempt to spread the tissue into a thin section. Examine the fibres under high power of the microscope.

2. Cooking losses in meat products
Losses are caused by moisture and fat separating from the product, producing noticeable shrinkage. Try the following experiment on sausages, meat burgers and minced meat:
Weigh the product. Weigh 60g of lard and add to a frying pan and heat. Fry the product for 10 minutes. Reweigh the drained product and weigh the fat from the pan (*when cooled*). Calculate the weight loss of the product, fat loss and moisture loss.

3. Fish filleting
Evaluation of the degree of wastage associated with filleting different species. Prepare two fillets from a weighed fish. Weigh the fillets and calculate the percentage yield of fillets. The fillets may then be frozen or used in other work.

4 Eggs – physical characteristics
Note nature of egg shell. Carefully break an egg on to a plate. Measure the yolk height and width, and calculate the yolk index. Test the egg parts with universal pH papers and note the pH. Try to observe each part of the egg structure.

7. Emulsifying property of egg yolk
Mix a drop of oil with some water, and shake. Note the speed of separation. Repeat using washing-up liquid, and then with some egg yolk. Note emulsification produced.

Chapter 3
Fruit and Vegetables

PREVIEW

- **Composition of fruits and vegetables**
  - mainly water, contributes minerals and vitamins, some roughage. Some products good carbohydrate sources, *eg* banana
  - turgid cell – at maximum water content
  - turgor pressure in cell balanced by elasticity of cell wall
  - transpiration of harvest produce causes turgor loss and wilting
  - colour pigments occur in plastids
  - cell wall made up of cellulose, hemicellulose and pectin
  - malic and citric acids most common
  - highly coloured and tropical fruits richer in Vitamin C
  - some products contain poison precursors, *eg* linamarin in cassava can break down   to release hydrocyanic acid

- **Post-harvest changes**
  - length of storage depends on:
    - (1) chemical composition
    - (2) resistance to microbial attack
    - (3) external temperature
    - (4) presence of gases in the store
  - respiration major process of interest
  - climacteric fruits show rapid rise in rate of respiration after harvesting
  - non-climacteric fruits and most vegetables show no rapid increase in respiration, but changes in composition are gradual
  - ethylene (ethene) stimulates ripening process
  - pectin broken down progressively:
    protopectin → pectinic acid → pectic acid → galacturonic acids
  - chlorophyll broken down to reveal other pigments *eg* carotenes
    or other, *eg* lycopene is synthesised during ripening
  - in vegetables, such as peas and beans, starch is synthesised from sugar
  - at lower temperatures starch is not synthesised and sugars accumulate, respiration increases

- **Storage**
  - respiration and ripening controlled by:
    - (1) reducing the temperature
    - (2) increasing CO_2 levels
    - (3) decreasing O_2 levels
    - (4) lowering atmospheric pressure (hypobaric storage)
    - (5) use of special surface coatings such as 'Pro-long'

- **Processing**
  - peeling, essential before further processing, can be by:
    - (1) hand peeling
    - (2) steam or hot water
    - (3) lye peeling using sodium hydroxide solution

(4) freeze peeling using liquid oxygen

     (5) acid peeling

- dehydration – traditional products made by sun-drying
- many products produced using tunnel driers
- best products freeze-dried (AFD)
- juice extraction
- low viscosity juices, *eg* apple, are clear and need the action of pectolytic enzymes
- high viscosity juices require pectin to maintain consistency, therefore, pectolytic enzymes should be inactivated, *eg* hot-break method for tomato juice
- pickles – rely on salt and acid for preservation
- acid may be added, *eg* vinegar, or produced by fermentation, *eg* lactic acid preserves
- use under-ripe fruit or add pectin
- conserves rich in fruit with added nuts
- candied fruit, slices of fruit dehydrated by strong solutions

The botanical term fruit refers to the organ that carries the seed. However, some fruits are used as vegetables, for example, tomatoes. Vegetables are from all other edible parts of a plant, such as the leaves, stem, roots and any storage organs. It is simpler to divide the two as follows: fruit have fragrant flavours and are usually sweet (or have sugar added); vegetables are plant products eaten with animal products and are not sweet but usually salted.

Many special varieties of fruit and vegetables have been developed by plant breeders for individual food processes. Carrots, for example, for canning, must be small, of even colour throughout and straight-sided. Darker peas have been developed for freezing, but paler types are better for canning. The crop must ripen at one and the same time to permit one destructive harvest, whereas it is beneficial for garden crops to ripen a little at a time so that they can be used in a fresh condition.

THE COMPOSITION OF FRUITS AND VEGETABLES

Being principally water, most fruit and vegetables provide to the average diet only minerals and some vitamins, and perhaps some roughage. However, these additions, particularly of vitamins such as ascorbic acid, can be of immense value in some diets. Some products, however, are good sources of carbohydrate, *eg* banana. In some parts of the world some crops form a significant part of the diet and in world tonnage potato, cassava and banana are the most consumed. Some 300,000,000 people are thought to live mainly on cassava in the equatorial belt of the world.

Plant tissues assume a characteristic maximum water content and at this level the tissue is said to be *turgid* or in a complete state of *turgor*.

A typical plant cell is somewhat like a balloon; however, it is not blown up with air but with water. The internal pressure in the cell, called *turgor pressure* can be as high as nine times atmospheric pressure. In a normal cell in full turgor this pressure is equalized by the elasticity of the cell wall, Figure 2.10.

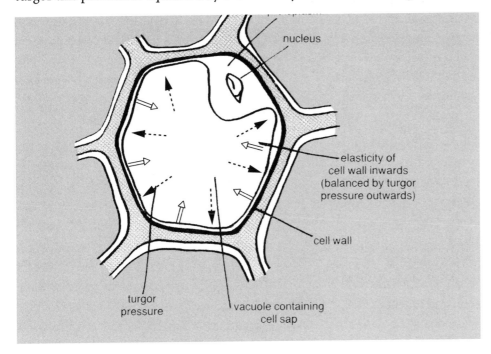

nucleus

elasticity of
cell wall inwards
(balanced by turgor
pressure outwards)

cell wall

turgor
pressure

vacuole containing
cell sap

Figure 2.10
Typical plant cell in full turgor

Once the supply of water is reduced or cut off to the cell, water is gradually lost from the plant by *transpiration* and the turgor pressure cannot be maintained. The elasticity of the cell wall now exceeds the outward turgor pressure and the cell starts to collapse. This is repeated throughout the plant which 'wilts' like a newly planted cabbage seedling on a hot day. Harvested leafy vegetables, such as lettuce remain turgid for only short periods before becoming limp. As plant cells become older a complex substance *lignin* is deposited on the cell wall, thus making it tougher. However, lignified tissues are old and poor to eat, whereas most vegetables should be eaten when small and tender.

Water enters the plant cell by the process of *osmosis* as the cell contains a concentrated solution of sugars and acids in the form of *cell sap*. The cell membranes maintain the cell in a fully turgid state but this also depends on the presence of supporting tissues and the cohesiveness of the cells. About one third of the measured texture (firmness) of a small, fresh carrot is due to turgor pressure.

The *colour* of fruit and vegetables is an important attractive feature, and most pigments occur in *plastids* which are specialized bodies lying in the *protoplasm* of the cell. Chlorophylls occur in the chloroplasts which are bodies containing the green pigment. The carotenoids are also present in these chloroplasts but until the fruit ripens and masked by the chlorophylls. Many of the bright reds, violets and blue colours and due to the anthocyanin group of colours (see pigments section).

Simple sugars are present in most fruit and vegetables, particularly sucrose, fructose and glucose. The latter two reducing sugars usually predominate, but in some fruits sucrose is most dominant, for example, in onion, carrot, pea, banana and melon.

The *cell wall* of fruit and vegetable cells is built up from a number of carbohydrates, cellulose being the main one, supported by pectins and hemicelluloses. Cells are held together by pectins and hemicelluloses which occur in the *middle lamella*. Changes in these occur in ripening so the cells part easily, leading to a softer texture. Starch is the second most common carbohydrate after cellulose and is the main food material in most vegetables, particularly in storage organs such as tubers, for example, potatoes and Jerusalem artichokes.

There is very little *lipid* in fruit and vegetables, but some occurs as 'cutin' which controls water loss from fruits such as apples. The *protein* content of fruit and vegetables varies enormously, and unfortunately some staple foods such as cassava are very low in protein and lack many of the essential amino acids. Legumes, *ie* peas and beans, are richer in proteins than most plant products, containing often about 8% protein. Much of the protein, however, is in the form of enzymes, which control the composition and ripening after harvesting in many fruits and vegetables.

Fruit and vegetables are normally acidic in nature, having a pH between 2 and 4. Malic and citric acids are the most common acids, sometimes one predominates, sometimes the other. Avocados are deficient in both and grapes when ripe have tartaric acid. Citrus fruits such as blackcurrants, raspberries, pears, potato, legumes and tomato have citric acid as their main acid. Malic acid dominates in apples, apricots, cherries, plums, bananas, lettuce, onion and carrot. Many other acids have been reported in smaller quantities, and many have important roles in metabolism (refer to Kreb's cycle). The most important acid, which is also a vitamin, is of course ascorbic acid. The outside layers of most fruits contain more than the inside, similarly fruits grown in the sun are richer than those in the shade. The West Indian cherry (Acerola) contains 1500mg/100g of ascorbic acid which compares with most oranges at 40-60mg/100g. As a rough guide, highly coloured fruit are richer in vitamin C than less coloured fruit.

The flavour compounds in fruits are largely oxygenated compounds such as esters, alcohols, acids, aldehydes and ketones, many being derivatives of the monoterpenes. Vegetables have a limited range of volatile odoriferous compounds, esters are generally lacking, but individual acids, alcohols, aldehydes and ketones may be found. Many sulphur-containing compounds may occur in the cabbage family and onions.

Some fruits and vegetables unfortunately contain small amount of complex substances which are *poison precursors*. Cassava contains the substances *linamarin* which is a glucose derivative containing a cyanide group. In certain traditional methods of preparing cassava an enzyme breaks down this substances to release free hydrocyanic acid. Gradual cyanide poisoning can occur as a result of this and in its mildest form can cause *goitre* and cretinism in people already on poor diets. Potatoes contain the glycoside solanine which can cause mild stomach upsets but in green potatoes levels of solanine can reach more dangerous levels.

POST-HARVEST CHANGES IN FRUIT AND VEGETABLES

When detached from the tree, or dug from the ground, a fruit or vegetable can continue to live and respire for a period of time, which, for some products, may be a number of months. This period of existence obviously uses up storage material within the product and gradually its quality falls until finally it undergoes senescence and decay. The length of storage of a plant product depends on: its chemical composition; resistance to microbial attack; external temperature; presence of various gasses in the storage atmosphere.

Respiration is the major process of interest in post-harvest fruit and vegetables. The rate of respiration, which involves the oxidation of energy-rich organic compounds to form simpler compounds and yield energy, is indicative of the rapidity with which compositional changes in fruit and vegetables are taking place.

Fruit and vegetables can be divided into two groups according to their respiratory behaviour. *Climacteric* fruit are generally 'fleshy' fruits that show a rapid rise in the rate of respiration after harvesting which leads to ripening and then senescence of the fruit. *Non-climacteric* fruits and most vegetables (except tomato) show no rapid increase in the respiration and changes in ripening and maturation are gradual. The characteristic climacteric pattern is shown in Figure 2.11, but, with the exception of the avocado, few fruits follow exactly this pattern.

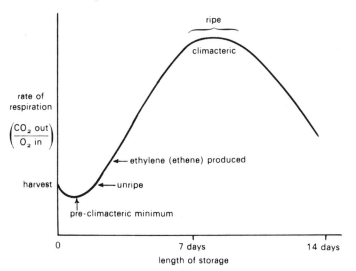

Figure 2.11
The climacteric in fruits

Climacteric fruits include banana, mango, pear and avocado. The fruit normally attains the stage ripeness best for eating at the climacteric or some time after the peak. Ripeness is a somewhat variable term, as ripeness for eating is overripe, for example, for jam-making where more pectin is required, but under ripe for juice extraction where a soft, juicy fruit is required.

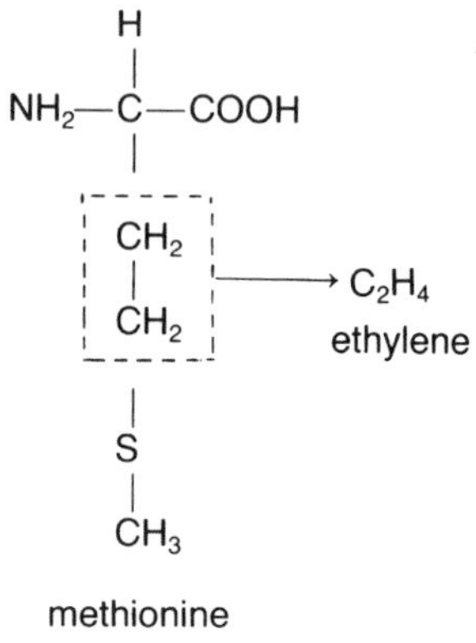

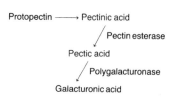

Figure 2.12

Production of ethylene (ethene)

Protopectin ──→ Pectinic acid
                    ╱ Pectin esterase
            Pectic acid
                    ╱ Polygalacturonase
        Galacturonic acid

Figure 2.13

Pectin breakdown during ripening

Figure 2.14

Respiration and starch synthesis competition in vegetables

Non-climacteric fruit include the citrus group, pineapple, fig and grape and also most vegetables do not show a climacteric. However, some fruits show a shallow peak. Fruits, which do not show the climacteric keep well for long periods under normal conditions, whereas climacteric fruit quickly ripen and deteriorate, presenting many problems in storage.

It has been known for some years that the gas ethylene (ethene) acts as a plant hormone and stimulates the ripening process. Ethylene is produced in the fruit at the beginning of the climacteric peak, thought to be from the amino acid methionine, as shown in Figure 2.12. Ethylene can be applied externally to cause ripening. Unripe fruit ripens rapidly when stored with already ripe fruit.

As ripening proceeds enzyme systems become active, resulting in a number of changes. The most important changes are in the carbohydrates contained in the fruit. Sugars increase at the expense of polysaccharides such as starch, and cell wall polysaccharides are broken down which leads to a softer texture in the fruit. The pectic substances are progressively broken down as ripening proceeds, as shown in Figure 2.13, which eventually leads to a very soft product.

Acid levels fall during ripening in some fruit, but are masked by the increase in sweetness due to sugars being produced. The most obvious changes in fruits during ripening are in their pigments, as chlorophyll is broken down to reveal other colours such as the yellow/reds of the carotenoids. Some pigments are synthesised during ripening, for example the anthocyanins and lycopene.

Changes are gradual in most vegetables and non-climacteric fruit. Changes occurring depend on which part of the plant the vegetable constitutes, as shoots, for example, continue to grow and lengthen. In vegetables with pods, such as beans and peas, protein is broken down in the pods and the resulting amino acids are translocated to the seeds and resynthesised into protein. Starch is synthesised from sugars during the post-harvest period of vegetables, which is the converse of what occurs in fruits. However, there appears to be a competition between the synthesis of starch, and the use of sugar for respiration and temperature appears to control this.

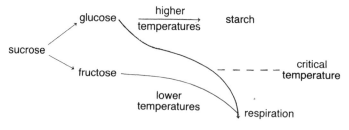

The *critical temperature* is a characteristic of each vegetable and, in potato, it varies from about 1.5–4.5C. In tropical products the critical temperature is much higher, usually around 13–16C. Above the critical temperature starch is synthesised, but below the temperature starch is broken down, sugars accumulate and respiration increases. This is clearly shown in winter, when potatoes are stored at too low a temperature. They contain too much sugar, *ie* reducing sugars glucose and fructose, and produce very dark chips and crisps on frying.

STORAGE OF FRUIT AND VEGETABLES

Until they are consumed or processed, fruit and vegetables are living, respiring biological systems. Respiration, and consequently ripening may be inhibited by: controlling temperature during storage; lowering the available oxygen in the store; increasing carbon dioxide levels; lowering atmospheric pressure; or using special coatings.

TEMPERATURE

Respiration slows down as the temperature of the environment decreases and thus ripening and senescence are delayed. However, chilling some fruit, particularly those of tropical origin, may cause considerable damage below a certain temperature. Below about 13C some enzyme systems are inhibited in tropical fruit while others continue, causing the accumulation of toxic intermediate products. This can cause discolouration, flavour and texture change in the fruit leading to rots and bacterial decay. Try storing a banana in a refrigerator!

CONTROLLED ATMOSPHERE STORAGE

Controlling the atmosphere in a store can slow respiration and delay ripening. The oxygen level can be lowered or the carbon dioxide level can be increased. This is called *controlled atmosphere*, CA, or *modified atmosphere*, MA, storage. The term MA is now being used for modified atmosphere within packaging films. It may be used in conjunction with temperature control. However, physiological disorders can readily occur if the gas levels are incorrect, as too high a CO_2 or too low an oxygen level can cause *anaerobic respiration* leading to the accumulation of damaging toxic compounds in the fruit. A simple way to make a CA store is just to allow the fruit to respire for a time to lower the oxygen and increase the CO_2 levels. This is generally unsatisfactory as respiration has started and will try to continue at a higher rate leading to spoilage. Correctly blended gases from cylinders are usually fed into a chamber from which most of the air has been removed.

Together with temperature control this is a very good system for storing many fruits and vegetables. Excess CO_2 is often removed by 'scrubbing' with sodium hydroxide, which absorbs the gas.

HYPOBARIC (LOW PRESSURE) STORAGE

This is a type of CA storage in which the atmospheric pressure in the store is reduced, so lowering the oxygen level and causing ethylene to diffuse out of the fruit, thus delaying ripening. Although the method has produced some good results, it is very expensive and difficult to perfect.

SPECIAL COATINGS

For a number of years some fruits have been waxed to prevent dehydration and to retard ripening. One of the most significant developments in food technology in recent years has been the development of an edible coating which can retard the ripening of most fruits.

A mixture of lipids (sucrose esters of some fatty acids) mixed with a polysaccharide is **marketed under the trade mark 'Pro-long'**. The powdered mixture is dispersed and dissolved in water; and the fruit and vegetables are dipped into it and allowed to dry. The result is the formation of a semi-permeable gas barrier which allows oxygen to diffuse into the fruit but retains some of the carbon dioxide produced during respiration. This mixture of internal gases reduces the metabolic rate of the product. It has a number of other advantages, such as reducing water loss and controlling some spoilage diseases. The treated produce can be stored at higher temperatures and therefore the method offers considerable savings on any other system at present in use. Ideally, crops should be treated as soon as possible after harvesting.

The potential of extending the storage life of many crops by up to three times by this method offers many new possibilities for the marketing of unusual tropical fruits. Developing countries can make use of a simple technique like this in order to develop an export trade of fruit and vegetables, which are cheap to produce and often under-exploited.

FRUIT AND VEGETABLE PROCESSING

Fruit and vegetables need to be peeled before they undergo further processing and preservation by canning, drying, freezing or in preserves. In the kitchen it is simple to peel by hand, but obviously this would be labour-intensive and expensive in a large factory. Boiling water and steam can be used to 'scald' produce in about $\frac{1}{2}$–3 minutes, in order to loosen the peel which can then be removed by rotating brushes and cold water sprays.

'Lye peeling' involves the use of a solution of caustic soda (sodium hydroxide) which dissolves the walls of the cells making up the peel, causing the peel to disintegrate. This common method will remove the peel and areas of bruised tissue in an economical manner. The lye can be neutralised with a solution of citric acid after peeling.

It is possible to freeze-peel by spraying liquid nitrogen on to the fruit, which on thawing can be easily brushed to remove the damaged peel. Acid solutions, particularly hydrochloric (0.1%) and tartaric (0.1%) have also been used for peeling a number of products and have the advantage of inhibiting any enzymic browning which might occur.

Dehydration

Many dried fruits are produced by the traditional sun-drying process in hotter countries. Obviously there is little or no control over this method and quality of the product is variable. Tunnel driers have been used extensively for drying fruit and vegetables, which are usually in a cube form, *ie* diced. The highest quality dried products are produced by freeze-drying and particularly by accelerated freeze-drying, AFD. However, the relatively high cost of the process necessitates a higher price for the product, which is not usually justified for cheaper fruits and vegetables.

Juice extraction

Juices can be squeezed from many different fruit and vegetables by a number of methods. It is often beneficial to macerate the product before extraction or to treat it with enzymes, particularly pectolytic enzymes, to increase the yield of the extracted juice. There are two main groups of juices, low viscosity and high viscosity juices.

Low viscosity juices, such as apple juice, are clear without any suspended matter. The apples are macerated to form a pulp which is pressed in a rack-and-cloth press to release the juice. Pectolytic enzymes and sometimes amylases are added to clear the juice, and any suspended particles are removed by filtration. The juice is then pasteurized before bottling or canning. Centrifuges are sometimes used in addition to the press to increase the yield.

Tomato juice is a typical *high viscosity juice* and the higher the viscosity the better the quality. The consistency of the juice is controlled by the method of manufacture and is not solely related to the solids content of the juice. In the *cold-break* method raw tomatoes are macerated at room temperature, then the seeds and skin are filtered from the juice. This process yields a juice of lower viscosity as the pectins are degraded by pectolytic enzymes; however the juice has excellent flavour and colour. In the *hot-break* method, most favoured by industry, tomatoes are macerated and heated to 85C to inactivate the pectolytic enzymes. The viscosity of juice is higher but the flavour and colour are not as in the cold-break method. Often hydrochloric acid is added during maceration, as this improves consistency, and is then neutralised after juice extraction with sodium hydroxide solution, which, with the acid, forms sodium chloride giving a degree of saltiness to the product.

Pickling

Pickles are usually made from cucumbers, onions, cauliflower and cabbage, but virtually any product can be used, and the practice of pickling dates back many thousands of years. The product in a pickle is preserved and flavoured by a solution of salt and edible acid, usually vinegar. The acid is either added or produced by fermentation, as nearly all vegetables can be fermented by lactic acid bacteria to yield a sufficient level of lactic acid. Preservation of vegetables by fermentation depends on: the reduction of the activity of the natural enzymes of the product; inhibition of oxidative chemical changes; and inhibition of the growth of spoilage organisms. Pickles can be prepared directly from vegetables without fermentation, by adding salt and vinegar.

Some products are allowed to ferment in a weak brine solution, for example, the expensive 'dill' pickles. Other products are fermented in a high-salt brine and then later converted into mixed pickle, *eg* 'salt-stock' pickles.

A traditional method is to fill a wooden vat about one-third full of a10% brine into which the cucumbers or other vegetables are filled. Dry salt is added to try to keep the salt solution at 10%. Brine is again added to cover the cucumbers completely so that fermentation can occur in the absence of air. As the bacteria multiply the brine becomes cloudy. Lactic acid is produced and, together with the salt, preserves the product.

Preserves

Many fruits are made into preserves which include jellies, jams, marmalades, conserves and candied fruit. (Table jelly is made from gelatine not pectin.) As gel formation is an essential part of a preserve, underripe fruit, rich in pectin, is the ideal material to use but lacking this, pectin may be added. Fruit pulp is often frozen or canned and stored to be made into jam out of season. Often sulphur dioxide is added to prevent microbial growth and discolouration, but is boiled off during jam manufacture.

In the traditional *jam-making* process, sugar is added to an equal weight of fruit, but, in reality, the amount of sugar used depends on the acidity of the fruit, the sugar content of the fruit, ripeness of the fruit and the type of product being made. The mixture is boiled, generally under reduced pressure, to reach the required total soluble solids content of about 68%.

Marmalades contain fruit pulp and peel, and being made from under-ripe fruit are particularly rich in pectin and acid. Citrus fruits are commonly used but pineapple, ginger, pear and grape marmalades are gaining popularity.

Conserves are generally similar to jams, but as they contain much more fruit they are expensive. Often chopped nuts, such as walnuts, are added to give texture and flavour to the product.

Crystallized or candied fruit is a traditional product, particularly in the Middle East. Strong sugar solutions are added to prepared slices of fruit which become dehydrated by the osmotic effect of the solution and are thus well preserved. Glace cherries, citrus peels and mixed cake decorations are produced in this manner. In the manufacture of glace cherries the cherries, de-stoned, are heated to 60C for up to 20 minutes and a small amount of calcium chloride is added to firm the tissues. The cherries are then added to boiling syrup and may stand in the syrup for some time. The prepared cherries are very sensitive to high humidity and must be stored at below 50% Relative Humidity and 10C.

PRACTICAL EXERCISES: FRUIT AND VEGETABLES

1. Microscope examination
Prepare the sections of a number of products, using a scalpel. Examine cellular structure. Stain some samples with a drop of iodine and examine for starch.

2. Storage of fruit
Take samples of two different fruits, *eg* apples and bananas. Store for several weeks: at room temperature; in a refrigerator; near a boiler; in an air-tight tin. Observe the overall quality of the product every week and note changes taking place. Cut open some of the fruit and note internal changes.

3. Peeling of vegetables
Compare the efficiency of peeling methods by weighing a sample of vegetables (potato, carrot or small turnips) before and after peeling.

Methods
  (a) Hand peeling
  (b) Lye peeling – immerse vegetables in a boiling solution of 5% sodium hydroxide solution (CARE!) for a timed period. Remove and drain, wash off skin under a running tap and weigh product.
  (c) Steam peeling – place vegetables in a pressure cooker and steam for 2, 4, 6 and 8 minutes. Wash off peel under the tap and weigh vegetables.
  (d) Abrasive peeling – if available use a peeling attachment for a domestic mixer or processor.

Peeling must be efficiently carried out, but with the minimum weighed loss. Which method meets these criteria?

Chapter 4

Cereals and Baked Products

PREVIEW

- **Cereals**
  - belong to grass family – *Gramineae*
  - most have similar chemical compositions
  - composition varies with variety, weather, growing conditions
  - moisture level 10-14%, protein content 7-13%
  - all cereal grains have: an embryo, endosperm and bran
  - vitamins, particularly B complex, found in bran

- **Wheat milling**
  - 'Strong' wheats have higher protein content – good for bread
  - 'Weak' wheats have lower protein content – good for cakes and biscuits
  - milling divided into:
    (1) cleaning and conditioning
    (2) size reduction and separation
  - moisture content important in milling – condition to 15-17½ % moisture
  - low extraction rates – up to 75% – mean white flour
  - high extraction rates – up to 95% for wholemeal flours
  - flour must be aged to improve bread-making properties
  - *Improvers,* usually oxidizing agents, added to accelerate ageing

- **Bread-making**
  - bread made from flour, water, salt, yeast and some fat
  - straight dough method – relies on wheat to produce CO_2 which stretches dough to produce honeycombed bread texture
  - Chorleywood process uses rapid mechanical development of dough plus rapid
  - oxidation of sulphydryl groups (-SH) and form disulphide bridges (-S-S-)
  - Chemical and physical changes
    (1) during mixing protein and starch become hydrated
    (2) gluten formed from gliadin and glutenin
    (3) fermentation converts sugars to alcohol, then a- and b-amylases attack starch to release maltose which is fermented
    (4) gluten retains CO_2 produced, but shows elasticity and extensibility -SH groups converted to –S-S- bridges
    (5) during baking starch gelatinized and protein coagulated
    (6) crust formed – colour due to Maillard reaction

- **Cakes, biscuit and pastry**
  - do not require gluten network
  - use 'weak' flours of lower protein content
  - 'high ratio flours' – small starch particles and low in protein
  - baking powders used as raising agents:
  - sodium hydrogen carbonate, a slow acting acid and starch
  - air must be whipped into batter

- 'Superglycerinated' fat contain more emulsifying agents – allow more water in a cake batter and therefore more sugar – result in a sweeter, longer lasting cake
- in biscuits more fat used to disrupt gluten and produce crumbly texture
- in pastry gluten restricted and layered to produce flakes

- **Other cereals**

Barley	– used to produce malt for beer
	– must be allowed to germinate to activate amylases to break down s starch
Rye	– some gluten – produces poor loaves
	– dough often soured by starter cultures
Maize	– (corn) little free nicotinic acid
	– released by cooking with alkaline water
	– cornflour main product
Rice	– par boil to cause vitamins to migrate to endosperm from bran
Oat	– higher on fats than others and contain more phytic acid
Breakfast cereals	– whole or part grains
	– starch pre-gelatinized then puffed, shredded or flaked
Pasta products	– made from Durum wheat
	– tough endosperms producing semolina

Cereal grains are one of the most important sources of carbohydrate and hence energy in the diet. Cereals belong to the grass family, *Gramineae*, and there are many thousands of varieties which have been cultivated since the beginning of civilization. The grains may be consumed whole or processed by many methods into flour, starch, bran, sugar, syrups and some oil. Rice alone feeds over half the world's population, particularly in the East where 93% of all rice is produced. The area of the world devoted to wheat production is double that of rice, but rice yields over double the grain produced from wheat.

COMPOSITION OF CEREALS

Most of the cereals have similar chemical compositions as they belong to the same family of plants. However, composition depends upon variety, weather and growing conditions. The moisture content of cereals is always higher after harvesting, but if properly handled the grain will attain a lower figure of about 10 – 14%, at which level germination of the grain is inhibited and moulds and bacterial rots do not usually occur.

The composition of cereals, in general terms, is given in Table 2.7

Table 2.7

General composition of cereals

Constituent	%	Example showing highest figure
Carbohydrate	58–72	Maize
Protein	7–13	Wheat
Moisture	1–14	Barley
Fat	1–7	Oats
Fibre	2–10	Oats
Vitamins:		
Thiamin	3–90 µg/g	Oats
Riboflavin	1.1–1.6 µg/g	Rye
Niacin	15–100 µg/g	Barley
Pantothenic acid	4.41–17 uµg/g	Rice

STRUCTURE OF A CEREAL GRAIN

All cereal grains share three main features. The first feature is an embryo or germ (hence wheatgerm) from which the root and shoot sprout. Secondly, the endosperm is a store of starch which is broken down to glucose to supply energy for the growing embryo. The third feature is known collectively as the bran, which is just several layers which cover and protect the grain. The wheat grain shows these features well and in Figure 2.15 the various parts of the grain are labeled.

Figure 2.15

Structure of a wheat grain

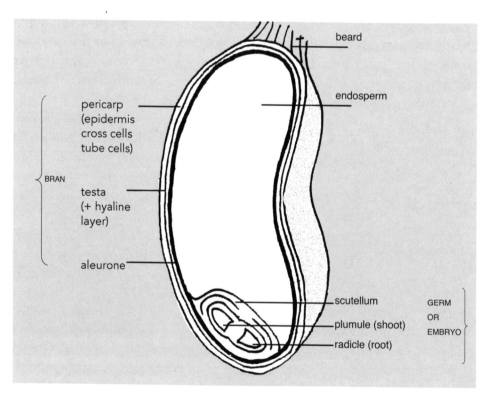

The distribution of nutrients is obviously uneven throughout the grain as the starch is concentrated in the endosperm and many of the B complex vitamins are in the outer bran layers, which is clearly illustrated by thiamin distribution. About 60% of thiamin is in the bran, 24% in the endosperm and 16% in the germ.

The germs of many cereal grains contain vitamin E (tocopherols) but this can readily be lost by oxidation.

WHEAT MILLING

Although rye has some bread-making qualities, most bread is made from wheat. The wheat grain has to be milled and separated into a number of suitable fractions to make flour which can be used for baking.

When we buy flour from the supermarket we expect it to be of a consistent quality and able to produce bread, or cakes or biscuits as required. To produce flours of the required different characteristics a number of different wheat strains are blended in the mixture fed into the mill (the grist).

'Strong' wheats have a higher protein content and produce bread of good loaf volume and good texture. 'Weak' wheats are lower in protein and are more suitable for cakes and biscuits. American wheats are particularly strong wheats, whereas European wheats are weak. However, there are new European wheats, for example, the English variety 'Avalon' which are stronger than former varieties and are good for bread-making. It is possible to extract protein from strong wheats and add to weak wheats to improve their bread-making performance.

The terms 'hardness' and 'softness' of wheats are sometimes encountered and these refer to milling characteristics of the grains. Hardness refers to the ease with which the endosperm disintegrates during milling. In hard wheats the endosperm separates more easily and intact from the bran, whereas in the soft wheats, the endosperm breaks down easily and does not separate.

The milling process can be divided into preliminary cleaning and conditioning, and secondly, size reduction of the grain and separation from the bran.

Preliminary cleaning and conditioning

A number of different specialized machines are used to remove all contaminants such as stones, string, metal, straw and other seeds. Sieving and blowing air through the grain will remove some contaminants. A disc separator uses discs with indents into which the wheat grains fall while other grains, such as oats and barley, pass through the machine. The disc rotates and then discharges the caught wheat grains, which then pass to magnets to remove metal particles. The grains are washed in a moving stream of water, and then surplus water is removed in a type of centrifuge, the 'whizzer'. It is important after this stage to 'condition' the grain to the required moisture content.

The moisture content of a grain influences its milling ability. As moisture levels increase in the grain, the bran toughens but the endosperm becomes more easily broken down. The ideal occurs at 15.0%-17.5% moisture content and is attained by conditioning at 25C for 48 hours or for shorter periods at higher temperatures. At higher moisture levels the bran will stick to the endosperm and not separate easily. Harder wheats are conditioned to higher moisture levels than soft wheats.

The *milling process* itself involves a series of disintegrations followed by sievings or 'siftings'. The first operation in the process is the use of the *break rolls,* usually five sets, which break open the grain. The break rolls have grooves and one roller rotates $2\frac{1}{2}$ times as fast as the other. As grains pass between the rollers, through the 'nip', one roller holds the grain back effectively as the other roller hits and breaks the grain open; see Figure 2.16.

Large particles are produced at this stage but with a little flour. The particles pass to sifters which separate the large particles; these pass to the second break rolls, which operate closer together and have more grooves. Up to five sets of break rolls may be used in this way; see Figure 2.17.

Figure 2.16
Break rolls

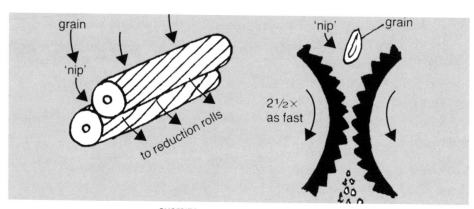

Figure 2.17
Wheat milling (simplified)

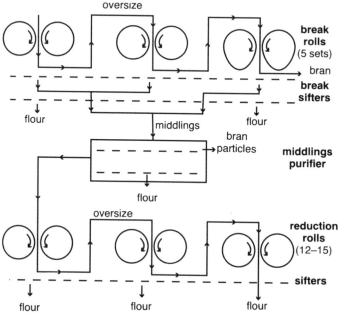

Small particles of endosperm, known as 'middlings' are separated in 'purifiers' and converted into flour by a number of smooth, *reduction rolls.* The reduction rolls are very close together, producing a fine flour with some starch damaged in the process. This latter fact is important in bread making.

The milling operation can be controlled to give flours of varying *extraction rate*. This term is a little confusing as a low extraction rate means a whiter flour and higher rate means the inclusion of more bran and, hence, a browner flour.

'Wholemeal' flour has had only coarse bran removed and has an extraction rate of 95%. Although the endosperm makes up to 82% of a wheat grain, it is only possible to have a maximum extraction rate of 75% of white flour as bits of bran can contaminate it at higher figures.

White flour always commanded a better price and was in greater demand by the public. However, there is something of a revolution taking place, as a result of the need to eat more roughage, and white flour is declining and wholemeal and other higher extraction flours are becoming more popular. White flours contain little lipid and therefore keep well, whereas wholemeal flours have a shorter shelf-life and have the added problem of containing some *phytic acid* which binds calcium.

Ageing of wheat flours

Flour used immediately after milling does not produce the best loaves. Ideally, flour should be stored for one or two months to allow improvement to take place, particularly in the wheat proteins. Oxidation of pigments (carotenoids) occurs so that the flour becomes whiter. However, the most significant changes occur in the disulphide bonds (-S-S-) which increase, joining the protein chains of flour.

These groups are important in giving the properties to dough of elasticity and extensibility.

Chemicals can be added to flour to improve its baking quality. These *improvers* used at very low levels of only 10-20ppm are generally oxidizing agents. Examples of improvers include potassium bromate, chlorine dioxide, azodicarbonamide and ascorbic acid (converted in dough to dehydroascorbic acid which is an oxidising agent).

BREAD-MAKING

Bread is made from flour, water, salt and yeast. Usually a small amount of fat is also added. From these ingredients a dough has to be made which can be fermented by yeasts. The desired dough condition is obtained by mechanical activity, particularly by stretching and folding.

Straight dough system

The ingredients for a 'one-sack' dough would include flour (127kg), yeast (1.6kg), salt (2.27kg) and water (68-70 litres). The ingredients are mixed with water at 27C and the dough is put into a warm place to ferment. After two hours the dough is 'knocked back' by kneading it to even out the temperature and ensure thorough mixing. Any gas (CO_2) is pushed out at this stage. The dough is allowed to rise for a further one hour when it is divided into portions which are roughly shaped. The dough is rested for about 15 minutes, which is known as the 'first proof', and is then moulded into the final shape and placed into tins. The dough is then rested for a further 45 minutes, the 'final proof', during which time it rises in the tin. The tins are placed in an oven, where the dough still rises slightly until the yeast is killed, usually at a temperature of 232-260C for 40-50 minutes. Steam is often injected to produce an attractive glaze on the bread nearer to the end of the baking process, and steam also reduces weight losses by evaporation.

Chemical and physical changes occurring in bread-making

When the ingredients are *mixed* they become hydrated with the water and a great deal of the water is absorbed into the mix. The flour proteins become hydrated forming the *gluten* (see the next section for further details). After mixing, fermentation begins and involves the conversion of sugars into carbon dioxide and alcohol by the yeast. Naturally occurring sugars, *eg* sucrose, glucose and maltose are fermented initially, but the amylases start to break down the starch of the flour to form maltose. The amylases, however, attack the damaged starch, as they find it more difficult to attack the starch tightly packed in intact granules. It is, therefore, important to have the right amount of damaged starch resulting from the milling process. Too much damaged starch can allow the production of too many dextrins by α-amylase which lead to a sticky dough, producing denser loaves of poor volume.

The carbon dioxide causes the dough to rise and the gluten retains the gas but also has elasticity and allows the dough's expansion. The production of carbon dioxide and the growth of some lactic acid bacteria results in the dough becoming more acidic. The 'proving' periods are rest periods in the fermentation process and allow the dough to recover from the effects of cutting and moulding. Unless properly controlled, proving can cause poor texture because of unequal gas production in different pats of the dough. The ideal conditions for proving are 32C and 85% relative humidity.

During the first stages of baking, enzyme and yeast activity increases and gas volume increases because of the temperature rise. These three factors cause the dough to rise rapidly and sometimes to overflow the sides of the tin occasionally to collapse when there is uneven mixing, resulting in large localized gas bubbles. The yeast activity declines at about 45C and is killed at 55C. However, the amylases are a little more heat-resistant and continue to break down starch up to 70C. Physical changes begin to occur rapidly in the dough as the temperature increases, particularly at 65C. The starch begins to gelatinise and the proteins coagulate at 75C.

Obviously the outside of the loaf reaches a much higher temperature in the oven than the inside, which rarely exceeds 100C. This results in the brown crust which is due to the Maillard reaction and the textural changes due to the production of dextrins from starch. The attractive flavour of the crust is a result of these reactions and from the fact that alcohol is driven from the dough and some is trapped and converted into ester in the crust. The alcohol causes a beer-like smell to emanate from the oven.

The role of wheat proteins in baking

The proteins in wheat are gliadin (40-50%), glutenin (40-50%) and smaller amounts of albumin, globulin and proteose. The wheat *gluten* is a blend of the two protein fractions, gliadin and glutenin. Gluten can be prepared by taking a bread flour and adding 60% of water and allowing it to stand for 30 minutes. Under running water the starch can then be washed away to leave the elastic, somewhat sticky, but tough, gluten.

Gluten can be considered as a system of proteins containing a number of bonding methods. The most significant bonding in operation is the disulphide bridge (-S-S-) between the cysteine amino acid units. As the dough expands there is an interchange between the disulphide bridges (-S-S-) and sulphydryl groups (-SH), and this process releases the pressure as the dough expands. However, as the disulphide bridges reform quickly the dough retains its elasticity, whilst at the same time having this extensibility. Extensibility of the dough may also be due to lipoproteins, which form 'slip-planes' in the dough. On baking in the oven the proteins coagulate and with the gelatinized starch form the honeycombed structure typical of the leavened loaf.

Rapid dough processes

A number of processes have been developed to speed up the dough-making process but still to produce bread of the normal texture and quality. Basically, the main fermentation processes, which take several hours, are replaced by rapid methods involving oxidation of sulphydryl groups (-SH) and considerable mechanical development of the dough.

The Chorleywood process is used extensively as it produces consistently good loaves of increased yield, and large amounts of weaker flours can be used. The dough is thoroughly mixed and stretched over a period of five minutes, during which time rapid oxidation of the sulphydryl groups occurs. Extra fat, water and yeast are needed. The oxidation of the sulphydryl groups is achieved by using 75ppm of ascorbic acid. This may be confusing as ascorbic acid is a reducing agent, *ie* it has the ability to add hydrogen or remove oxygen. However, in the dough the ascorbic acid is converted by enzyme action to dehydroascorbic acid. Dehydroascorbic acid is an oxidising agent and removes the hydrogen from the sulphydryl groups –SH, thus forming the disulphide bridges –S-S- very rapidly.

In this way the dough structure is quickly formed and tightens. The violent mixing carried out in the process corresponds to the gradual stretching achieved during the normal fermentation process. Sometimes the amino acid L-cysteine is added, which tends to make gluten uncoil a little and expose the sulphydryl groups which can be oxidised.

Figure 2.18

Action of ascorbic acid in the Chorleywood process

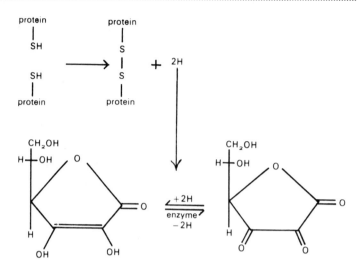

CAKES, BISCUITS AND PASTRY

Unlike in bread, the gluten network is undesirable in most other baked products. The property of extensibility is often required, however, but without the elasticity. If the shape of a biscuit is cut out then it would be unacceptable for this to contract due to the properties of gluten. In general, flours produced from soft wheats (*ie* low in protein) yield better cakes than those from hard wheats. Special cake flours called 'high-ratio flours' are available to industry. These specially milled and sieved flours contain more starch and less protein, thus producing the best cakes. The particles in the flour must be carefully controlled and must be as small as is possible.

In addition to flour, *simple cakes* also require as ingredients sugar, fat, eggs and often baking powder. It is not proposed to discuss the various cakes and how they are made but to review some general principles.

A satisfactory cake can only be produced from a batter in which there has been adequate gas produced and retained. Air can be beaten into the mix and retained with the help of egg and by creaming with suitable fat. Baking powder is often used to produce carbon dioxide in the moist batter and during the earlier stages of baking. Baking powder is formed from sodium hydrogen carbonate (biocarbonate), a slow acting acid and starch. The starch helps keep the other two ingredients dry and the mixture free-flowing. Baking powders often use calcium phosphate $(Ca(H_2PO_4)_2)$ or disodium pyrophosphate $(Na_2H_2P_2O_7)$ as the acid ingredient. Traditional baking powder contained cream of tartar (potassium hydrogen tartrate) and sometimes tartaric acid. These acid constituents react at room temperature to produce carbon dioxide, but some of the gas may escape before baking. Sodium aluminum sulphate has been used as the acid as it reacts only at oven temperatures, but can produce an unpleasant off-flavour. The acidic derivative of glucose, glucono-delta-lactone, is often used in a similar manner.

Air must be whipped into the mix for most cakes, as it influences the final cake volume. The batter must stretch round and retain the air as it is mixed into the mix. The proteins from the flour and eggs do this, but too much protein produces a rubbery cake. This rubbery texture is minimised by the incorporation of fat and sugar into the mix.

Fats interfere with the development of the gluten network and allow the protein particles to slide on each other, which leads to a more tender product. Emulsifying agents, such as mono- and diglycerides and lecithin, are added to the fats; sometimes large amounts are added to form 'super-glycinerated fats'. These w enable more water to be mixed into the batter, which in turn allows more sugar to be added. As a result of these additions a sweeter, more moist cake is produced, which, because of the higher water content, stales more slowly.

Sugar not only provides sweetness to the cake but is also responsible, along with fats, for tenderness. Sugar has the tendency to slow down the development of the gluten. Cakes containing a lot of sugar require more mixing than those with less sugar, otherwise a lower cake volume is obtained after baking.

The amount of moisture in a cake is an important determinant of quality. During the mixing process water dissolves the sugar and hydrates the starch and protein. The protein and starch hold water through hydrogen bonds, even though the protein becomes denatured during baking. When a cake becomes *stale*, moisture is lost and this is due to changes in the starch. A process similar to *retrogradation* occurs in which hydrogen-bonding of water to the starch alters and water is eliminated from the starch gel.

The high moisture content of cakes can readily lead to mould growth, partricularly in wrapped goods. Sodium and calcium propanoates (propionates) will prevent mould growth, and similarly sorbic acid has been found to be useful.

The mixes for *biscuits* and *pastries* are dough-like and are rolled and kneaded, unlike the liquid-like batters for cake-making. In biscuits a large amount of fat is used to ensure disruption of the gluten, so that a crumbly or brittle texture is produced. Baking powder is used but only a small degree of gas production is usually required.

In *pastry* tenderness and a degree of flakiness are fundamental requirements. Ingredients must be mixed carefully and the creaming of the fat must be such that it shows some 'plasticity'. Although the gluten development is again retarded, a layering of the gluten is encouraged to give flakiness to the product.

SOME OTHER CEREALS

Barley

This very hardy cereal is grown extensively for the brewing industry and to a lesser extent for other purposes, such as animal feed.

Malt and a range of malt products are made from germinating barley. The barley is allowed to sprout under moist, warm conditions so the α- and β-amylases become active and start to break down the starch endosperm. When the desired amount of maltose has been produced, the grain or the malt is extracted for use in beer making, malt whisky and in vinegar. 'Pearl barley' is grain from which most of the bran and the germ have been removed.

Rye

This cereal is preferred to wheat in colder and most arid regions as it can withstand adverse conditions. The rye protein contains some gluten but it lacks elasticity and so produces loaves of poor volume and dense texture. Doughs made from rye are unusual in that often they are soured with starter culture which gives acidity and characteristic flavour to the rye bread.

Maize

Maize, or corn in many parts of the world, is popular in many poorer countries, but unfortunately it is also poorer nutritionally. The grain is deficient in lysine and tryptophan and low in free nicotinic acid as most of it is bound and unavailable. The disease pellagra has been common when maize was the staple diet. Boiling maize with alkaline water, such as lime water, releases the nicotinic acid from the bound form, and this is practised in South America and Mexico. Cornflour is an important product from maize and is used extensively in many forms in cooking and food processing.

Rice

It is estimated that over half the world's population depends on rice as food. Milling then 'polishing' rice removes the bran to leave the white grain, and in so doing removes most of the B complex vitamins. Parboiling rice before milling causes migration of thiamin particularly into the grain so that it is not lost in milling. Parboiling also toughens the grain and makes it less susceptible to insect attack.

Nutrients are lost from the grain during cooking; and so rice should be boiled in a minimum of water so that loss of nutrient is prevented. 'Quick cook' rice has been pre-cooked to gelatinize the internal structure. This gives the product a somewhat sponge-like interior capable of rapidly absorbing water during cooking.

Oats

This cereal is unusual in containing more fat (7%) than other cereals (1-2%). It is also fairly rich in protein, but does not contain bread-making gluten. The fat content can cause problems in becoming rancid during storage. In 1987 oats were shown to lower blood cholesterol levels.

Phytic acid occurs in oats and can combine with calcium, in extreme cases causing calcium deficiency leading to rickets. Soaking the grain for long periods reduces the problem. Oats are used mainly in porridges, but can be used in biscuits and animal food.

BREAKFAST CEREALS

Cereal grains and part grains are used extensively in many modified forms as breakfast cereals which are especially popular in Britain. To reduce the consumers' preparation time the starch of the endosperm must be pre-gelatinised by some method which involves the reduction of the B complex vitamins. Vitamins B_1, B_2, B_6, D_3 and niacin, in addition to iron, are often added so that, it is claimed, many cereals provide over a third of the daily requirements of these vitamins. Three types of breakfast cereals will be discussed below, but the range of products is ever increasing in this highly competitive food sector.

Cornflakes are made from white maize which must be thoroughly cleaned and shelled and must have all bran and germ removed. The white endosperm is broken into pieces which are then steamed for about three hours to gelatinise the starch. A number of additions are made which include salt, sugar, malt and vitamins. The mixture is cooled and then is passed through smooth rollers under tremendous pressure. The flakes produced by this rolling are heated in an oven to toast them and give a somewhat 'bubbly' appearance.

Shredded wheat is made from whole wheat, which is added to an equal amount of water and pressure-cooked to gelatinize the starch. The grains now soft are shredded by two rollers that produce a continuous flow of strands which are built into layers of the required thickness for the 'biscuit'. The edges of the biscuit are crimped and the product is dried in an oven at about 250C for about 20 minutes.

Puffed cereals have been popular for many years and can be made from barley, maize, rye, wheat, rice and even soya beans. In the case of puffed wheat the grains are placed in a special puffing gun into which steam is injected to increase the pressure and cook the grains. The pressure is suddenly released and this causes rapid expansion of the water vapour within the grains causing them to double their size. This process leads to open honeycombed texture typical of this type of product.

PASTA PRODUCTS

Pasta products are made from the Durum group of wheats, characterized by having tough endosperms, which produce a yellow coloured semolina on milling due to carotenoid pigments. Semolina is granular starch from the endosperm of hard wheat and it is better than flour because less water is needed to make the pasta dough, thus facilitating drying of the pasta product subsequently. There are many different types of pasta and some are enriched with egg or soya flour. Generally there are four stages in the manufacture of these products. The wheat semolina is mixed with salt and water to form a crumbly mixture that is kneaded and worked between heavy rollers to make a dough. The dough must be stiff, yet show a degree of 'plasticity', which is obtained after a short resting period. Shaping the dough is performed using a special press with the appropriate die to obtain the right shape and size of the emerging pasta stream. The extruded pasta is cut into standard lengths corresponding to each product type and is then dried in a special drying room, taking up to three or four days. In hot climates, sun-drying has been used for drying pasta, but can take up to two weeks.

PRACTICAL EXERCISES: CEREALS

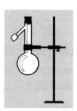

1. Microscope examination
Prepare the sections of a number of products, using a sca

1. Microscopic examination of dough
Add a small amount of water to a bread flour. Knead and work into a dough. Take a small amount and make a thin slide preparation. Cover with a cover-slip and place a drop of iodine next to the cover-slip. Starch will be stained and gluten will clearly be distinguished.

2. Separation of gluten
Make a dough as in 1. Cover with tap water for half an hour. Place dough in muslin and work between fingers under a running tap to eliminate starch. Gluten remains in the muslin.

3. Water absorption
Weigh 20g of flour into a dish and add water from a burette. Mix the flour and water and note the amount of water used to produce a dough of normal bread consistency. Compare the water absorption of different flours.

4. Yeast
Examine a suspension of fresh yeast and dried yeast under the microscope. Try to observe the multiplication of the yeast cells by 'budding'.

5. Comparison of bread-making potential of flours
Make a mixture of 40g flour, 60cm3 of water and 3g of yeast. Pour into a measuring cylinder (250 or 500cm3). Note initial level. Observe the rise in the 'dough' as the yeast fermentation proceeds. Note the height achieved by each and conclude which flour is best for bread-making, taking into account its elasticity and retention of gas.

6. Flour additives
Test samples of flour for:

(a) ascorbic acid:
add 1 drop of dichlorophenol indophenol (DCPIP) to a suspension of flour in dilute acetic acid. The pink colour will be decolourised by ascorbic acid.

(b) potassium bromate:
Make a paste of flour in water and add some potassium iodide in hydrochloric acid. The bromate will be coloured black.

Chapter 5

Beverages

PREVIEW

- **Carbonated drinks**
  - carbon dioxide from sodium carbonate and weak acid – hence 'sodas'
  - sucrose used for sweetening and to give body
  - in dietetic drinks – saccharin, acesulfame K or aspartame used and carboxy-methyl cellulose to give body
  - natural flavours and colours inferior to synthetic versions
  - acidity from dissolved CO_2 and other acids, such as citric, and phosphoric in 'cola'

- **Tea**
  - young leaves of tea bush
  - contains caffeine
  - can inhibit over 60% of iron absorption in a meal
  - colour, strength, body and stringency due to tannin
  - three types, green, black and oolong
  - black and oolong need active enzymes (polyphenolases) to give colour

- **Coffee**
  - coffee beans enclosed in pulp and skin as a 'cherry'
  - fermentation required to remove mucilage
  - drying develops colour and flavour
  - roasting further develops flavour
  - constituents, up to $\frac{1}{3}$ extracted by brewing
  - instant coffee made by dehydrating brew by spray-drying or AFD
  - coffee attracts attention as possible health hazard – some correlation between coffee consumption and increase in cholesterol in blood

- **Cocoa**
  - contains less caffeine, but also stimulant, theobromine
  - chocolate liquor used for chocolate manufacture, remaining cake used for drinking chocolate

- **Wine**
  - quality and characteristics depend on variety of grape, climate, soil, method of manufacture and maturation
  - red wines produced from black grapes by fermenting pulp and skins
  - rose wines only short period of pulp fermentation
  - white wines press out juice and ferment in absence of skins
  - alcohol content depends on sugar content, type of yeast and presence of moulds which can concentrate juice within grapes, *eg* Sauternes
  - sparkling wines require secondary fermentation in bottle, *eg* Champagne
  - semi-sparkling wines depend on malo-lactic fermentation
  - fortified wines have added spirit, *eg* brandy

- **Beer**
  - more complex than wine-making
  - must extract fermentable sugars from grain, *eg* barley
  - barley must be malted to produce sugars
  - hops add bitterness, flavour, preservatives and protein coagulants
  - British beer – top-fermenting yeasts
  - lagers – bottom – fermenting yeasts

- **Spirits**
  - must distil and collect alcohol carefully
  - raw spirit needs long maturation
  - liqueur: spirit with added syrup and flavour, such as essential oils

The body needs to take in a large amount of water daily, between one and two litres. This water is taken in as food, any food products being at least 80% water, and in the form of drinks. Beverages are not normally consumed for their food value but for thirst-quenching and often for their stimulating effects! It is convenient to divide beverages into those which are non-alcoholic *eg* tea, coffee, cocoa and carbonated soft drinks, and alcoholic drinks which include wine, beer, cider and spirits.

NON-ALCOHOLIC BEVERAGES

CARBONATED DRINKS – MINERAL WATER

Artificially carbonated water was first produced in the 18th century and has been popular ever since. Carbonated drinks are sweetened, flavoured, acidified, coloured, artificially carbonated and often chemically preserved. The carbon dioxide was originally obtained from sodium carbonate or hydrogen carbonate by the action of a weak acid in the drink. As sodium salts were used, the name 'soda' was adopted and can still be seen today, *eg* strawberry cream soda.

Sweetening of these drinks has been traditionally carried out using sucrose as a colourless syrup to give the finished drink about 12% sugar on average. Sugar also has the advantage of giving 'body' and some degree of mouth-feel to the drink. There has been an enormous increase in drinks with reduced sugar levels for slimming diets. Sucrose is significantly reduced or totally replaced by saccharin, or any other approved sweetener such as aspartame* or acesulfame K, and the body of the drink produced by adding a small amount of pectin or carboxymethyl cellulose.

*Breaks down under acid conditions giving a slightly shorter shelf-life

Carbonated drinks must have an attractive flavour which must also be stable under acid conditions in the drink and unaffected by light entering the bottle. Natural flavour extracts do present some problems, as, for example, terpenes change in the presence of acid. A small amount of emulsifier is often added to prevent separation of essential oils on standing. Synthetic flavours offer many advantages to the manufacturer and are often used.

Synthetic *colours*, particularly coal tar dyes, are used for similar reasons and in cola-type drinks caramel is used. Natural colours generally do not posses sufficient pigment depth and are often not stable in the acidic drinks.

The *acidity* will in part come from the dissolution of carbon dioxide in the water to form carbonic acid.

$$CO_2 + H_2O = H_2CO_3$$

Further acids are used to enhance particular flavours, citric, tartaric and malic acids are common, but phosphoric acid is used in cola-type drinks. The final pH is about 3. Although acids help preserve the drink, long-term keeping quality is only obtained by using preservatives, usually benzoic acid. Often sodium benzonate is used as this breaks down to release benzoic acid in the acidic drink.

Carbonation of the drink is achieved by exposing a large surface area of the cooled drink to pressurized jets of carbon dioxide. The gas is more soluble in water at lower temperatures that at higher temperatures. After carbonation the drink can be filled into bottles or cans.

TEA

Tea comes from only the young leaves of the evergreen tea bush, which yields suitable leaves after three years and up to 50 years afterwards. Like coffee, tea is a stimulating drink as it contains caffeine. (figure 2.19)

The colour and strength of the tea, together with some body and, often considerable, astringency are due to the *tannins* in the tea. Tea aroma is produced by a small amount of essential oil in the best and most expensive types of tea. Tea taken with a meal has been shown to reduce the absorption of iron by as much as 64% and may cause anaemia in high tea consuming communities like China.

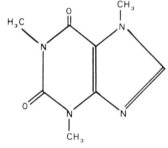

Figure 2.19
Caffeine

The *processing* of the tea can produce three main types – green, black or oolong. Enzyme activity (polyphenolases) is responsible for black tea and partly for the lighter oolong tea, but the enzymes are inactivated in green tea.

To produce *black tea* the leaves must wither and soften and partially dried. The cell walls are ruptured by passing the leaves between rollers to release the juices and, thus, activate the enzymes. The enzymes are active for up to five hours before they are inactivated by drying at about 93C. Finally the moisture content is brought down to below 5%.

To produce green tea the enzymes must be inactivated usually by steaming the leaves. The leaves are then simply rolled and dried.

Oolong tea is intermediate in being partially steamed, thus allowing some polyphenolase activity.

COFFEE

Coffee trees are also evergreen, but produce fruit after five years, which when ripe are red and often called 'cherries', see figure 2.20.

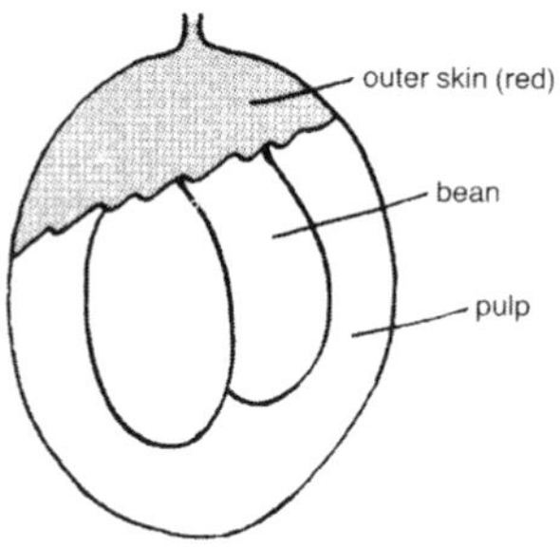

Figure 2.20
Coffee 'cherry'

The 'cherry' contains two coffee beans enclosed in a tough skin. To remove the beans, the ripe cherries are passed to pulping machines, which remove the pulp of the cherry to leave the two beans surrounded by a coating of mucilage. This mucilage is removed by natural fermentation of the beans or special washing techniques. The beans are dried to a moisture content of about 12% and undergo flavour and colour changes during the process.

The dry hulls of the beans are removed by friction and the beans are carefully sorted and graded for size, colour and potential brewing quality.

The flavour of coffee is further developed during *roasting* which is carried out at about 205C for five minutes. Essential oils are given off with the fragrant aroma of roasted coffee. The coffee is ground down to size depending on its intended use as different particle sizes affect brewing time.

In brewing coffee, about one-third of the constituents are extracted by hot water. Caffeine is extracted easily and almost completely after ten minutes brewing; however, shorter brewing times are better to avoid extracting bitter phenolic compounds. The composition of coffee is complex, and over 200 compounds have been identified. As well as caffeine, chlorogenic acids and nicotinic acid derivatives are important.

Instant coffee is made by dehydrating the brew from large percolators. Generally spray-drying is used, but high quality coffee is made by accelerated freeze-drying (see section on drying processes). However, even the best instant coffee can lack the full flavour of freshly brewed coffee. Volatile constituents can be trapped and recovered during roasting, grinding and extraction to be added back to the coffee.

Coffee consumption has attracted attention as a possible health hazard. Studies have shown possible connections between coffee and coronary heart disease, high blood pressure, some forms of cancer and diabetes. In all cases results are inconclusive.

COCOA AND DRINKING CHOCOLATE

Cocoa, like tea and coffee contains some caffeine, but also it contains another stimulant, theobromine. Cocoa beans grow in pods, with 25 or so beans arranged in rows in each pod. The beans are surrounded by mucus and pulp, which is removed by fermentation carried out traditionally by heaping the beans and covering then with leaves. During fermentation colour and flavour are developed. The beans are dried to about 7% moisture and later roasted to develop their flavour further. Special crushing machines and 'winnowners' are used to separate the grain and hull from the remainder known as the *nibs*. The nibs are passed through various mills where they are torn apart and ground releasing fat from the cells. The heat of the grinding process melts the fat and this liquid product is known as *chocolate liquor*, the essential ingredient of chocolate. After removing the chocolate liquor the cake left is prepared for cocoa powder, which is lower in fat. The cocoa powder may be treated with weak alkali, *eg* potassium carbonate which improves the solubility of the cocoa and darkens the colour. Often sugar, vanilla essence and salt are added to cocoa to produce a typical drinking chocolate.

ALCOHOLIC BEVERAGES

WINE
Grapes have been fermented by yeasts to make wine since at least 4000B.C. Although other fruits can be used to make wine, grape is the most suitable. Yeasts naturally occur on the surface of grapes as bloom and will readily ferment the crushed grapes. Wine production, therefore, can be carried out with the minimum of equipment. However, the enormous demands for consistent and high quality wines has led to elaborate procedures being developed.

The quality and characteristics of a wine depend on: variety of grape, climate, soil, method of manufacture and maturation.

GENERAL CHARACTERISTICS OF WINES
Colour
Red wines are produced from black grapes, *eg Pinot noir,* which are pulped and fermented with the skins present. The pigment of the skins, mainly anthocyanins, is extracted and as alcohol is produced during fermentation this extraction is accelerated. The longer the skins remain in the fermentation the darker the colour. The pulp is strained off and then fermentation proceeds to completion.

Rose wines are produced in a similar way, but the skins only remain for about 24 hours before straining.

White wines can be made from most grapes, even black ones, as the flesh of the grapes is seldom coloured. The grapes are crushed and the resulting pulp is hydraulically pressed (formerly this was done with the feet) to separate juices from the pulp. A yeast starter culture is added to ferment the juice, which is often treated before to this with sulphate to kill 'wild' yeasts and bacteria.

Alcohol content and sweetness
Obviously, the sugars of the juice are fermented to produce alcohol and in so doing the sweetness of the juice decreases. If all the sugars are fermented, a *dry wine* results, and the alcohol content will be between 9-14% usually. In warmer climates the grapes will fully ripen and contain more sugar, which

leads to a wine with more alcohol and possibly one, which is sweet. Yeasts generally can only ferment up to about 14 or 15% alcohol before they are inhibited then killed by the alcohol.

Some wines, such as Sauternes, are very sweet because the grapes used have been 'attacked' by a mould – *La pourriture noble* – the noble rot. This mould concentrates the sugars in the grapes, making them almost raisin-like, and also the mould produces glycerol which adds to sweetness.

Fortified wines have alcohol contents of 17-21%. To achieve this, spirit, usually brandy of lower quality, is added to fortify a normal wine.

Sparkling wines

During fermentation carbon dioxide is produced; in a number of sparkling wines this gas is retained to give the bubbles. Special alcohol-tolerant strains of yeast are used and residual sugar is involved in a secondary fermentation in the bottle. Champagne is the best sparkling wine as it has small, long-lasting bubbles.

Semi-sparkling wines, eg Mateus Rosé, are produced by a special fermentation, the malo-lactic fermentation. Malic acid is broken down, by certain bacteria, to give lactic acid and liberate carbon dioxide, as shown in the following equation:

$$\begin{array}{c} CH_2COOH \\ | \\ CH(OH)COOH \\ \text{malic acid} \end{array} \rightarrow CH_3CH(OH)COOH + CO_2 \\ \qquad\qquad\qquad \text{lactic acid}$$

Wine-making

The yeast used for wine making is a variety of the common yeast *Saccharomyces cerevisiae* and has an ellipsoidal shape, hence *S.cerevisiae var. ellipsoideus.* The yeast acquires individual characteristics when growing on different grapes in different areas, for example, the ability to produce more alcohol. The grapes are crushed and an active yeast culture ferments the sugars until either all the sugar is used; the yeast is poisoned by high alcohol levels; or additional alcohol is added. Sometimes benzoates can be added to stop further fermentation.

After fermentation, 'racking' is carried out to separate the wine from the sediment, particularly dead yeast, which starts to break down. The wine may be aged in casks or tanks for several months, or even years, for heavy red wines. Red wines require a long maturation period to break down their high content of tannin. After maturation, the wine is filtered and stabilized by the addition of benzoate or sulphites. Crystals of salts of tartaric acid are often removed at this stage. Some wines are pasteurized before bottling.

During 1986 and 1987 some Austrian and German wines were found to be sweetened with an industrial solvent, diethylene glycol to give the appearance of a better wine. (Anti-freeze is ethylene glycol.)

BEERS, ALES AND LAGERS

Beer-making is more complex than wine-making, as fermentable sugars must be extracted from grain, particularly from barley. Malting of barley must be carried out to produce maltose and other fermentable sugars. Other grains can be used to extend the malt, since the amylase content of malt is capable of breaking down more starch than is present in barley itself. These grains, usually boiled, modify the flavour of beer and minimise the formation of protein hazes.

The malt and cereal grains are roughly milled and hot water is added in a large container – the mash tun. The temperature is controlled at about 65C and takes about three hours, after which the liquid, *the wort,* which is rich in dissolved sugars, is allowed to drain from the grains. The wort is passed to a copper where it is boiled and hops are added. The hops add flavour, bitterness, natural preservatives and protein coagulants to the wort. The wort is then filtered and rapidly cooled. Fermentation is carried out at about 15C.

In typical British beers the carbon dioxide produced during fermentation carries the yeast to the top, and is called top-fermenting. In lagers, the yeast is bottom-fermenting. Finings may be added to clarify the beer, or it is filtered to remove yeast, then bottled or kegged. Carbonation is carried out by sugaring barrels in a traditional process or by injection of carbon dioxide.

Compared with wines the alcohol content of beers is lower at about 2-5%. Beers which are heavier with more 'body' are richer in carbohydrates and proteins. These beers are also richer in minerals and are good nutritionally.

SPIRITS

Distillation is the only method of producing drinks with alcohol concentrations above 20%. Distillation is dependant on the difference in volatility between water and ethanol. In heating a wine or beer both water and alcohol are distilled, but as alcohol boils at 78C, compared with water at 100C, the alcohol concentrates in the vapour and must be trapped and condensed. This is a difficult process for a number of reasons. Rapid heating during distillation can cause loss of alcohol and unwanted chemical reactions. During the initial stages of distillation methanol, which is toxic, can be given off and therefore the 'spirit' collected at first must be discarded.

The raw spirit must be aged over long periods in wooden barrels. Some oxidation occurs producing flavours and some flavour is picked up from the cask, ideally made of oak.

Liqueurs are produced by adding a special flavouring, such as an essential oil, to a spirit and usually syrup for sweetening.

PRACTICAL EXERCISES: BEVERAGES

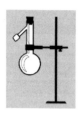

1. pH and titratable acidity
Compare the pH of a range of juices and soft drinks, using pH meter (if available) or pH papers. Titrate 10cm^3 samples of drink with 0.1M sodium hydroxide, using phenolphthalein as indicator. A light pink colour indicates the end-point. Record volume of hydroxide used.

2. Saccharin identification in drinks
To a sample of drink, add a small amount of resorcinol. Add a few drops of concentrated sulphuric acid (CARE!). Heat in a water bath until a green colour is produced. Cool completely, then add some water and sodium hydroxide solution. A fluorescent green is produced, indicating the presence of saccharin.

3. Effects of pH
To a coloured drink, for example blackcurrant juice, add varying amounts of acids and alkalis. Record the pH and note the colour change.

4. Effect of pH on tea and coffee
Prepare brews for tea and coffee, and filter. Repeat 3.

Chapter 6
Chocolate and Confectionery

PREVIEW

- **Chocolate**
  - chocolate liquor: 55% fat, 17% carbohydrate, 11% protein
  - contains stimulant, theobromine
  - cocoa butter – fat from chocolate liquor: unusually hard at room temperature, but melts just under body temperature
  - unstable crystal forms of cocoa butter can cause white bloom on chocolate
  - conching helps develop flavour and aroma and with tempering develops right texture
  - milk chocolate – added condensed milk

- **Confectionery**
  - control of sugar crystal size and ratio of sugar: moisture
  - crystalline products-
  - large crystals – rock
  - small crystals – fudge, fondant
  - non-crystalline products – boiled sweets, butterscotch, gums
  - caramelisation must be controlled to prevent bitter and dark coloured products
  - invert sugar important to add sweetness and control sucrose crystallization

CHOCOLATE

Cocoa is processed to produce *chocolate liquor*. (See beverages section) This liquor is about 55% fat, 17% carbohydrate and 11% protein. In addition it contains about 6% tannin and 1.5% theobromine, a stimulant similar to caffeine. The presence of this substance explains the slightly addictive nature of some chocolate. On cooking this liquor a bitter chocolate is produced which can be used in baking. Further processing is necessary with sugar to yield sweet chocolate and with sugar and milk to produce milk chocolate.

Cocoa butter is the fat which is removed from chocolate liquor; and in many ways it is an unusual fat. Cocoa butter is quite hard at normal temperatures but melts quickly at just under body temperature. This characteristic enables chocolate to be made into various shapes and bars and to be used as coatings for sweets and biscuits, where it remains solid until it is eaten, when it softens readily in the mouth. Processing of chocolate is designed to ensure that the cocoa butter crystallizes in a stable form in the chocolate.

There are three unstable forms which can lead to poor texture and the formation of white 'bloom' on the surface of the product, particularly when the chocolate melts then curls again.

Plain chocolate is made from chocolate liquor, or cocoa nibs, to which is added cocoa butter and some sugar. Cocoa beans must be carefully selected and roasted to give the distinctive flavour of plain chocolate. The ingredients are mixed in a special mixer, which has scraper blades and heavy crushing rollers. An even paste is produced in this mixing process and is ground to reduce the particle size until it is completely smooth. Large steel rollers carry out this grinding process and are referred to as *refiners*. A film of chocolate is passed from one roller to the next and there are usually five in all. Often plain chocolate is refined several times before the final process of *conching*.

Conching is performed in a large metal vat with a large roller and is a slow process, sometimes taking up to two days at 65C. The warm chocolate from the refining process is poured into the vat and extra cocoa butter and some vanilla flavouring are added. The roller moves backwards and forwards in the vat moving the chocolate continually. In this manner the chocolate is helped to develop its full flavour and aroma, and the right texture.

The chocolate can now be cooled and moulded. However, to obtain a glossy finish the chocolate is cooled until it thickens slightly and then is warmed again. This process is *tempering*. The warm, tempered chocolate flows into moulds where it cools and sets in a controlled manner.

Milk chocolate contains milk in addition to the constituents of plain chocolate. Milk must be condensed under vacuum and usually sugar is added to produce a sweetened condensed milk, which is mixed with chocolate liquor and dried to produce a powdery solid. This powder is made into chocolate by being mixed with cocoa butter and refined and conched as for plain chocolate.

CONFECTIONERY

The vast range of confectionery products manufactured is based on the ability to manipulate sugar, the principal ingredient. This manipulation is accomplished by controlling the state of crystallization of the sugar and the sugar: moisture ratio. The sugar may be in the form of large or small crystals or it may be non-crystalline and glass-like. The mixture may be hard or soft according to the moisture level, and air may be whipped into the product. If the sugar is *crystalline* it may be in the form of one crystal forming the whole product, such as in 'rock'. Very small crystals exist in fudges and fondants, *eg* chocolate fillings.

Non-crystalline sugar forms hard or brittle, or chewy sweets and gums. The sugar is amorphous and the water content varies from about 8% and up to 15% to produce the softer products. Marshmallows are very soft as air is whipped into them.

If sugar is added to water in a ratio of 2:1, a final solution of 66% sugar results which, on cooling, becomes *supersaturated*. Upon further cooling and with some agitation the sugar crystallizes. This crystallisation can be accelerated by 'seeding' with just one sucrose crystal. Very high concentrations of sugar may solidify as an amorphous mass, for example in the manufacture of boiled sweets.

Invert sugar is an important ingredient in many sweets as it is sweeter than sucrose but also controls its crystallisation. Invert sugar encourages the formation of small crystals essential to the smoothness of many products such as fondants, fudge and soft mints. Corn syrup and special fructose syrup are now often used.

Caramelisation is an important process in the production of a number of products. If sucrose is heated, either as a solid or solution, it undergoes decomposition to produce a range of brown products collectively known as *caramel*. Often in the production of caramels milk powder is added in a small amount to facilitate the Maillard reaction, rather than just allowing the process of caramelisation to proceed alone.

PRACTICAL EXERCISE: CONFECTIONERY

1. Caramelisation of sugar
Heat sugar in a ignition tube, note production of brown colour and typical smell. On further heating note the production of unpleasant and acrid odour of burnt caramel.

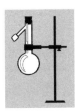

2 Inversion of sucrose
Make a solution of sucrose and test with the Fehling's test. Add 1cm³ of dilute sulphuric acid to a second solution of sucrose and heat in a water-bath. Test with Fehling's solution and note the positive result due to the production of invert sugar.

3. Crystallisation of sucrose
Crystallise sugar in a number of ways to make crystals of different sizes and different products:
    (i)   make a strong solution of sugar in water by heating, cool and allow to crystallize
    (ii)   repeat (i) but seed with small crystals of sugar
    (iii)   repeat (ii) but stir
    (iv)   repeat (ii) and add a small amount of cream of tartar.

Chapter 7

Microbiology

PREVIEW

- **Micro-organisms**   – main groups bacteria, moulds, yeasts, algae and viruses.

- **Naming**
  - names in italics or underlined
  - name in two parts – genus (capital letters) and species (small letters)
    eg Pseudomonas fluorescens

- **Growth of Bacteria**
  - increase in numbers, can double in twenty minutes
  - bacterial growth cycle: lag phase, log phase, stationary phase, death phase
  - main growth influences: temperature, moisture, pH and gas.

- **Food Spoilage** – spoilage depends on:
  - initial bacterial load in food
  - influence of growth factors e.g. temperature
  - storage conditions of food

- **Food Poisoning**   – some organisms produce toxins
  - some infect gut or body
  - examples: *Staphylococcus aureus*
              Clostridium botulinum, Salmonella

- **Current microbial problems**
  Salmonella
  Listeria
  Botulism
  E coli

- **Food Hygiene** – need to consider:
  food premises
  hygiene practices
  personal hygiene

Microbiology is the study of micro-organisms, *ie* bacteria, fungi, protozoa, some algae and viruses. They are generally too small to be seen with the naked eye.

Foods, as well as meeting the nutritional requirement of humans, also meet the nutritional needs of a vast range of micro-organisms. Given the right conditions, micro-organisms will multiply rapidly in food and usually produce changes in flavour, aroma and texture. At the same time, a more sinister population of micro-organisms might become established in the food without any noticeable change in the organoleptic properties of the food. These organisms might cause an outbreak of food poisoning when the apparently wholesome food is consumed.

WHAT ARE MICRO-ORGANISMS?

Micro-organisms are microscopic living things, mainly belonging to the plant kingdom, but some, protozoa are animals. The main groups of micro-organisms are the *bacteria, moulds, yeasts, algae* and *viruses*. The one common aspect of these simple organisms is that they are small. Bacteria are often around 1micron (1/1000mm) across, yeasts are somewhat bigger at about 10microns and moulds can be larger as they form long thread-like structures.

Three of these microbial types are of significance in foods: *bacteria, moulds* and *yeasts*.

- **Bacteria**   are extremely widespread and cause food spoilage, even food poisoning.
- **Moulds**   are very common with their spores floating in the air ready to fall on and colonise a suitable food. Some moulds can produce toxins which cause disease.
- **Yeasts**   spoil foods, particularly those of a higher sugar or salt content.

HOW ORGANISMS ARE NAMED

All living organisms are named using the system developed by the taxonomist Linnaeus. Each name has two parts (binomial). The first part is the generic name (or genus) and is given a capital letter, and the second part is the specific name (or species) given a small letter. Names are in italics or underlined when written,

   eg Pseudomonas fluorescens

After mentioning the first time, the organism's name can be abbreviated.

Full Name	Abbreviation
Escherichia coli	E. coli
Clostridium botulinum	C. botulinum
Saccharomyces cerevisiae	Sacc. cerevisiae
Staphylococcus aureus	Staph. aureus

NB. Bacterium is singular, bacteria plural.

THE GROWTH OF BACTERIA

The multiplication of micro-organisms is generally referred to as 'growth' and as numbers of bacteria increase we say they are 'growing'. This does not mean the bacteria are increasing in size, only in numbers; since they can divide rapidly, their population can sometimes double in about 20 minutes.

(a) The growth of bacteria is rather slow at first as the organisms become established in the food; this is the lag phase.

(b) Once established the bacterial cells start to divide ever more rapidly – the log or exponential phase. Sometimes at this stage the food might not show any outward signs of the bacterial population, although often obvious odours will be detected.

(c) As nutrients are used up in the food, the rapid rate of multiplication slows down and the number of cells being produced matches the number of bacteria dying. This is the stationary phase, when there is a constant level of micro-organisms.

(d) After a while the numbers dying exceed new cells and the growth cycle passes to the death phase. At this stage the food may well be 'off', but it may still be a good source of nutrients for a different group of bacteria which thrive in the conditions produced by the previous groups. In this way different groups of organisms can use the food as a source of nutrients until it is completely decayed. See Figure 2.21.

Figure 2.21

Bacterial growth cycle

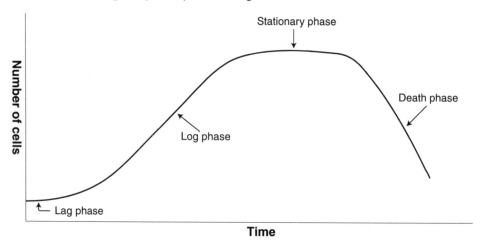

Bacteria will not grow on merely any food, under any condition. There are a number of factors which influence the growth of bacteria (but there are often quite large degrees of tolerance):

Temperature: although many bacteria can grow at widely differing temperatures, they often prefer to grow within a specific temperature range. Organisms which grow most readily at around room temperature and upwards (20—40C) are known as *mesophiles*. This group contains many food poisoning and spoilage organisms. Some organisms actually grow more rapidly at refrigeration temperatures (O—10C), this group contains the *psychrophiles*. Conversely, the *thermophiles* have an optimum at between 50C and 70C. The former cause spoilage in chilled foods, while the latter can withstand heat to quite high levels in cooked or processed food.

Moisture: micro-organisms require differing levels of moisture in order to grow in foods. Most bacteria require high moisture levels, whereas most moulds can grow under low moisture conditions, for example, on old leather. Some yeasts are capable of growing in high sugar products such as confectionery or salt products like pickles. A few years ago several million fondant-filled chocolate eggs exploded because they had become infected with a yeast which caused fermentation of the filling producing gas

pH Conditions: organisms have a preference for certain pH conditions, many prefer near neutral but some, particularly moulds, can grow under very acidic conditions.

Air: some organisms can only grow in the presence of oxygen (or air) and are known as *obligate aerobes*. Those organisms which can only grow in the absence of oxygen are *obligate anaerobes*, whereas those which are capable of either are *facultative anaerobes*.

In order to grow in a food the factors an organism requires for growth must be met. Some organisms are extremely demanding in their growth requirements, others are easily accommodated. Unfortunately, human food meets the requirements of most organisms without much difficulty.

FOOD SPOILAGE AND PRESERVATION

Micro-organisms eat our food in order to grow in much the same way as we do. They produce waste-products (sometimes toxic) and cause chemical changes in the food product. These changes can be detected as odour, flavour, colour and texture changes. Some are very noticeable and obnoxious, indicating that the food is 'bad'. Many of the changes produced by spoilage due to micro-organisms are obvious, like the rotting of fruit, souring of milk, putrefaction of meat and 'hairy' mould growth. Most of these foods are termed *perishable*, whereas foods like flour or spices are *stable*.

Whether or not spoilage occurs depends on a number of factors: (a) an initial load, perhaps of several million organisms, may be necessary to initiate spoilage; (b) the previously-described growth factors have to be met in the food; (c) the storage conditions under which the food is kept also affect the rate of spoilage. In the processes of food preservation, the growth factors of organisms are controlled so as to prevent or retard their growth.

(1) The temperature of storage may be reduced below the optimum growth temperature of most organisms present in the food. Thus in chilled foods only psychrophiles can grow.

(2) High temperatures may be used to kill all organisms present, for example, in canning.

(3) In the process of drying, water levels are reduced to below the moisture level requirement of organisms so they cannot grow.

(4) Products can be made more acid, in pickling or fermentation, so that the pH of the product is outside the growth range of the organisms.

(5) Food can be packed in a vacuum or gas flushed to prevent oxygen supporting the growth of obligate aerobes.

(6) A range of substances, preservatives, can be added to inhibit the growth of micro-organisms.

Food spoilage can occur in a product to produce noticeable spoilage so that people do not usually consume the product. However, some organisms can grow or be carried in a food without altering the food. These may then cause food-poisoning or some other disease.

FOOD POISONING

The number of cases of food poisoning caused by micro-organisms is increasing annually. In addition to the greater number of outbreaks, more groups of organisms are being recognised as capable of causing illness. The public is aware of food poisoning and will report cases more readily, rather than accepting their illness as another 'bilious' attack. There are greater numbers of small food outlets, cafes and fast-food establishments. Although many have very high standards, there are enough whose hygiene standards are below par to cause an increase in the outbreaks of food poisoning.

The presence of large numbers of micro-organisms in a food does not necessarily mean the food is a health risk. However, high numbers often imply poor hygiene standards at some time during the handling and preparation of the food. This poor hygiene could mean that the food has become contaminated with food poisoning organisms. For an outbreak of food poisoning to occur the food must become *contaminated with food poisoning organisms* and these must *grow to sufficient numbers* to cause illness. Some organisms produce toxins, sometimes very resistant to heat, which cause the poisoning and not the organisms themselves.

Contamination of foods by micro-organisms can occur from a variety of sources, not least humans. The air, soil, skin, animal feed and utensils can contaminate exposed foods. The contamination need not occur directly, but via a number of different vehicles. To illustrate the case of contamination of foods by micro-organisms a number of short case histories will be discussed.

Example 1

A common organism found on the skin, in the nose and in spots or boils is capable of growing in many foods and producing a toxin which causes food poisoning. This organism is called *Staphylococcus aureus*, or *Staph. aureus* for short.

A person preparing a trifle for a reception had a boil caused by *Staph. aureus* on the arm, but the plaster covering the boil came away. Whilst preparing the trifle the person had touched the boil and then the trifle ingredients. The trifle was now contaminated with *Staph. aureus*, which grew in the trifle until it was consumed at the reception. After about three or four hours people who had been to the reception were feeling dizzy, suffering from nausea and vomiting. Some older people were liable to become unconscious. When the toxin had been expelled from their bodies most people recovered within a day. Obviously, this was a case of poor hygiene and the boil should have been covered and not touched. Correct washing of hands and hygienic preparation of the food was essential.

Example 2

A very serious type of toxin food poisoning is caused by the organism *Clostridium botulinum*. This bacterium produces very heat-resistant spores.

In the 1930s and 40s home-canning was popular in the USA and, to a lesser extent, in the UK. Home produced canned vegetables, meat and fruits were popular. However, on occasions, products were insufficiently heat treated to sterilise the can contents. This was often carried out, after sealing the can, in a pressure cooker. Most organisms in the food would be destroyed by the heat but the spores of *Cl. botulinum* are more heat-resistant and therefore survived the process. The heat process stimulated the bacterial spores to germinate and to grow in the food in the can.

As the bacterium is an obligate anaerobe, conditions in the can of little or no oxygen are ideal. The bacteria multiply in the food and produce a toxin, neither of which can be detected in the apparently wholesome food. After eating the food, symptoms of food poisoning develop perhaps twelve hours later. The toxin is one of the deadliest poisons known and affects the central nervous system leading to paralysis and often death.

Example 3

The salmonella group of bacteria is well known for its food poisoning activities. In addition to causing food poisoning, it contains organisms capable of causing serious illness such as typhoid.

Salmonella causes food poisoning by infecting the gut of the victim and then multiplying inside the person. Irritation of the gut lining occurs and toxic by-products are produced leading to vomiting and diarrhoea. These symptoms vary from fairly mild to very severe resulting in death.

Salmonella can contaminate foods by various means.

(a) The bacteria may be carried by rodents, insects or birds which contaminate food directly, food preparation areas, or animal feed.

(b) Infected animals can pass the organisms to humans if the infection is not detected or eliminated in cooking or processing. It is well known that chicken must be thoroughly cooked with no red meat to ensure the elimination of salmonella.

(c) The most difficult form of contamination to trace is the human carrier. This is a person who does not show symptoms of a salmonella-type infection but has large numbers of the organism within the intestinal tract. Poor personal hygiene, particularly after using the toilet, can lead to contamination of food by the carrier's salmonella. Stool-testing of all personnel involved in the food operations is necessary to trace the carrier. The person should not be allowed in the factory or cafe until after at least two clear stool tests.

As the organisms need to grow in the gut before symptoms of food poisoning begin to occur, it may be several hours or days before an outbreak is discovered. In the case of some food-borne diseases, such as typhoid, very few organisms can cause the illness but then the incubation period may be two or three weeks. Obviously, to trace back to find the contaminated food is comparable to a murder investigation!

Example 4

Another type of food poisoning can occur in reheated meats. The organism *Clostridium perfringens* can contaminate meat during slaughter. Like *Cl. botulinum* the bacterium produces very heat-resistant spores which can survive the cooking of the meat. If the meat is stored for a time, the spores may germinate and the emergent bacterial cells will multiply. If the meat is only reheated and not thoroughly cooked again, the bacteria will survive and then increase in numbers. This occurs more rapidly in canteens with heated display counters. The contaminated meat, when consumed, releases its bacteria in the gut, where they produce a toxin resulting in food poisoning.

Other examples

Other groups of bacteria have been implicated in food poisoning from time to time.

(1) Another spore-former, *Bacillus cereus*, has been known to cause food poisoning in boiled rice and in some shellfish.

(2) Bacteria shaped like commas, known as *Vibrio cholerae* (or *V. comma*), can cause disease. A food-borne disease which has caused many deaths is of this type. As the name suggests, it causes cholera.

(3) A relative of the above bacterium has been implicated in food poisoning in some fish products, particularly in Japan. The bacterium is called *V. parahaemolyticus*.

(4) The genus *Campylobacter* is now the most common cause of food poisoning in the UK. The species particularly involved is *C. jejuni* which is found to contaminate foods of animal origin, eg chicken.

Food poisoning can also occur due to chemical contamination of foods, either deliberately or by accident. The contamination of cooking oil in Spain a few years ago was an example of this. However, food poisoning can and must be avoided and there is no excuse for poor hygiene in manufacturing or handling of foods.

CURRENT MICROBIAL PROBLEMS

In 1988 Edwina Currie, then junior Health Minister, made her now infamous remark that 'most of the egg production in this country, sadly, is now infected with salmonella'. This resulted in an immediate drop of 50% in egg sales, which subsequently levelled off to 10% below normal.

Salmonella

In fact, the Salmonella infection in eggs resulted from a type of contamination not encountered before. The organism involved is very specific and is called *Salmonella enteritidis* (phage type 4). The bacterium infects the ovaries of chickens and, from there, gains access to the yolk of eggs. Only the white of the egg has defence mechanisms against bacteria, not the yolk. Thus, the consumption of under-cooked eggs, particularly 'runny' yolks and egg mousses, could lead to a salmonella infection. In 1988 there were about 10,500 cases of this type of salmonella infection out of 30 million eggs consumed daily.

Listeria

At about the same time as the egg crisis another organism, *Listeria monocytogenes*, came to prominence. Listeria was found to contaminate 16% of cook-chilled foods in a survey conducted by the Department of Health. For many years the organism had been known as a cause of abortion in sheep. Among humans, in 1988, there were 287 known cases of listeriosis of which 50 of the sufferers died and 11 women had miscarriages. However, according to Sir Donald Acheson, the then Government's Chief Medical Officer, 'one person in twenty has listeria in the gut and is feeling quite well'. Clearly, compared with more than 24,000 reported cases of food poisoning in 1988, the number of known cases of listeriosis is very small. However, it should be realised that some minor cases of food poisoning may, in fact, be caused by listeria. It would therefore appear that the difference between a mild stomach upset and full listeriosis depends on individual susceptibility: foetuses, babies, the very elderly and those taking immuno-depressant drugs are most at risk.

Unfortunately, unlike most other bacteria, listeria can multiply rapidly if food is kept at a temperature of around 4C. Yet many supermarket display cabinets have been kept as high as 8C. This means that in such cases we cannot rely on the fact that spoilage organisms grow before food poisoning in chilled foods. The temperature is such that the food poisoning organisms rapidly multiply. As well as cook-chilled foods, salads, pates and certain soft cheeses, including goat, have been implicated.

Botulism

Botulism is a rare but deadly form of food poisoning in the UK. There are several strains of *Clostridium botulinum* which produce toxins of varying potency in food, type A being the deadliest poison known. In June 1989 there was an outbreak of botulism in hazelnut yoghurt. The organism grew in a puree of hazelnut used for flavouring which was then added to the yoghurt in the final mixing. The pH of yoghurt is low enough to prevent *Cl. botulinum* from multiplying. However, the toxin is unaffected by the low pH and, therefore, can cause severe food poisoning. A total of 27 cases of poisoning occurred.

E. coli

Escherichia coli is a widespread generally harmless bacterium found in the gut of humans and other animals. However, there are a number of varieties which are pathogens to humans. Some produce 'travellers' diarrhoea' as a result of poor personal hygiene, with food handlers passing on the contamination. However, there is one very serious type in the UK. This is called enterohaemorrhagic *E. coli (EHEC)* and the strain is numbered 0157 : H7.

The infected food may contain very few bacterial cells (10-100), which is unusual as most bacterial infections and food poisoning require large numbers. The incubation period can be 3-4 days and the symptoms include: diarrhoea, abdominal pain, blood in the stools and internal bleeding may occur. In severe cases kidney failure may occur and even brain damage.

The organism originates from the intestines of animals, particularly cattle, and gains access to food during handling including slaughter. It has been found in beef, burgers and dairy products. It has also been found in fruit juices and even under the skin of carrots. It is a tough organism and has shown resistance to acid, heat and antibiotics. Any faecal contamination is a possible cause of contamination of foods, even the use of natural fertilisers for organically-grown crops.

It is very easy to view these microbial problems superficially and generate, for example, 'listeria hysteria'. Although more cases of food poisoning are being reported, the actual number of cases may not be rising significantly. Reports of salmonellosis have shown an almost continuous annual increase since data were first collected in the 1940s. There is now a much greater public awareness of food poisoning and a willingness to report cases. Analytical and assay techniques have improved considerably so foods can be readily shown to contain food poisoning organisms. However, the number of organisms present may not be large enough to cause poisoning, since in most cases considerable numbers are required.

The current preoccupation with food hygiene is a mixed blessing. In earlier times people lived with a greater range of infection risks and children acquired immunity at an early age from low-level infection. Most people live in daily microbial risk with no ill effect due to their immunological systems. The removal of all bacteria, if that were ever possible, would compromise our immunity systems so that exposure to any organism would have a devastating effect.

FOOD HYGIENE

The main regulations relating to hygiene are the Food Hygiene (General) Regulations. These cover any food business, including shops, cafes, canteens, clubs, boarding houses, schools and factories. Anyone involved in handling food is subject to the Regulations. They also apply to all foods and drinks and also to any ingredient.

Food premises

- The premises used in the food business must be clean and in good condition. The position and construction of the premises must not allow contamination of food in any way. The floors, walls and ceilings must be kept clean and so must every toilet facility provided.
- There must be an adequate, constant supply of clean, potable water, both hot and cold. Sanitary conveniences must be clean, with a 'Now Wash Your Hands' notice. Food handlers must have adequate hand-washing facilities, with soap, brushes and drying facilities (hot air drier or paper towels).
- A first aid kit must be readily available, with waterproof, brightly coloured plasters.
- Staff should be provided with clothing lockers.
- Equipment used for processing and handling must be in good condition and clean. Containers should be non-absorbent and capable of easy cleaning.

HYGIENIC PRACTICES

- Provision must be made for separating and disposing of unsound food in a different part of the premises.
- Food placed in the open for sale must be screened or covered if any risk of contamination is likely.
- Foods intended for immediate consumption require special precautions, particularly meat, poultry, fish, gravy and imitation cream, and any product prepared from them. These foods must not be kept between temperatures of 10C and 62.7C; consequently they must be cooled or kept really hot. Food poisoning organisms multiply rapidly at lukewarm temperatures.
- Everyone involved in the food business should do all in his/her power to protect the food from contamination. Cleanliness is of utmost importance at all times.

  (a) Food must not be placed where there is a risk of contamination. This means that it must be kept at least 45cm from the ground.
  (b) Food must not be packed in packaging materials that are not clean. Newspapers can be used as an outer wrapper for some products.
  (c) Animals, poultry or animal feed should not come into contact with food or packaging materials.

PERSONAL HYGIENE

There are six rules for personal cleanliness to prevent micro-organisms from entering food.

(1) Cleanliness of hands or other parts of the body in contact with food is very important. Hair nets should be used as hair can carry bacteria.

(2) Clothing and protective overalls must be kept clean and changed often.

(3) All cuts and grazes should be covered with a waterproof, brightly coloured dressing.

(4) Food handlers must not spit and must not smoke while handling food or while in a room containing food.

(5) Personal health is important and employees must report cases of diarrhoea, vomiting, septic sores and boils, discharges from the ear, nose or eye. 'Carriers' of diseases must declare the fact if known.

(6) Serious diseases should be reported to the Medical Officer of Health and include typhoid, paratyphoid, salmonella infections, dysentery and staphylococcal infection.

Most of these points are obvious and are routinely carried out or avoided, as the case may be, by competent food handlers. Failure to comply can lead to prosecution or perhaps, worse still, to an outbreak of food poisoning resulting in total loss of future business.

Section 3
HANDLING AND PREPARATION OF FOOD RAW MATERIALS

This section of the book covers the storage of raw materials before processing and preservation, and handling and preparation of these materials to make 'convenience' foods. All operations required to be carried out before preservation are covered here.

Convenience foods may be defined* as foods for which the degree of culinary preparation has been carried to an advanced stage by the manufacturer and which may be used as labour-saving alternatives to less highly-processed products. This preparation of the food means that the product is easier and quicker to use than the basic product available to consumers.

Foods are convenient for different reasons. They may be convenient to buy, being more economical in the long run with less wastage; they may be convenient to carry home, one tin of dried milk will perhaps make three litres of liquid milk. Convenience in storage is an important factor as canned and packeted foods easily store in a cupboard or pantry and most homes now have a freezer to store frozen goods. The speed and convenience of preparation are probably the most important factors in evaluating a convenience food. The old type of field-dried peas (marrowfat) are a convenience food in that they are sorted, cleaned and pods are removed; however they take all night to rehydrate, which is hardly convenient! Packaging a food into convenient serving sizes is another aspect of convenience. Fully-prepared convenience foods are relatively new and in these foods convenience should be in their completeness.

The food factory takes in a large quantity of food material which must be stored until required. The food material is then prepared in a number of ways which include: cleaning, sorting, grading, size reduction, mixing, concentration, filtration and blanching. Following the relevant procedures required, the product is preserved and packaged.

*National Food Survey Committee

Chapter 1

Storage of Raw Materials

PREVIEW

- **Chilled storage**

    food kept above –1C and below 4C

    reduces spoilage by micro-organisms and enzymes

    inhibits the growth of thermophilic organisms

    (grow at 50-70C)

    most mesophilic organisms (grow at 20-40C)

    some mesophiles can grow at 5C, all pyschrophilic organisms (0-10C) can grow in
        chill stores and spoil food

    some enzymes similarly can grow at chill temperatures

    chilled foods deteriorate gradually

    chilled foods must be handled carefully and hygienically

    chilled foods for sale must be labelled with either 'sell by' or 'best before' dates

    chilled stores may be more efficient if gas added (CA stores), particularly about
        10% carbon dioxide

- **Frozen storage**

    products must be frozen quickly and maintained at the same temperature without
        fluctuations

    best storage at –29C

    temperature fluctuations can cause loss of weight due to sublimation of ice and a
        number of chemical changes, such as rancidity in fat

    'freezer-burn' is surface dehydration of the food caused by sublimation of ice

    frozen foods can cause tainting problems

    some foods give out odours and some readily accept odours

Factors controlling the quality of stored fresh fruit and vegetables include temperature, use of gases, reduction in pressure and the specialized use of coatings. These methods can be applied to the storage of a wide range of food products, and even the use of special coatings might have applications in other products yet to be investigated.

CHILLED STORAGE

A 'chilled food' is 'a perishable food which, to extend the time during which it remains wholesome, is kept within controlled ranges of temperature above – 1C and below 4C'. Chilling cannot preserve a food indefinitely but can reduce spoilage caused by micro-organisms and enzymes. Micro-organisms grow in certain temperature ranges and each type of organism has an optimum temperature for rapid multiplication, *ie* growth.

Thermophilic organisms, usually bacteria, grow best at 50–70C and they are usually very heat-resistant. Chilled storage will completely inhibit these organisms. The *mesophilic organisms* have optimum growth in the range 20-40C and are common spoilage organisms of food. Generally they are inhibited in chilled stores but occasionally some can grow at 5C. The *psychrophilic* organisms are low temperature organisms growing rapidly at 0-10C and even below 0C if water is available. This group of micro-organisms includes a number of bacteria which readily spoil chilled foods. The growth of *Listeria* , a widespread pathogen capable of causing many diseases including meningitis, can be attributed to chilled temperatures.

Enzymes are similar to micro-organisms in having optimum temperatures or ranges for their activity. In figure 3.1 the typical shape of a curve showing enzyme activity against temperature can be seen. Like micro-organisms some enzymes are active at chilled temperatures and cause changes in the product particularly in flavour, colour and texture.

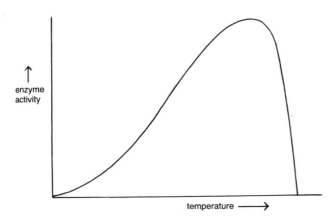

Figure 3.1
Enzyme activity and temperature

It is essential to chill food as quickly as possible and keep it chilled. Chilled foods must be handled hygienically and with care to avoid damage such as bruising.

Chilling is **not** freezing, as in the latter case water in the food is frozen and the temperature of the frozen food will be well below freezing point.

During *storage* chilled products gradually deteriorate and any quality loss cannot later be recovered during processing. The storage of chilled products, whether in a factory or in the home, is subject to certain commonsense rules. Raw meat, fish or poultry should be stored so they do not drip on to other foods, particularly those which have been cooked or processed and will be eaten without further cooking. Leafy vegetables should be covered or packed in such a way as to control the loss of moisture by evaporation. Prepared salads such as cole-slaw can also dehydrate readily. The domestic refrigerator is similar to the factory chill-store, but on a smaller scale, and generally maintains a temperature of 7C or over.

Although many raw materials are stored in a chilled form before further processing, there is a large sale of fresh chilled foods which have not been processed further. The *Food Labelling Regulations require chilled foods,* among others, to be labelled with either, 'sell by' or 'best before' dates on the package. The 'sell by' date is the latest recommended date of sale of the food, and also includes an indication of the period after purchase for which the food will retain its freshness, if stored according to the instructions supplied. The 'best before' date is the date up to which the food can be expected to retain its freshness and eating qualities. It must be remembered that those dates are approximations, as the food does not suddenly become unpalatable but gradually deteriorates.

CONTROLLED ATMOSPHERE STORAGE

Gas storage, in addition to chilling, can greatly extend the storage life of many food materials. Controlled atmosphere (CA) and modified atmosphere (MA) have been discussed for use with fruits and vegetables. Other products can benefit from the addition of about 10% carbon dioxide to the store, as it is particularly effective against moulds and some bacteria. Chilled beef will keep for longer periods if 10-15% carbon dioxide is added to the store. Higher concentrations, however, cause the meat to lose its bright red colour due to the loss of oxymyoglobin in the diminished concentration of oxygen. Myoglobin and possibly brown metmyoglobin is produced which changes the meat to dull red and brown.

Eggs can be stored with only about 2?% added carbon dioxide. This reduces the loss of carbon dioxide from the eggs and the corresponding rise in pH is inhibited, thus retarding changes leading to lower quality.

Hypobaric storage (low pressure) has been used for a range of products. However, it is very expensive and similar results can be obtained using cheaper CA methods.

FROZEN STORAGE

Food products must be frozen quickly and maintained at an even, low temperature during storage. The freezing techniques and the effects on food quality are reviewed later.

In the factory the cold-store corresponds to the domestic freezer. After being frozen quickly by some freezing technique (see section on freezing) the product must be stored in a cold-store at the recommended temperature. Ideally, the lower the temperature of the store the better the quality of the product after thawing. A temperature of –29C has been found to give better results with most food materials, compared with a temperature of –18C, which used to be in widespread usage.

If the temperature of storage is allowed to fluctuate a number of problems can develop. AT –18C it has been found that a temperature fluctuation of ±3C caused green vegetables to start to change to a dull greyish colour due to pheophytin production from chlorophyll.

Similarly mince beef was found to start to become rancid.

Fluctuating temperatures also cause loss of weight of the product as ice will sublime to water vapour. If the product is well packed the water vapour may condense and refreeze on the inside of the packaging material, producing frost, which falls out when the package is opened. This is frequently seen in domestic freezers and with products such as frozen bread. In exposed areas of a food, particularly in meat and fish, the water vapour will leave the surface of the product and cause local dehydration: curiously this dehydration is called 'freezer-burn'. Freezer-burn results in discolouration, texture changes and poorer eating quality. Surprisingly, many enzymes are active during the frozen storage and can produce changes in colour, flavour and texture in the food. Enzymes must be inactivated by blanching to prevent this occurring. However, recent work has shown that blanching can only inactivate some enzymes for a limited period and they are able to reactivate themselves during frozen storage.

When storing foods in a factory cold-store or a domestic freezer care must be taken to avoid tainting. Some foods, even when frozen, give out odours, which are picked up by other foods, thus tainting them. It is estimated that only about 15% of all causes of tainting of frozen foods are discovered. The reason probably for this is that the taint may produce some off flavour which might be described only as mousy, cat-like, mushroom like and so on! Highly spiced foods, meats, fish and many fruit products give off odours, whereas fats, particularly butter, meat and egg products, readily pick up odours. Good housekeeping is therefore essential when storing frozen food to prevent odour transfers.

Chapter 2

Cleaning, Sorting and Grading

PREVIEW

- **Cleaning**

  can be with or without water

  contamination of food with stones, leaves, twigs and animal parts has increased due to mechanisation of harvesting

  use of chemicals in growing crops has increased chemical contamination

  cleaning is a separation process

  screening used extensively to separate soil and stones from food

  very dusty process but cheap and efficient

  aspiration using air blast to remove lighter particles from food

  water must be hygienic for wet cleaning techniques such as soaking spraying and flotation washing

- **Sorting**

  one characteristic considering such as size, weight or colour

  sorted foods better for mechanised operations, essential where heat transfer processes are used

  sorted foods easier to handle and pack into supermarket containers

- **Grading**

  quality separation

  a number of factors must be considered simultaneously such as shape colour, size, freedom from damage and contamination

  rarely will one attribute indicate quality

CLEANING OF FOOD RAW MATERIAL

If a particular crop is harvested by hand the picker is usually very careful to avoid anything other than the particular food material. Other parts of the plant such as twigs, leaves and flowers are avoided. Similarly the picker will ensure that the product is not contaminated with stones, earth, string, weeds and obviously not insects, excreta or small animals. *Mechanised picking machines and combined-harvesters* although efficient do pick up some contamination. In addition the machines can on rare occasions lose nuts and bolts, and drop grease or oil on to the food. Modern agricultural techniques make use of insecticides, herbicides and many fertilizers, all of which can leave residues on the food factory.

Cleaning is a *separation process* as the contamination has to be separated from the food. This separation can be achieved with or without water, but generally several stages are necessary to ensure that a product is thoroughly clean.

Cleaning *without using water* usually takes the form of sieving or screening any contamination from the product. Screens of different sizes can be used to separate large and small particles from the food material. This method of cleaning is cheap and fairly efficient, but with very dusty products there is a risk of recontamination from dust in the air. Like most continuous processes, continuous screening is more efficient and less labour intensive. In Figure 3.2 a continuous drum screen is shown in a simplified form.

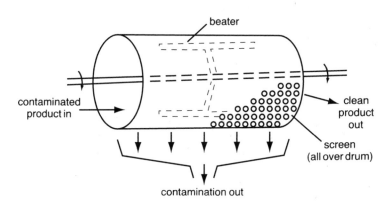

Figure 3.2

Continuous drum screen

Root vegetables can be partially cleaned by rotating brushes which remove dried soil. *Aspiration* or winnowing is a development of the ancient process of throwing chaff and grain into the wind to separate then after threshing. The process depends on a strong upward air-current and the fact that the product and contaminants will have different buoyancies in this air stream.

Modern harvesting equipment has increased the occurrence of pieces of metal contaminating food materials. Should this metal reach the consumer in a prepared food product the manufacturer would be subject to a heavy fine. Magnetic material can be removed by powerful magnets, but aluminium and

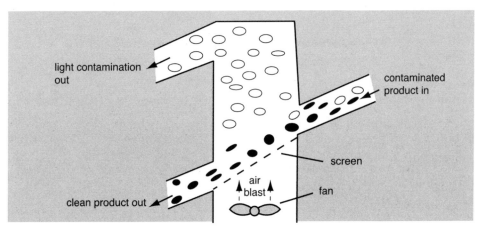

Figure 3.3

Aspiration

stainless steel, commonly found in food processing equipment, are non-magnetic. Metal detectors must be employed, therefore, to look for non-magnetic metals in the food.

When *water* is used for cleaning it obviously must be free from contamination itself and should be free from bacteria and chemical contamination. Unfortunately in some parts of the world this is not the case and food products may become infected with typhoid, cholera and other diseases, and sometimes with poisonous chemical residues.

Heavily soiled vegetables can be *soaked* in water as a preliminary to further cleaning. The efficiency of soaking can be improved by agitation of the water. Spray washing is one of the most widely used methods of wet cleaning. A small volume of water at high pressure is used as the force of the spray cleans the food and it is not just a washing process with water running over the product.

Figure 3.4

Spraying washing

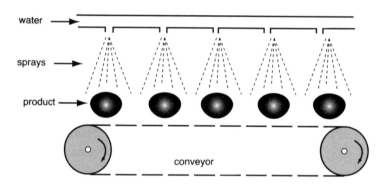

More complicated washing systems are used in some factories, for example, *flotation washing*. This system depends on a difference in buoyancy in water between the food and the contaminants. The food passes through a number of weirs and is forced under the water by slowly rotating paddles.

Figure 3.5

Flotation washing

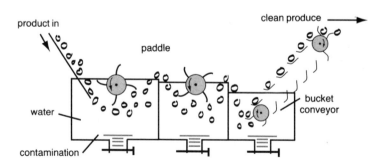

Generally a food material cannot be cleaned by just one method and it is necessary to employ perhaps three different methods to ensure that the product is properly cleaned. This is the first process involved in preparing a convenience food.

SORTING AND GRADING

Like cleaning, sorting and grading are separation processes; sometimes, similar equipment may be used, for example, screens are used to sort by size. *Sorting* should be reserved for the process of separating foods into categories of a single physical property, such as size, shape, colour or weight. *Grading* is quality separation and a number of factors may have to be assessed before a food can be graded into a certain category of quality.

SORTING

If individual food products are required to be processed mechanically then the job is made much easier if the food items are all of the same size. Filleting of fish can be performed mechanically, but fish must be of the same size, otherwise only a small fillet will be obtained from one fish and a large fillet from another including undesirable parts of the gut. Vegetables and fruit particularly can be sold in a supermarket in small trays and stretch-wrapped. Items, which have been sorted into similar categories of size or weight, are much easier to pack in such containers.

In processing involving heat penetration, such as blanching and canning, or in processes involving heat loss, such as chilling and freezing, uniformity of size is important. Large food items will be underprocessed and small items may be overprocessed.

Many fresh food items sold in supermarkets, such as meat cuts, are automatically sorted by *weight*, packaged and labelled. Small vegetables such as peas and beans, eggs, fruits and nuts are often sorted by weight.

A number of food raw materials are sorted according to *size* and a range of screens can be employed to do this. Round items are best suited to this type of process and they must be able to withstand quite rough handling. Fruits are often sorted by size, but care must be exercised to avoid bruising.

The natural *colour* variation of food products is normally acceptable to the consumer; however, discolouration due to rots, bruising and bad handling is not acceptable. Sometimes growing conditions and bad weather produce products with a lot of discolouration. Sorting by colour was carried out extensively using trained operatives in a tedious, labour-intensive manner. Unfortunately, this still cannot be avoided for some products. However, the process can be carried out mechanically employing a complex electronic system using photoelectric cells which compare the colour of the product with a standard colour background. Any of the products not matching the background are rejected, usually by a blast of compressed air. The method has been used successfully for many products, including dried peas, rice, coffee beans, grain, potatoes and onions.

GRADING

Grading is separation into different categories according to the overall quality of the food. The term 'quality' is somewhat subjective as what is good eating quality in a product for one person may not be for another. Take apples, for example; some people would consider an apple as good quality if it is firm and slightly acidic, whereas others consider a good eating apple to be soft, juicy and sweet. A good quality fruit for jam-making much be rich in pectin, but a fruit for juice production must be low in pectin, soft and juicy. In this case quality is dependent on the final end-use of the product. Normally the quality of a food cannot be judged by examining one aspect only. A number of factors have to be considered simultaneously to assess the food's quality, and obviously it is virtually impossible to mechanise this operation.

First quality food products must be free from damage, contamination and undesirable parts of the raw material, and must be within a specified range of shape, size and colour. Texture also is an important factor in determining quality in such products as some fruits, vegetables, cakes and potato crisps.

Chapter 3
Size Reduction and Mixing

PREVIEW

- **Size reduction**

  - important in a number of processes as original material may be too large or wrong shape

  - crushing – preliminary to other size-reduction processes

  - grinding processes common, eg use of hammer, disc, pin and ball mills

  - mills rely on fragility of product and are of no use for fibrous material, eg slicing, dicing and also shredding and pulping may be used for some products

- **Mixing**

  - the closer the particles are in size the easier the mixing process. Large particles are difficult to mix with small particles

  - liquids easier to mix

  - emulsification is necessary for liquids which are immiscible

  - homogenisation involves reduction of the droplet size of one liquid

  - when mixing liquids, turbulence should be encouraged

  - powder and particle mixers rely on displacing parts of the mix in relation to other parts by some form of agitation

  - tumbler mixer or ribbon mixers are common

  - doughs and pastes require powerful mixers with heavy mixing elements

  - pressure homogeniser used for liquids, colloid mill for homogenising pastes

SIZE REDUCTION

If you look at many packet, tinned and frozen foods you will notice the products are not in the original size and shape but have been reduced or modified into a different shape. Obviously it is impossible to can a whole pineapple; make fish fingers from a whole fish, or bottle a fruit and call it juice. Size reduction plays an important role in the preparation of convenience foods and in preparing raw materials for other processes such as juice extraction.

We have seen in the processing of wheat into flour that the grain is *crushed* between grooved and then smooth rollers. Crushing is only used as a preliminary stage to further size reduction, but *grinding processes* are much more common. Special grinding machines include hammer, disc, pin and ball mills.

The *hammer mill* (Figure 3.6) is useful in shattering fragile material into small fragments. It is probable that this size reduction occurs in two stages. Firstly, the product fractures along existing fissures and defects, and then secondly new fissures are formed, followed by fracture along these fissures.

Disc mills use rotating discs with studs to break the product and *pin mills* use rotating plates with a large number of short metal rods and pins. *Ball mills* are tumbling mills consisting of a drum containing balls or rods which crush the product as the drum rotates. (Figure 3.7).

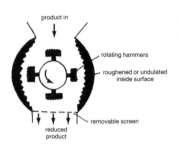

Figure 3.6 (above)

Hammer mill

Figure 3.7 (right)

Ball mill

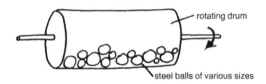

These types of mills rely on the fragility of the product and are totally ineffective for any fibrous, elastic or viscous product.

Fibrous materials have to be cut and cannot be reduced in size by crushing or impact. Sharp knife edges or saws are employed. Rotary cutting knives are often used for slicing meat products, fruit and some vegetables. Often slices are further reduced into cubes by the process of *dicing* in which cross-knives are used. Diced meat and vegetables are used in soups, dried products and some prepared complete meals.

Sometimes a food material is *shredded* as a preliminary operation to dehydration, where the large surface area aids the rate of water loss. Lower grade fruit is often *pulped* by high speed paddles, and is then used in jam-making or frozen for future use.

MIXING

If you look at the list of ingredients on the side of a packet of dried vegetable soup you will see that there may be twelve or more different ingredients. If you open the packet you will notice large, medium and small particles of dried vegetables and a lot of powder. To blend these ingredients into a uniform mix is extremely difficult. The closer the particles are in size the easier the mixing process and the more difficult it becomes as particle sizes vary. Large variations in particle sizes can result in 'demixing' during a blending operation, so after a period of time the product may be less uniform than it was earlier in the process. When small quantities of one component have to be blended uniformly into large quantities of other components, some pre-mixing of the smaller component will be necessary in part of the larger component.

Liquids obviously do not have these problems of particle size and, therefore, mix easily when they are miscible. Some liquids separate out after mixing, *eg* oils and water and therefore *emulsification* is necessary. *Homogenisation* goes further than emulsification and is a mixing process combined with size reduction, as the dispersed liquid droplets are reduced in size in the crude emulsion and are mixed uniformly.

MIXING EQUIPMENT

Mixing machines are very diverse and some are very specialized, for example, dough mixers. Some mixers have more widespread uses and the mixing parts or *elements* can be interchanged, such as those on a kitchen mixer. *Liquid mixers* are designed to stir liquid, but not in a regular flow pattern. When stirring a liquid in a bowl with a spoon it is normal to reverse the stirring action every few minutes in order to cause turbulence and thus better mixing. This idea is practical in large-scale mixing, but baffles have to be used to obtain the turbulence, as shown in Figure 3.8.

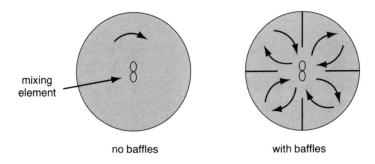

mixing element

no baffles   with baffles

Figure 3.8
Turbulence in mixing liquids

The high speed propeller mixer is probably the most commonly used mixer for liquids, and is mounted off-centre in the mixing vessel to obtain turbulence (Figure 3.9).

Powder and *particle* mixers rely on displacing parts of the mix in relation to other parts by some form of agitation. *Tumbler mixers* are used commonly for this purpose and revolve rapidly to tumble the mix. These mixers come in many shapes from cubes to double cones.

The *ribbon blender* is often used for dry mixes such as dried soups, instant dessert and bakery products. The mixer consists of a trough in which rotates a shaft with

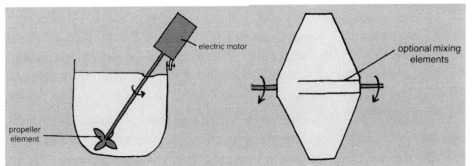

electric motor

optional mixing elements

propeller element

Figure 3.9 (left)
Propeller mixer

Figure 3.10 (right)
Tumbler mixer

two helical screws, one screw being left-handed and the other right-handed. As the mixer operates one screw takes the mix in one direction while the other screw tries to bring the mix back again. Thus, thorough mixing is achieved.

Doughs and pasts are very difficult to mix because of their high viscosity, and mixers must be powerful with mixing elements capable of reaching all the 'dead spots' of the mixing vessel. This can be seen by observing the action of a dough-hook attachment for a kitchen mixer. 'Z'-blade mixers are used for pastes in the food industry and consist of heavy mixing elements in the form of a 'Z' which twist in and out of the path of each other.

HOMOGENISATION

During homogenisation two liquids are mixed and the particle size of one liquid, usually a fat, is reduced and then dispersed in the other liquid. Often an emulsifier is also needed to ensure long-term stability of the emulsion which is produced. In the case of homogenised milk (Section 2.1.1.2) the emulsifying system is naturally occurring.

To break down the liquid droplets the crude emulsion is forced through a narrow opening at high velocity. A *pressure homogeniser* is used for this and consists of a homogenising valve, or often two valves, and a high pressure pump (Figure 3.11).

Figure 3.11

Pressure homogeniser

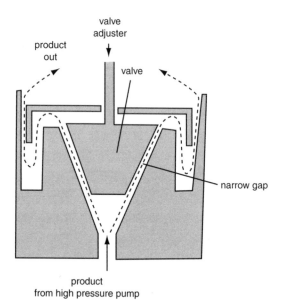

This type of homogeniser cannot be used for more viscous materials. The *colloid mill* can be used to homogenise more viscous products, such as mayonnaise. A rough or corrugated rotor revolves and the material passes between this rotor and the side of the mill through a very narrow gap. Homogenisation is thus achieved by this 'grinding action' in the limited space between the rotor and the side of the mill.

Chapter 4
Filtration and Blanching

PREVIEW

- **Filtration**

  - separation of solid from liquid

  - clarification to remove small quantities of solid from a liquid

  - filtrate liquid passing through filter medium, solids remaining referred to as filter cake

  - filter media include fabrics, paper, sand, porous carbon and porcelain

  - filter aids, large inert particles speed up filtration

  - plate and frame press common pressure filter

  - continuous rotary drum filter – works by vacuum to draw filtrate through medium

  - centrifugation alternative to filtration

- **Blanching**

  - purpose to inactivate enzymes as they can damage product during canning, freezing and drying

  - also blanching causes shrinkage by expelling air and some water

  - blanching also cleans product, may improve texture and colour

  - efficiency checked by peroxidase test

  - water-blanching can cause loss of soluble materials, eg water-soluble vitamins

  - additives, eg ascorbic acid, may be added to blanching water

  - steam blanching does not cause losses due to leaching

  - microwave blanching new development

FILTRATION

Filtration in the food industry involves a very wide range of applications in separating liquids from solids. Sometimes the solid is retained for further processing, sometimes the liquid. In the process of *clarification*, filtration is carried out to remove small quantities of solid from a liquid, *eg* finely suspended material from wines.

Some terms used in filtration can be confusing. The *filtrate* is the liquid which passes through the filter and the filter membrane itself is referred to as the *filter medium*. Separated solids accumulate on the filter medium and these solids can be referred to as the *filter cake* or filter residue.

Filter media include fabrics, such as cotton, silk and nylon, paper, sand, charcoal, porous carbon and porcelain. The type used often depends on a particular application. The holes in the medium will vary in size in some materials, but can readily be blocked by solid particles during filtration. For this reason *filter aids* are often used. Filter aids consist of large particles of unreactive material, such as paper pulp and Kieselguhr, which form a lattice-like structure on the medium. The liquid can freely run through the lattice as the holes remain clear in the medium.

Figure 3.12

Action of a filter aid

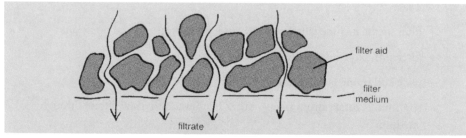

Figure 3.13

Section of a plate-and-frame press

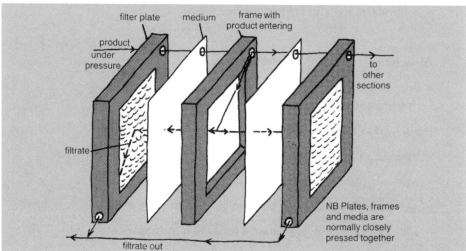

A very common filter used in many food industries is the *plate-and-frame press* (figure 3.13). Special plates covered with filter medium alternate with hallow frames in a special rack. The plates, media and frames are squeezed together by an adjustable screw. The liquid to be filtered enters the frame and the solids build up on the medium while the pressure applied to the filter forces the liquid through the medium on to the plate. This is repeated in a number of sections in the filter.

As an alternative to applying pressure to speed up the filtration process, a vacuum may be applied to help draw the filtrate through the medium. *Continuous rotary drum vacuum filters* are commonly used as they are continuous and cheap to operate.

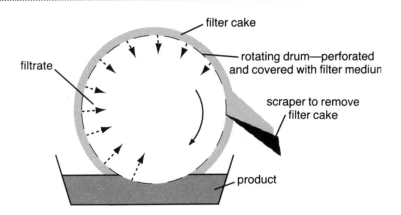

Figure 3.14
Rotary drum vacuum filter

CENTRIFUGATION

Instead of removing solid particles from a liquid by filtration, they may be removed in many cases by centrifugation. One application is in the separation of cream from milk. Centrifuges are used in purifying oils, clarification of beer, separation of yeast and in sugar refining.

BLANCHING

Blanching is a necessary preliminary operation in the preparation of vegetables for canning, freezing or drying. There are a number of purposes for blanching. *Enzymes* must be inactivated by blanching before further heat processing otherwise they may cause flavour, texture and colour changes in the product. During canning, for example, until the temperature reaches a high enough level to inactivate the enzymes they will be extremely active.

It is, therefore, desirable to inactivate them by blanching before canning. In frozen products many enzymes show some activity, although often only slight in some products. This activity is enough to cause a loss in quality of a stored frozen product. (See section on physiologically active proteins) Animal products are not blanched as enzymes are necessary to produce the desired flavour and sometimes texture. Fruits are rarely blanched since losses of volatile flavour compounds may be more critical than changes produced by subsequent enzyme activity.

An equally important aspect of blanching is the *shrinkage* it produces in a product, usually by the expulsion of trapped air or gases and the loss of some water. Mushrooms illustrate this problem well, as they contain much trapped air. If they are canned without blanching, the air is expelled in the can so that the can appears to be one-third or fewer mushrooms, one-third water and the rest air. Blanching reduces the mushrooms in size and expels most of the air. The filled mushrooms in the can still show some shrinkage during heat processing, but considerably less than previously. Cooking of mushrooms, of course, causes considerable contraction, so canned mushrooms should be compared with the normal cooked product.

Blanching has a number of side effects, some of which are beneficial, some deleterious. Blanching will help clean the product and will reduce the bacterial population. However, if the product is left wet and warm, bacteria will multiply rapidly and may exceed their original numbers before further processing. In the case of some products, texture and colour are improved by blanching. Undesirable changes include losses in heat-labile nutrients, particularly vitamins may be lost by leaching.

In blanching, foods are heated rapidly to a certain temperature, normally near 100C, for the required time, then cooled quickly, or processed further without delay.

BLANCHING METHODS

The food material is dipped into *hot* or *boiling* water for a short period, usually 30 seconds to three or four minutes. In continuous blanchers the material passes through the water on a moving belt or rotating screw. The combination of time of blanching and the temperature is dependent on the size of the food material. The *peroxidase test* (see enzymes) is used to determine the efficiency of blanching. Water blanching can cause high losses of soluble material in some products. In other cases additives can be placed in the blanching water to improve the product; these have included sulphites, citric acid and ascorbic acid (vitamin C).

Steam blanching uses saturated steam in a closed vessel through which the food is conveyed, usually by a rotating screw. Steam blanching offers advantages over the previous method in reducing losses soluble material, but additives cannot be used. Other methods of blanching have been investigated and *microwave* blanching offers a possible alternative method.

Products frozen in a domestic freezer are often used within, perhaps, three months. The likelihood of any changes being caused by enzymes is fairly remote. Many home-grown vegetables are frozen whole, *eg* cauliflowers, and it is impossible to blanch them satisfactorily when this large. The commercial frozen food company perhaps takes up to a year to prepare, store and distribute its products. Enzyme changes can be considerable in this period. Hence the need to blanch products for commercial frozen storage.

PRACTICAL EXERCISES: *PREPARATION OF FOOD RAW MATERIALS*

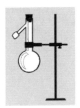

Frozen storage
Store samples of fish fillets in a freezer, both unpacked and packed well in polythene bags. Look for freezer-burn.

Cleaning
Use a sample of well-soiled carrots or potatoes.
(a) brush, with a small stiff brush, individual vegetables and note the inefficiency and difficult of the process.
(b) soak vegetables in cold water and note the time most soil is removed. Agitate the water and note improvement in cleaning.
(c) Attach a rubber tube or nozzle to a cold tap, squeeze and spray the vegetables with a blast of cold water. Rotate the vegetables whilst spraying and note the time necessary to obtain a clean product.

Sorting and grading
Examine a range of convenience foods and note evidence of sorting and grading. Establish those criteria used for the grading of a particular product.

Mixing
Weigh equal amounts of sugar (say 200g) and dried peas. Place in a large tin and seal. Shake for a few minutes. Remove a sample of the mixture and weigh. Separate out the peas and weigh. Repeat for varying lengths of time. The best mix is when the peas and sugar are in equal quantities. Repeat the experiment using a variety of mixing elements for a domestic mixer.

Filtration
Mix a sample of flour with water. Filter through normal filter paper. Note the filtering process becomes sluggish as the paper becomes blocked. Some starch will form a colloidal dispersion and pass through the filter. Repeat, adding a small amount of Kieselguhr to the mixture, note improved speed of filtration.

Blanching
Use a vegetable such as carrot or potato. Dice into ? cm3 cubes.
(a) Water blanching – boil a saucepan of water. Place equal quantities of dried vegetable into three small muslin bags. Dip these bags containing the vegetables into the boiling water for 1, 2 and 3 minutes respectively. Cool immediately in cold water. Test for peroxidase activity as detailed below.
(b) Steam blanching – fill a pressure cooker with water just below the level of the trivet and heat to boiling. Repeat as for water blanching by placing a small bag of vegetables in the pressure cooker and then putting the lid on but not the pressure weight. Repeat for 1, 2 and 3 minutes steaming.

(c) Microwave blanching – place a bag of vegetables in a microwave oven, and 'cook' for 1, 2 and 3 minutes. Test for peroxidase activity.

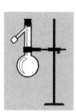

The peroxidase test

A spot of freshly prepared guaiacol solution (1%) is mixed with an equal volume of hydrogen peroxide (5 volume solution) and then placed on to the food. If peroxidase is still active in the vegetable a red/brown colour appears on the sample within one minute.

Section 4
PRESERVATION PROCESSES

If a food is not preserved by some method it will undergo spoilage by the action of micro-organisms and enzymes, and possibly by chemical reactions. Chemical reactions such as rancidity do not occur in all foods and are often a long-term spoilage. In most cases the preservation of a food is concerned with the destruction of spoilage organisms and enzymes, or in their inhibition over long periods of time. Heat processing is an example of the former in destroying organisms and enzymes by heat, and freezing is an example of the latter in that the organisms and enzymes can become active again on thawing.

Spoilage of foods by enzymes is often not so obvious, or as rapid, or such a potential health hazard as is spoilage caused by the growth of bacteria, fungi or other micro-organisms. A number of factors affect microbial growth and these can be made use of in the preservation of foods.

Exposing micro-organisms to *temperatures* above their maximum growth temperature will kill the cells of the organism, usually by denaturing the enzymes necessary for normal life functions. Some species produce very resistant spores which are difficult to destroy by heat. Temperatures below the minimum growth temperature of the organisms will retard growth (*ie* multiplication of cells) and freezing will halt growth completely. This is said to be *bacteriostatic* process, as opposed to a process such as canning, which kills the bacteria, hence *bacteriocidal*.

Micro-organisms require *water* for growth; however, some can grow at very low moisture levels. Removal of water from a food will inhibit the growth of organisms. Water can be removed by drying a food, but the water can also be made unavailable by freezing. Similarly, the addition of sugar and salt can deny micro-organisms their requirements for water by osmotic effects.

There are a number of products that are preserved by lowering of *pH*. These include products where acid is added, *eg* pickles, or where acid is produced by fermentation, *eg* cheese, yoghurt and some pickles.

Some bacteria require *oxygen* to survive and similarly most fungi require oxygen. Some organisms, however, grow in the absence of oxygen, and some actually cannot grow in its presence. Organisms requiring oxygen are inhibited in a number of processes, such as canning, gas-packing and vacuum-packing by ensuring all oxygen is removed.

A range of chemical substances is permitted for use as *preservatives*. Antibiotics were once used for this purpose, but it was soon realised that bacteria could become immune to these substances, and could, on occasions, pass on this immunity to disease-causing organisms.

Micro-organisms can be destroyed or severely inhibited by a range of *radiation sources,* in much the same way as any living organism.

Preservation of food sometimes relies on making use of more than one of these factors. Heat processing of canned foods which are acidic is normally less severe because of the lower pH.

Preserved foods must be packed into containers that prevent their recontamination. For this reason food packaging is included in this section.

Chapter 1
Heat Processing

PREVIEW

- **Preservation processes in general**
  - food spoil by action of micro-organisms, enzymes and chemicals
  - number of factors affect microbial growth:
    - (a) temperature
    - (b) water
    - (c) oxygen
    - (d) pH
    - (e) preservatives
    - (f) radiations

- **Heat processing**
  - foods preserved by application of sufficient heat to kill micro-organisms and enzymes
  - but pasteurization kills all pathogens and some spoilage organisms
  - sterilization more severe, kills all cells and more spores
  - 'commercial sterility' achieved in canning as some spores may survive
  - severity of heat treatment lessened in the presence of acid or osmotically active substances such as sugar
  - Clostridium botulinum – dangerous food-poisoning organism – inhibited usually below pH 4.5
  - low acid foods pH 4.5 or higher require sterilisation
  - acid foods pH 4.5 down to 3.7 require pasteurization
  - high acid foods pH below 3.7 require blanching only

- **The heat process**
  - 'cold point' part of can which is slowest to heat up
  - in solid packs heat transfer is by conduction
  - in liquid packs heat transfer is by convection
  - combinations of temperature and time required to kill organisms
  - higher temperature = shorter time
  - Decimal reduction time or D value is time to reduce spores to 1/10 of original level
  - F value is the number of minutes at 121C which will have a sterilizing effect equivalent to that of the process

• The canning process

- pack food into container, seal then heat process until contents are 'commercially sterile'
- canning process must include:
  - **(1)** cleaning of raw material
  - **(2)** blanching
  - **(3)** filling – addition of brine or sauce
  - **(4)** sealing – double seam formed
  - **(5)** sterilization – in retorts
  - **(6)** cooling
  - **(7)** labelling

- retorts operate usually at 121C
- all air must be expelled before processing to avoid pockets of air where under-processing will occur
- cooling water must be chlorinated to avoid 'leaker-spoilage'
- sterilisable pouches (laminates of foil and plastics) and toughened glass alternative for cans
- aseptic packaging – product sterilised by high temperature, short time process then filled into sterilized containers under sterile conditions
- cans may spoil if under-pressure, as spores will survive to produce gas, souring or sulphide discolouration
- 'leaker-spoilage' may occur if seams damaged or can is dented – any organism can be involved

Foods can be preserved by the application of heat in sufficient quantity to kill all micro-organisms and to inactivate all enzymes. There are, in fact, two levels of heat processing dependent on combinations of temperature and time. *Pasteurisation* is heat processing designed to kill all pathogenic organisms, and in so doing to kill most spoilage organisms. This extends the storage life of the product a little but makes it bacteriologically safe.

Sterilisation is a much more severe heat process aimed to destroy all micro-organisms. Absolute sterility is difficult to obtain as some bacterial spores may survive the process. *Commercial sterility* is the state achieved in most canning processes, and is heat processing designed to kill virtually all micro-organisms, and most spores, which would be capable of growing during storage.

The severity of the heat treatment of food to be preserved can be lessened if the food contains acid or osmotically active substances such as salt or sugar. Acidity is the most important factor affecting heat processing and its inhibiting effect on spoilage organisms starts at about pH 5.3. The presence of larger than usual amounts of fat, starch or sugar has been shown on occasions to protect micro-organisms at lower pH values than 5.3. The most important pH is 4.5, as below this pH the very dangerous organism *Clostridium botulinum* is inhibited. However, certain strains of the organism have survived lower pH values. The bacterium produces a very powerful toxin, if it survives heat processing of a canned food. The toxin has a mortality rate of about 70%. The spores of *Cl.botulinum* are very heat resistant and the canning industry is designed to ensure their elimination in canned foods.

Low acid foods have pH values of 4.5 of higher, and must be sterilized during heat processing. *Acid foods* have pH values of 4.5 down to 3.7 and a less severe pasteurization process will be sufficient to preserve them. At pH values below 3.7 only few fungi can grow and in most cases the food can be considered a *high acid* food which may only require blanching to inactivate enzymes.

Foods must be heat processed in a container which will not be affected by heat and one which is sealed to prevent recontamination of the product. Traditionally foods were heat processed in cans and glass bottles, but now there is a rapid growth of pouches made of foil, plastics and special laminates capable of withstanding the process.

THE HEAT PROCESS

If you look at the vast range of canned products you will notice that some contain liquid foods, *eg* soups; some solids suspended in liquids, *eg* canned peas; and some are completely solid *eg* some canned meats. In the heat process the right quantity of heat must penetrate the can and its contents as far as the point in the can which is known as the 'cold point'. In a *solid pack* such as canned meat the cold point is on the centre of the can and heat takes a long time to reach this point by the process of *conduction*. In the case of a *liquid pack,* such as soup, convection currents ensure rapid heat penetration into the product, and the cold point is moved slightly from the centre of the can.

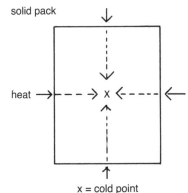

x = cold point

If a special thermocouple (thermometer) is inserted at the cold point of a can the temperature history of the can may be recorded throughout the sterilization process.

As the food is heated the slope of the graph will be steeper if the food is a liquid pack until the holding temperature is reached, the plateau part of the graph. Usually, the holding temperature is 121C, but a lower temperature is used for acid foods.

Some organisms, especially those of the genera *Bacillus* and *Clostridium*, produce heat- resistant spores. Some of these spores may survive the heat process to germinate and grow in the food to spoil it or produce toxic substances. *Cl.botulinum*, as mentioned above, produces a powerful toxin and is, therefore, used as an indicator organism in canning processes.

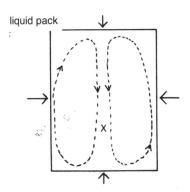

Figure 4.1

Heat penetration into cans

Like other organisms and spores, the spores of *Cl.botulinum* are destroyed by

Figure 4.2

Temperature history in heat processing a canned food

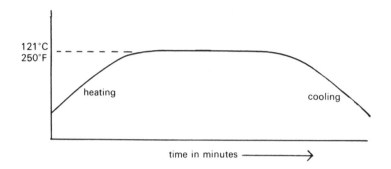

heat at rates which depend on the temperature. At higher temperatures the rate of spore destruction is greater, and at lower temperatures spores are killed more slowly.

However, at any given temperature the spores are more heat resistant than others. It can take a very long time at a certain temperature to destroy all spores and so a statistical approach is taken in evaluating the heat process and the heat resistance of organisms.

At a certain temperature, usually 121C, after a period of time, 90% of the spores will have been killed and after a further similar length of time, 90% of the remaining spores will be killed, *ie* 1000 spores will be reduced to 100, then 100 spores to 10. This period of time is known as the *decimal reduction time* or *D value*. At a higher temperature a shorter time or D value will be required to kill 90% of the spores. In Figure 4.2 the warming up, holding and cooling periods of the combination of time and temperature can be calculated and added together to give the F_0 *value* of the process. The F_0 value denotes the sterilizing value of the process and is defined as the number of minutes at 121C which will have a sterilizing effect equivalent to that of the process. F_0 values will depend on the nature of the product and the size of the can involved, for example, beans in tomato sauce require F_0 values from 4-6 minutes, while meat in gravy requires an F_0 value of 12-15 minutes.

THE CANNING PROCESS

The traditional canning process involves packing the food into a container, and then heating the container until its content are 'commercially sterile'. Canning cannot improve the quality of a food raw material and at the very best can only maintain the harvested quality of the product. In general, however, there is a decrease in the quality of the product, which is often only slight using modern techniques. Unfortunately, in many parts of the world canned foods have a poor reputation, which is due in most cases to the use of low quality raw materials.

Canned foods are convenience foods and are intended to be ready to eat. Food raw materials must be cleaned effectively and free from all contaminants and inedible parts. The microbial load must be kept as low as possible before heat processing to minimise the risk of contamination with heat resistant spores. Canned foods usually require some size reduction, such as slicing or dicing.

Blanching must be carried out quickly after size reduction to avoid enzymic reactions, particularly browning reactions. The main purposes of blanching, in canning are to expel air and shrink the product and to inactivate enzymes. After blanching the product is filled automatically either by weight or volume into the cans. Often with vegetables a 1-2% brine is added, which may contain other additives such as citric acid, colour and flavour compounds. Sometimes a sauce is added with a complex mixture of thickening agents, spices and herbs. The food is filled whilst hot and usually right to the top of the can.

The cans are passed to a special seamer where a vacuum is applied to draw out air from the can as the lid is sealed into place. A double seam is employed and involves rolling the 'hook' of the lid under the hook of the body of the can and then pressing it flat.

Usually some of the product spills out of the can and on to the outside during sealings, and this must be washed off. The cans are then heat processed in a retort (or autoclave) which is effectively a large pressure cooker.

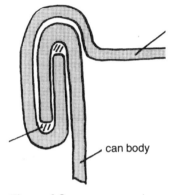

Figure 4.3
Double seam on can rim

The cans are usually placed in baskets that are lifted or wheeled on trolleys into the retort. The retort is closed and steam is allowed to enter. All air must be driven out of the retort by the steam, in much the same way as air is driven out of a pressure cooker. When steam is coming out freely from the vents of the retort all air is expelled. Any air pockets between cans will cause under-exposure to the heat which might result in dangerous bacteria surviving in a can. The vents of the retort are closed, and the pressure rises in the retort, usually to 15 psi/1bar, which corresponds to a temperature of 121C. After holding at this temperature for the required processing time the cans are cooled by spraying with cold water. Sudden application of cold water will cause the steam to condense too rapidly and the pressure developed in the can, which is equal to the outside pressure of the steam, will push the can walls outwards and distort the shape of the can, straining its seams. For this reason, compressed air is supplied to the retort as cooling begins to avoid this sudden pressure drop. Cans are often removed from the retort after partial cooling and are passed through a bath of chlorinated water to cool them to about 40C. The remaining heat in the can dries off any residual water on the surface of the can after cooling and this prevents any rusting. Cans are then labeled with special printed labels. In many cases now the cans are printed before the process and so labeling is obviated.

Cans which have been heat-processed must be handled with care especially if still wet. As the contents of the can cool a very strong vacuum builds up in the can. If there is any defect in the can or seam a small amount of water from the outside of the can may be drawn into the can. This water may be contaminated with food poisoning organisms which can infect the food and cause an outbreak of food poisoning some time later. For this reason cooling water must be free from bacteria and should be chlorinated. A severe outbreak of typhoid was caused in Aberdeen when imported corned beef from Argentina had been infected by contaminated cooling water. The water used in the cooling bath for the large cans of corned beef was river water, from a river carrying typhoid organisms, and this water was not chlorinated.

Figure 4.4 is a typical flow diagram of a canning line, in this case showing canning of mushrooms. Other lines will be similar but with variations particularly in size-reduction and mixing equipment for sauces and other additions.

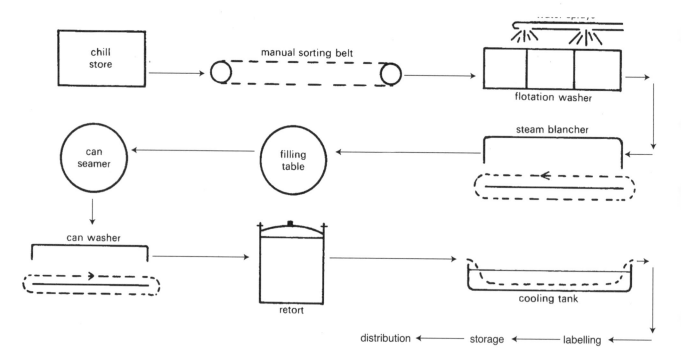

Figure 4.4

Canning mushrooms

Canning lines can readily be made continuous and very large throughputs can be obtained using continuous retorts. *Continuous* or *hydrostatic* retorts are extremely large and heads of water are used to maintain the pressure within the interior of the chamber of the retort.

STERILISABLE POUCHES AND GLASS

Tinplate for cans has become increasingly expensive, and although very thin plate is now used, the can is often more expensive than the food raw material. This has resulted in declining sales of canned foods, compared with frozen products, which have shown a corresponding increase in sales. The flexible pouch, which is often a special laminate of foil and plastics, is an alternative to the can and has other advantages. The pouches are flat and therefore allow more rapid heat penetration during the sterilization process and processing times may be reduced by as much as 50%. However, pouches can be damaged easily and are often difficult to seal. Rates of production of pouches, therefore, do not compare with traditional canning lines at the moment.

Glassmaking is one of the oldest technologies and use of glass in food preservation dates back to the 19th century. The most marked improvement in glass has been the production of lightweight but strong glass. Lightweight bottles, combined with widemouth closures, have resulted in a container, which can rival the can for vegetables, fruits, beer and soft drinks.

ASEPTIC PACKAGING

The problem of sterilizing milk, with particular reference to the production of a 'cooked- milk flavour', led to the development of the UHT process to sterilize the milk without causing the flavour changes. This technology can be applied to a range of products, which are rapidly sterilized then packaged into sterilized containers.

Aseptic packaging can be defined as the filling of a commercially sterilised product into a container, previously sterilized, and applying a sterilized seal in a sterile environment to obtain a hermetic seal. The food is heated to a high temperature of 150C for a short period of only a few minutes and the cooled. Direct injection of steam may be used for some products to obtain the same result. The sterilized product is filled into sterile cans, in a sterile environment, which are then hermetically sealed.

There are a number of plants operating this system for soups, ice-cream mixes and custards. Work is being carried out with the use of special micro-filters to remove bacteria and thus sterilize the product, where the product is particularly heat-sensitive.

SPOILAGE OF CANNED FOODS

In 1812 the firm Hall & Donkin (England) used tinplate to produce cans of roast veal. In 1818, some 46,000lb of these canned foods were purchased by the Admiralty. A few remaining cans were opened in 1938 and were found to be in perfect condition. However, on occasions cans, which were usually too large, were under-processed and food poisoning outbreaks resulted. It was not until 1922 that the current style of can was generally accepted.

Under-processing of cans now is a rarity, but trouble can occur due to the presence of very heat resistant spores. *Thermophilic gas spoilage* is caused by the growth of *Clostridium thermosaccharolyticum* which has particularly heat resistant spores. The organism produces large amounts of hydrogen which causes the can to bulge and even burst. Some bacteria can produce souring of products which are normally low in acid but without the obvious production of gas. *Bacillus stearothermophilus* is a common causative organism of this problem, which is only detected when the can is opened and the content tested. *Clostridium nigrificans* produces hydrogen sulphide which can blacken the contents of an under-processed can of non-acid foods. Sometimes, however, bulging of cans and some discolouration can be caused by natural acids in the food, for example, canned tomatoes often show some swelling.

Poor seams and can defects can lead to '*leaker spoilage*'. Unlike under-processed foods, even bacteria which show no heat resistance may contaminate the product. Bacteria entering the can may spoil the product and produce gas, causing the can to swell. Sometimes, harmful bacteria may grow in the product without any gas production. *Salmonella typhi* (typhoid) normally produces gas in cans so they can be discarded as obviously being infected. However, in the Aberdeen typhoid outbreak the nitrate of the corned beef inhibited the gas production and the organisms grew and eventually caused the outbreak of typhoid.

Damaged cans usually have experienced strain on their seams and organisms may have entered. Damaged cans should be avoided, as should any showing swelling.

PRACTICAL EXERCISES: *HEAT PROCESSING*

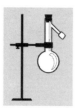

Heat penetration

Take a can of tomato soup and a can of meat (dog food will suffice), and remove lids. Suspend a thermometer or probe from digitial thermometer in the centre of the can contents, using a retort stand. Place the cans in a water bath and boil. Record the rise in temperature of the product against time, and plot a curve of heat penetration, with temperature against time in minutes.

Effect of metals on texture of heat processed vegetables

Make up solution (0.5litre) of sodium hydrogen carbonate (bicarbonate) and calcium chloride in strengths of 1%, 2%, 5% and 10%. Boil samples of vegetables such as peas, carrots or diced potatoes for one minute in each of these solutions and in water. Cover sample of each in a beaker and keep in a refrigerator for several days. Note any change in texture as the firming effect of calcium may take several days. Sodium samples should be noticeably softer.

Can examination

Examine the outside of the can and note body seams, reinforcement rings and labelling. Open the can and look for presence of lacquer on the inside of the body and the lid. Cut into the side of the can and cut across the double seam with a suitable saw. Examine the seam with a hand lens.

Chapter 2
Freezing

PREVIEW

- **Freezing**
  - preserves by :
    (1) low temperature
    (2) withdrawn water in the form of ice
  - dissolved substances lower freezing point below 0C, food begins to freeze at about –1C
  - thermal arrest period – the time the food takes to pass through the part of the freezing cycle where water is frozen into ice
  - slow freezing leads to low quality produce as water is withdrawn from the cells
  - large ice crystals form outside the cells; on thawing form 'drip'
  - rapid freezing produces small ice crystals, a higher quality product and less drip
  - 'quick freezing' – thermal arrest time as short as possible and product reduced to final temperature quickly
  - 'deep freezing' – average temperature of the product is reduced to -17.8C then kept at this temperature or lower
  - individually – quick – frozen (IQF)
  - individual freezing, eg of peas

- **Refrigeration cycle**
  - main system involves vapour compression
  - refrigerant takes up heat in evaporator from the food – vapour formed pumped away
  - compressed then condensed back to liquid
  - liquid passes to pressure release valve
  - enters evaporator and cycle is repeated

- **Freezing methods**
  (1) Immersion freezing – use brines or refrigerants
  (2) Plate freezing – freezing by contact with refrigerated plate, can be horizontal or vertical
  (3) Blast freezing – cold air blown on to food of any shape
      – temperature and speed of air control rate of freezing
      – fluidised bed-freezers use vertical blast of air
  (4) Cryogenic freezing – use of liquified gases at very low temperature, usually nitrogen or CO_2

• **The cold chain**

– frozen food has to travel down cold chain:

– freezer → bulk cold store →refrigerated

– vehicles → wholesalers → retailers → home

– heat gain at all points leading to quality loss

– display cabinets can be over filled and strip lighting can warm product

– product may thaw after purchase if journey home is too long

– star marking used to indicate storage life of a product and storage potential of an appliance

If foods to be frozen are placed in a cold store, a very poor quality product is produced. However, the quality of most frozen foods can, by careful control of the freezing process, be equal to that of the original 'fresh' food material.

Freezing preserves foods by two principles. The very low temperatures involved inhibit microbial growth, often causing the death of some organisms, and also retard the action of enzymes or chemicals. The production of ice during freezing causes water to be withdrawn from the food, and this dehydration effect also prevents microbial growth.

Most foods contain a large amount of water, which is normally in the form of solutions of sugar, salts, acids and other substances. These substances lower the freezing point of water and so food normally freezes at a temperature below 0C. During a freezing process, most foods begin to freeze at about –1C. It takes some time for all the water in a food to freeze, particularly in large items. As water is withdrawn to make ice crystals, the dissolved substances become more and more concentrated. The increase in concentration of the solutions in the food depresses the freezing point further. Often the temperature must fall to about -5C before most of the water is frozen. Even at this temperature concentrated solutions will remain unfrozen and may contain up to 20% of the original water. When no more ice crystals are formed, the food cools rapidly, usually to about –30C. This last part of the cycle (see Figure 4.5) is called 'tempering'.

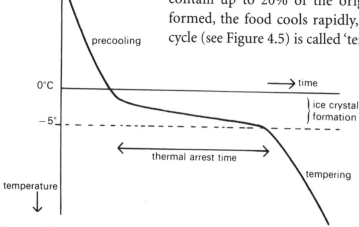

Figure 4.5

Freezing cycle of a food

The 'thermal arrest period' is the time the food takes to pass through the part of the cycle where water is frozen into ice (–1C to –5C). To produce high quality frozen foods it is necessary for this period to be as short as possible. The thermal arrest period will depend on the size of the product. For peas the period will be, perhaps, one second, but a side of beef may take 36 hours to pass through the period.

When plant materials are frozen, the solutions outside the cells freeze first of all as they are less concentrated than solutions inside the cell. Ice crystals begin to form in this way between the cells and steadily increase in size (see Figure 4.6). Slow freezing rates allow water to be withdrawn from the cells to form large ice crystals outside the cells.

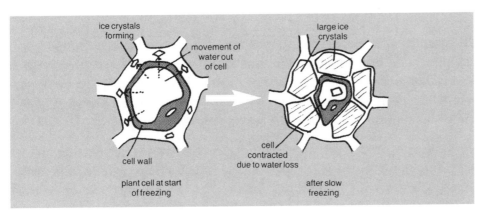

Figure 4.6

Ice crystal formation in plant products

The cells become dehydrated by this means, and on thawing they will be found to have lost all their turgor pressure and will be in a collapsed state. The large ice crystals outside the cells may push into the cells and cause some damage, but on thawing they will produce a lot of water, which is not within the cells, giving a very watery texture to the product. Slow freezing causes the concentration of substances in the cells because of this water loss, and these solutions may damage the proteins or other cellular constituents. If the temperature is lowered rapidly the water outside the cells is again first to freeze, but is rapidly followed by freezing of the water within the cells. Only small ice crystals are produced which do not cause concentration of solutions within the cells and the accompanying damage. On thawing the water produced from melting ice is still within the cells and the texture of the product is closer to that of the original product.

Fish and meat products do not have such an obvious cellular structure, but have different types of tissue. Water can be withdrawn in a similar manner from the tissues, and, on thawing, produces a pool of water around the product. This water is known as 'drip' and is noticeable in fish that has been frozen slowly.

The highest quality foods, therefore, must be frozen quickly and must have their final temperature as low as is practicable. The term 'quick-freezing' is a vague term which is often used. The term means that the thermal arrest period is as short as possible and the product is reduced to its final storage temperature quickly. For fish, which is quick-frozen, the thermal arrest period should be less then two hours and the final recommended temperature should be –30C.

Deep freezing has been defined by the **International Institute of Refrigeration** as a process whereby the average temperature of the product is reduced to –17.8C, then kept at this temperature or lower. This definition does not take into account the rate of freezing which can be slow producing a lower quality product.

An old term, '*sharp-freezing*', is misleading The rate of freezing is often very slow. In a domestic freezer this rate of freezing is sufficient if individual items are frozen on a tray, then packaged afterwards. Packing before freezing will result in a very slow freezing process.

In commercial freezing operations, high quality products are produced by adopting this individual freezing method, the products are referred to as *individual-quick-frozen* (IQF). The method is particularly useful for vegetables, such as peas, and berry-type fruits, such as raspberries. The IQF process is continuous, followed by packing into bags for supermarket sale.

Re-freezing of frozen products should always be avoided, as quality will fall each time the product is frozen. Bacteria, which often are only inhibited by freezing will begin to multiply in the thawed product and may reach dangerous levels. On re-freezing, then thawing again, levels of organisms may be high enough to cause food poisoning.

THE REFRIGERATION CYCLE

The most common system employed in freezers and other refrigeration systems is that of *vapour compression.* Refrigeration is generally understood to be the method of causing heat to flow in a direction which is not natural, for example, from a cold substance to a hotter one. This reversal of flow of heat is obtained using a *refrigerant,* which is a substance having a high latent heat capacity on changing state from gas to liquid and back again.

Exchange of heat occurs at two surfaces, an evaporator and a condenser. These surfaces are joined and connected to a compressor and expansion valve, as shown in Figure 4.7.

Liquid refrigerant takes up heat in the evaporator from the food to be frozen. The heat causes the refrigerant to evaporate and the vapour formed is pumped away from the evaporator by the compressor, where it is compressed, and then condensed back into liquid refrigerant in the condenser. The liquid passes round the circuit to the expansion valve which releases it into the evaporator to complete another cycle.

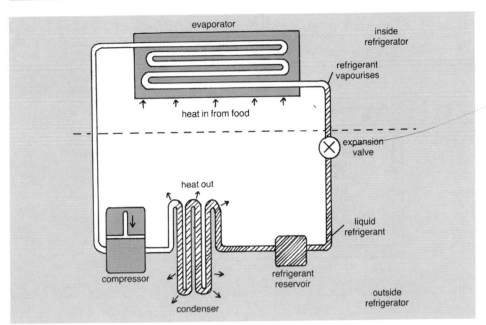

Figure 4.7

Vapour compression refrigeration cycle

Ammonia has been used extensively as a refrigerant, but the freon group of organic compounds is now used widely, particularly in smaller refrigeration systems.

FREEZING METHODS

Immersion-freezing was one of the first methods generally employed for freezing foods. It is a slow method with little control. Brines were prepared from salt and ice; as more and more ice was added the temperature fell to a suitable level for freezing. The food was then immersed in this brine for several hours. Modern methods have used refrigerants which have been sprayed onto the food. The method is little used as the following methods offer greater advantages.

Plate-freezing has played a major role on making available a wide range of frozen produce, and has only been replaced by other methods in the last few years for some products. The food is prepared in the normal way and is packed into a flat container, usually a cardboard-based container, often with a polythene or wax lining. The container is placed between flat, hollow, refrigerated metal plates and the plates are adjusted to press tightly against the pack. The method depends on contact between the pack and the freezing plate and any air gaps will slow heat transfer from the product, thus greatly increasing the freezing time.

The plates may be horizontal (see Figure 4.8) or vertical. The horizontal type was commonly used for many types of food products, but the vertical type is used mainly for bulk items. Vertical plate-freezers are often used on board trawlers for freezing fish fillets into blocks, which can be sawn up into fish fingers at a later stage.

Figure 4.8

Horizontal plate-freezer

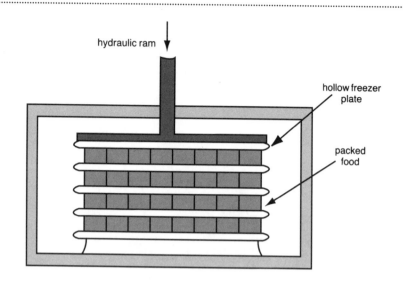

The main disadvantage of plate-freezers is that they cannot easily freeze irregular shaped food materials. The *blast-freezer* is ideally suited for this type of operation.

Generally a blast-freezer is a large cabinet in which a fan has been introduced to move the air over the product. Stationary air acts as an insulator, but moving air readily takes up heat and loses it again quickly. The effect can be experienced by blowing on the back of your hand, especially when wet. Ideally the air should have a temperature of –25C or lower and should move with a velocity of about 400m/min. The blast-freezer (see Figure 4.9) generally is a batch system and as such has disadvantages, being only suitable for a low throughput of product. Continuous systems have been developed and have much larger throughputs.

Figure 4.9

Blast-freezer

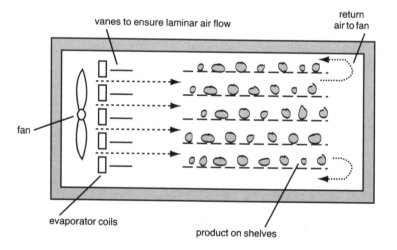

Fluidised-bed freezers are blast-freezers with a vertical air blast of sufficient velocity to 'fluidise' the product in the air stream. To fluidise a product, such as peas, beans, chipped potatoes and soft fruit, the product must be suspended on jets of refrigerated air. Freezing takes between four and ten minutes and such freezers are continuous, often with throughputs of 10tons/hour (see Figure 4.10).

Some modern systems are constructed in the form of a spiral to reduce floor space.

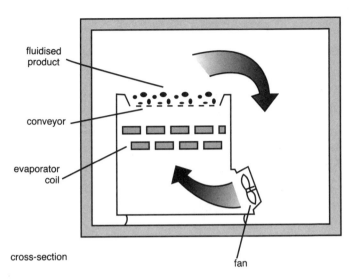

Figure 4.10
Fluidised-bed freezer

Cyogenic-freezers make use of very cold *liquified* gases, such as nitrogen and carbon dioxide. Freezing is so rapid for some products that they suffer thermal shock because of the rapid contraction caused by the sudden lowering of temperature. Liquid nitrogen (at –196C) is sprayed on to the food on a conveyer-belt in a tunnel (see Figure 4.11). Nitrogen gas is removed by fans to the entrance of the tunnel to pre-chill foods before the actual freezing stage, to reduce thermal shock. The method is good for soft fruits and products such as prawns, but not larger items, as too much nitrogen will be used.

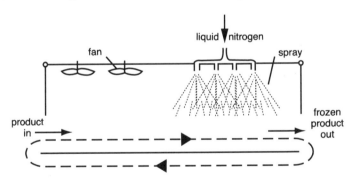

Figure 4.11
Liquid nitrogen freezer

Liquid CO_2 freezers work at a higher temperature (–78C). However, the system is more economical than the nitrogen system and the gas can be recovered and re-used. Because liquid CO_2 cannot exist at atmospheric pressure, it is stored in bulk under pressure and reduced temperature. As soon as the pressure is released the CO_2 converts to a fine powder of carbon dioxide snow and an equal amount of CO_2 gas. The CO_2 snow has a surface temperature of –78C and converts directly to CO_2 gas on contact with the food, thus achieving rapid freezing rates. The carbon dioxide is also a bacteriostat and helps preserve the food product. Frozen storage systems have been developed, with liquid CO_2 for use on airliners.

THE COLD CHAIN

All frozen food has to travel down the 'cold chain', from freezer to the bulk cold store, via refrigerated vehicles to wholesalers, then retailers and finally to the home. As we saw in the section on the storage of raw materials, fluctuating temperatures during the storage of frozen products can lead to considerable loss in quality. Freezing and storage in the factory should be at −30C for best results and long storage potential. Some heat gain will occur when the product is transferred from the cold store to the transport vehicle. The vehicle itself, although it is refrigerated with a mechanical refrigeration or liquid nitrogen system, can only maintain the temperature of the load. The vehicle's refrigeration system can only cope with heat coming through the insulation, doors and floor, and cannot reduce the temperature of the product.

The wholesaler's cold room will not be at such a low temperature as that of the factory, and may only be at −20C, or occasionally −25C. Smaller vehicles, possibly relying on insulation and without a refrigeration system, may transfer the product to the retailer where the cold room will be at −18C or higher.

The retailer usually makes use of open-top display cabinets for frozen products. These cabinets have caused numerous problems at this stage of the cold chain. Over filling will mean that packs on the top will be at too high a temperature, and the use of strip lighting may warm packs close to the top and back of the cabinet. The cabinet should be nevertheless, at about −15C and never warmer than −12C.

Figure 4.12

Star marking recommended storage times for frozen foods

When a pack of frozen food is bought, it is perhaps carried round the supermarket, put in a bag and then taken home during a time period possibly of hours. Some products can thaw out completely during this time. Frozen packs used to be wrapped in newspaper, a moderate insulator, but now a token plastic bag is used.

If the food is used immediately the quality loss resulting from the journey home will not matter; however, if the food is placed in a freezer problems may result. A partially thawed food will re-freeze at a much slower rate, producing large ice crystals and a product of lower quality.

A star marking system is used for frozen foods and also for domestic freezers and refrigerators. The star markings are given in Figure 4.12.

The use of similar markings on the food packs and appliances give easy cross-reference. A further symbol (see Figure 4.13) is used to indicate a freezer capable of freezing food as well as storing frozen food.

Figure 4.13

Symbol indicating food-freezing capability

When this symbol is used on a freezer the manufacturer must state the weight of food which can be frozen in each 24 hours. This weight factor is called the *rated freezing capacity* of the appliance. The three stars, as before, indicate that frozen foods can be stored up to three months.

The cold chain is represented graphically in Figure 4.14. Any method of *Diagram* handling and storage, which reduces the slope of the graph, will improve the final quality of the product.

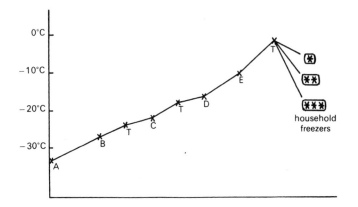

Figure 4.14

The cold chain

A: factory freezers
B: factory cold-store
C: distribution/wholesalers cold-stc
D: retail cold store
E: display cabinet
T: transport

PRACTICAL EXERCISES: FREEZING

Freezing of meat

Take a sample of minced meat and form into a burger. Insert a thermometer into the centre of the burger, or, if available, use a thermocouple and digital thermometer. Place in freezer; repeat with a sample in a quick-freeze section and in the freezer compartment of a refrigerator. Every five minutes observe the temperature and plot the freezing curve. (The process may take some time as the rate of freezing will be slow.)

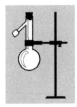

Observations of frozen food

Observe the levels of filling products into retailer display units. Note the time taken to buy a frozen food and take it home. Look for any evidence of thawing out. Place in a domestic freezer and note the time taken to re-freeze (this will not always be possible with well packed foods).

Construct a diagram representing the cold chain for the product.

Chilling of fish

Take a whole fish and take its temperature. Pack crushed ice around the fish and record the temperature and time. Plot the cooling curve for the fish. Make a 1% salt solution and add some ice to bring the temperature down to 0C. Immerse the fish and repeat the cooling process. Compare the ice and chilled water (corresponding to refΩrigerated seawater) for their ability to chill fish.

Chapter 3

Dehydration

PREVIEW

- • **Dehydration**
  - – amount of available water in a food, describe in terms of water activity (a_w) where pure water has an aw of 1.0
  - – lower a_w levels are achieved by use of sugar, salt and dehydration
  - – some water is bound in foods and difficult to remove by drying
  - – quick drying causes less shrinkage than slow drying and produces a product which rehydrates more easily
  - – soluble solids move to surface during drying – some diffuse back to centre
  - – case-hardening – skin on surface caused by soluble solids, heat and changes in proteins. Slows dehydration and inhibits rehydration in water

- • **Drying processes**
  - – pre-treatment necessary: size reduction, eg dicing, blanching, sulphiting
  - – sun-drying – slow, uncontrolled, but popular in hot countries
  - – warm air-drying – kiln drier, simple method
  - – tunnel driers popular for vegetables
  - – concurrent drier – less shrinkage, good rehydration characteristics in product, but final moisture levels higher
  - – countercurrent drier – more shrinkage, poorer rehydration but low moisture levels
  - – for liquids – roller drier – high product temperatures, bacteria destroyed but loss in quality and browning may result
  - – spray drier – very popular, rapid method producing fine powder – bacteria may survive, heat pretreatment necessary
  - – freeze-drying – very high quality product
  - – freeze product then subject it to high vacuum to cause sublimation of ice to leave
  - – product free of water – AFD – some heat applied to accelerate process

Water is required by micro-organisms for them to maintain a normal population growth. Removal of water by dehydration does not kill the microbes but just stops their growth, in a comparable manner to freezing. If the moisture level of the dried product rises due to pick-up of water from the atmosphere or any other source, micro-organisms will again resume their activity and reproduce, ultimately to spoil the food.

Some micro-organisms require a high level of moisture to be able to grow, whereas some, such as osmophilic yeasts, can grow at very low moisture levels. The amount of available water in a food is described in terms of water activity (a_w). Moisture levels are compared with pure water which has an a_w of 1.0. Table 4.1 lists ranges of water activities which are required by certain micro-organisms. Drying is carried out to reduce moisture levels to a very low figure, but as we have seen in Section 2 some products are preserved by salt and sugar which reduce the a_w by osmotic effects. Typical examples of lowered water activity are found in jams, salted foods and sugar products.

Table 4.1

Water activity ranges

Water activity	Organisms which grow in this range
0.90 and above	Most bacteria
0.85–0.90	Yeasts
0.80–0.85	Moulds
0.75	Halophilic bacteria (spoil salted products)
0.60–0.75	Osmophilic yeasts (spoil products high in sugar)

Some water in food is *bound* and cannot be easily removed by dehydration. However, nearly all water normally present in a food can be removed by one of a number of drying processes. The loss of water results in a significant reduction in the weight and bulk of a product, as well as preserving it. This enables a greater weight of actual food nutrients to be transported in a given volume of a container or vehicle. Famine relief measures clearly indicate this useful aspect of dehydration, as, for example, large amounts of dried milk powder are sent to disaster areas and not bulk containers of liquid milk.

Any drying method will therefore cause shrinkage of a food material, but this is minimal with freeze-drying techniques. Rapid drying systems cause the outer edges and corners of the food piece to become dried out and rigid and thus fix the shape of the dried food pieces early in the process. Water is removed from the centre of the food to produce a light honeycomb product which readily rehydrates when added to water. Slow drying allows the product to shrink further and produce a dense dried food, which is difficult to rehydrate.

As a food dries, water moves to the surface where it is evaporated. Water is always in the form of a solution in foods and the substances dissolved in the water cannot escape by evaporating and so accumulate at the surface of the product. While there is still water in the food some of these substances will diffuse back into the centre. However, in many foods there is an accumulation of soluble solids at the surface of the dried product. These solids may prevent complete dehydration and slow rehydration of the product when it is used.

Sometimes the accumulation of salts and sugars at the surface, combined with heat, causes a skin to be formed which is known as *case-hardening*. This has been known to occur when drying fruit, meat and some fish products. Case-hardening prevents complete dehydration and inhibits rehydration. To minimise the problem some products are pierced with a pinhole before drying.

Many drying processes involve heat which causes the destruction of some vitamins, particularly C and B_1. In dried foods containing fats the loss of moisture and the concentration of salts has been shown to accelerate oxidative rancidity reactions. There is always a change in shape, colour and eating quality after drying, but the process of freeze-drying has been found to minimise these changes.

DRYING PROCESSES

Certain pre-treatments are necessary before dehydration can be carried out on a particular food. Food materials dry more rapidly if they are reduced in size and this produces a greater surface area for water loss. Many products, such as vegetables and meat, are diced before drying. Enzymes will become very active in these initial stages of a drying process and so they should be inactivated by blanching. Some products are also treated with a variety of substances, for example, sulphite may be added to the product to minimise enzymic browning reactions, or non-enzymic reactions such as Maillard reaction.

Sun-drying is an ancient process which is still one of the main methods of drying a food in some countries. In hotter countries, a vast range of products is dried by the sun, particularly fruit, fish and meat products. The method is often slow and is uncontrolled. There are often considerable problems with insect infestation, particularly of fish. The product can shrink excessively and can take a considerable time to rehydrate. In Britain, peas (marrowfats) used to be dried in the field but produced a variable product which had to be soaked, sometimes all night, to rehydrate completely.

Warm air driers are very common in producing a wide range of products particularly cheap dried vegetables. A simple system in the *kiln drier* which is often a two storey building, with a furnace on the ground floor producing warm air which rises through a slatted floor to dry the product (see Figure 4.15). (This method has been used for hops for many years.)

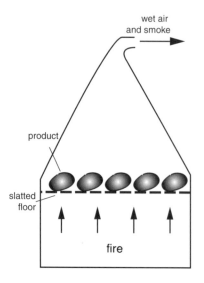

Figure 4.15

Kiln drier

Tunnel driers are a very common type of hot air drier. Some produce rapid drying of the product with little shrinkage, but do not obtain very low final moisture levels (the concurrent type Figure 4.16). Other types slowly dry the product, making it shrink more and is of poorer rehydration ability, but in very low final moisture levels (the counter-have become current type.)

These tunnel driers are comparable with blast-freezers and in a similar manner it is possible to make use of the air-flow to 'fluidise' the product in a *fluidised bed dried* (see Figure 4.17). A fluidised bed drier can be a continuous drier producing a product of low shrinkage and good rehydration characteristics. Its use is limited to products which are small enough to fluidise by the upward blast of hot air in the drier.

None of the driers described so far can be used for liquid foods. A common method, which was used for some time was the *roller* or *drum drier.* This method was used for milk products, baby foods and breakfast cereals. In most

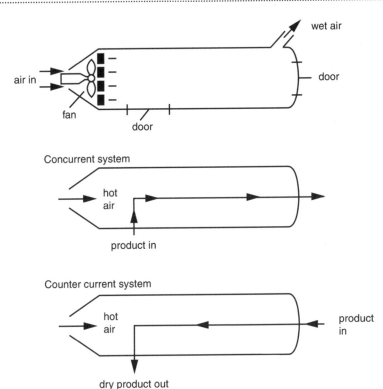

Figure 4.16 (left)
Tunnel drier

Concurrent system

Counter current system

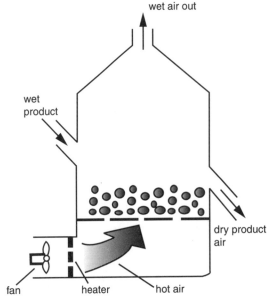

Figure 4.17 (above)
Fluidised bed drier

cases it has been superseded by the spray drier. A large stainless-steel drum is heated internally by steam and this drum rotates slowly. A paste or concentrated mixture of the product is picked up by the drum and is dried as the drum rotates, to be scraped off by knives on the opposite side,(see Figure 4.18). Sometimes two drums are used which rotate towards each other. High product temperatures can be achieved, which produce a sterile product, but one which may be heat-damaged, causing browning reactions, loss of vitamins and decrease in protein quality or solubility.

The *spray drier* is used extensively to dry a wide range of liquid foods, particularly milk, egg products and products such as desserts. A fine spray of the product is produced by an atomizer that is built into the top of a large conical shaped chamber. On entering the chamber the spray of food is met by a blast of hot air, which dries the food into a fine powder within seconds. As the process is so fast bacteria survive, and so it is necessary to heat-

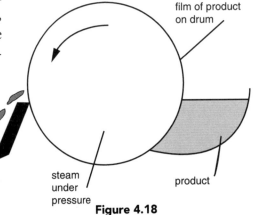

Figure 4.18
Roller or drum drier

process the liquid before drying. Milk powder produced by this method is a very fine powder, which does not wet or disperse well in water. To improve the wetability, dispersability and ultimately the solubility of the product, it is often re-wetted! This re-wetting causes the powder particles to clump together to make sponge-like structures which are dried by warm air in a fluidised-bed drier. The sponge like structures absorb water rapidly and disperse and dissolve in it quickly. As an alternative to re-wetting the powder may be only partially dried initially.

All the drying processes described above have involved heating to some extent with the accompanying changes produced in the product. *Freeze-drying* produces a very high quality product as it involves little or no heating. As a consequence of this there is little shrinkage in the product; fewer flavour changes; no case-hardening; good rehydration characteristics. The product is very friable, however, and its honeycombed structure readily crumbles if not carefully handled.

The process of freeze-drying involves freezing the product by a normal freezing method and then subjecting the frozen product to a strong vacuum. Instead of the ice melting it sublimes to leave the product in a dry state. However, as the process is very slow, and therefore expensive, the process of *accelerated freeze-drying* (AFD) was developed. The product is subjected to a strong vacuum and a small amount of heat by conduction, radiation heating or microwaves. The sublimation process is, therefore, accelerated and costs are reduced.

Figure 4.19

The principle of accelerated freeze-drying

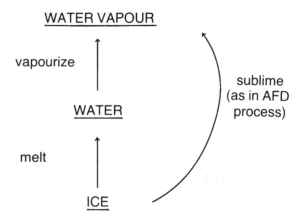

Very high quality products, particularly dried fruit and vegetables, meat and coffee have been made by this method.

The economics of any food factory necessitate the operation of large, continuous processes. The technology involved in drying has made greater advances because it has been actively involved in the development of such convenience foods such as dehydrated vegetables, soup powders, instant coffee, desserts and instant mashed potato. The products are convenient to carry; they store easily; and they can be used often to make a meal in a few minutes involving minimal preparation.

PRACTICAL EXERCISES: *DEHYDRATION*

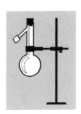

Drying vegetables

Dice a number of carrots evenly into about 1cm³ cubes. Weigh a sample of about 40g. Place on a tray or, if available, on a fine mesh wire-rack. Place in a fan-assisted oven at the lowest temperature setting, usually about 70C. Remove the sample every 10 minutes and re-weigh. Plot a curve of weight against time until the product is dry. Repeat at a number of other temperatures. Repeat using diced carrots, which have been blanched for two minutes in boiling water. Note the physical characteristic of each dried sample.

Rehydration of dried vegetables

Add samples of dried vegetables to water and gently heat. Note the time and extent of rehydration. Compare with commercial samples dried by known methods such as tunnel drying and AFD.

Chapter 4
Irradiation of foods

PREVIEW

- **Irradiation**

  - potential to reduce:

    (1) microbial spoilage
    (2) insect damage
    (3) need for chemical additives, also to improve organoleptic and keeping qualities of unrefrigerated foods. Inhibition of sprouting and ripening in fruit and vegetables

- **Wholesomeness of irradiated foods**

  - extensive tests have shown there are no risks with irradiated foods
  - in some products high dosage levels can cause flavour, colour and texture changes
  - irradiated foods are permitted in many countries
  - irradiation in the UK permitted in the Food Safety Act from January 1 1991

- **Irradiation processes**

  - plant is expensive as it needs extensive screening for operatives
  - two types of radiation:-

    (1) electrons produced from radioactive sources in a linear accelerator
    (2) gamma rays emitted from cobalt 60 or caesium 137
  - electrons have poor penetration, gamma rays cheaper, with better penetration but not directional
  - radiation sterilisation (radappertisation)
  - high dose levels 10kGy (kilogray) to 30kGy
  - causes colour, flavour and texture changes in some products
  - radiation pasteurisation (radurisation) similar to pasteurization in killing pathogens and some spoilage organisms, dose about 2.5kGy
  - very low levels (0.1kGy) found to be useful in inhibiting potato sprouting
  - largest use in Japan

So far, only one method to have a lethal effect on micro-organisms, and that is sterilization by heat, has been covered. Irradiation is the only other technology which has a lethal effect and can be compared with heat processing in a number of respects.

At first irradiation was thought to have great potential as a means of reducing microbial spoilage and insect damage; improving opanoleptic properties of foods; obviating the need for some chemical additives; extending the life of unrefrigerated foods. All other technologies were thought to be on the verge of redundancy. Research has continued throughout the world, particularly with regard to the wholesomeness of irradiated foods, but the main problem is acceptance by the consumer.

WHOLESOMENESS OF IRRADIATED FOODS

All organisms can be damaged or changed in some way by a number of radiation sources. Spoilage and food poisoning organisms can be destroyed by radiation at a certain level, but sometimes this is much higher than would kill a human being. Ionisation of a food component can occur when the food is irradiated, leading to the formation of reactive molecules and free radicals.

Other side-reactions might include the production of off-flavours and the destruction of vitamins.

The irradiation process will not induce radioactivity in foods. However, the chance of residual radioactivity in irradiated foods has caused considerable consumer resistance to the possible use of this technology on a large scale. Any doubts about this residual activity have now been removed by extensive animal feeding studies and by chemical tests. These investigations have produced no evidence of adverse effects as a result of irradiation. Breakdown products of food components, *ie* water, carbohydrates, fat and protein in irradiated foods are the same regardless of the food, and therefore toxicity testing of all food irradiated will less than 10 kilogray (kGy) is not necessary. Most of these breakdown products are also found in other processed foods, particularly those which have been heat processed. These breakdown products are known to be safe and there is no evidence of toxicity.

LEGISLATION

Irradiated foods are permitted in many countries and are quite widely accepted in a number of these. In 1986 a report was published by the Advisory Committee on Irradiated and Novel Foods which concluded that the irradiation of foods proved to have no significant disadvantages or risk to health. From January 1 1991 the use of irradiation was legalised in the UK for some vegetables, spices and poultry products.

IRRADIATION PROCESSES

Irradiation plant is expensive, particularly because of the heavy screening to protect operatives. To operate economically plant must be used continuously. As only a few commodities can be irradiated legally in some countries, economical operation is extremely difficult.

Two types of radiation are used: electrons produced in a linear accelerator from radioactive sources, and gamma rays from the radioactive decay of cobalt 60 and caesium 137 sources. The electron beams are restricted to foods of less than 5cm in thickness because of their poor penetrability. Gamma rays, which unlike electron beams cannot be directed, are more common and cheaper to use.

In a continuous irradiation operation the food material should be exposed to the radiation source at various angles to minimise any penetration problems.

Radiation sterilisation or *radappertisation* is intended to produce a sterile product similar to a canned food. Doses of radiation have to be high, in excess of 10kGy and often as high as 30kGy. Unfortunately, high dosages of radiation on a number of products, particularly fruit and vegetables, have been found to cause changes in colour, texture and flavour. Most development in recent years has therefore been carried out at low dosage levels.

Radiation pasteurisation or *radurisation* gives a significant reduction in the number of spoilage organisms and destroys pathogenic organisms. Levels of radiation of the order of 2.5kGy are used, but changes in the spoilage pattern may result. Very large quantities of potatoes have been irradiated in Japan to inhibit sprouting (dose level 0.1kGy). In Holland, chicken has been treated by irradiation. Also the Dutch have irradiated successfully smaller quantities of diced vegetables, shrimps, frog legs and spices.

In South Africa a range of products has been treated, usually at a dose level of 0.7kGy. The range of products includes potatoes, chicken, mangoes, strawberries, bananas, onions, garlic and avocados.

Products, such as potatoes, other vegetables and fruit receive low dosage levels to inhibit sprouting or ripening. However, controlled atmosphere storage or refrigeration may still be necessary to ensure prolonged storage. Products which are sterilised by irradiation must be aseptically packaged, and, as with heat processed foods, recontamination should be made impossible.

Chapter 5
Packaging

PREVIEW

- **Packaging**
  - must protect against mechanical forces, climatic conditions and contamination
  - must contain the product
  - must identify the product: name, storage conditions, serving instructions, ingredients declaration and average filled weight

- **Packaging materials**
  - cans – low carbon-steel protected by thin layer of tin
  - lacquer to protect against sulphur staining of product, colour changes, eg anthocyanins with iron, and acid attack
  - paper and board – most common method of packaging
  - solid white board made from chemical woodpulp
  - chipboard made from recycled paper
  - plastics- either flexible or rigid
  - most common 'polythene', ie low density polyethene (polyethylene)
  - high density polyethene resists boiling temperatures
  - polythene – poor barrier to oxygen
  - 'nylon' (polyamide) good oxygen barrier
  - aluminium foil can be laminated with polythene
  - new plastic bottles – PET (polyethylene terephthalate), very light but strong
  - cellulose films – 'cellophane' – wide range of types, denoted by letter codes, eg P permeable, M moisture proof
  - glass – new lightweight, but strong glass.

- **Packaging individual foods**
  - need to know nature of food and degree of protection required
  - fresh fruit and vegetables require oxygen, but must allow loss of some moisture
  - fresh meat requires oxygen to form bright red oxymyoglobin
  - cured meat needs protection against oxygen to prevent discolouration
  - dehydrated foods protect against moisture, oxygen and mechanical damage
  - frozen foods protect against moisture loss to prevent 'freezer–burn' and require
    - low oxygen permeability to minimise tainting problems

From the earliest times some form of packaging has been necessary for food. The prime functions of packaging have remained the same throughout time – to protect, contain and identify the product. Prevention of recontamination of a preserved product is the prime purpose of many examples of packaging, particularly in canning, and is the reason for including packaging in the preservation section of the book.

Natural materials such as leather, pottery, wood, gourds and baskets were used for thousands of years. Processed material came into use perhaps three hundred years ago with the adaptation of glass, paper and metal. It is only in the last forty years that synthetic materials, such as cellulose and polythene films, have been available. These materials have been adapted to rapid changes in the food industry, particularly to increasing rates of production demanding cheap but strong packaging materials.

The packaging of food must *protect* the food during storage, transport, sale and the journey to the home.

The packaging must protect against *mechanical* forces, such as impact, vibration or compression. Very fragile foods, such as *AFD* foods, need to be well protected, usually by packing into a can or foil laminate. Fibrous and tougher food products require less protection against mechanical force. A number of *climatic conditions* can affect foods. Some foods are susceptible to humidity, high temperatures, light and various gases. These facts must be considered when choosing a package material for a particular food. The packaging material must prevent *contamination* of food by micro-organisms, insects, chemicals or soil. A packaging must be shaped to *contain* the food conveniently, but sometimes this is difficult. Problems are often overcome by other means, for example, special small cylindrical carrots are grown exclusively for canning. The normal tapered carrots of varying sizes are difficult to can.

To *identify* the product the package is labelled, often with considerable detail about the product, serving instructions, ingredient declarations and average weight of product. Very tight regulations govern the labelling of foods, and even the name of the product is carefully regulated. For example, a can labelled 'Beef Curry' must contain at least 35% beef. The label on a package is designed to be attractive and 'eye catching' by using different colours, shapes and designs. Often a photograph of the product is used, but this must not be misleading. To return to the example of beef curry, the label would show a picture of the curry served with rice. This would imply, at first sight, that the can included rice as well as curry. The words 'serving suggestion' are often inlcuded under the photograph, and other articles not included in the package are often slightly out of focus.

PACKAGING MATERIALS

FOOD CANS

Food cans consist of a body with a fixed end, into which the food is filled, to be followed by sealing an identical end on the top of the can. Cans were rather heavy and consequently with rises in the cost of materials became more expensive than some of the products they contained. Weights of cans have now been reduced by over 50%, with thinner walls supported by strengthening ribs.

Traditional cans are made from tinplate, which consists of thin low–carbon steel protected from corrosion by a thin layer of tin. New developments are taking place to eliminate the tin coating and replace it with special lacquers. The use of aluminium has increased enormously particularly for drinks.

Electrolytic action can result in the dissolution of any exposed iron, and sometimes, in the presence of acid, hydrogen gas is evolved. *Lacquers* are often used to prevent any interaction between the package and the product. These lacquers are wax-like materials with specific functions.

During heat processing, sulphur-containing amino acids such as cysteine can be broken down to liberate sulphur compounds, particularly hydrogen sulphide. This hydrogen sulphide will react with the can and produce black iron and tin sulphides, which will discolour the product. For this reason, when canning fish or meat products, a sulphur-resisting lacquer (epoxy-phenolic lacquer) is used on the tinplate and ends of the can. In some liquid packs, such as peas and soups, sulphur compounds can accumulate in any head-space in the can, giving an unpleasant smell when the can is opened. Sulphur-absorbing lacquer (oleo-resinous lacquer) is used with zinc oxide, which produces white zinc sulphide and is not noticeable. Acids will attack the tin-plate, and if lacquered inadequately gas production will result. Acid will concentrate its attack through any pin-holes in the lacquer and will produce a 'hydrogen-swell'. Recent lacquering techniques have lessened this problem.

Some food pigments, notably the anthocyanins, react with tinplate. The pigments produce a grey sludge in the can and the can must be totally lacquered to prevent it.

PAPER AND BOARD

Paper and board are still the most used packaging materials. Raw materials include chemical woodpulp, which is mainly cellulose; mechanical woodpulp, which is cheaper and brittle; and recycled waste paper.

Board must be specially prepared for direct contact with food. *Solid white board* is commonly used and is produced from chemical woodpulp that is bleached. Other board, such as *chipboard*, is produced from recycled waste paper, which has a natural grey colour. The board is used for outer containers, not in contact with the food. Wax coating or polythene may be applied, particularly for packaging frozen foods.

No major changes have occurred in many of these packaging materials for several years. However, a recent innovation is the 'ovenable' board used to make shallow trays for prepared or frozen foods which are cooked by microwaves. The carton board is coated with polypropene which can resist temperatures up to 140C. Foil trays cannot be used in microwave ovens.

PLASTICS

A very wide range of plastics is used for food packaging either as flexible or rigid containers. These materials include 'polythene'* (low density polyethene), ethene vinyl acetate (EVA), polyamide (nylon) and polyvinylidene chloride (PVDC). Each film can be made in a variety of densities and often with a range of properties.

The most common plastic packaging film for food is 'polythene', which is low density polyethene (polyethylene). It is a relatively cheap film, offering good properties, which include: particularly good heat sealing water vapour resistance, strength and low temperature resistance. However, it is not a good oxygen barrier and cannot withstand temperatures above about 90C. High density polythene will resist boiling temperatures and has been used for 'boil-in-the-bag' products. Linear low-density polythene is a new development produced by a low pressure process. The film has improved temperature resistance and greater strength, allowing thinner film to be used.

The poor oxygen barrier characteristic of polythene can be improved if it is laminated with another film, particularly polyamide (nylon) which is a very good barrier to oxygen. This is essential for vacuum packaging a number of foods, which deteriorate in the presence of oxygen, for example, foods containing fat. A new development, which may offer advantages for some products, is the production of vacuum-metallised films in which a minute layer of aluminium is deposited in a vacuum chamber on to a plastic film base. This can be made into **retortable** pouches. If better barrier properties are required the aluminium foil is laminated with paper and polythene. The paper carries the label and provides strength. The foil provides a very good barrier to gases, moisture and light, and the polythene provides a heat sealing facility with some protection for the foil.

PET (polythene terephthalate) bottles have made a significant impact on the soft-drinks industry, as they offer reduced container weight, large size, and little risk of breakage. The plastic is rigid enough, but is aided by gas pressure, to which it has excellent barrier properties.

*NB 'polythene' is the common name for polyethene (polyethylene formerly)

Polystyrene in a number of forms is used for trays and insulated containers. Supermarket trays are made of expanded polystyrene which can be used to keep produce cool.

CELLULOSE FILMS

Cellulose films are available in a range of densities, characteristics and uses. The films are coded by letters which have specific meanings, as shown in Table 4.2.

Letter(s)	Meaning
P	Permeable (not a moisture barrier)
M	Moisture proof (nitrocellulose coated on both sides)
DM	Demi-moisture proof (coated on one side)
QM	Quasi-moisture proof (slightly moisture proof)
MXXT	Very good moisture barrier (PVDC coated)
MXDT	Good moisture barrier (PVDC coated on one side)
B	Opaque
C	Coloured
S	Heat sealable

Table 4.2
Cellulose film codes

GLASS

Glass has been used for food packaging for a considerable time. However, for high speed production in a food factory glass had severe limitations, because of the ease of breaking. New lightweight but tough glass containers have changed this. Wide-mouth closures and lightweight bottles are gaining popularity for beers, soft drinks and some jars are available for fruit and vegetables. A sleeve of expanded polystyrene, which may be printed, can be used to protect some types of bottles.

PACKAGING INDIVIDUAL FOODS

The technologist needs to know the nature of the food to be packaged and the degree of protection required. A few examples of the problems involved are given below.

Fresh *fruit and vegetables* continue to respire and transpire in a package. The package must be permeable to gases, as oxygen is required for respiration. A somewhat decreased oxygen supply may prolong storage life. Continued transpiration, however, causes the accumulation of water droplets on the inside of the package, which is likely to facilitate mould growth. Packaging films are often perforated to release this moisture. Leafy vegetables are packed to control too much water loss, to prevent wilting.

Fresh *meat* requires oxygen in order to maintain its bright red colour. In the absence of oxygen, oxymyoglobin is lost and myoglobin, a dull red, is formed.

A good moisture barrier is needed to prevent too much weight loss in the form of water vapour, but it must be a barrier which will allow the passage of gases, particularly oxygen. *Cured meats* do not require oxygen, which may damage their colour by causing the formation of brown metmyoglobin. A film impermeable to oxygen, and gas packaging, would be beneficial for these products.

Dehydrated foods must be kept dry and only a small amount of moisture can cause a loss in keeping quality. Many dried products are easily oxidized and so a barrier impermeable to moisture and oxygen should be used. Often dried foods are fragile and some protection is needed against mechanical change, by using a can or foil laminate.

Packaging materials for *frozen foods* must have low moisture permeability to prevent 'freezer burn', which is surface dehydration. Gaps between the food and the packaging material must be avoided, otherwise sublimation of the ice from the food may occur and this will refreeze next to the packaging material, producing 'frost', which is unsightly and also result in product weight loss. Low oxygen permeability is desirable to minimise flavour exchange and tainting problems in a cold store.

BAR CODING

Figure 4.20

Bar code

This system of coding packaged articles was introduced in 1978, although it has been in operation in US since 1973. Every product is assigned its own particular number, which also indicates its price and description. The number appears in the pack in the form of bar symbols, which can be read rapidly by electronic scanners at the supermarket checkout. The system ensures rapid 'checkout', which is also totally accurate and avoids human errors. Movement of the bar symbol over the scanner automatically signals a computer which feeds back data, such as price, and this is automatically printed in the till ticket.

An example of the European Article Number (EAN) is given in Figure 4.20. This system uses a thirteen digit symbol.

PRACTICAL EXERCISES : PACKAGING FILM

Try the following on samples of packaging films

1 Water tap test –

hold a piece of film under a running tap. Film which is not moisture proof soon becomes saturated and limp

2 Breath test –

breathe on a sample of film; a moisture-proof film will cloud over.

3 Burn test –

light with a match one end of a small, tight roll of film. Observe the burning, smoke and odour produced. Does the material drip moist beads?

Cellulose films – burn sometimes slowly, do not melt or drip, eg P, MS & DMS

Polystyrene – burns with black smoke and melts

Polyester – does not burn easily, but melts

Polythene – burns slowly, melts and drips

4 Tear test –

tear a piece of film.

Cellulose film is easy to tear

Polyester shows some tear resistance

Polythene is difficult to tear

Section 5
PRODUCT ANALYSIS AND THE CONSUMER

This section of the book covers all the consumer issues that affect food production from the design of the label to consumer issues through to current trends.

In addition, aspects of food control which govern the composition of foods is looked at with what is permissible for food manufacturers to undertake in food product development and manufacture.

Aspects of food modifications are covered, particularly the current issues of good manufacturing practice, risk assessment and HACCP, the use of ICT in food manufacture, and genetic modifications.

Chapter 1

Product Analysis

PREVIEW

- **Looking at the Food Label**
  - name of the food
  - list of ingredients
  - storage conditions
  - durability
  - name and address of manufacturer
  - instructions for use
  - average weight of contents

- **Nutritional Labelling**
  - energy, protein, carbohydrate, fat, fibre, sodium, vitamins and minerals

- **Examples of product analysis for:**
  horseradish sauce
  ice-cream
  canned sauce
  mayonnaise.

A great deal of information can be obtained about a food product by looking at the label on the packet or tin. A number of regulations control what is permissible on a food product label:

    (1) Name of the food
    (2) List of ingredients
    (3) Any special storage conditions or conditions of use
    (4) Indication of durability
    (5) The name and address of the manufacturer
    (6) Instructions for use if necessary
    (7) Average weight of contents.

NAME OF THE FOOD

Regulations control the use and form of names. 'Chicken curry' indicates a certain level of meat content but 'Curry with chicken' means there is a lot less chicken present. If no name prescribed by law exists, then a name can be used which enables the food to be distinguished from other products.

LIST OF INGREDIENTS

Ingredients must be listed in order of descending weight, which is determined at the time of their use in the preparation of the food. Exceptions can be found in a number of products.

(1) If an ingredient is dehydrated or in a concentrated form, it may be positioned in the list according to its weight before dehydration, *ie*, fresh.

(2) Similarly reconstituted foods may be listed after reconstitution.

(3) Water and volatile products used as ingredients must be listed in order of their weight in the finished product.

(4) Mixtures of ingredients like nuts, vegetables and herbs can be put under a heading 'in variable proportions', provided no single one dominates.

The naming of ingredients is important, *eg* 'fish' can be used for any species, 'fat' for any refined fat, 'sugar' for any type of sucrose.

Flavouring is identified by the word 'flavouring', the word 'natural' may be added for naturally occurring products. Additives can be listed by either the principal function they serve, followed by the name or by their E numbers (see later), *eg* flavour enhancer – monosodium glutamate or E621.

The list of permitted titles for additives is given below.

Acid	Emulsifying salts	Preservation
Acidity regulator	Firming agent	Propellant gas
Anti-caking agent	Flavour enhancer	Raising agent
Anti-foaming agent	Flour treatment agent	Stabiliser
Antioxidant	Gelling agent	Sweetener
Bulking agent	Glazing agent	Thickener
Colour	Humectant	
Emulsifier	Modified starch*	

Table 5.1
Permitted additives

*The specific name of the starch is not required.

INDICATION OF DURABILITY

<u>Minimum</u> durability is indicated by 'best before' followed by the date up to which the food remains in first class condition if stored correctly.

Date to be declared	Period of durability
'Best before ' – day/month	Within 3 months
'Best before end' – month/year	3–18 months
'Best before end' – month/year or year	More than 18 months

The 'use by' date should be indicated by 'use by' followed by the date (day/month or for longer periods day/month/year). Details of necessary storage conditions must be given.

	per serving (x-g) and per 100 g
Energy	kJ and kcal
Protein	g
Carbohydrate, of which:	
– sugars	g
– polyols	g
– starch	g
Fat, of which	
– saturates	g
– mono-unsaturates	g
– poly-unsaturates	g
– cholesterol	mg
Fibre	g
Sodium	g
Vitamins*	units as appropriate
Minerals*	units as appropriate

* Names to be given and relevant units, eg vitamin C 60mg, folacin 600µg.

Figure 5.1

Example of a food label from an orange drink

NUTRITIONAL LABELLING

This must be in tabular form as shown below or in linear form on small labels.

In calculating energy the following conversion factors are used:

Ingredient	Energy supplied
1g of carbohydrate (not polyols)	17kJ (4kcal)
1g of polyols, eg sorbitol	10kJ (2.4kcal)
1g of protein	17kJ (4kcal)
1g of fat	37kJ (9kcal)
1g of ethanol	29kJ (7kcal)
1g of organic acid	13kJ (3kcal)

Misleading descriptions:

Words or claim	Conditions of use of words
Food with implied flavour	Flavour must come from the food only and not added
'Dietary' or 'dietetic'	Used only for foods for a particular nutritional use, eg for people with digestive problems
'Ice-cream'	Must be frozen with minimum of 5% fat and 2.5% milk proteins and obtained from an emulsion of fat, milk solids and sugar with other substances
'Dairy ice-cream'	Minimum 5% fat must be milk fat
'Starch-reduced'	Only if carbohydrate is less than 50% of the dry matter
'Low calories'	Only to be used for soft drinks with a maximum of 42kJ (10kcal) per 100ml
'Non-alcoholic'	Cannot be used with a name commonly associated with an alcoholic drink except 'non-alcoholic wine'

LOOKING AT THE FOOD LABEL

Below is given a typical ingredient declaration with an exploration of each ingredient:

This food manufacturer has chosen to use the chemical names of additives instead of their E numbers, eg Sodium metabisulphite Only the category name need be included for flavourings	Ingredients, after dilution: water, sugar, glucose syrup, comminuted oranges, citric acid, preservatives: sodium benzoate and sodium metabisulphite, artificial sweetener (saccharin), vitamin C, flavourings. colour (ß-carotene – provides vitamin A)	It is not necessary to use the category name for additives which function as 'acids' in foods and whose chemical name includes the word 'acid' Citric acid
Although ß-carotene is a permitted colour, and is being used as a colour in this drink, it is also a source of vitamin A (ß- carotene provides vitamin A)		Vitamin C is the same chemical as the antioxidant E300, L-ascorbic acid. Here, however, it is being used as a vitamin Vitamin C

Source: *Food Additives – the Balanced Approach*, Ministry of Agriculture, Fisheries and Foods, HMSO, © Crown Copyright 1987.

Examples of some ingredient lists are given below.

Example 1 – horseradish sauce

Horseradish (fresh), malt vinegar, sugar, vegetable oil, cream, salt, skimmed milk powder, acetic acid, pasteurised dried egg, mustard, stabilisers (E412, E415), colour (E171), tartaric acid, lactic acid and flavouring.

The points mentioned on acids and flavouring can be seen in the list, and other ingredients are clearly understandable. The stabilisers are E412, guar gum and E415, xanthan gum. The colour used, E171, is titanium dioxide.

Example 2 – an ice-cream

Reconstituted dried skimmed milk, sugar, dextrose, vegetable oil, whey powder, emulsifier (E471), stabilisers (E412, E407), natural colours (annatto, curcumin), flavouring.

The emulsifier used, E471, is a monoglyceride or a mixture of mono- or diglycerides of fatty acids. The stabilisers prevent the formation of large ice crystals and control thawing. Here E412, guar gum and E407, carrageenan, are used.

Example 3 – a canned sauce

Tomatoes, onions, modified starch, sugar, mushrooms, salt, hydrolysed vegetable protein, vegetable oil, citric acid, spices, herbs.

Apparently a 'natural product' with no *E* numbers! The modified starch does not have to be named.

Example 4 – mayonnaise

Water, vegetable oil (with antioxidant E320), modified starch, egg yolk, sugar, spirit vinegar, salt, lemon juice, stabilisers E405, E415, preservative E202, flavourings.

This product, although traditional in many respects, will have a long, stable shelf-life. Antioxidant is contained in the vegetable oil and cannot be ignored. Here E320, butylated hydroxyanisole, is used. Stabilisers prevent the high level of oil from separating out, an alginate E405 and xanthan gum (E415) are used. This product contains the preservative E202, potassium sorbate, which is effective against moulds in particular.

Chapter 2

Consumer Product Management

Author: Suzan Green BSc, MSc

Senior Lecturer in Consumer Behaviour, Centre for Food, Sheffield Hallam University, UK

PREVIEW

- **Consumer Behaviour**
  - rights of the consumer, responsibilities of organisations
  - decision making, purchasing process, consumption experience of food products
  - consumer attitudes and perceptions. Information gathering processes.

- **Consumer and Society**
  - characteristics, lifestyles of consumers
  - demographics, ageing population linked to food marketing
  - effects of culture on product purchasing trends in food consumption.

- **Product Design and Development**
  - reasons for needing new products
  - factors influencing new food product development:
    socio-cultural
    market
    industrial
  - how consumers evaluate products
  - concepts of "quality of design" and value for money.

- **Influence of Food Retailers**
  - survey of UK food retailing
  - influence of retailers on food products
  - influence of retailers on new product development
  - merchandising and product management.

- **Emerging Trends**
  - influence of ethnic foods
  - concepts of ethnic fusion and hybrid cuisine
  - leisure and sport products and necessary nutritional concepts
  - influence of ageing population.

- **Marketing and Market Research**
  - importance of market research in decision making
  - process of market research and gathering of information
  - design elements of questionnaires
  - analysis of results
  - strategic planning
  - developing a marketing plan for food products
  - advertising and public relations

- **Financial Aspects**
  - costing food products
  - fixed factory costs, variable costs in production
  - concept of break-even point
  - costs of new product launch
  - consumer reactions to pricing.

CONSUMER BEHAVIOUR

Consumer behaviour looks at the relationship between how individuals (consumers, purchasers) make decisions about how to spend their available resources (money, time, effort) on goods and services and how producers (suppliers, manufacturers, retailers) act to meet/create their needs and wants. It includes the study of who buys what, when they buy it, why they buy it, how they buy it, where they buy it and how often they buy it. Being fmcgs (fast moving consumer goods), there are special problems (perishability, availability, seasonality) and opportunities (innovative product/packaging designs) attached to food products.

CONSUMER RIGHTS AND RESPONSIBILITIES

Organisations are constantly seeking to produce existing products more cheaply or to launch winning new products on to the market to maximise sales and profits. The ways in which they do this have increasingly become the subject of public scrutiny as consumers seek to reassure themselves that 'cost-cutting' does not mean unsafe or unethical practices. For example, the process of the mechanical recovery of meat (mrm) – which entails removing every last shred of flesh from the bones of animals for use in meat products – has been under the spotlight in recent years due to fears associated with the BSE crisis in beef.

The main consumer rights include:

(1) the right to safety (*eg* no harmful microbiological contamination, hygienic production methods, packaging which will not injure the consumer)

(2) the right to information (*eg* accurate nutritional, labelling and marketing [especially advertising] information)

(3) the right to consumer education (*eg* access to knowledge about the products)

(4) the right to a safe environment (*eg* free from pollution and hazardous waste and positive steps such as recyclable packaging and pump dispensers rather than aerosols)

(5) the right to redress (*eg* compensation for unsafe or misleading products).

Organisations are required to behave in an ethical and socially responsible manner. They must ensure that production, advertising and selling practices do not violate consumer rights through deception, misrepresentation or misinformation. Any information provided should be of a reasonable amount, be easy to understand and easy and practical to use. Consumer and environmental protection policies should take conservation and sustainability of resources into account.

In addition to increased legislative rights brought about by the UK's membership of the EU, consumer rights are established and protected through a variety of different organisations. These fall into three categories.

(1) **Government agencies** (eg MAFF – Ministry of Agriculture, Fisheries and Food
    NACNE – National Advisory Committee on Nutritional Education
    COMA – Committee on Medical Aspects of food policy)

(2) **Industry self-regulatory bodies** (*eg* ASA – Advertising Standards Authority
    IBA – Independent Broadcasting Authority)

(3) **Consumer groups**, local and national (*eg* The Consumers Association, The
    Soil Association).

In addition, the FSA – Food Standards Agency – an independent advisory body, has recently been set up in response to pressure for independent policy making.

In recent years, the trade press (*eg Grocer* magazine), media (*eg Consumer Which*, lifestyle supplements of broadsheets, food magazines, TV) and the Internet have played an increasingly important role in bringing food related issues to the attention of the general public.

CONSUMER DECISION-MAKING,

THE PURCHASING PROCESS AND CONSUMPTION EXPERIENCE RELATED TO FOOD PRODUCTS

In consumer behaviour textbooks, many models of consumer decision-making are presented. They all try to account for behaviour, but differ in the number of variables and the extent of their effects in influencing consumer purchasing patterns. Some factors are specific to food products and those listed in Table 5.2 are relevant to food purchasing behaviour.

Table 5.2

Factors affecting food purchasing and consumption

Type of factor	Examples
Cultural	Cultural trends and norms, customs, religion, myths symbolism, local / regional / national preferences, habits
Economic	Income, prices, taxes
Marketing	Advertising and promotion, distribution, store location,size, product portfolio and layout
Physiological	Heredity, allergy, taste, food acceptability / intolerance
Political	EU legislation, food policy, Common Agricultural Policy
Psychographic	Personality, self-concept, lifestyle, values, attitudes, beliefs, emotions, mood, preferences, significance of food
Social	Social class, reference groups, household size, family life cycle stage, demography, (nutritional) educational level
Technical	Food processing and preparation methods, cooking andstorage options, packaging materials and type, natureof ingredients
Other	Seasonality, perishability, portability

Dependent on individual products and the circumstances of the consumer, all of these factors will have some bearing on what products are selected, in what quantity, when and how often. However, factors affecting purchasing decisions may be taken for granted (eg habit) or unconscious (green colour is associated with organics/freshness/ health) or not explicitly recognised ('I just fancied it') by the consumer at the point of selection or purchase.

Models are most often of the sequential type (a then b then c) and typically involve four stages.

1 – noticing	2 – choosing	3 – acting	4 – assessing
'I'm hungry' 'That looks tasty'	'I feel like a snack' 'I like that brand / flavour'	'I'll buy that to eat now' 'Just a small packet will do'	'I prefer the one I usually buy' 'That was good value for money'

Consumers may be conscious of all or none of these stages. Sometimes decisions, purchases and consumption experiences are done on 'autopilot' (inertia), sometimes one stage may dominate "I'm hungry" (the first thing I can grab will do). All stages will be affected to some extent by the factors given in Table 5.2 on page 234

INFORMATION GATHERING AND PROCESSING, CONSUMER ATTITUDES AND PERCEPTIONS

Information is gained through the process of perception – the way in which consumers select, organise and interpret stimuli to make sense of them. These stimuli are interpreted through the five senses – sight, sound, taste, touch and smell – all of which are very important for food products (fruit, herbs, freshly baked bread etc.).

Information originates from both internal sources (memory, previous experience and learning) and external sources such as the product itself (attributes such as appearance, smell); from marketing sources (advertising, product packaging, tasting sessions); from personal sources (friends, neighbours, other purchasers); or from impersonal sources (government, its agencies or consumer organisations) "Eat five fruits and vegetables a day"!

Consumers can acquire information both actively (deliberately – eg by looking at how many grams of salt a product contains) or passively (incidentally – eg going past a billposter whilst on a bus).

Information acquisition is limited by the amount of information consumers are able to process effectively. Once attention is paid to stimuli and they have been understood (acquisition), consumers must then be able to remember, retain and recall information in order to fully process it. Once processed, information stored in the memory forms the associations that the consumer makes with brands, products or companies. The nature of the association (positive/negative, accepting/rejecting) forms the basis of the consumers' product/brand evaluation.

If there are simply too many stimuli to take in, the consumer filters out what is not a priority (maybe they do not want to consider all the different brands of coffee but simply choose the brand they bought last time). Selective rejection of stimuli is most likely when consumers are indifferent to the product for one reason or another. The more significant/important the product, the more the consumer is said to be 'involved' with it. Levels of involvement tend to be associated with the 'risk' of the purchase, eg cost (higher risk with lobster than mackerel); image (one is more likely to serve exotic vegetables than tinned peas and carrots at a dinner party) etc.

Since consumers filter out certain stimuli, companies devote considerable time and money to finding out why. They are interested in consumers', attitudes because the intention to buy depends both on information processes and on beliefs (feelings/evaluation) about the product (brand/company). The most commonly used traditional attitude measurement scales are:

(1)   the semantic differential – items are rated using a battery of (usually) seven-point bipolar opposite scales, eg excellent value for money versus poor value for money, convenient location versus remote location etc.

(2)   Likert Scales – usually take the form of a statement followed by a five-point range of responses, eg "produce in this store is always very fresh"–strongly agree, agree, not sure, disagree, strongly disagree

(3)   Thurstone Scales – usually take the form of a graded range of statements and consumers choose the one they most agree with, eg

– I always choose superpremium brands because they are the best quality
– I always choose the brand leader, irrespective of price
– I usually choose the brand leader, but not if another brand has a promotional offer
– I always choose own-label, because they are better value
– I always choose value lines, they are the same as own-label, anyway.

However, one of the most contentious issues in consumer research is whether attitudes predict actual behaviour as opposed to intended behaviour.

THE CONSUMER AND SOCIETY

THE INDIVIDUAL CONSUMER – CHARACTERISTICS AND LIFESTYLE

There are some key political (eg Food Standards Agency), economic (eg year on year falling costs of food supermarket shopping), social (eg changing role of women) and technological (eg availability of very long-life chilled ready meals) issues which impact on all our daily lives in respect of food consumption. At the same time, there are other interactive, individual, personal variables such as personality and motivation which vary from one consumer to another, but which are nevertheless influential on our individual and collective behaviour.

Personality theories attempt to establish the idea that aspects of a person's character will influence their purchasing behaviour, whilst motivation theories suggest that a series of evermore sophisticated needs, drives and wants (physiological, psychological and existential) seek expression and satisfaction through products purchased.

On the whole, personality and motivational research alone have failed to show a clear and consistent link between these individual human characteristics and purchasing behaviour for food products – although some evidence shows that certain personality traits are predictive of alchohol consumption!!

More success has been achieved in identifying groups of consumers who exhibit similar purchasing behaviour (these are called segments) in their responses to products, packaging and advertising when additional factors are taken into account. If personal values and beliefs are assessed along with personality and motivation variables, purchase choices can be be predicted more accurately. Consumer behaviour can be most reliably predicted though, when lifestyle factors are also considered.

Lifestyles are actual patterns of behaviour and are constructed by measuring consumers' activities, interests and opinions (AIOs).

Activities	Interests	Opinions	Demographics
Work	Family	Themselves	Age
Hobbies	Home	Social issues	Education
Social events	Job	Politics	Income
Vacation	Community	Business	Occupation
Entertainment	Recreation	Economics	Family size
Club membership	Fashion	Education	Dwelling
Community	Food	Products	Geography
Shopping	Media	Future	City size
Sports	Achievements	Culture	Stage in life cycle

Source: Plummer, (1974)

Table 5.3

Activities, interests and opinions

The following examples are similar to the types of statements related to food that would be used in an AIO analysis.

> I really like to go shopping for food
> I am never sure which foods are good for my family
> I prefer microwaveable foods that are fast to cook
> If both partners work full time, men should do their share of the cooking
> I buy the best food I can afford.

Consumers' lifestyles depend on how they spend their time and money, what they think is important and how they react when asked for their opinions on different subjects. The different consumer lifestyles below show, just how different food purchasing decisions are likely to be for the examples given.

(1) Environmentally-conscious and active consumer rights supporter,

member of the Soil Association, single, vegetarian, working as a part-time conservation volunteer

Likely to seek budget lines, fresh produce (organic if affordable), no meat or fish or products containing animal fats, but more cheese, eggs and pulses, low-salt, high-fibre and healthy foods

(2) Busy professional city couple with no children, a high disposable income who travel extensively for work and pleasure both in the UK and abroad. Belong to a local gym and enjoy entertaining friends for meals at home

Likely to seek branded goods, often premium brands; chilled ready meals and high value added items such as pre-prepared salads, exotic and adventurous ingredients and products, luxury and indulgent items. Lots of wine, fresh herbs, fresh pasta, selected frozen foods and functional foods/nutraceuticals (energy drinks and vitamin enriched products). No price-conscious lines, few tinned or heavily processed items other than ready meals

(3) Large, young, inner city family, single parent, unemployed. Struggle to subsist on state benefits. Leisure confined to television, window shopping and the occasional magazine

Likely to seek the cheapest items, value lines, promotions and reduced-price items. Purchase bulky carbohydrates to stem hunger–bread, potatoes, chips and low-cost protein additions – tinned sausages and beans, cheap cuts of meat, frozen mince etc. Diet is likely be low in fibre, fresh fruit and vegetables, which can be expensive, but high in sugary, high-fat products such as biscuits, cheap savoury snacks and confectionery (treats).

DEMOGRAPHICS AND LIFESTYLES LINKED TO FOOD MARKETING

When lifestyles, personality, values and attitudes are considered in tandem with demographics (objective measures of population size and make up such as age, income, employment, household size etc.) marketers use the term 'psychographics' to describe consumer profiles or 'typologies'. These profiles form the basis of 'market segments' – groups of consumers who can be expected to behave in a similar way towards the products targeted at them and how they are marketed.

The most widely known psychographic tool originated in the USA (SRI International, California) in the early 1980s and is called VALS (Value and Lifestyle Survey). This instrument defines eight international consumer segments based on a combination of psychological characteristics (do principles, status or action tendencies define self-orientation?) and resource accessibility (time, money, effort, energy).

In Europe, RISC (Research Institute into Social Change, Paris) identified 10 lifestyles/value segments based on attitudes expressed in relation to social trends, whilst Socioconsult (Paris) constructed nine 'Social Milieux' segments on the basis of consumers sharing common values and outlooks on life.

All are widely used on an international level to assess general lifestyles and can be applied to consumption profiling. However, one French research agency, CCA (Centre de Communication Avancé) has developed Sociostyles, a lifestyle classification system, for identifying and targeting specific markets and consumers. For Europe, 16 basic groupings are identified, but this system is then able to map these onto areas of specific interest – say food product trends.

These applications can be micro-sectorial in nature (*eg* attitudes to meal preferences), but can also be used to take a wider view, for example, to segment product markets or to identify behavioural or psychological trends.

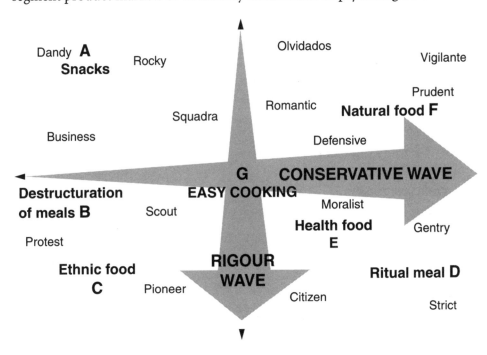

Figure 5.2

Integration map of food preference trends and lifestyle types

Source: Euro-Socio Styles © CCA& Europanel

Figure 1 associates lifestyle types with food choices and meal types. For example, the snack sector, A, is most favoured by the 'Dandy' segment ("hedonist youth with modest income, seeking welfare structures") followed by Rocky, Business and Squadra types. It reflects a preference for prepared fast-food dishes which can be nibbled or eaten without cutlery, without a table, by oneself, at any time of the day or night and whilst doing something else. It reflects trends towards working without formal breaks, for eating 'on-the-hoof', to more consumption autonomy (more singles, destructuring of the family unit and unified eating occasions/menus) and an imitation of the 'American way'.

With such knowledge, food marketers can more effectively target consumers of interest to them.

The media and television have focused more and more on lifestyle issues in recent years and food/cookery and consumer items/programmes feature prominently in these and are very popular. TV exposure has created surges in demand for food ingredients and products such as limes, cranberries, coconut milk and Thai fish sauce. In this way consumers learn how to use food products and so generate new or increased levels of demand. Lifestyle preferences for more 'al fresco' living and eating are directly connected to this

CULTURAL INFLUENCES ON PRODUCT PURCHASING

Whilst food needs to be consumed for physiological reasons – survival – it is not only this functional or instrumental value which determines the individual's reaction to it. Psychological needs can also be met through buying food (it can be a feast for the eyes), preparing it (a sense of being a provider or a form of creative expression) and eating it (people enjoy the social interaction when eating together). Therefore, both the functional or utilitarian value of food and its symbolic significance are influential in food purchasing decisions.

Cultural influences are very important, too. A culture is sometimes described as society's personality. It is the accumulation of shared meanings, rituals, norms and traditions among the members of that society. A culture also includes its values, norms, ethics and material objects. Core cultural values describe those ideals which are commonly endorsed and accepted as a 'good thing' by the majority and determine the overall priorities a consumer attaches to different products and services.

Some core contemporary values in western society and their possible influences in the food arena are shown in the table opposite.

TRENDS IN FOOD PURCHASING AND CONSUMPTION

Taking an overview, food purchasing and consumption are becoming increasingly fragmented. More people are consuming more varied food and drink products on more occasions than ever before. One in every four eating events is estimated to be 'on-the-move', with purchases from take-aways, sandwich and snack bars, drive-throughs and vending machines at new highs. One in six of these products is consumed in a vehicle – so-called 'dashboard dining'. Traditional meal occasions based on the whole family sitting together eating the same food, at the same time, in the same room, have rapidly diminished and been replaced with more snacks, TV dinners and microwaved convenience (often ethnic) products. There is more variety in what is eaten and when: the emphasis on convenience relates both to autonomy in timing and type of food.

'Grazing' – nibbling a bit of this and a bit of that at intervals to suit throughout the day and night, is becoming a norm amongst certain social segments (students, young single householders) who almost exclusively consume convenience products which are ready to eat or very quick to

Core cultural values	Food production/purchasing impliation
A more casual lifestyle with less formality	Destructuring of meal occasions and more individual autonomy over what is eaten, multiple product choices consumed at the same meal time by different people and less formal meals and meal times. Increase in ready and microwaveable products, big 'snacks', single portions and on-the-go products
Pleasure seeking and novelty – a desire for products and services which make life more fun	Constant innovation and product differentiationin all aspects – taste, texture, portion size,packaging advertising, branding, product concepts etc. Food as entertainment, eg, string-type cheese, stackable lunch packs. Character merchandising and growth in products especially geared to children. In 1999,174 such new products were successfully launched in the UK
Consumerism – increased concern over value for money with rising expectations about quality and performance	Strengthening of value and own-brand lines, cut price and discount stores. Rise in 'groceraunt' products – restaurant style food available to take home, for 'eating out, staying in'. Increase in functional foods, eg, energy drinks, vitamin enriched products
Instant gratification – living for today and intolerance of non-immediate availability	Rise in treats, indulgence and luxury items, superpremium lines and convenient packaging formats. More convenient access and availability through wider distribution, vending and specialist in-house provision (eg patisserie)
Simplification – a removal of time and energy spent on'unnecessary' things or tasks	More pre-prepared, prepacked, processed and added-value lines for consumption at once or after microwaving to cut down effort in productselection, preparation, cooking and clearing away. Disposable integral plates/bowls/cups etc. eating implements and packaging
Time conservation – time has to be used effectively	Rise in consumption of freezables to reduceshopping occasions, pre/part-prepared, completeor partial ready meals
Concern with appearance and health, youth, keeping fit and looking good	Expansion/creation of calorie-light product ranges. Increase in low-fat, low-calorie, low-salt, high-fibre products and substitutes. More product innovation in the areas of functional foods and nutraceuticals. Meat reduction and meat substitutes (mycoprotein, soya, tofu). Eat yourself healthy campaign – 'five fruits and vegetables a day', Mediterranean 'superfoods' (eg, garlic, olive oil, red wine, red peppers, sun-dried tomatoes, pasta, rice, fish and shellfish)

prepare. As a consequence, markets for the following product categories, which all support meal destructuring, have expanded substantially in the last five years, in terms of both value (£) and volume (units sold).

Frozen food

This market has nearly quadrupled in the last 20 years, and was worth almost £5 billion in 1999. A massive £1.3 billion of this was accounted for by ice-cream alone. In this sector, the fastest growing products in 1999 were burgers (+21%), pizzas (+18%) and chips (+14%). The frozen ready meals market forms a significant subsector of the frozen market as a whole, accounting for about 15% by value, although growth in this market from 1994 to 1999 was steady but slow – around 9% from £627 million to £683 million. This modest but sustained growth is expected to prevail. Most of the considerable growth in the ready meals sector has come from the following:

Chilled ready meals

This sector now marginally outstrips the frozen ready meals market in terms of value, currently being worth around £700 million – an overall increase of 83% in the five year period to 1999. The pace of expansion of this market is accelerating, with 23% growth from 1998 to 1999, and this trend is expected to continue.

Ambient ready meals

Ambient ready meals showed consistent growth from 1994 (£107 million) to 1999 (£137 million), 16% by value, in real terms.

The 'eating out' market increased by 25% from £16.52 billion in 1994 to £20.6 billion in 1999, with fast food (burgers, pizzas, chicken, take-aways etc.) marginally outsizing hotel and restaurant trade in this sector.

Fast food

The UK fast food market was worth over £7 billion in 1999. Sales of sandwiches comprised almost £3 billion, or over 40% of this total. The classic 'hot trio' – burgers, chicken and pizza – also held around 40% of this market, with sales of over £2.7 billion. Some of these more mature markets are nearing saturation (meeting definitive possible demand).

Savoury snacks

Over the last five years, the savoury snack market has also grown substantially, from £1.6 billion in 1994 to £2.25 billion in 1999 – an overall increase of 40% by value. In real terms (adjusted for inflation) the two key sub sectors in this market – crisps and savouries (all other snacks) – showed different rates of growth: crisps by 11%, savouries by 30%. Tower stacking products are the fastest movers in the snack sector, with the market leader at number 20 in the 'Top 20 grocery products' for 1999. Market value indicates that, on average, every household in the UK consumes more than £100 of savoury snacks each year!

Confectionery

This sector has two subsectors, chocolate: valued at around £4 billion, and sugar, £2 billion, in 1999 – a £6 billion industry. From 1994 to 1999 growth was much faster in the sugar sector (40% – fruit products show strongest growth) than for chocolate (25%). Much of the increase in sales has been due to a fast developing importing trend – up 20%, year on year, since 1998.

Soft drinks

This complex market was worth £3.6 billion in 1999 and includes four main subsectors – carbonates, fruit juices, waters and 'others' (energy and isotonic drinks, concentrates [squashes] and iced teas). Two subsectors are showing very fast growth, in response to consumer demand for 'indulgent yet healthy' alternatives to sugar-laden carbonates. These are waters and adult sport and energy drinks. The latter market has grown by 73% by volume, 81% by value since 1994. In 1999, 228 million litres were consumed.

Interestingly, of the Top 20 UK individual grocery brands by value in 1999, no less than eight fell into the market sectors described above. Coca-Cola was the top performer with sales of £395.9 million, whilst Walkers crisps were third, with sales of £343.6 million.

There is no doubt then, that traditional eating patterns have changed forever: with more mobility, more grazing, more variety, more novelty, more convenience and more ready-to-eat products being key characteristics of the new wave of product selection and consumption in the new millenium.

PRODUCT DESIGN AND DEVELOPMENT

ANALYSING THE NEED FOR NEW PRODUCTS

The stimulus for new products is two-fold. First, *producers* need new products to survive in the marketplace as there will always be products in their portfolio which are (or will be) declining and becoming less profitable. New products are needed to keep ahead of the competition, to defend market share and to retain and promote a strong brand name and up-to-date image.

New products can be developed proactively (ahead of the competition) or reactively (in response to a market aggressor or entrant). Since proactive new product development can bring about 'pioneering advantage' (a long-term consumer preference for the first brand in the market), the rewards for successful innovation can be great. As well as totally new product concepts, innovations can be worked into 'problem' aspects of existing, promising, but ailing products. These might be new packaging, size format or distribution solutions, for example.

Second, new food products are continually required by *consumers*. They constantly seek some elements of novelty, variety and choice in their food shopping alongside the food staples and favourite 'must buy' brands which are regularly purchased.

However, it is unusual for consumers to offer completely innovative product concepts directly to the market; rather they tend to suggest modifications to existing products through various forms of feedback, both solicited (through market research) and co-incidental (via customer complaints). Neverthless, valuable changes can emerge from these communication channels, such as the additions of new flavours to limited ranges (*eg* mango to apple juice, or integral spouts to waxed paper milk/fruit juice cartons).

Consumer demand for new products is driven by contemporary social and cultural trends which impact on consumers, real and perceived needs and wants.

FACTORS AFFECTING NEW FOOD PRODUCT DEVELOPMENTS

Socio-cultural factors

The ageing population, the older first-time parent, the rise in single and child-free households and the increasing role of women as consumers are key *social* trends which will affect new product demands in the coming decade. When these are combined with *cultural* trends towards convenience, time saving and instant gratification and *lifestyle* preferences motivated by health concerns, quality of life and leisure pursuits, the opportunities for new products to meet consumers' needs and wants are considerable.

For example, health awareness trends have been vigorously translated into new product trends in recent years. Over 20% of new food products launched in 1997 and 1998 were 'lite' (low-fat/reduced-calorie) products.

Similarly, today's more hectic lifestyles have spawned the new 'portables' – products designed to be consumed 'on-the-go' (fewer cans, more screw-top bottles, integral/disposable straws/plastic cutlery, more individual portions, more 'bars', more mobile-friendly packaging).

Market factors

Market factors are those which have to do with the business environment within which products are created and sold. The most fundamental of these is *business confidence* because it governs the financial climate within which all business activity takes place. Issues such as stability and strength in the stock market, favourable interest and foreign exchange rates and a strong national economy positively affect the potential for new products as producers are more willing to take risks and to invest money and resources when the economic climate is buoyant.

Second, *legislative factors* are important because they set the framework for legal practice and thereby the constraints on production and advertising. Recent examples of legislation-led new products include the removal/reduction in levels of certain colours and additives to comply with EU laws. Product opportunities in one area can also emerge from legislative constraints in another. So, for example, the BSE crisis resulted in certain beef products being banned, whilst social reaction led to a demand for more meat alternatives and the expansion of mycoprotein (Quorn) and other substitute products such as Tofu and Khero.

Third, *political factors* are important, because they can profoundly determine the supply, cost and availability of ingredients. For example, as a result of the Common Agricultural Policy, there is an over-supply of many products which has forced prices down. This simultaneously means that, as ingredients, such products become more attractive as the basis for added-value lines, such as meat-based ready meals.

Finally, *competition* is a key market factor affecting new product development. In order to compete effectively in the marketplace new products which are different or superior to existing ones need to be created. 'Product differentiation' is an increasing trend in the market, to the extent that 'product fragmentation' (more and more subtle/minor differences between very similar products) is becoming the norm in some product categories (*eg* yoghurt, some pre-packed delicatessen products).

Manufacturers are forced into such strategies in very tightly contested (highly competitive), or mature (well developed and established), or saturated (at the limit of potential consumer demand) markets.

Industrial factors
Industrial factors are connected with aspects of the production process. They include factors such as *technological developments* in plant and machinery which make new industrial processes possible (protective atmospheric wrapping films, Internet shopping); *microbiological factors* affecting the safety of new products (such as BSE and the genetic modification of organisms); *engineering/ergonomic* factors which can improve productive capacity or efficiency and so reduce production costs. In this case, there will be economic implications to consider. Cheaper production could either mean that more funds could be channelled into another phase of the development process (say advertising), or the savings could be passed directly on to the consumer in the form of a lower unit price.

Finally – and much more difficult to pinpoint because it is really a human factor of production – the 'spirit of innovation' and 'entrepreneurship' within the industry. To what extent are new ideas encouraged? Are producers committed to 'making things happen'? How disabling of the innovation process can 'territorial' in-fighting (for example, between R&D and marketing) be? If product innovation is stifled from the start, no combination of social, cultural, market or industrial factors will be able effectively to deliver new products to the market.

Certain sectors are known to be particularly dynamic – both proactive and responsive to consumer trends. Current examples include the adult soft drinks sector, the 'outdoor foods' sector and the children's sector. These change over time according to market opportunity.

CONSUMER EVALUATION OF PRODUCTS
Consumers make evaluations of products based on many different criteria, such as whether the product was satisfactory, fit for the purpose for which it was bought, whether it was good value for money ...

Consumers also make evaluations of products at different stages of the consumer behaviour process. For example, they may reject a product before the *acquisition* stage (it contains too much fat) and not buy it. Or, they may buy it and make judgements during some aspect of the *consumption* [in-use] stage (this packet is difficult to open, this product tastes too sweet). The product may also be evaluated at the *disposition* [disposal or handing-on] stage (this packaging is not recyclable, the amount of waste from this product makes it very expensive). Consumers might make such judgements at none, some, or all of these stages. New food product developers, therefore, need to consider the total product and not simply the part which is eaten.

Consumers make evaluations on the basis of their attitudes towards various 'attributes' (features) of the product. Attitudes consist of two components: beliefs and judgements. The consumer might believe that a product (olive oil spread) is healthy, modestly priced and readily available. They might judge that this is a 'good' thing.

Attitudes which combine favourable judgements with a positive assessment of product attributes are likely to result in the product being purchased. Producers are therefore always looking for ways to create positive attitudes towards their products and, indeed, one way in which they try to broaden the market for a product is by changing consumers' evaluations of the product to be more positive.

Unless new products are unique, they are rarely evaluated 'in a vacuum'. Almost (if not) always, products are evaluated with reference to other similar, competitive products which form a basis for comparison. Here product preferences are expressed – evaluative judgements which involve comparisons (I prefer olive oil spread to vegetable fat spread because it is healthier). Typically then, new product developers need to know consumers' attitudes towards competitive products when they are involved in developing new product concepts.

Another key issue concerns who is doing the evaluation. Someone may make the purchase decision (mother buys prawn flavour fish bites) but may not be the consumer of the product (six year old son). In this case there might be a positive attitude in the acquisition stage ('I think Jack will like these, they look fun') and a negative one in the consumption stage ('Yuk, I hate these pink things, I prefer fish fingers'). In this case, only consumer research will help the manufacturer to know that the product failed because the child (consumer) rather than the mother (purchaser) rejected the product.

Consumers are continually interested in new food products to bring variety and novelty into their routine purchasing patterns. However, consumers are also more educated and more discerning about products than ever before. They are constantly evaluating products both consciously (they are aware of their thoughts) and automatically (they make judgements but do not make a 'mental note' of them). New product developers need to be very well informed to ensure positive attitudes to their new products which will result in repeat purchasing.

QUALITY OF DESIGN

Quality of design is vital if a product is to succeed in the marketplace. Estimates as to how many products make it from product concept to established product vary widely, but the percentage is very low. On average about 1 in a 100 (1%) ideas are developed into new product concepts. Of these, around 1 in 20 (5%) are developed to the launch stage. More than one-third (35%) fail at the launch stage (*ie* to cover all development costs, or 'break even'), and of the reminder, only 5 –10% make substantial profits.

Quality design is most likely to come about when producers have:

(1)   an in-depth knowledge of consumers' preferences
(2)   an integrated business whose different departments (marketing, finance, R&D, production etc.) work effectively together as a team to satisfy customers' preferences and exceed their expectations.

Quality design will therefore result from a process whereby the technical aspects of production (what it is possible to make) are constantly informed by the cost implications (how expensive the process will make the product) and how well these match with consumer wants and needs (based on market intelligence about product preferences).

New food products are most likely to be successful when:

(1)   they are unique or superior in some way to competing products (eg 'Pringles' – as a new product it was unique [there are now copycat versions like 'Stackers'], lighter, crunchier and fresher than competing snack products)

(2)   a good marketing strategy is employed
      (*eg* 'Pringles' – had a strong advertising campaign with the challenging slogan "When you pop you can't stop" and powerful promotional gimmicks and merchandising – *eg* special, limited edition 'Pringles' pocket packs)

(3)   the technical production is flawless
      (*eg* 'Pringles' – the product keeps its unique shape, does not break in transit and is kept superfresh in attention-grabbing, resealable packaging).

If all three criteria are met, the chances of post-launch success increase to 90%!

VALUE FOR MONEY

Through constant increases in general levels of affluence and the overall standard of living over the last 50 years, consumers now expect that the food products they buy will be of a decent quality. However, they are also interested in reasonable prices, and these are made possible by the amount of competition on the market.

In the UK, the percentage of money spent on food per head of the population is the lowest in the European Union in relation to income, at 11% (of Gross Domestic Product or GDP). This is partly a measure of the relative 'cheapness' of food in this country but also a reflection of our affluence (we have more money to spend) and of our motivation towards food in general (a cultural norm). In the UK, food is simply not the priority area of expenditure it is, say, for the French or the Italians.

In general, consumers assume that there is a positive relationship between price and quality – the more you pay, the better the product – referred to as 'the price – quality relationship', but at the same time they also seek 'value for money'. From a range of similar products on offer, they will select what they consider to be the best balance between a particular level of quality and what they are required to pay for it, according to the usage situation for which it is being bought. For example, they might be quite content to buy a lesser quality, own-label, ambient, fruit juice for a children's party since they need 20 litres (50 pence per litre) but would choose a fresh, chilled, premium-brand, litre pack to take to a friend in hospital (£2.25 pence per litre).

INFLUENCE OF FOOD RETAILERS

SURVEY OF FOOD RETAILING IN THE UK

Food retailers are very powerful in the UK, in 1999 accounting for around 46% of total retail sales, a figure which has gradually increased throughout the last decade at the expense of non-store retailing (mail order). This position is likely to change radically in the coming decade as e-commerce and e-tailing (Internet retailing) expand.

The food sector is dominated by large grocery multiples (including the 'Big 4' – Tesco, Sainsbury's, Asda and Safeway – together with Somerfield, Kwik Save, Morrisons, Marks & Spencer, Waitrose and Iceland). Taken together, these market players now account for approximately 90% of total trade in the sector (by value, £).

Concentration of activity is increasing year on year, with the 'Big 4' increasing their combined strength from 51% of sales in 1994 to 70% in 1999. Concentration has been achieved both through merger (Somerfield, Kwik Save in 1998) and acquisition (Asda, by Walmart, the US food giant, in 1999).

However, the fortunes of the 'Big 4' have varied in the last five years. Tesco achieved the highest growth rate (sales) from 1994 to 1999 (64% in real terms) and toppled Sainsbury's from its position as market leader. Over the same period, the rate of growth of Sainsbury's slowed considerably, to only 34%. Safeway turned in a weaker performance still – just 29% growth, whilst Asda fared much better, with 56% growth over the five years.

Of the smaller chains, both Waitrose (48%) and Morrisons (42%) showed strong growth. Most of the others made relatively modest growth or stood still, with the exception of Iceland (22%).

In terms of operating profits, Tesco and Morrisons were the only food multiples to show growth in 1998/9, whilst the most profitable food multiple is Morrisons with overall margins of 6.7%. Tesco are expected to challenge and overtake Sainsbury's in respect of operating margins in 1999/2000.

As far as asset utilisation is concerned (profit per square foot), the operators with the highest proportion of large format stores reported the best figures, with Tesco in the number one position.

Whilst the financially robust position outlined reflects the power of the grocery giants, these companies have had to work hard to achieve their buoyant position in difficult trading conditions. Factors such as negligible population growth, static demand and fierce competition have combined with changed patterns in food consumption and some key declining markets (eg red meat) to force food retailers to adopt competitive pricing strategies which have included an explosion in own-label goods, the introduction of basic 'value' lines (often 'loss-leaders') and massive cost cutting on certain lines to compete with the foreign-owned discounters. Among these, Netto (Denmark) and Aldi and Lidl (Germany) are the most significant. Warehouse clubs – like Costco – introduced from the USA, who are also contenders in a tight market. Recent evidence indicates that the discounters are struggling to compete with the multiples' aggressive price initiatives as their market growth slows, or levels out.

The major retailers have had increasingly to look to non-food added-value services such as petrol, banking, pharmaceuticals, dry cleaning, audio, books and magazines, video rental and photographic services, as well as increasing their proportion of the 'mobile' food sector (sandwiches, snacks and 'lunchables') and introducing food service operations in the form of convenient, in-house, catering for hungry shoppers on-the-go.

Loyalty cards, widely introduced in recent years, and initially seen as a perk, are increasingly viewed as 'golden handcuffs' as shoppers come to understand from experience their marginal value in real terms, and realise how little protected they are from the manipulation of the detailed data they willingly provide about their shopping habits, choices and expenditure.

OTHER FOOD RETAILERS

The independent sector of food retailers (sole traders) contracted in the 1990s by around 20%, whereas small retail chains (multiple ownership) increased by about 40%: a less significant, but nevertheless clear additional indicator of retail concentration.

WHO'S SHOPPING WHERE?

Shoppers are using a wider variety of stores for food shopping than five years ago. A typical household uses five outlets regularly: two or three major retailers and selected local shops or convenience stores. This means that the main weekly/monthly shop (primary shop) is more widely dispersed across the major retailers, but also that more substantial 'secondary' shopping is conducted at the favoured 'alternate' supermarket. Morrisons and Tesco alone gained more 'primary' shoppers in 1999, partly due to expansion in the number of their outlets in 'new' regions and the proliferation of town and city centre stores, but also to the upsizing of existing stores and the extension of their product portfolios.

THE FUTURE?

If the stringent planning arrangements of the 1990s are relaxed, the major retailers will look to increase the proportion of out-of-town hypermarkets and superstores in their outlet portfolios as these are their most profitable formats. Otherwise, profits will be squeezed from a further range of value-adding services: through extension into non-food product categories (focus on leisure and home sectors), from more intense price competition between the multiples and with the discounters and by further eating into the declining independent and small multiply owned sector.

The most significant change and anticipated growth is likely to come from the expansion in Internet shopping (where Tesco and Sainsbury's lead the way), from hard-wired terminals as well as from mobile phones using the latest WAP (wireless application protocol) technology and from home shopping via digital television. Perhaps, more mundanely (and maybe sooner?) also from home delivery and personal 'food shopper' services.

INFLUENCE OF RETAILERS ON FOOD PRODUCTS,
CONSUMPTION, EXPENDITURE AND AVAILABILITY

Retail concentration among grocery multiples ultimately reduces choice for the consumer as supply is limited to fewer differentiated outlets. But concentration also leads to buying power in the market with manufacturers and other suppliers. For this reason the major retailers have been able to drive down manufacturers' margins with some consequent price benefits for the consumer. (This point is, however, hotly contested, with supermarkets' alleged 'unbridled' profits under scrutiny by the Office of Fair Trading.) In fact, the proportion of household income spent on food has been declining constantly for the last 50 years, and now stands at around 11% – the lowest in the EU.

Purchasing power means that global imports of a very wide range of goods are now commonplace, with more and more 'exotic' ingredients as well as processed products on the shelves. As well as thinking globally, retailers have been forced to a recognition through consumer pressure groups that, in the longer term, 'acting local' is also in their best interest. Home-grown produce is fresher, cheaper, in season, avoids the environmental impacts created by international freighting (the food miles debate) and supports the local, regional and national economy as the growing crisis in agriculture deepens. In addition, it offsets claims about unethical practices (for example, the 'exporting' of employment abroad) and feeds a growing consumer movement in favour of 'authenticity' and known-origin goods.

These concerns are linked to recent health scares over BSE and more widely to worries about genetically modified foods. In response to consumer pressure, all the major retailers have now moved against GMOs with the result that trials have been limited and full-scale production delayed. The power of the retailers is such that it can force such policy decisions through, even at a national, governmental level.

In the search for new buyers, food products are becoming ever more differentiated and markets fragmented. Just think of how many different lines of yoghurt are presented in the average food superstore! Within food retailing, all the major multiples now sell products in four main strata – something to appeal to every taste and pocket.

(1) Luxury, premium quality, high-price, indulgence and treat ranges which include restaurant quality meal components (appetisers, starters, main courses, vegetables, salads, desserts, wines, drinks) global 'exotica', treats and special event foods

(2) Mainstream, everyday, major (Heinz beans, Nescafe, Coca-Cola) and niche (Marmite, Bisto gravy granules) brands, consistently priced other than frequent promotional offers

(3) Own-label goods – typically high-volume, safe, proven and traditional lines to compete with brands but sold at lower prices on the 'value for money' ticket

(4) Budget or low-priced goods aimed at the price-conscious shopper – more limited ranges of the most basic products (including staples [bread, tea] and necessities [toilet roll, washing up liquid]) sold at very low prices, often 'loss leaders'

Large food retailers typically stock up to 40,000 lines, usually with most choice in the own-label category. However, once own-label goods exceed 55% of the product portfolio, overall sales have been shown to decline as there is insufficient variety and access to branded, luxury or value lines. Offering lines in each of these different product strata means that some products are attractive to all socio-economic groups from the affluent or indiscriminant to the most price-conscious shopper.

Consumption is partly determined by product availability (ie retailer supply), but equally by consumer demand. This has been demonstrated in very clear ways in relation to environmental concerns such as food scares (reduction in beef consumption following deaths from CJD, the human form of BSE), refusal to purchase products containing GMOs (soya, tomato puree), but also more subtly in respect of wider political, social and technological matters. (Boycotting of French products when France rejected re-introduction of exported British beef, acceptance of South African products after the breakdown of apartheid, the 'rush for limes' after celebrity endorsement on TV cookery programmes, rise in crisp sales following introduction of new 'extra-fresh' foil packaging etc., etc.).

The type of shopping available is significant in that the large grocery multiples, having for the most part replaced specialist high street retailers, are increasingly providing 'copycat' shops within their stores. Whilst delicatessens are long-standing examples of this, fresh meat, fish and bakery counters are becoming more prevalent over time and their product ranges increasingly contain more value-added products (such as BBQ-ready marinated meats). Through such provision, the major retailers aim to extend their (in-house own-label) ranges and provide one-stop shopping for all their customers' needs, so increasing average expenditure. If successful, this strategy could minimise sales lost to secondary sources.

Discounters, by contrast, operate on a very different basis. Instead of competing on service, choice, quality and a pleasant shopping environment, their operations are almost exclusively price driven. The 'pile 'em high, sell 'em cheap' philosophy relies on fast, high-volume throughput in order to pass on bulk purchasing benefits to the consumer through low mark-ups. As a consequence, discounters' product margins are typically 8–10% instead of the 20–25% expected, by most multiples. The available number of lines is hence very limited (3–5000), when compared with the superstores which stock 10–15 times as many. No thrills, no frills.

The geographical dispersion of the major retailers means that some regional strongholds are identifiable, *eg* Tesco and Waitrose in London and the south-east, Asda and Morrisons in the north. Store location clearly affects consumer choice as most consumers will not make detours to shop if there is a large, local, food superstore. To this extent, the location of a new store is critical, both in terms of the size and the socio-economic profile of the catchment area that it supports, since product portfolios are closely geared to these factors.

A further factor recently affecting availability has been the elastification of store opening hours. Although far from uniform across the country, and variable by organisation, most supermarkets are now open seven days a week, typically from 8 or 9am until 9 or 10pm Monday to Saturday and 10am to 4pm or similar on Sunday (due only to legislative constraints). Some of the largest outlets or those located in areas of urban concentration are open 24 hours a day on one (usually Friday) or more days of the week. This practice has enfranchised a new breed of shopper – young night-owls, late shift workers, taxi drivers and other night workers.

RETAILER INFLUENCES ON NEW PRODUCT DEVELOPMENTS,
SALES OF NEW FOOD PRODUCTS AND THE 'OWN-LABEL' CONCEPT

Both in response to consumer trends or their own ideas for product-led innovations, the major retailers are powerful enough to commission products directly from the manufacturers. The majority of these are sold under own-label packaging, but – sometimes manufacturers will be asked to develop lines on the retailers behalf – it boils down to where the research and development and marketing costs are to be borne.

Manufacturers vary in their willingness to make own-label products, often viewing these as a challenge to their existing brands. Even when their brand images are very robust, they fear an association with cheaper copycat products which might dilute the hard-won quality images they seek to perpetuate and which keep them at the top of the market. Coca-Cola have battled with both Sainsbury's and Virgin on this point, as they, along with companies like Kelloggs and Mars, have steadfastly refused to make own-label products. Kelloggs have gone so far as to use this as an advertising strategy for the cornflakes brand "We don't make cornflakes for anyone else".

Other major manufacturers such as Nestlé and Unilever do make products to retailers' own specifications which are sold as own-brand, but principally only to mop up excess productive capacity. At the other end of the scale, United Biscuits has a large, specially built plant for own-label products which generates in excess of a third of their total sales.

International comparisons show that the rise in own-label products is linked to retail concentration, the fewer powerful hands that dominate the market, the more likely own brands are to be available, and the higher the proportion of these is likely to be. So, for example, in Portugal, where the structure of food retailing is very fragmented, there are very few own-label products (less than 5%), whereas this figure reaches 50–55% in the UK's most powerful retailers.

As the major multiples can effectively showcase own-label products – giving them preferential shelf positioning or 'facings' (prime selling space) they are able to promote these products on the back of the reputation of and familiarity with established brands through (cheaper) promotion rather than (expensive) advertising. Growth of own brands is hence often at the expense of the weaker competitive branded products.

ASPECTS OF MERCHANDISING AND PRODUCT MANAGEMENT WITHIN SUPERMARKETS

It has already been noted that consumer attitudes and perceptions can affect the intention to buy a product but do not necessarily translate into an actual purchase. In order to achieve this the major retailers take great care to manage their product portfolios effectively, both through store and product management and merchandising.

Merchandising

Merchandising aims to prompt purchase at the point of sale. One key issue is to increase the visibility of the product, since 'noticing' is a required first stage in the process leading to a purchase. Visibility is increased by shelf positioning, price tickets, specialist displays and bin-dumps (free-standing displays usually separate from the main shopping aisles). Indirect sources of stimuli can also prompt consumer reaction such as music (speed will affect the pace of shopping) and real/artificial odours (such as newly baked bread in the bakery or the smell of 'fresh-bread' pumped through the air-conditioning), which stimulate the appetite and make people buy more.

Merchandising is also used because the majority of purchases are either unplanned or on impulse. Accordingly, in-store stimuli can either prompt consumers to recall that they *need* the product (they have run out at home, but it was not on their shopping list) or, through drawing attention to the product make them feel that that they '*want*' it, and so buy on a whim.

Product management

Product management is essential because of the many different categories of product which all require different methods of storage, handling, display and stock rotation. Fresh fruit, for example, requires much more careful attention than say, tinned vegetables due to its perishability (it will degrade if kept in warm, moist conditions), fragility (it will bruise if not handled and displayed with care) and shelf-life (it has a short 'buying window' before its sell-by date)

In major supermarkets which carry 30,000 – 40,000 lines, the stores' products are often organised according to categories, of which there might be around 400. Each of these can be managed like a small business as an independent 'cost centre'. Through barcode scanning at the checkouts, direct product profitability analysis (DPP) can be undertaken to see how well each category is doing and what contribution it is making to the overall profitability of the store. Category management is also useful in providing information about the 'brand mix' (how much space to allocate to each brand in proportion to how much is sold) and scanning also automatically triggers re-ordering and re-stocking.

The positioning of these categories around the store is also important. Staple items like tea, bread, milk and eggs are positioned to pull customers past as many other products as possible. Fruit and vegetables are often placed just inside the entrance because their colour, shapes, variety and attractive displays are inviting. Certain areas of the store sell better than others – eye-level shelves, outer aisles, aisle-ends and checkouts, for example.

Overall, store design is also important both psychologically and practically. Factors such as ease of parking, appropriate trolleys and wide aisles all increase consumer expenditure. Overcrowding reduces shopping time and lowers purchasing levels. The latest trends are for spacious, uncluttered, open environments with lower aisles so that consumers can see beyond their immediate horizon. 'Rustic' fixtures and fittings and the use of natural colours (green, cream) and materials (wood, paper) are also in vogue. One major food retailer has created fun visual cues (further visual stimuli) in the form of very large, moving glass fibre animals to help locate products and attract consumers (especially through kid-appeal) to them (*eg* cows for dairy products, penguins above the freezers). The term to describe in-store environmental manipulation to enhance shopping is 'retail atmospherics'.

Stock rotation (constantly keeping products with the shortest shelf-life at the front of displays) and re-stocking shelves can be problematic if the amount of product on display is out of proportion to its sales. Stores constantly monitor this to ensure that the space allocation is appropriate and that the product is always displayed when available from the storage facility.

More widely, retailers try to maintain consistency in the availability of the widest range of products – if it is not for sale it cannot be bought and a sale is lost. Factors such as seasonality will clearly affect availability of fresh fruit and vegetables, but is the store geared up with barbeque products in April in case of an unanticipated warm weekend?

When all these factors are considered together, it becomes clear that merchandising and product management within supermarkets are linked to consumer behaviour in a quite deliberate and strategic way. Getting these things right is the key to maximising sales and profits for the store.

EMERGING TRENDS

Demographic and lifestyle changes originating in the 1990s are set to continue over the next 10–20 years and so impact directly on the UK food and drinks markets. The main demographic changes include the rise of the single person household (SPH), the increasing role of economically active women, the continued decline of the traditional family unit and the ageing population. Lifestyles have become more time-pressured and hectic, more sophisticated, more individualistic, more self-reliant and more leisure oriented. These, together with other 'social drivers' of food consumption such as:

– the desires for convenience, time-saving and novelty
– technology (introduction of new cooking devices)
– major food scares (BSE and *E.Coli*)
– the growth of the health lobby.

These have all contributed to radical changes in consumer eating habits in the last decade. Some trends, considered in more detail below, are particularly significant, and can be expected to have a dynamic impact on the food industry in coming years.

ETHNIC FOODS, ETHNIC FUSION AND HYBRID CUISINE

Six percent of the total UK population (3.5 million people) are of ethnic origin, of which around two million are Asian. In the UK today, there are approximately 25,000 ethnic restaurants; the UK is reputedly the most ethnocentric nation in western Europe in terms of attitudes towards, and acceptance of, the cuisines of its ethnic minorities. London, for example, has more than double the number of ethnic food service outlets per million of the population (around 150) than Paris (around 65) and more than seven times as many as Rome (20).

Consumption of ethnic food is as much associated with lifestyles and aspirations as it is with the food itself. Consumers are drawn to ethnic foods because of many of the social drivers identified in the previous section, but particularly because they are novelty seeking and want to see themselves as adventurous in their eating habits.

Many ethnic cuisines are unfamiliar or complicated to make and require specialist knowledge, cooking utensils and ingredients. Therefore, many initial explorations into ethnic foods begin with sampling meals at ethnic restaurants, the purchase of ethnic ready meals or the use of ethnic convenience products such as cooking sauces. The interaction of all these has created a much increased demand for ethnic foods.

The ethnic restaurant and take-away market was worth around £3.5 billlion in 1999, with its key advantage of 'authenticity' for the consumer. However, this does not include frozen, chilled and ambient ethnic ready meals and a burgeoning range of *ingredients* (herbs, spices), *accompaniments* (specialist rices, grains and breads), *sundries* (sauces, pickles and condiments) and ethnic *convenience products* (cooking sauces, pastes, stir fry mixes etc.).

At present, the most popular ethnic foods are Indian, Chinese and Italian, but South East Asian (Thai, Malaysian and Indonesian), Japanese, Caribbean and Tex-Mex foods are gaining in market presence and strength. In the strongest and best established sectors, product differentiation is becoming more commonplace. Product segmentation is taking place on the basis of regionality as well as taste preferences and types. 'Chicken curry' is no longer a simple choice. Is it Goan or Bombay chicken curry? Or is it from Malaysia or Indonesia? Is it a mild Indian chicken curry (khorma) or a very hot (vindaloo) one?

Other related trends include ethnic fusion which involves taking successful concepts from the cuisines of different regions/nations/cultures and blending them together such as chicken tikka lasagna (Indian and Italian) or hot chilli beef pizza (Mexican and Italian). This produces a hybrid cuisine where the taste sensations are already known to be palatable (and therefore commercially attractive) in their own right, but which are perceived by consumers to fulfil novelty as well as added (taste) value benefits when sold together as a new product innovation.

Creolisation involves the blending of various eating traditions into new ones to make the tastes of one regional/national cuisine fit the mainstream culture of another. In the UK context, this 'product localisation' means, for example, Mexican food with less chilli, or indianised sandwiches (onion bhaji, raita and salad are already on the market!).

LEISURE AND SPORTS PRODUCTS

A relatively new and potentially very lucrative market is for the specialised food/drink products which are currently being sold and developed for use in sports and leisure activities. These can range from adaptations to existing products by reformulation through the use of innovative packaging designs and formats which are more portable – such as screw-top bottles and re-usable dose-spout bottles for sipping – right through to products which are designed to perform a particular task (such as the replacement of lost body salts and fluids, the enhancement of energy levels through stimulants, or supplementing daily vitamin intake). Where products are specifically designed for such purposes they are termed *functional foods*. If they have an explicit medical purpose they are referred to as *nutraceuticals*.

CONCEPTS FOR SPORTS NUTRITION

General interest in and growing awareness of health issues in the wider population has led to more demand for lighter and healthier alternatives which add fibre and cut down on the 'empty' calories, fat, sugar, salt, additives (flavourings, colourings) and preservatives contained in many modern foodstuffs.

Nutritional experts advocate such dietary revisions not only in order to reduce overweight and obesity, which are contributing to major health problems in our society, but also in the positive interests of health and fitness. Sportsmen and women have a particular interest in these recommendations as they require a diet which complements their form of exercise and enables them to achieve optimal performance. In order to do this they need a balanced diet which will maximise strength, stamina and flexibility whilst helping to build/maintain appropriate muscle and minimise unwanted weight gain. Specialist products are needed to match different training needs (ie for carbohydrate loading in advance of marathons); whilst the recent controversy about 'banned substances' contained or released through product consumption (such as nandrolone), have alerted manufacturers that certain additives need to be positively avoided.

For general health and fitness enthusiasts, the most important types of products in this sector have been those which control energy production – either by reducing it through low-calorie foods (fruits, vegetables, lean meat and fish, rice and pasta) or by providing a fast energy release/stimulant when needed (such as fruit and cereal bars and drinks containing caffeine, taurine and guarana).

INFLUENCE OF THE AGEING POPULATION

From demographic data it is known that the UK population is an ageing one. This is due to three key factors.

First, *people are living longer* (increased longevity). Over the 40-year period from 1991 to 2031, the number of 'old people' (65–79) will increase from around 7 million to 9.5 million (+35%). Over the same period, numbers of the very old (80+) will grow by 60%. Those aged 65 or more will then account for almost a quarter of the population, or one in every four people.

At the same time, the numbers of those aged under 40 will constantly decline, as will the 40–65 age group after 2010. In sum, this means that in the next decade, the only age groups growing in the population are those aged 40 plus.

Second, *fewer babies are being born.* This means that the young are a declining proportion of the population and, indeed, by 2021, it is estimated that this situation will be further intensified as the *replacement rate* becomes negative. At this point, annual deaths will exceed annual births. The overall size of the population will further decrease and the percentage of the young (under 40, but especially under 16) will diminish.

These factors will have a profound effect on product availability and new product development. Older consumers are known to be more settled and stable, set in their ways, less accepting of change and less likely to embrace innovative new product concepts.

Empty nesters (householders without children) and post-family (children have left home) lifestagers are growing both in numbers and affluence. More older people will have more money to spend. They will also tend to have more time to spend on leisure activities, so new products targeted at them are likely to be of a luxurious, indulgent nature: more geared to 'al fresco' lifestyles, home entertainment, hobbies and travel.

On the other hand, people who are old now or will be in the coming decades, experienced food rationing during and post-war (WW2). As a result of this and higher levels of physical exercise in years gone by (*eg* more walking and exercise-intensive domestic duties like washing and mowing the lawn without mechanised, automatic machines), they led more active lives when young. For many, this has left them with an abiding interest in remaining fit and healthy so food products designed to satisfy these needs are also likely to be favoured. Functional foods, and in particular nutraceuticals, will experience growth in the 'grey' consumer segments.

Through nostalgia, this group are also likely to be strong in their pursuit of 'authenticity' in products ('bacon which tastes like it used to') and so provide a kickback against the cheaper but mass-produced, mass-marketed, highly processed and lower quality goods which are the norm today.

For this group, 'added-value' will paradoxically come from 'taking away' (growth hormones, additives and preservatives).

MARKETING AND MARKET RESEARCH

INTRODUCTION

Market research in the food industry has two basic purposes:

(1) to reduce uncertainty when launching new products or making changes to already established food products (*eg* re-packaging, re-branding)

(2) to monitor performance of food products in the marketplace so that informed management decision-making can be undertaken to improve performance through strategic (product) planning and management.

The marketing research process is continuous and circular: ideally, market research is conducted throughout the whole food product development process from the new product concept right through to its final launch. Product monitoring is then undertaken and the outcome in turn feeds back into the development of further new product ideas which initiate the whole process anew.

THE ROLE OF MARKET RESEARCH IN MANAGEMENT DECISION-MAKING

Market research can take many different forms and employ a wide range of techniques to help support sound management decision-making whether this be connected with new product launch or product monitoring.

	Role of Market Research	Examples of management decision-making
Managing change effectively	• To test out different ideas before investing significant resources	• Selection of product concept to be developed • Selection of new brand image
Monitoring performance	• To analyse consumer buying behaviour • To analyse sales data	• Decision to spend more money on advertising • Sales analysis indicates changes in distribution of product are needed

Based on the rationale for undertaking the research, the market researcher will decide which technique is most appropriate for generating the type of information required. The most important issues to be addressed in the market research process will also be identified before any actual research.

The market research process

The starting point for any market research is the question "What is the rationale for undertaking this research?" Answers to this question can be categorised into three broad types:

(1) *Exploratory design studies*

These studies are used to help define and understand the new product concept and identify and evaluate creative new solutions to existing management problems (how can we prevent our snacks from getting into tiny bits before the consumer buys them?)

(2) *Descriptive studies*

Here research is undertaken to 'capture' information which already exists and which could be related to food product performance – distribution channels or market share, for example

(3) *Causal studies*

Studies of this type attempt to identify the key factors which influence consumer behaviour. For example, the degree to which advertising campaigns affect sales. This type of study is notoriously difficult to design and will often provide ambiguous results.

Irrespective of the type of study undertaken, the stages of the market research process remain common to them all.

Stage 1	Research brief	➡	Manufacturer and researcher work together to agree a clearly defined rationale and goals and objectives for the research
Stage 2	Research proposal	➡	A work plan and budget are agreed and the most appropriate research method is agreed
Stage 3	Data collection	➡	Reliable and valid data is collectied with careful control of the data collection process
Stage 4	Data analaysis and interpretation	➡	The data is processed to provide meaningful results
Stage 5	Presentation of research report	➡	The results, conclusions and recommendations are presented in a form that will allow effective management decisions to be made

QUALITATIVE RESEARCH AND DATA COLLECTION

Qualitative research

Two techniques are commonly used in qualitative research: in-depth interviews and focus groups (sometimes called buying panels). In both cases an experienced researcher trained in the technique will engage the individual or group in a series of structured discussions to gain insights into *subjective* aspects of consumer behaviour (perceptions, attitudes, beliefs, values etc). Advertisers can use this technique to gauge consumer reactions to different styles or types of packaging or to help create a consumer profile for a particular market segment.

Qualitative research tries to answer 'how' and 'why' questions.

Quantitative research

Quantitative research, by contrast, is concerned with the collection of data for statistical analysis. This type of research considers *objective* (factual) information such as the size and composition of markets, demographics and sales figure.

In the food retailing industry, significant advances in data collection have been brought about by technological means. Two of the most important are:

(1)   *Scanning technology*
      Sales at the checkout are registered using barcodes (formally termed universal product codes [UPCs]) which, in conjunction with customer loyalty cards, provide large amounts of consumer purchasing data

(2)   *Internet use*
      Provides information relating not only to actual purchases but also browsing behaviour.

Quantitative research tries to answer 'where', 'when' and 'how many' questions.

In spite of these advances, one of the more traditional techniques, still widely used in the food industry today, is the questionnaire.

QUESTIONNAIRE DESIGN

Following the launch of a new product, manufacturers will often conduct a market survey based on administering a questionnaire to a carefully selected sample of around 1000 consumers. This sampling may be conducted with different market segments and repeated over time to monitor how the product is moving from novelty buy to regular purchase.

The questionnaire is designed to produce both qualitative and quantitative data using different question styles.

Open Questions

Open questions (do not limit the answer) produce qualitative data (descriptions in words), *eg*

> "What do you think of the colour of brand X?"

Closed questions
Closed questions (confine the answer options) produce quantitative data (comparable numerical information), *eg*

> "How often do you buy brand X?" (tick the most appropriate box)

once a week	once a month	once a year	never
☐	☐	☐	☐

When conducting a questionnaire it is vital that the sample (the people selected to complete the questionnaire) is *representative*. This means it must be a fair reflection of a cross-section of the population who might be expected to buy the product.

ANALYSIS OF RESULTS

Market research data can be analysed in two different ways. In descriptive terms, or in terms of relationships.

Descriptive statistics

Results are presented in a clear and simple way to show what has been found. Information is often presented in simple mathematical terms (eg percentages or fractions).

For example, a quantitative survey of 1000 respondents assessing natural fruit juice consumption shows that:

- 23% drink fruit juice every day
- 27% drink fruit juice four or more times per week
- 14% drink fruit juice once a week
- 36% drink fruit juice occasionally.

This information can be presented in a different way:

- around 1 in 4 drink fruit juice every day
- around 1 in 4 drink fruit juice four or more times per week
- around 1 in 7 drink fruit juice once a week
- around 1 in 3 drink fruit juice occasionally.

The popularity of fruit juice flavours might be:

- 29% orange
- 20% apple
- 14% grapefruit
- 11% red berries
- 11% blackcurrant
- 15% others.

Qualitative data from discussion in a focus group may reveal multiple answers to the question: "Why do you drink fruit juice?"

- "I like the taste"
- "It makes me feel healthy"
- "It is thirst quenching"
- "It is good for you".

Relational data

Results are analysed to look for links between different parts of the data. So, using the example above about fruit juice, of the 29% who stated that orange was their favourite flavour, maybe 80% were male and 20% were female. Therefore, there is a positive relationship between gender and orange juice consumption. (Orange juice is more likely to be preferred by men.)

Further discussion in the focus group may reveal that people feel that "drinking fruit juice is healthy" because of strong associations with, or links to, youth, sport, fitness and an 'outdoor lifestyle'.

STRATEGIC PLANNING

A recent survey of the top 100 UK grocery brands yielded the surprising fact that 38 of these products were launched over 51 years ago, as Table 5.4 shows!

In contrast to these exceptional and mostly 'classic' food products, the majority of new products launched will go through a life cycle which rarely exceeds 18 months. Given the huge costs in terms of time and money invested in new product developments, producers are constantly searching for strategies to extend the product life cycle.

To plan strategically, producers must take into account both internal and external factors to manage the process of change from newly launched product to established brand leader.

External factors include competition and market reaction.

Internal factors include expansion of scale of manufacture and changing distribution channels.

Years from launch	Number of brands
51+	38
31–50	27
21–30	15
11–20	10
less than 10	10

Table 5.4

Top 100 UK grocery brands

DEVELOPING, AND IMPLEMENTING, A MARKETING PLAN FOR FOOD PRODUCTS

For each new product, therefore, a marketing plan is needed which is adapted to take it through the various stages of the product life cycle shown in Figure 5.3.

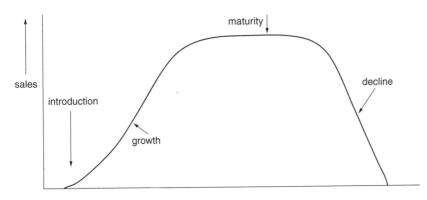

Figure 5.3

The product life cycle

Table 5.5, shows how marketing activity has to be planned for and altered as each stage of the product life cycle is reached. It is vital to have good market

Table 5.5

Marketing activity at different stages of the product life cycle

Life cycle stage	Description	Marketing plan
Introduction	New product launch	Market launch, strong; advertising
Growth	Sales are increasing and break-even point for product launch costs is exceeded	Develop productive and distribution capacity and increase retail outlets
Maturity	Sales reach a high point and product becomes a brand leader	Marketing to sustain prime brand image and promotions to fight off competition
Decline	Sales begin to decrease as better rival products are introduced by competitiors	Either: (a) re-brand, re-package, improve and relaunch or (b) withdraw from marketplace and replace with new product

intelligence, sales data and consumer feedback to recognise each stage in the life cycle. The objective of the marketing plan is to maximise the period of maturity (and so profit) for the product. Exceptions to this are few but include food products deliberately introduced as novelty/seasonal items.

THE ROLE OF MARKETING IN DEVELOPING AND MANAGING PRODUCTS

The marketing department needs to have an involvement in all stages of the development and management of food products because it performs an intermediary role between what the producer supplies to the marketplace and what the consumer needs or wants from the product. Producers do not want to be stuck with failed products which will not sell, and consumers do not want products thrust upon them which are of no interest to them and which they will not buy. The marketing function tries to match up supply and demand through a detailed knowledge of what the producer can make and what the consumer will be prepared to buy. This knowledge means that marketing are constantly trying to 'fine-tune' different factors of production at each stage of the production process. This might involve making changes to food product prototypes as a result of market testing, whilst at the same time setting a price which will meet costs, yet be attractive enough to consumers to make a profit.

Marketing, therefore, has a central role in the organisation. To work most effectively it requires both very efficient marketing information systems for monitoring product performance and strong communications systems – internally with all functional areas of the organisation (eg finance, R&D, quality control etc.) and externally – in communications with the consumer – through its role in advertising, promotion and public relations.

ADVERTISING AND PUBLIC RELATIONS

Advertising

The two main aspects of marketing communications that are visible to the consumer are advertising/promotions and public relations (customer care). Food products can be advertised to consumers in four different ways:

(1) *Paid for commercials*
These can include poster campaigns, TV, newspaper, magazine and Internet advertisements

(2) *Promotional offers*
Often found on the supermarket shelf and through in-store advertising. Examples include 'buy one get one half price', price reductions, bonus loyalty card points and in-store tasting sessions. May also take the form of 'money off' vouchers in magazines or through the letterbox

(3) *Direct selling*
The most common method is direct mail which may include a 'taster

sample'. Other methods include mail order/Internet shopping (e-tailing) and home shopping via digital television

(4) *Free publicity*
This may occur, for example, as part of a magazine article or feature (sometimes called advertorial) or recipe, or through the endorsement of the product by a 'celebrity chef'.

Public relations
Public relations forms the final way in which consumer reactions can be monitored. In particular, monitoring customer complaints can provide a useful tool for quality control of the product. In addition, a positive customer care policy will enhance the overall image of the company and reinforce the image of its commitment to the brand in the eyes of consumers.

FINANCIAL ASPECTS

Financial aspects of any food product need to be fully understood if a business is to survive and thrive. Often the difference between success and failure will rest on achieving a careful control of costs combined with a well thought-out pricing policy.

BASICS OF COSTING FOOD PRODUCTS

In economic terms there are several stages in the food production process where costs can be incurred, and these are ultimately passed on to the consumer.

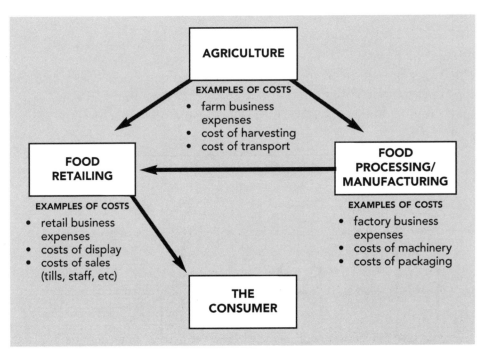

Figure 5.4

Costs incurred at different stages of the food chain

For each stage in the process detailed costs need to be worked out to ensure that a correct charge is made to make a profit. To achieve this, all the costs incurred are compiled and are compared against sales figures, which are carefully monitored. This allows each business to calculate the cost per unit of production. So for a farm business this may be the cost per kilo of wheat produced, whilst for the cereal manufacturer it may be the cost per packet of cereal.

FIXED AND VARIABLE COSTS OF FOOD MANUFACTURE

At each stage in the production process, costs can be divided into two categories:

– fixed costs   – variable costs

Fixed costs do not vary with the level of output (production). For a food manufacturer they might include staff wages (as long as they are not on piece work!), heating and lighting, insurance premiums etc..

Variable costs do change with the level of output. For the same food manufacturer they would include cost of ingredients, running costs of machinery, packaging materials etc..

The total costs of manufacture will be:

Total costs = fixed costs + variable costs

Figure 5.5 shows that as the number of units of food being processsed increases, the fixed costs become less important relative to the variable

Figure 5.5

Costs of manufacture

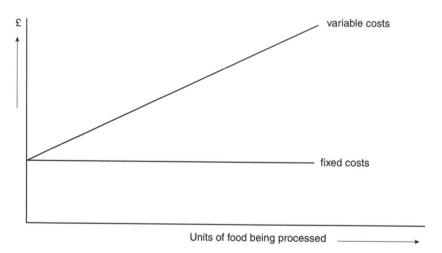

Figure 5.6

Unit costs to produce a tin of beans

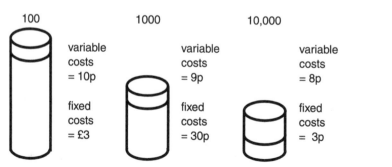

costs. This is termed an 'economy of scale'. This economy of scale can be further enhanced because the cost of some of the variable factors of production (*eg* ingredients) can be reduced by negotiating a discount for bulk purchasing.

BREAK-EVEN POINT

As has been shown, the total cost of manufacturing a food product can be calculated and this will vary with the level of production. Depending on the level of production, a unit cost can be ascertained.

The total revenue (income) gained from production can be calculated by multiplying the unit price by the number of units sold.

> Revenue = price per unit x number of units sold

In order to make a profit, a selling (unit) price must be established such that all the costs of production are exceeded by the revenue from the number of units sold.

The break-even point occurs when all the production costs are equal to the revenue gained from the sale of units of the product.

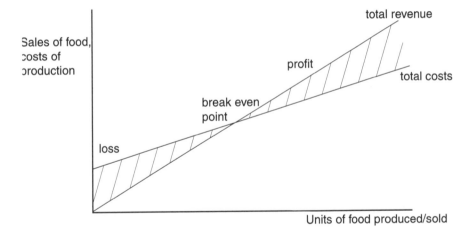

Figure 5.7
Break-even graph

The break-even point for production will vary depending on:

> – the volume of production
> – the price charged per unit.

COSTS OF LAUNCHING NEW PRODUCTS

The new product development process is shown right.

Different businesses in the food production chain may be involved directly in all or only parts of the product development process, as illustrated by the following example. A new dairy product is developed which must be stored under specific conditions of temperature and pressure. This will generate costs for

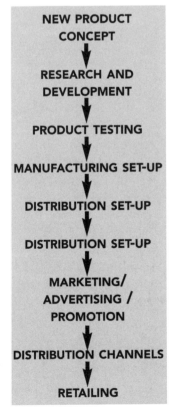

manufacturing equipment and processes (to the producer), new technology to develop storage facilities (producer, distributor and retailer), new forms of packaging (producer), transportation (distributor) and finally display (retailer).

One of the most difficult equations to get right is the marketing costs associated with a new product launch. Food manufacturers will monitor the effectiveness of their marketing by conducting consumer research. Typically they consider two aspects:

– consumer awareness of the new product (% of consumers asked)
– consumer purchases of the product (% of consumers asked).

The ratio of consumer purchases to consumer awareness is then calculated. Food products will yield quite different rates. For example, the ratio for a new breakfast cereal might be 3:5 (ie for every five people who have heard about the product, three will buy it), whereas the ratio for a new ethnic ready meal might only be 1:5 (as this is a much more 'risky' product: higher cost, less familiar type of product for many consumers, more chance of rejection on grounds of taste etc.). Typical 'success' rates will be established for different products against which marketing activity will be judged.

CONSUMER REACTIONS TO PRICING

This section has illustrated several reasons for developing high-volume production. In retailing, this approach is translated into a 'pile 'em high, sell 'em cheap', high–volume sales philosophy. However, consumer reactions to pricing do not always bear out the basic economic principle that as price falls, more is purchased.

Consumers are influenced by many features of products in addition to price, and for many food products there is a clear perception that price is linked to quality, particularly when there are several apparently similar lines in a product range and the focus is on establishing the differences between them (this is termed product line pricing). Prepackaged ham is a good example here. Often the differences boil down to how much water is added to the product, or what production processes have been used (boiling, baking, steaming etc).

Many food products can increase sales volumes by reducing prices. However, beyond a certain level of price reduction, consumers will become convinced that the quality of the product must also have been lowered and sales may actually nosedive rather than rise.

In fact, the quality of the product may not have been compromised in any way and the price reduction could have come about as a genuine economy of scale generated by an increased volume of production. This illustrates the power of consumer perceptions, irrespective of the facts.

Chapter 3
Food Control and Modification

PREVIEW

- **Good Manufacturing Practice**
  - basic principles of correct manufacturing procedures
  - effective manufacturing operations
  - effective food control
  - quality control and quality assurance
  - esponsible management
  - product specifications.

- **Genetic Modifications**
  - methods used for GM foods
  - potential benefits
  - safety and ethical issues.

- **Risk Assessment and HACCP**
  - risk of food contamination
  - HACCP, planned systematic procedure used to identify and assess hazards
  - seven basic concepts of HACCP:
    analyse process
    recognise critical control points
    decide on target levels
    develop monitoring system
    establish corrective action
    install verification process
    develop documentation
  - implemented in fourteen stages.

- **Use of ICT in Food Manufacture**
  - sprocess control, automation and robotics
  - sautomated processes
  - use in retailing and distribution.

GOOD MANUFACTURING PRACTICE

Good manufacturing practice (GMP) is an all-embracing management operation which ensures that food products are manufactured to consistent quality standards. GMP embraces both the total manufacturing process and the quality assurance procedures aimed at maintaining quality.

The Basis for GMP *

GMP has two complementary and interacting components: the manu-facturing operations and the quality control/quality assurance system. Both of these components must be well designed and effectively implemented. The same complementary nature and interaction must apply to the respective managements of these two functions, with the authority and responsibilities of each clearly defined, agreed and mutually recognised. This is not to ignore or belittle the importance of other key functions essential to the well-being and progress of a company, or indeed of those functions contributing direct services or advice to the manufacturing operation (*eg* purchasing, cost accounting, work study, production planning and engineering maintenance).

What constitutes well-designed in these two contexts mentioned above is not just a matter of common sense or something that would be self-evident to non-technical business people. As well as management skills, extensive and up to date knowledge of food science and technology relating to the ingredients, processes, packaging and products concerned are also necessary.

Effective manufacturing operations *
GMP requires that every aspect of the manufacture is fully specified in advance and that all the resources and facilities specified – namely

- measures and precautions at critical control points based on hazard analysis
- adequate premises and space
- correct and adequately maintained equipment
- appropriately trained people
- correct raw materials and packaging materials
- appropriate storage and transport facilities
- written operational procedures and cleaning schedules
- appropriate management and supervision
- adequate technical, administrative and maintenance services

are in fact provided, in the right quantities, at the right times and places, and are utilised as intended.

In order to ensure that operations do go according to plan, it is also necessary to

- provide operators with written procedures in clear unambiguous instructional language (with due regard to reading and language problems of some)
- train the operators to carry out the procedures correctly
- avoid if possible incentive bonus schemes *eg* with adequate safeguards against unauthorised short-cuts
- provide a food control service working along the lines indicated below
- ensure that records are made during production to show that specified procedures were in fact complied with and to enable the history of manufacture and distribution of a batch subsequently to be traced should a problem arise or recall be necessary
- establish a well-planned and effective system to carry out a product recall, should that prove necessary
- establish a tried and proved crisis management procedure in case of need.

Effective food control *

The other and complementary major component of GMP is effective food control. Effectiveness requires:

- well-qualified and appropriately experienced food control management participating in the drawing up of specifications
- adequate staff and facilities to do all the relevant inspection, sampling and testing of materials and monitoring of process conditions and relevant aspects of the production environment (including all aspects of hygiene)
- rapid feedback of information (accompanied where necessary by advice) to manufacturing personnel, thereby enabling prompt adjustment or corrective action to be taken and processed material either to be passed as fit for further processing or for sale as the case may be, or to be segregated for treatment or disposal as appropriate.

Responsible management *

Of course, the requirements of effective manufacturing operations and effective food control mentioned above are merely headings; within each there are many aspects.

GMP can only stem from policy firmly and uncompromisingly stated and continuously pursued by a company board and general management, which, moreover, provides adequate resources for the purpose.

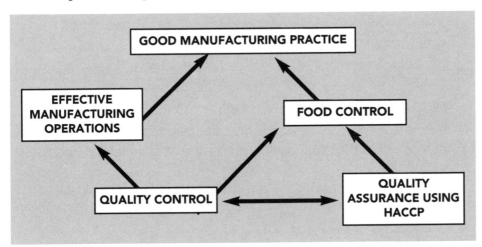

The ability to demonstrate that the principles of GMP have been fully and effectively implemented could assist a manufacturer in defending a prosecution for infringement of any food legal requirement.

According to the Food Safety Act 1998 'it shall be a defence for the person charged to prove that all reasonable precautions were taken and all *due diligence* exercised to avoid the commission of the offence by himself or a person under his control'. Due diligence is the reducing to a minimum practicable level the risks of contamination in manufacture and of contaminated products leaving the manufacturing source. This is achieved by means of GMP.

The food manufacturer *must* comply with a large range of legal requirements covering product composition, hygiene, safety and labelling. The market at which the product is aimed determines the product quality as shown in its appearance, texture, flavour, nutritional status, convenience, shelf-life and presentation. The product quality is expressed in a comprehensive product specification.

GENERAL PRINCIPLES FOR PRODUCING PRODUCT SPECIFICATIONS

(1) Specifications should embrace ALL aspects of the product, *ie,*

    (a)   raw material procurement and storage

    (b)   manufacturing process

    (c)   product inspection and storage

    (d)   distribution to consumer outlets.

(2) The product and process specifications should reflect the customer's requirements in precise measurable terms, as far as is practicable, *eg* measurements of appearance, flavour, odour and texture.

(3) The product and process specifications should meet the requirements of any government legislation, *eg* minimum compositional standards, food additives, contaminants, chemical and microbiological quality criteria and packaging material quality.

(4) All specifications must be realistic and achievable within the normal limits of people, machinery and materials.

(5) Where possible, realistic tolerances should be placed on all relevant quality parameters.

(6) The 'critical points' in the process should be identified where maximum sampling and testing need to be carried out. A HACCP flow diagram should be included (see previous page).

(7) Finished product inspection should be reduced to the minimum level compatible with the confidence justified by the raw material and process controls.

(8) Alternative procedures and quality contingency plans should be drawn up to take account of, *eg* unavailability of a specific raw material, or unavailability of a material of the specified quality.

(9) Product specifications should be kept under constant review.

THE PRODUCT SPECIFICATION

The product specification will include the following information as standard:

– *Product name*
  Including a brief description of the product

– *Product code*
  Each product will have a unique code. Variations of product, *eg* different size packs, will have codes with a common base but with some different digit

- *Name and address of manufacturer*

- *List of ingredients*
  Including acceptable sources of supply

- *Composition of product (the recipe)*
  This will include any relevant quality parameters, *eg* size of carrot dices, to be used in a canned ready meal

- *Standards to which the finished product must conform:*
  physical standards
  analytical standards
  organoleptic standards
  microbiological standards.
  If relevant, photographs may be included to demonstrate the appearance of the acceptable product and to illustrate the limits of tolerances

- *Nutritional data*

- *Product selling weight*

- *Packaging details*
  Including details of both inner and outer packaging

- *Handling and storage requirements*
  Details of storage temperature and any requirements as to storage away from other products in order to prevent picking up taints. Need for storage off the floor, etc.

- *Minimum durability/shelf life*

- *Health and safety requirements*
  Any relevant considerations that apply to the manufacture, handling, storage or use of the product

- *Legal requirements*

Details of the manufacturing process will include:

- *Process flow diagram*
  This will define the stages in the process

- *HACCP flow diagram*
  Manufacturers are required to adhere to the Food Safety (General Food Hygiene) Regulations 1995

- *On-line QA requirements*
  Details of checks and the frequency with which they must be carried out during processing

- *Finished product tests*
  These are the tests whose results will be required to show that the product conforms to the standards previously listed.

*reproduced with the permission of the Institute of Food Science and Technology (UK), from the *Food and Drink – Good Manufacturing Practice – (A Guide to its Responsible Management)* ISBN 0 905 367 154.

GENETIC MODIFICATION

Genetic modification (GM) is currently the most disputed food topic, but it has to be recognised that it has the potential to offer vast changes in the quality, variety and quantity of food available worldwide.

Genetic modification of food is a branch of biotechnology and can also be referred to as gene technology, genetic engineering and genetic manipulating. The term 'genetically modified organism (GMO)' has been used widely to describe plants, animals or micro-organisms to which DNA has been added other than by conventional means, *eg* during reproduction.

Selective breeding has been undertaken to produce food crops and improved livestock for many years. Gene technology makes a more organised approach to this, it is quicker and can cross species and barriers. It is the latter point that causes concern as it is against nature.

Methods of genetic modification

Genes are contained in the genome (nucleus) and each gene is made in the same way. This new technology has allowed the transfer of genes with their individual characteristics from one plant or organism to another.

GM involves actually copying the genes which govern a particular characteristic from one organism and transferring them to another. GM enables transfer between different species and between plants and animals.

An early example was the modification of soya, which was given a gene to make it resistant to the herbicide glyphosate. The crop could be sprayed and all weeds would be killed, leaving the soya growing without any competition. This caused concerns because many people thought that this herbicide resistance could be passed to other species, particularly weeds, which would then show the same herbicide resistance.

Potential benefits of genetic modification

Compared with conventional selective breeding of crops and animals, GM has the following advantages:

- a very wide range of potential improvements are available, *eg* pest resistance, increased yield, better quality and nutritional aspects
- it is quicker and can be achieved in a few generations – some traditional selective breeding programmes have taken 20 years
- greater accuracy can be achieved in selecting particular characteristics

According to the Institute of Food Science and Technology (UK)* the benefits to the food industry could be considerable:

- improved agricultural performance with reduced use of chemical pesticides
- greater ability for crops to grow in inhospitable environments, *eg* those susceptible to drought

- improved ability to feed an increasing world population
- improved sensory characteristics of food, *eg* flavour, texture, colour
- improved nutritional status, such as increased vitamin levels
- improved processing characteristics and reduced wastage.

Safety of GM foods

This has become a very emotive issue, particularly concerning environmental aspects. Past experience has shown that problems of a new or modified species in a difficult environment take several generations to become apparent. Cross pollination from GM crops is a concern, particularly on transferring characteristics to weeds and 'contaminating' organic crops.

There is concern that the allergic properties of some crops may be transferred to others and genes transferred to bacteria, thus altering their characteristics and possibly turning them into emerging pathogens. The possible production of toxic substances in GM foods is also of concern.

Much is still not known, but work must continue to solve any problems and reap the enormous potential benefits.

(Further reading: *Guide to Food Biotechnology*, published by the Institute of Food Science and Technology (UK), 5 Cambridge Court, 210 Shepherd's Bush Road, London W6 7NJ (ISBN 0 905367 13 8); *GM Crops and The Environment   Benefits & Risks*, published by: The Food and Drink Federation, 6 Catherine Street, London WC2B 5JD.)

RISK ASSESSMENT AND HACCP

Food processing involves many stages, often many different materials and many people. There are risks of contamination of the food occurring at many stages in some processes. It is important for manufacturers to be aware of all the risks of contamination and what to do about them.

Hazard analysis critical control point (HACCP) is now in widespread use in the food industry and is an essential component of quality assurance procedures. HACCP is a planned systematic procedure used to identify and assess hazards and risks in the food manufacturing operation. This is followed by the identification of the means to control these risks. Hazards are specific threats, *eg* foreign body or microbial contamination, which have the potential of harming the consumer. Malpractice during the manufacturing process is also considered a hazard. During a manufacturing process there are a number of stages or points in the production line where potential hazards may occur, the so called critical control points (CCPs). Controls are applied at the CCPs to remove or minimise the hazard to an acceptable level. Target levels, or values of a parameter, *eg* temperatures are set at the CCPs and these levels have been shown to control the hazard. There are seven basic concepts in HACCP.

These are:

(1)   Analysis of the process (usually a flow diagram)

(2)   Recognise CCPs
(3)   Decide on target levels
(4)   Develop a monitoring system
(5)   Establish corrective action
(6)   Install a verification process
(7)   Develop documentation.

These seven principles of HACCP are implemented in a total of 14 stages.

Stage 1 : Draw up a plan

Decide which process line is to be investigated and whether microbial, chemical or physical hazards will be involved. Clearly establish the extent of the plan, *eg* when the food leaves the line, factory or when it arrives at the consumer outlet.

Stage 2 : Build a team

The people involved in HACCP will include production personnel, quality assurance/control staff, chemists, microbiologists and engineers. All must be convinced of the value of carrying out HACCP.

Stage 3 : Describe the product

The composition and processing of the food will need to be known in detail. Knowledge of the following is required:

* composition/structure
* processing
* packaging
* storage/handling/distribution
* shelf-life required
* correct image.

In addition, there should be checklists for the formulation and processing:

Formulation check list
* raw materials used
* micro-organisms possibly present
* possible toxicity of ingredients
* action of any preservatives in preventing microbial growth
* pH influence on microbial growth
* water activity (^{a}w) influence on microbial growth

Processing check lists
* recognise likelihood of contaminants reaching the product during manufacture
* establish if micro-organisms or toxins are destroyed in processing
* investigate the possibility of post-processing contamination
* identify the influence of packaging on microbial growth
* assess the conditions of distribution.

Stage 4 : Identify the intended use of the product

After the product leaves the factory how will it be handled and stored? Factors including chilling and temperature control must be considered. Will the product be reheated sufficiently to kill all micro-organisms. After heating, will the product be held hot or at room temperature? Will there be a risk of further post-heating contamination?

Stage 5 : Draw a flow diagram of the process

Draw up a diagram correcting each stage of the process starting with raw materials through all stages of processing, packaging, storage and distribution (if necessary).

Stage 6 : Check the flow diagram

Take the diagram out on the factory floor and confirm its accuracy. Ensure the process is not influenced by changes in work patterns such as shift work.

Stage 7 : List all hazards and their prevention

All hazards need to be identified throughout the process, starting with the raw materials and finishing with the product leaving the factory. Once the hazards are known, control and prevention measures can be developed.

Potential microbiological hazards

It is essential that these are identified, particularly where there is a risk of contamination with pathogens. The following will have to be established:

- does the pathogen (bacterium probably) come with raw materials
- does the process destroy the pathogen
- can the pathogen contaminate the product post-processing
- can the pathogen multiply in a particular type of food.

Physical and chemical hazards

Consumer complaints and company quality control records are a good source of possible hazards, *eg* metal contamination. Physical methods of removing the hazards can be established.

Risk assessment

Risk is defined as the likelihood that a hazard will occur. An approach is to describe the food as belonging to a risk category which can be high, medium or low.

Category 1 – High risk products
(i)   products needing refrigeration – containing fish, egg, vegetables, cereal or dairy ingredients
(ii) raw products – meat, fish and dairy
(iii) products with pH values above 4.6 which have been sterilised and sealed into containers for distribution at normal temperatures
(iv) infant foods.

Category 2 – Medium risk products
(i)   dried or frozen products – containing meat, egg, fish, vegetables, cereal or dairy ingredients
(ii) sandwiches and meat pies (fresh consumption)
(iii) fat-based products – magarines, spreads, mayonnaise and dressings.

Category 3 – Low risk products
(i)   acidic products (pH less than 4.6) – pickles, acidic beverages
(ii) raw vegetables (not processed or packed)
(iii) jams and preserves
(iv) sugar-based confectionery
(v)   edible oils and fats.

Prevention measures

After the nature of the hazard has been established, preventative measures can be developed. Sometimes more than one method will be needed to eliminate a hazard.

Stage 8 : Identification of critical control points (CCPs)

The next stage in the HACCP process is to identify the points in the manufacturing process at which control of safety is critical. The CCPs highlight for the manufacturer where particular care has to be concentrated in the implementation of prevention measures. There can be any number of CCPs that should be kept to a minimum so that full prevention measures can be applied to achieve food safety.

Stage 9 : Target levels

Prevention and control measures are identified for each of the CCPs. Often it is easy to establish a target value, but sometimes critical limits have to be established, *eg*

(1) absence of metal, no level of metal in a product is acceptable
(2) heat processing – there will be a target temperature but this will vary between certain critical limits.

Stage 10 : Develop a monitoring system

A series of observations and measurements are needed to ensure that the preventative measures have been implemented correctly.

Monitoring enables management to detect any loss of control in food safety at a CCP. It is important, therefore, to state clearly who, how and when monitoring is to be performed and recorded. Measurement techniques include chemical, microbiological and physical methods, *eg* temperature, pH, presence of contaminants and microbial contamination.

Stage 11 : Corrective action plans

If a problem or failure of a preventative measure occurs, a corrective action plan has to be put into effect. The plan should contain details of:

(1) immediate action to be taken and by whom
(2) investigate how the loss of control occurred
(3) who is to assume responsibility for making decisions
(4) what to do with defective products.

Stage 12 : Develop verification procedures

Microbial examination and analysis of both intermediate and final products play an important role in verification. If HACCP is working, bacterial counts tend to show lower variations.

Stage 13 : Establish documentation and record keeping

HACCP to work efficiently needs efficient and accurate documentation; this can often be achieved in tabular form as shown below:

HACCP

Product name:

Flow diagram of process:

Step No.	Hazard	Prevention measure	CCPs	Target levels	Monitoring how/who	Corrective actions

Stage 14 : Review of the HACCP plan

A review of the whole process is carried out at intervals and when changes occur, *eg* in raw materials or processing.

This is a brief review of the essential process of HACCP. Further reading: *How to HACCP* by Mike Dillon and Chris Griffith, ISBN 1 900134004.

USE OF ICT IN FOOD MANUFACTURE

For many years processes in the food industry were batch processes, which entailed filling equipment with raw materials, processing and then emptying the equipment. Modern processing is continuous and at high rates and volumes.

The texture analyser produced by Stable Micro Systems (SMS) is an example of the level of advancement achieved in this type of control. Products can be processed to a controlled level of hardness, brittleness, softness or stickiness, which can be immediately compared with stored information and visually against control graphs.

This type of production needs elaborate control systems at all stages, particularly in the blending of raw materials, monitoring the process and packaging operations. The use of information and communications technology (ICT) is therefore widespread throughout the food industry in the 21st century.

Process control and automation

To ensure product uniformity and production efficiency, process control of food manufacture is essential. Process control is used mainly in the following:

- scheduling of raw materials
- controlling the flow of product through the process
- evaluation and control of the process and product
- making technical and design decisions.

Control systems which actually perform the function vary from local equipment controllers to process computers, which feed information into an overall supervisory computer.

The systems will not work without the use of special sensors at various parts of the process. A sensor can measure any one process variable such as temperature, pH, moisture level, weight or colour. In the food industry solid-state electronic sensors are used. Biological sensors are being developed and are linked to microprocessor control, which enables quality characteristics such as colour and texture to be measured and large amounts of information about the food to be stored, measured and compared with specifications.

The texture analyser produced by Stable Micro Systems (SMS) is an example of the level of advancement achieved in this type of control. Products can be processed to a controlled level of hardness, brittleness, softness or stickiness, which can be immediately compared with stored information and visually against control graphs.

Automated process
Each stage of a process can be under computer control from the ordering of raw materials to the distribution of finished goods. The advantages of automation are given below:

(1) more frequent checking at critical control parts
(2) improved productivity and reduced wastage
(3) improved product quality
(4) rapid diagnosis of faults in plant equipment
(5) lower risk to operatives
(6) low labour costs.

In some plants, closed-circuit television is used to view the plant and relay information to viewing monitors in a central control area.

Distribution and retailing
Many large food retailers rely on daily deliveries of fresh (chilled) products. The distribution system is under computer control and ensures rapid communications and accurate information for ordering. The system works as follows:

• the stores within the retailing group have computer links to their head-office and pass their daily requirements through the links so that the head-office can then request the food manufacturers to produce the right quantity of each product

• the chilled products are transported to a central distribution point, where the deliveries are broken down into small lots for delivery to individual stores

• the central distribution point receives computer data from the head-office as to where to deliver the chilled foods and in what quantity

- experience has shown it may take four hours, for example, to reach a particular store, so the transport vehicle leaves with its load of chilled foods at about 4.30am to arrive at the store just before opening, usually each day
- the product will probably only have a shelf-life of a day or two so fresh deliveries are needed continually.

The product mix going to a particular store could be enormous so computer control is essential.

OTHER AREAS IN THE FOOD INDUSTRY WHERE ICT IS USED

Computer aided design (CAD)

This is used to assist in designing equipment, production lines, but occasionally more complex products.

Formulation of products

Varying formulations to reduce cost without lowering the quality is a main objective here.

Robotics

Robots can be programmed to take over repetitive and boring tasks within a production line.

Nutritional analysis

The composition of a product can be quickly analysed and its contribution to nutrition can be assessed.

Managing and monitoring

There are many applications, particularly in HACCP and production control.

APPENDICES

Appendix 1

Complete List of Permitted Additives *(NB. This list is subject to review on occasions)*

COLOURS

No	Name	Products in which found
E100	Curcumin	Flour confectionery, margarine, rice
E101	Riboflavin	Sauces, processed cheese
E101(a)	Riboflavin-5 '-phosphate	Preserves
E102 E104	Tartrazine Quinoline yellow	Soft drinks (formerly in many Yellow/orange products)
E110	Sunset yellow FCF	Scotch eggs
E120	Cochineal	Biscuits, soups, Swiss rolls
E122	Carmoisine	Alcoholic drinks
E123	Amaranth	Jams, preserves, soups, sweets
E124	Ponceau 4R	Cake mixes, soups
E127	Erythrosine	Dessert mixes, soups
E128	Red 2G	Glacé cherries, trifle mix
E131	Patent blue V	Sausages
E132	Indigo carmine	Scotch eggs
E133	Brilliant blue FCF	Biscuits, sweets
E140	Chlorophyll	Canned vegetables
E141	Copper complexes of chlorophyll and chlorophyllins	Soap, oils Green vegetables in liquid
E142	Green S	Pastilles, tinned peas
E150	Caramel	Beer, soft drinks, sauces, gravy browning
E151	Black PN	Sauces
E153	Carbon black (vegetable carbon)	Liquorice, preserves
E154	Brown FK	Kippers (will be deleted when suitable replacement available)
E155	Brown HT (chocolate brown HT)	Chocolate cake
E160(a)	Alpha-carotene; beta-carotene; Gamma-carotene	Margarine, soft drinks
E160(b)	Annatto; bixin; norbixin	
E160(c)	Capsanthin; capsorubin	Crisps, butter, coleslaw
E160(d)	Lycopene	Cheese slices
E160(e) E160(f) E161(b) E161(g)	Beta-apo-8'-carotenal Ethyl ester of beta-apo-8'-carotenoic acid Lutein Canthaxanthin	 Biscuits (likely to be deleted)
E162	Beetroot red (betanin)	Ice-cream, liquorice
E163	Anthocyanins	Yoghurts
E170	Calcium carbonate	
E171	Titanium dioxide	Sweets, horseradish sauce
E172	Iron oxides; iron hydroxides	Dessert mixes, cake mixes
E173 E174 E175	Aluminium Silver Gold	Sugar, confectionery, cake decorations
E180	Pigment rubine (lithol rubine BK)	Rind of cheese

PRESERVATIVES

No	Name	Products in which found
E200	Sorbic acid	Soft drinks, fruit yoghurts, processed cheese slices,sweets
E202	Potassium sorbate	Pizza, cheese spread, cakes
E203	Calcium sorbate	
E210	Benzoic acid	
E211	Sodium benzoate	
E212	Potassium benzoate	Pickles, cheesecake mix, sauces, flavourings, beer, jam, salad cream, soft drinks, fruit pulp, fruit-based pie fillings, marinated herring and mackerel, desserts
E213	Calcium benzoate	
E214	Ethyl 4-hydroxybenzoate (ethyl para-hydroxybenzoate)	
E215	Ethyl 4-hydroxybenzoate, sodium salt (sodium ethyl parahydroxybenzoate)	
E216	Propyl 4-hydroxybenzoate (propyl para-hydroxybenzoate)	
E217	Propyl 4-hydroxybenzoate, sodium salt (sodium propyl para- hydroxybenzoate)	
E218	Methyl 4-bydroxybenzoate (methyl para-hydroxybenzoate) methyl 4-	
E219	Hydroxybenzoate, sodium salt (sodium methyl para hydroxybenzoate)	
E220	Sulphur dioxide	Dried fruit, dehydrated vegetables, fruit juices, fruit pulp, fruit syrups, drinks, wine, egg yolk, pickles
E221	Sodium sulphite	
E222	Sodium hydrogen sulphite (sodium bisulphite)	
E223	Sodium metabisulphite postassium	
E224	Metabisulphite	Dried fruit, dehydrated vegetables, fruit juices, fruit pulp, fruit syrups, drinks, wine, egg yolk, pickles
E226	Calcium sulphite	
E227	Calcium hydrogen sulphite (calcium bisulphite)	
E228	Potassium hydrogen sulphite	Wines
E230	Biphenyl (diphenyl)	Fruit skins, surface of citrus fruits, surface treatment of bananas
E231	2-hydroxybiophenyl (orthophenylphenate)	
E232	Sodium biphenyl -2-yl oxide (sodium orthophenylphenate)	
E233	2-(thiazol-4-yl) benzimidazole (thiabendazole)	
E234	Nisin	Cheese, clotted cream, canned foods marinated herring and mackerel
E239	Hexamine (hexamethylenetetramine)	
E242	Dimethyl discarbonate	
E249	Potassium nitrite	Soft drinks, alcohol-free wines
E250	Sodium nitrite	
E251	Sodium nitrate	Cooked meats, bacon, ham, cured meats, corned beef, tongue, some cheeses,
E252	Potassium nitrate	
E280	Propionic acid	
E281	Sodium propionate	Bread, flour confectionery, dairy products, pizza, Christmas pudding
E282	Calcium propionate	
E283	Potassium propionate	
E284	Boric acid	Caviar
E285	Sodium tetraborate	
E1105	Lysozyme	Cheese

ANTIOXIDANTS

No	Name	Products in which found
E300	L-ascorbic acid	Fruit drinks, also used to improve flour and bread dough, dried potato, sausages, meat loaf, Scotch eggs, steak cubes
E301	Sodium L-ascorbate	
E302	Calcium L-ascorbate	
E304	i) ascorbyl palmitate or ii) ascorbyl stearate	
E306	Extracts of natural origin rich in tocopherols	Vegetable oils, cereal-based baby foods
E307	Synthetic alpha-tocopherol	
E308	Synthetic gamma-tocopherol	
E309	Synthetic delta-tocopherol	Vegetable oils, chewing gum, margarine
E310	Propyl gallate	
E311	Octyl gallate	Meat and fish products
E312	Dodecyl gallate	Beef stock cubes, cheese spread, biscuits, convenience foods
E315	Erythorbic acid	
E316	Sodium erythorbate	Chewing gum
E320	Butylated hydroxyanisole (BHA)	
E321	Butylated hydroxytoluene (BHT)	

EMULSIFIERS, STABILISERS, THICKENERS AND GELLING AGENTS

No	Name	Products in which found
E322	Lecithins	Low fat spreads, in chocolate as an emulsifier, confectionery, many other applications
E400	Alginic acid	Ice-cream, soft and processed cheese, cake mixes, salad dressings, cottage cheese, synthetic cream
E401	Sodium alginate	
E402	Potassium alginate	
E403	Ammonium alginate	
E404	Calcium alginate	
E405	Propane-1,2-diol alginate (propylene glycol alginace)	
E406	Agar	Ice-cream, frozen trifle
E407	Carrageenan	Quick setting jelly mixes, milk shakes
E410	Locust bean gum (carob gum)	Salad cream
E412	Guar gum	Packet soups, meringue mixes, sauces
E413	Tragacanth	Salad dressings, processed cheese, cream cheese
E414	Gum arabic (acacia)	Confectionery
E415	Xanthan gum	Sweet pickle, coleslaw, horseradish cream
E416	Karaya gum	Soft cheese, brown sauce
E417	Tara gum	
E418	Gellan gum	
E432	Polyoxyethylene (20) sorbitan monolaurate (Polysorbate 20)	Bakery products, confectionery creams, cakes
E433	Polyoxyethylene (20) sorbitan mono-oleate (Polysorbate 80)	
E434	Polyoxyethylene (20) sorbitan monopalmitate (l'olysorbace 40)	
E435	Polyoxyethylene (20) sorbitan monostearate (Polysorbate 60)	
E436	Polyoxyethylene (20) sorbitan tristearate (Polysorbate 65)	
E440(a) E440(b)	Pectin Amidated pectin pectin extract	Jams, preserves, desserts

EMULSIFIERS, STABILISERS, THICKENERS AND GELLING AGENTS

No	Name	Products in which found
E442	Ammonium phosphatides	Cocoa and chocolate products
E460	Microcrystalline cellulose; powdered cellulose	
E461	Methylcellulose	High-fibre bread, grated cheese, low fat spreads, edible ices, gateaux
E463	Hydroxypropylcellulose	
E464	Hydroxypropylmethylcellulose	
E465	Ethylmethylcellulose	
E466	Carboxymethylcellulose, sodium salt (CMC)	Jelly, pie filling
E470(a)	Sodium, potassium and calcium salts of fatty acids	Cake mixes
E470(b)	Magnesium salts of fatty acids	
E471	Mono- and diglycerides of fatty acids	
E472(a)	Acetic acid esters of mono- and diglycerides of fatty acids	
E472(b)	Lactic acid esters of mono- and di-glycerides of fatty acids	Frozen desserts, dessert toppings, mousse mixes, continental sausages bread frozen pizza
E472(c)	Citric acid esters of mono- and diglycerides of fatty acids	
E472(e)	Mono- and diacetyltartaric acid esters of mono- and diglycerides of fatty acids	
E472(f)	Mixed acetic and tartaric acid esters of mono – and diglycerides of fatty acids	
E473	Sucrose esters of fatty acids	Coatings for fruit
E474	Sucroglycerides	Edible ices
E475	Polyglycerol esters of fatty acids	Cakes and gateaux
E476	Polyglycerol esters of polycondensed fatty acids of castor oil (polyglycerol polyricinoleate)	Chocolate-flavour coatings for cakes
E477	Propane-1, 2-diol esters of fatty acids	Instant desserts
E481	Sodium stearoyl-2-lactylate	
E482	Calcium stearoyl-2-laccylate	
E483	Stearyl tartrate	Bread, cakes, biscuits, gravy granules
E491	Sorbitan monostearate	
E492	Sorbitan tristearate	
E493	Sorbitan monolaurate	
E494	Sorbitan mono-oleate	
E495	Sorbitan monopalmitate	Cake mixes

SWEETENERS

No	Name	Products in which found
E420	Sorbitol; sorbitol syrup	Sugar-free confectionery, jams for diabetics
E421	Mannitol	Sugar-free confectionery
E950	Acesulfame potassium (k)	Canned foods, soft drinks, table-top sweeteners
E951	Aspartame	Soft drinks, yoghurts, dessert and drink
E952	Cyclamic acid and its sodium and calcium salts	Mixes, sweetening tablets
E953	Isomalt	
E954	Saccharin, potassium saccharin sodium saccharin calcium saccharin	Soft drinks, cider, sweetening tablets
E957	Thaumatin	Table-top sweeteners, yoghurt
E959	Neohesperidine DC	Soft drinks, desserts
E965	Maltitol	
E966	Lactitol	Sugar-free chewing gum
E967	Xylitol	

OTHERS

No	Name	Products in which found	Use
E170	Calcium carbonate		Base, firming release agent
E260	Acetic acid	Pickles, crisps, salad cream, bread	Acid/acidity regulators
E261	Potassium acetate		
E262(i)	Sodium acetate		
E262(ii)	Sodium hydrogen diacetate		
E263	Calcium acetate	Quick-set jelly mix	Firming agent
E270	Lactic acid	Salad dressing, margarine	Acid antifungal action carbonating agent, packaging gas
E290	Carbon dioxide	Fizzy drinks	
E296	DL-malic acid; L-malic acid	Low calorie squash, soup	Acid
E297	Fumaric acid	Soft drinks, sweets, biscuits, dessert mixes, pie fillings	Acid
E325	Sodium lactate	Jams, preserves, sweets, flour confectionery	Buffer/humectant
E326	Potassium lactate	Jams, preserves, jellies, canned fruit, fruit pie filling, many products	Buffer/humectant
E327	Calcium lactate		
E330	Citric acid		Acid
E331	Sodium dihydrogen citrate (monosodium citrate); disodium citrate; trisodium citrate	Sweets, gateaux mixes, soft drinks, jams, preserves, sweets, processed cheese, canned fruit, dessert mixes	Acid/flavour buffer, sequestrants, calcium salts are firming agents
E332	Potassium dihydrogen citrate (monopotassium citrate); tripotassium citrate		
E333	Monocalcium citrate; dicalcium citrate; tricalcium citrate		
E334	L-(+)-tartaric acid		

No	Name	Products in which found	Use
E335	Monosodium L-(+)-tartrate; disodium L-(+)-tartrate	Confectionery, drinks, preserves, meringue pie mix, soft drinks, biscuit creams and fillings, dessert mixes, processed cheese	Acid/flavouring, buffer, emulsifying salts, sequestrants
E336	Monopotassium L-(+)-tartrate (cream of tartare); dipotassium L-(+)-tartrate		
E337	Potassium sodium L-(+)- tartrate		
E338	Orthophosphoric acid (phosphoric acid)		
E339	Sodium dihydrogen orthophosphate; disodium hydrogen orthophosphate; trisodium orthophosphate		
E340	Potassium dihydrogen orthosphosphate; dipotassium hydrogen orthophosphate; tripotassium orthophosphate	Soft drinks, cocoa, dessert mixes, non-dairy creamers, processed cheese	Acid/flavouring, sequestrants, emulsifying agents, buffers
E341	Calcium tetrahydrogen diorthophosphate; calcium, hydrogen orthophosphate; tricalcium diorthophosphate		
E350	Sodium malate, sodium hydrogen malate	Jams, sweets, cakes, biscuits, processed fruit and vegetables	Buffers, humectants, calcium salts are firming agents in canned fruit and vegetables
E351	Potassium malate		
E352	Calcium malate, calcium hydrogen malate		
E353	Metatartaric acid	Wine	Sequestrant
E354	Calcium tartrate		
E355	Adipic acid	Sweets, synthetic cream Desserts	Buffer/flavouring
E356	Sodium adipate		
E357	Potassium adipate		
E363	Succinic acid	Dry food and beverage mixes	Buffer, flavouring
E380	Triammonium citrate	Processed cheese	
E385	Calcium disordium ethylenediamine-NNN N' – tetra-acetate (calcium disodium EDTA)	Canned shellfish	Sequestrant
E422	Glycerol	Cake-icing, confectionery	Humectant, solvent
E450(i)	Disodium diphosphate		
E450(ii)	Trisodium diphosphate		
E450(iii)	Tetrasodium diphosphate		
E450(iv)	Dipotassium diphosphate	Whipping cream, meat products, bread, processed cheese, canned vegetables	Buffers, sequestrants, emulsifying salts, stabilisers, raising agents
E450(v)	Tetrapotassium diphosphate		
E450(vi)	Dicalcium diphosphate		
E450(vii)	Calcium dihydrogen diphosphate		
E450(c)	Sodium polyphosphates, potassium polyphosphates		
E451	Triphosphates		Emulsifiers, Sequestrants
E452	Polyphosphates		
E479(b)	Thermally oxidised soya bean oil		
E500	Sodium carbonate, sodium hydrogen carbonate (bicarbonate of soda), sodium sesquicarbonate		

No	Name	Products in which found	Use
E501	Potassium carbonate, potassium hydrogen carbonate	Jams, jellies, self-raising flour, wine, cocoa, biscuits, icing sugar	Bases, aerating agents, anti-caking agents
E503	Ammonium carbonate; ammonium hydrogen carbonate		
E504	Magnesium carbonate	Tomato juice	
E507	Hydrochloric acid	table salt replacement	Processing aid
E508	Potassium chloride	canned fruit and vegetables	Gelling agent, salt substitute
E509	Calcium chloride		
E513	Sulphuric acid	Colours	Firming agent
E514	Sodium sulphate	Salt	
E515	Potassium sulphate	Bread	Diluent
E516	Calcium sulphate		Salt substitute
E517	Ammonium sulphate		Firming agent, yeast food
E520	Aluminium sulphate		Carrier for food additive
E521	Aluminium sodium sulphate		
E522	Aluminium potassium sulphate		
E523	Aluminium ammonium sulphate	Cocoa, jams, sweets	
E524	Sodium hydroxide	Sweets	
E525	Potassium hydroxide	Sweets	Base
E526	Calcium hydroxide	Cocoa, food colouring	Base Firming agent, neutralising agent
E527	Ammonium hydroxide	Sweets	Diluent and solvent for food, colours, base
E528	Magnesium hydroxide	Sweets	
E529	Calcium oxide	Cocoa products	Base
E530	Magnesium oxide		Base
E535	Sodium ferrocyanide	Salt, wine	Anti-caking agent
E536	Potassium ferrocyanide	Salt	
E538	Calcium ferrocyanide	Cake mixes, self-raising flour, biscuits	Anti-caking agent
E541	Sodium aluminium phosphate		Acid, raising agent
E551	Silicon dioxide (silica)	Skimmed milk powder, sweeteners	Anti-caking agent
E552	Calcium silicate	Icing sugar, sweets	Anti-caking agent, release agent
E553(a)	Magnesium silicate synthetic; magnesium trisilicate	Sugar confectionery	Anti-caking agent
E553(b)	Talc	Tabletted confectionery	
E554	Aluminium sodium silicate	Packet noodles	Release agent
E555	Potassium aluminium silicate		Anti-caking agent
E556	Aluminium calcium silicate		Anti-caking agent
E559	Kaolin		Anti-caking agent
E570	Stearic acid		Anti-caking agent
E574	Gluconic acid		Emulsifier, release agent
E575	D-glucono-1,5-lactone (glucono delta-lactone)	Cake mixes, continental Sausages	Acid, sequestrant
E576	Sodium gluconate		Sequestrants, buffer, firming agent
E577	Potassium gluconate	Dietary supplement, jams, dessert mixes	
E578	Calcium gluconate		
E620	L-glutamic acid		
E621	Sodium hydrogen L-glutamate (monosodium glutamate; MSG)		
E622	Potassium hydrogen L-glutamate (monopotassium glutamate)		
E623	Calcium dihydrogen di-L-glutamate (calcium glutamate)		

No	Name	Products in which found	Use
E624	Monoammonium glutamate	Savoury foods and snacks, soups, sauces, meat products	Flavour enhancers
E625	Magnesium diglutamate		
E627	Guanosine 5-disodium phosphate (sodium guanylate)		
E628	Dipotassium guanylate		
E629	Calcium guanylate		
E630	Inosinic acid		
E631	Disodium inosinate		
E632	Dipotassium inosinate		
E633	Calcium inosinate		
E634	Calcium 5'ribonucleotide		
E635	Sodium 5'-ribonucleotide		
E900	Dimethylpolysiloxane		Anti-foaming agent
E901	Beeswax	Sugar, chocolate confectionery	Glazing agent
E902	Candelilla wax		
E903	Carnauba wax	Sugar, chocolate confectionery	Glazing agent
E904	Shellac	Apples	Waxing agent
E912	Montan acid esters		
E914	Oxidised polyethylene wax	Citrus fruit	Glazing agent
E920	L-cysteine hydrochloride		
E925	Chlorine		
E926	Chlorine dioxide		
E927(b)	Carbonamide	Chocolate-coated cherries	Firming agent
E938	Argon		
E939	Helium		
E941	Nitrogen		Gas flushing/packaging
E942	Nitrous oxide propane butane iso-butane		Propellant gas
E948	Oxygen		Packaging gas
E953	Isomalt		Humectant
E999	Quillaia extract	Drinks	Foaming agent
E1200	Polydextrose	Low calorie foods	Bulking agent
E1201	Polyvinylpyrrolidone		
E1202	Polyvinylpolypyrrolidone		
E1404	Oxidised starch		
E1410	Monostarch phosphate		
E1412	Distarch phosphate		
E1413	Phosphated distarch phosphate		
E1414	Acetylated starch		
E1422	Acetylated distarch adipate		
E1440	Hydroxyl propyl starch		
E1442	Hydroxy propyl distarch phosphate		
E1450	Starch sodium octenyl succinate	Many foods	Modified starch – thickening
E1505	Triethyl citrate		
E1518	Glyceryl triacetate (triacetin)-propan-1,2-diol (propylene glycol)		Carrier for additives

Appendix 2
Food Terminology

Acesulfame K

Water-soluble artificial sweetener similar to saccharin but with no after-taste.

Acids

Most foods are acidic. In fruits and vegetables *citric* and *malic* acids are the most common. In fermented products, such as yoghurt, *lactic acid* predominates. Acid is added to manufactured foods to improve flavour and to balance excessive sweetness.

Acraldehyde see *Acrolein*

Acrolein

Also known as acraldehyde. This is a breakdown product when glycerol, fats or oils are heated to a high temperature. It appears as vapour with an acrid odour.

Additives

Chemicals, both synthetic and natural, which are used to give various functional properties to foods. In the quantities used, additives are edible but are not foods in their own right. Permitted additives within the EU are usually given E numbers.

Adenosine

A combination of adenine (a base) with the sugar ribose. Adenosine monophosphate contains one phosphate residue, diphosphate two, and triphosphate three. The latter, adenosine triphosphate (ATP) is important in the liberation of energy from foodstuffs. It is also involved in supplying energy to muscles during contraction.

Ageing
– of eggs
Thick white of the egg becomes thinner, and membranes around the yolk weaken. Foaming properties of white improve with ageing.

– of flour
Flour improves by keeping for several months. *Pigments* are bleached by oxidation, and *protein* quality is improved. Accelerated ageing is obtained by using oxidising agents.

– of meat
Enzymes break down large *protein* molecules after *rigor mortis* to make meat more tender. Free *amino acids* and *fatty acids* are produced to contribute to meat flavour.

– of wine
A slow oxidation process that reduces astringency due to *tannin* in red wines. The production of *esters* is encouraged and a smoother wine with a bouquet is produced.

Alginates

Produced from giant kelp; sodium alginate is the most common form. Widely used as additives, properties include: emulsifying, stabilising, gel-forming, film-forming and thickening.

Amino acids

Proteins are built up of amino acids which must contain an amino group ($-NH_2$) and a carboxyl group ($-COOH$). Amino acids are linked by *peptide* bridges ($-CONH-$) to form *peptides*, *polypeptides* and *proteins*.
– essential amino acids

These must be included in the diet and cannot be synthesised in the body. Eight come in this category: valine, leucine, isoleucine, phenylalanine, threonine, methionine, tryptophan, lysine.

Children also require histidine and some people only synthesise arginine slowly.

Amylases

Enzymes which break down starch. α-amylase (or dextrinogenic amylase) attacks starch molecules randomly to produce *dextrins*. β-amylase systematically removes *maltose* from starch molecules. The two enzymes together are called *diastase*.

Amylopectin

One structural form of *starch*, the other being *amylose*. Composed of interconnected short chains of a-glucose to give a much branched, tree-like structure. Amylopectin is more difficult to *gelatinise* than amylose but forms stable gels resistant to *retrogradation*.

Amylose

A straight chain form of *starch* made of α-glucose units. The chain takes the form of a spiral or helix, with six *glucose* units per turn. Amylose readily undergoes *gelatinisation* but after a time *retro-gradation* occurs with the gel contracting and releasing water (*syneresis*).

Anaerobic respiration

Metabolism that occurs in the absence of oxygen. Compared with aerobic respiration it is much less efficient in producing energy and leads to the accumulation of products such as alcohol, which may eventually have a toxic effect.

Anthocyanidins

The basis of a group of water-soluble pigments in plants, *benzopyran derivatives* with two ring structures (benzene derivatives) joined by a bridge. The basis of *anthocyanins* when combined with sugars. Substitution of different groups into the ring structures can lead to different coloured *pigments* in fruit, vegetables and flowers. An increase in –OH groups gives blue colours and increase in –OCH_3, gives red.

Their names indicate the colours they produce by association with flowers: *eg*
- peonidin – red
- delphinidin – blue
- petunidin – mauve.

Anthocyanins
Made from an *anthocyanidin* joined to a sugar or sugars such as *glucose*. Form a wide range of water-soluble *pigments* with colours ranging from blue to red. They are pH sensitive, like litmus paper, becoming red at lower pH and blue at higher pH. (See *Anthocyanidins*.)

Anti-caking agents
Absorb moisture from dried foods without themselves becoming wet. Addition to powders ensures free-flowing characteristics, eg. salt. Common examples: magnesium oxide, silicates, calcium phosphates, salts of some long chain *fatty acids* such as stearic and palmitic.

Antioxidants
Prevent *rancidity* developing in fats by either absorbing oxygen or preventing chemical changes involved in rancidity. Antioxidants which absorb oxygen, include: *ascorbic acid* (vitamin C), gallates, and *tocopherols* (vitamin E). Chemical reactions involved in rancidity are prevented by BHA (butylated hydroxyanisole) or BHT (butylated hydroxytoluene). *Hydrolytic rancidity* cannot be prevented by antioxidants.

Ascorbic acid
Ascorbic acid is vitamin C in either its oxidised or reduced form. The latter is a powerful reducing agent and can be used as an *antioxidant*. Used in a number of products to protect flavours and fats against oxidation. Used in the Chorleywood bread process to speed dough development.

Naturally occurring in many fruits and vegetables, deficiency can lead to a range of diseases including bleeding of gums, bruising, internal bleeding and scurvy. The best sources are tropical fruits. Blackcurrants 200mg/100g, rose-hips 175mg/100g, oranges 50mg/l00g. Potatoes supply a significant amount in the British diet because of the large quantity eaten, but contain only 8–30mg/100g, or less, when stored for several months.

Aseptic packaging
A previously sterilised product is filled into a sterile container. The container is sealed in a sterile environment to obtain a hermetic seal. Used for custards, ice-cream mixes and soups.

Aspartame
A sweetener made from the combination of two *amino acids*, phenylalanine and aspartic acid. Nearly 200 times as sweet as *sucrose* with none of the after-taste of *saccharin*. Under acidic conditions and prolonged storage may break down.

Aspiration
A development of the ancient process of winnowing. A strong blast of air is used to separate food materials from contaminants, *eg* chaff from grain in wheat milling.

Avidin
An egg protein found in the white. Its anti-microbial properties as it binds the vitamin *biotin* make the latter unavailable to bacteria.

Bacteriophages
Viruses which attack bacteria only. They cause problems in *starter cultures* used in cheese-making by killing the bacteria in the cultures, thereby preventing development of acidity in the cheese. Abbreviated to 'phage'.

Baking powders
Used to produce carbon dioxide in cake mixes to help give the required texture to the cake. Formed from sodium hydrogen carbonate (bicarbonate), a slow acting acid and a starch filler. Acids used include *cream of tartar*, calcium phosphate, disodium pyrophosphate and glucono-δ-lactone.

Bar coding
A code in the form of bars on a pack that can be read rapidly by electronic scanners at checkouts. The scanner is linked to a computer which feeds data back to the checkout and which prints the data automatically onto the till ticket. The code bars are split into: prefix for the country of origin; manufacturer's number; item number and check digit.

Benzoic acid
A permitted *preservative* in a number of products. Like the benzoates (also permitted preservatives) it is used widely in soft drinks and similar products, but use is declining owing to allergic reactions in some people and the public's reaction to additives in general.

Benzoic sulphimide see *Saccharin*

Benzopyran derivatives
Formed from two benzene rings and a joining bridge. Basis for coloured *pigments* such as *anthocyanins*, anthoxanthins and flavone derivatives.

Beri-beri
A disease caused by the deficiency of vitamin B1 (thiamin). Symptoms include muscular weakness, palpitations, fever and heart failure. Outbreaks in the Far East have been caused by polishing rice, which removes the main source of vitamin B1.

Biosynthesized proteins
A *protein* produced by growing micro-organisms on suitable substrates, usually by a continuous fermentation method. Proteins have a good *amino acid* make-up but consumer resistance has been encountered.

Biotin
A *vitamin* synthesised in the human gut by bacteria. Deficiency is very rare. Egg protein *avidin* combines with biotin making it unavailable to micro-organisms.

Bitterness
A property of a range of organic and inorganic substances, particularly those containing magnesium, ammonium and calcium derivatives or quinine and *caffeine* in drinks.

Blanching
A short heat treatment carried out on vegetables before *canning, freezing* or *drying*. Main objectives are to inactivate enzymes and to shrink the product.

Efficiency of blanching tested by *peroxidase* test. Main methods are water- and steam-blanching. New developments include use of *microwaves*.

Blast-freezing
Cold air (at around –25C) is blown on to a food product of any shape to freeze it. The rate of freezing depends on the air temperature, its velocity used and the surface area of the food exposed. Fluidised bed freezers are a development in which air is blown upwards to 'fluidise' the product as well as freeze it.

'Boil-in-the-bag' products
Food products prepared and packed into bags which can be immersed into boiling water for rapid cooking. High-density polythene is commonly used, but new, thinner bags are available in linear low-density polythene.

Botulism
A dangerous disease with up to 70% mortality rates, caused by the ingestion of a toxin produced by the organism *Clostridium botulinum*. The organism produces heat resistant spores which can survive in canned foods that are underprocessed. The spores require a temperature of 120C and a pH less than 4.5 for complete destruction. The toxin, of which only minute quantities can be fatal, is destroyed above 63C.

Browning reactions
There are two main types:

– Non-enzymic
- caramelisation – breakdown of sugars at high temperatures to produce brown products
- *ascorbic acid* oxidation – slow process in some fruit juices leading to brown *pigments*
- Maillard reaction – *reducing sugars* and *amino acids* or *proteins* react together eventually to form brown *melanoidin pigments*. The reaction is quicker at higher temperatures and high pH.

– Enzymic
In some fruit and vegetables the *enzymes, polyphenolases*, react with phenolic substrates in the presence of oxygen to produce brown *pigment*. Ideally substrates are diphenols, eg *catechol* in apples. Browning results from bruising, cutting, or some processing.

Browning can be prevented by using sulphites or sulphur dioxide, by inactivating *enzymes* or by removing one or more of the reactants, eg by removing sugar to prevent the *Maillard reaction*.

Brucella
A genus of bacteria, of which *B. abortus* causes abortion in cattle and can contaminate milk. Disease in humans is an undulating flu-like disease. Cattle now tested for brucella and the organisms are usually destroyed in pasteurisation.

Buffers
Control and stabilise the pH of food. Some food components act as buffers, eg *amino acids* and *proteins*. Weak *acids* and their salts are used, eg *lactic, citric, malic* and *tartaric* acids.

Caffeine
A stimulant found in tea and coffee, considered to be addictive. Caffeine has been implicated as a possible cause of a number of disorders including nervous problems, but little has been proved. Coffee beans contain about 1% caffeine. Referred to as an alkaloid drug; also called *trimethylxanthine*.

Calciferols
There are two slightly different calciferols: cholecalciferol (vitamin D3) and ergocalciferol (vitamin D2), and both are related to *cholesterol*. Produced by action of sunlight on the skin or found in fish oils.

About 2.5µg per day is adequate; more can cause poisoning by damaging the kidneys. Involved with calcium absorption and deficiency leads to the disease *rickets*.

Calcium
Combines with phosphate to make up the structure of bones and teeth. Only about 40% of calcium in food can be absorbed by the body. Main sources are dairy products, bread and some vegetables. Deficiency a problem in old age, particularly in women, causing the disease osteoporosis.

Canning
The process by which food is hermetically sealed in a container and then heat processed. The heat process is sufficient to kill all micro-organisms and most of their spores. A few spores may survive so the product is termed 'commercially sterile'; absolute *sterility* is very difficult to attain.

Caramel
Produced when sugars are heated above their melting point. Caramel is a range of brown substances, of variable composition. Some components may have a bitter flavour. It is used as a brown colour for foods and as a flavouring agent.

Caramelisation
Process by which caramel is produced by heating sugars to high temperatures. A *browning reaction* in the absence of amino acid or proteins (see *Maillard reaction*).

Carbohydrates

Hydrates of carbon, made up of carbon, hydrogen and oxygen. Included in the group are sugars, oligosaccharides and *polysaccharides*. The process of photosynthesis is responsible for producing carbohydrates in plants.

Carbonated drinks

Soft drinks to which is added carbon dioxide to give sparkle, better mouthfeel and some acidity. Carbonated drinks are sweetened, flavoured, acidified, coloured and often chemically preserved.

Carob gum see *Locust bean gum*

Carotenoids

A group of fat-soluble *pigments* ranging from yellow to red in colour. All are similar to carotene, which, as the name suggests, is found in carrots.

True carotenoids contain 40 carbon atoms, and are built up from eight *isoprene* (C_5H_8) units. They are unsaturated hydrocarbon derivatives with conjugative double bond systems. Carotenoids with –OH groups present are called *xanthophylls*. Some have *pro-vitamin A* activity, *eg* β-carotene.

Case-hardening

A problem occurring in the dehydration of some foods, eg fruits, when a skin is produced on the surface which inhibits complete dehydration and retards rehydration. Usually caused by high temperatures, soluble solids and the denaturing of proteins on the surface of the produce.

Casein

The main milk *protein*, representing about 3% of milk. Precipitated by *acid* at about pH 4·6 and coagulated by *rennet* in cheese making. A mixture of phosphoproteins with different properties. α_s-casein is precipitated by calcium, whereas (κ)-casein is insensitive to calcium.

Catechol

A substrate (a diphenol) for the enzymes *polyphenolases* in apples which causes *enzymic browning* when apples are damaged, cut or eaten.

Cellulose

The most abundant *carbohydrate*, indigestible but a good source of fibre. Two types: crystalline and amorphous; the latter absorbs a considerable quantity of water and has been used in slimming foods. It is a *polysaccharide* composed of long chains of ß-glucose, providing the main support for cells in plants.

Chilling

A method of extending the storage life of a product by lowering its temperature to between –1 and 8C, but not by freezing the product. Current research indicates that a temperature of below 4C (and as close to 0C as possible without freezing) is preferable to ensure that the product is safe from Listeria infection.

'Chinese restaurant syndrome'

A feeling of dizziness and sickness apparently brought on by excessive consumption of *monosodium glutamate* (MSG), which was found to be used excessively in Chinese restaurants. However, MSG is naturally present in most foods, as it is a derivative of the *amino acid* glutamic acid. Also known as Kwok's disease.

Chlorogenic acids

Complex organic acids found in fruit and vegetables. As they contain *phenolic* groups (–OH) they are ready substrates for *polyphenolase* enzyme activity to produce brown *pigments*. Similarly, they are found in *tannins* and coffee.

Chlorophyll

The *green* pigment of plants, involved in photosynthesis, the process by which plants manufacture carbohydrate. Under acid conditions the pigment is broken down to a greyish/brown colour, called *pheophytin*. Chlorophyll is stable under alkaline conditions, hence the addition of bicarbonate of soda (sodium hydrogen carbonate) to green vegetables when cooking, which causes the pH to rise.

Cholesterol

A widely distributed sterol found in animal tissue. The body can produce up to twice its normal requirements. It has been implicated in circulatory diseases, particularly as it can be deposited on the walls of blood vessels. Related chemically to vitamin D.

Clarification

Process of removing suspended or colloidal material from liquid products, such as wine. Centrifugation, filtration and *enzymes* can be employed.

Climacteric (in fruit)

The peak of the rise in respiration shown in some fruit after harvesting. Climacteric fruit include: banana, avocado, mango and tomato. The rise in respiration is accompanied by changes associated with *ripening*.

Cold chain

A loose title for the course of events of transport and storage of frozen foods, from the *freezing* of foods, through storage and distribution, finally to the home.

Commercial sterility see *Sterilisation*

Conching

A process used in traditional chocolate manufacture to help develop the right texture.

Controlled atmosphere (CA) storage

The storage of food products, particularly fruit and vegetables, in an atmosphere modified in some way, usually by changes in temperature and gases, particularly oxygen and carbon dioxide. Lower temperature and lower oxygen or high carbon dioxide levels are common.

Cryogenic freezing

The use of liquified gases for *rapid freezing* of small food items, eg raspberries and prawns. The liquified gas, usually nitrogen or carbon dioxide, is sprayed onto the food product. Rapid freezing is possible for small items only.

Curd proteins

Clotted proteins produced by the action of *rennet* on milk. *Casein* is modified by the rennet allowing *calcium* to react with the k-casein, causing it to coagulate. The *whey proteins* are drained away to leave the curd which is transformed into cheese.

Curing

A term usually applied to meat which involves the development of colour, flavour and enhanced keeping qualities. Curing brine is added to meat and comprises salt, sodium nitrate, some sodium nitrite and sugar. Nitrate is converted to nitrite which combines with *pigments* in the meat to produce the characteristic pink/red colour.

Cutin

A general name for waxy substances found on the surface of fruit, eg on apples.

Cyanocobalamin

Vitamin B12, essential for the formation of red blood cells. Deficiency disease (the inability to absorb the vitamin) is pernicious anaemia. Found in animal products, a particularly rich source being liver.

D value

A *canning* term: the 'decimal reduction' value or 'D' value, refers to the reduction of bacterial spores to one-tenth of the original number in a canned product as a result of heat processing. For example, a D value of four means that it takes four minutes at 121C (250F) to reduce the number of bacterial spores to one-tenth of the original number.

Dark cutting beef

A defect of beef caused by too high a pH owing to insufficient *lactic acid* being produced after slaughter. Oxygen is unable to penetrate the meat to produce the bright red oxymyoglobin; a dark purplish/red product is therefore produced. On cooking, the meat is dark in colour and often tough.

Demersal fish

Fish which are bottom feeders and are usually 'white', eg cod, saithe, sole, haddock and whiting.

Denaturation

Generally refers to the uncoiling of *protein* chains caused by heat, changes in pH, agitation and sometimes light. Slight denaturation can be reversible and, in the case of *enzymes*, activity is regenerated.

Dextrins

Breakdown products of starch which are soluble, long chains of α-glucose units. They are formed when bread is toasted and are often used as edible adhesives.

Dextrose

Alternative name for α-D-glucose. Name originates from the ability of dextrose solution to rotate a plane of polarised light in a clockwise or dextro-rotatory fashion. Given the symbol (+), as opposed to laevorotatory, as in *fructose*, which is given the symbol (−).

Dextrose equivalent value (D.E.)

A value denoting the degree of conversion of *starch* into *glucose*. The higher the D.E., the more glucose (*dextrose*) present. Lower D.E. sugar syrups are less sweet but thickening and add body.

Diastase

The combination of α- and β-*amylases* which break down *starch*.

Dielectric heating

A form of heating produced in a material when it is subjected to an alternating electric field. Heating is caused by molecular friction due to rapid movement of molecules, such as water, in the alternating electric field. *Microwave* heating is similar, but is caused by electromagnetic radiation.

Diglycerides

Emulsifying agents, composed of *glycerol* and two *fatty acids*. Not as effective as *monoglycerides*.

Dipeptides

Two *amino acids* linked together by the *peptide* link or bridge (−CO−NH−). Formed in cheese *ripening* in some varieties.

Disaccharides

Sugars, such as *sucrose*, *lactose* and *maltose*, formed by the combination of two *monosaccharide* units with the elimination of a molecule of water.

sucrose = *fructose + glucose*
lactose = *galactose + glucose*
maltose = *glucose + glucose*

Disulphide bridge

A bridge or link formed between *protein* chains from the *amino acid* cysteine. The bridge (−S−S−) gives elasticity to dough during bread-making.

Diterpenes

Derivatives of isoprene (C_5H_8), all diterpenes are based on four isoprene units ($C_{20}H_{32}$). (See *Terpenoids*.)

Drip

The liquid which exudes from a frozen product on thawing. Found in fish and meat if frozen slowly.

Drying (dehydration)
Removal of water from a food to preserve it.

– Freeze drying
Food frozen then subjected to strong vacuum to sublime the ice and leave food dry; expensive.

– Roller drying
Used for liquids; product in contact with hot roller or drum; relatively slow drying for milk or whey.

– Spray drying
Liquid sprayed into chamber and met by a blast of hot air to produce a fine powder, *eg* coffee.

– Fluidised bed drying
Hot air blown upwards into a bed of product, which then acts as a fluid and dries fairly rapidly.

Electrophoresis
The movement of electrically-charged particles when an electric current is passed through a solution. Used to separate *proteins*. Fish can be recognized by the bands of proteins produced by electrophoresis of fish flesh within special gels, each fish species having its own unique band formation.

Emulsifying agents (emulsifiers)
Substances which enable the production of a stable dispersion of oil in water or vice versa. Examples include: *glyceryl monostearate* (GMS), *lecithin*, egg yolk, and *whey protein*. Some are more soluble in oil than water, but all orientate themselves at the interface between oil and water and prevent droplets of oil from coalescing and separating.

Enzymes
These substances are naturally occurring catalysts found in the cells of plants or animals. They exhibit the properties of *proteins* and may be very specific in their action. If not inactivated they can produce undesirable changes in processed foods, such as changes in flavour, colour or texture.

Enzymic browning see Browning

Erucic acid
A *fatty acid* (22 carbon atoms) found in rape seed oil. Implicated as a cause of heart disease. Modern varieties are bred to be free of the acid.

Essential amino acid see *Amino acid*

Essential oils
Natural oils which contribute to the flavour of foods, particularly fruits. Name is derived from 'essence' – they are not 'essential' for life. They are the basis of naturally occurring food flavours, such as citrus oils.

Esters
Formed from the reaction between organic acids and alcohols. Many have fruit-like flavours, *eg* ethyl ethanoate (acetate) which is like pear-drops.

Ethylene (ethene)
A gas which acts as a plant hormone, stimulating the *ripening* process and the increase in respiration rate in *climacteric* fruit. Thought to be produced by the breakdown of the *amino acid*, methionine. The gas can be added externally to ripen fruit, *eg* bananas.

Extraction rate of flour
Indicates the yield of flour obtained when milling wheat. Wholemeal flour is 100% extraction, *ie* the whole wheat grain. White flour is about 72% extraction as the bran and germ have been removed.

Extrusion
A process of making snack foods, particularly corn and potato-based products. The food material is heated under pressure in a barrel-shaped piece of equipment with either a single or double internal revolving screw. The revolving screw takes the product to a dye from which the product is released. The sudden pressure drop, on release from the dye, makes the product expand rapidly to produce a light porous texture. Various dyes are used to give products of different shapes and sizes.

F value
A term used in canning to denote the overall lethal effect of the heating process. It refers to the number of minutes at which the product is kept at 121C (250F) that give an equivalent sterilising effect to carrying out the whole sterilization process. The exact time is determined by that required to achieve 'commercial sterility', when the bacterial population has been reduced by 12D, ie down to 10^{-12} of the original level. (See *D–value*.)

Fatty acids
Organic acids containing a carboxyl group (–COOH); fatty acids are long-chain acids found in fats combined with *glycerol*.

– *Essential fatty acids*
Fatty acids required by the body, *eg* linoleic (the main one), linolenic and the third, arachidonic, which is produced by the body.

Fehling's test
A test for reducing substances, particularly *reducing sugars* such as *glucose, fructose, maltose* and *lactose*. Two solutions are mixed then boiled with the sample. Fehling's solution 1 is copper sulphate and solution 2 is a mixture of sodium hydroxide and tartrate buffer. When mixed and heated, reducing substances turn the blue solution to a brick red colour due to the production of copper 1 oxide.

Fermentation
The metabolism of organic compounds in the absence of oxygen. Yeast ferments sugar to produce alcohol. *Lactic acid* bacteria ferment *lactose* in milk in yoghurt manufacture. Fermentation produces energy for the organism, but inefficiently compared with aerobic respiration.

Fibre

The indigestible parts of food, generally consisting of *cellulose, hemicellulose* and pectin. Important in maintaining proper functioning of the digestive system. The NACNE report recommends a minimum of 30g per day.

Filled milk

A dried milk containing vegetable fat instead of butter-fat. Has better keeping qualities than whole-fat milk powder. Used by the catering industry.

Filter aid

A substance made up of large, inert particles that is mixed with the liquid to be filtered to prevent holes in the filter becoming blocked. The filter aid forms a porous structure on the filter allowing the liquid to flow through freely. Examples are kieselguhr, paper pulp and carbon.

Flavonoids

A large group of compounds found to be a basis of *pigments*, such as *anthocyanins*, and also some bitter components of foods. They can act as natural antioxidants in the body

Flavours

Flavours are detected by the nose and therefore volatile substances contribute most noticeably to them, *eg* fruit flavours. *Essential oils* from fruits are main flavour components. Synthetic flavours often contain *esters*. Nature-identical flavours contain the same chemical substances that are found in the natural product or flavour, but do not necessarily contain all the substances found in the natural product.

Flavour enhancers

Substances which enhance or improve a flavour. *Monosodium glutamate* (MSG) has been widely used in many products, particularly meat, fish and vegetable products. *Ribonucleotides* are similar to MSG but sometimes more effective. Only very small amounts are needed. Their action may be through the stimulation of the taste buds.

Flavour profile

A taste-panel procedure whereby a flavour is broken down into a number of factors or characteristics. The characteristics are often rated on a scale from 1 to 10.

Fluidised bed drying see *Drying*

Fluidised bed freezing see *Blast-freezing*

Folic acid

A vitamin essential in the synthesis of certain *amino acids* and similar components. Deficiency causes a form of anaemia. Widely found in foods, *eg* liver, vegetables and yeast.

Free radicals

Highly reactive chemical species formed from molecules with unpaired electrons. They are involved in initiating and perpetuating the reactions which cause fat to become *rancid*. The *antioxidants* BHA and BHT produce stable free radicals and stop the *rancidity* reactions. Free radicals have been implicated as possible causes of cancer and heart disease.

Freeze drying see *Drying*

Freezer burn

The drying out of the surface of a frozen food, particularly meat or fish, which is unwrapped. The problem is caused by the sublimation of ice crystals from the surface directly to water vapour. The thawed product is tougher or drier to the palate.

Freezing

The conversion of water from the liquid state to solid ice. The thermal arrest period of freezing is the time taken for all the available water to be formed into ice. Common methods:

- Immersion – food placed in a very cold brine
- Plate – freezing by contact with cooled flat surface
- Blast – cold air blown over the product to freeze it
- Cryogenic – liquid gases, nitrogen or carbon dioxide are sprayed over the food.

Freshwater fish

Fish that live in non-salt water and are unable usually to live in sea water, *eg* trout, pike, perch.

Fructose

Also known as *laevulose*. Rotates a plane of polarized light anti-clockwise, hence 'laevorotatory'. A very sweet sugar (*monosaccharide*) about 1·6 times as sweet as *sucrose*. Found in *invert sugar*, honey, jam and confectionery.

Fuller's earth

Used in the refining of oils to remove *pigments* such as *carotenoids*. Porous colloidal aluminium silicate is the main constituent.

Galactose

A *monosaccharide* and *reducing sugar*, found linked to *glucose* in *lactose* (milk sugar). It has a six-carbon ring structure similar to *glucose*, except for the position of the hydroxyl group on carbon atom four. Has about one-third the sweetness of *sucrose*.

Galacturonic acid

An acid derivative of *galactose* with a carboxyl group (–COOH) on carbon atom six. A component of pectin. Pectic acids are predominantly galacturonic acids in long chains.

- Methyl galacturonate
  Methyl ester formed from galacturonic acid. Found in *pectin*. *Pectinic acids* are predominately methyl galacturonate with some galacturonic acid in long chains. Pectinic acids are the main constituents of pectin used to set jam.

Gas chromatography

A type of chromatography using columns packed with a stationary phase through which is passed a carrier gas. Volatile substances are separated by the procedure and detected by special detectors, usually flame ionisation detectors. Useful for separation of *flavour* components.

Gelatin

Made from the collagen of connective tissues, bones and skin by acid or alkaline processes. Good gelling properties, commonly found as table jelly.

Gelatinisation

The process by which a gel is formed. In the case of *starch* a large quantity of water is absorbed and the starch eventually cross-links to form a three-dimensional network. Starches gelatinise at certain temperatures. Starches higher in *amylose* gelatinise at lower temperatures than those rich in *amylopectin*. The latter produces more stable gels.

Glucose

A *monosaccharide* containing six carbon atoms, also called *dextrose*. A reducing sugar of about 70–80% the sweetness level of sucrose.

Glucose syrup

A colourless syrup produced by hydrolysis of *starch*. Of variable composition including *glucose*, *dextrins* and *maltose*. Used as a sweetening agent in confectionery.

Gluten

The *protein* of wheat flour and, to a lesser extent, rye. Composed of two types of protein, gliadins and glutenins. Responsible for the extensibility and elasticity of dough in bread-making. Strong flours are richer in gluten. (see *Wheat proteins*.)

Glycerine see *Glycerol*

Glycerol

Commonly known as *glycerine*. A clear, viscous, sweet liquid. Chemically a trihydric alcohol, with three carbon atoms. Combines with *fatty acids* to form *triglycerides* which make up fats.

Glycerol monostearate (GMS)

An *emulsifier*, made from *glycerol* and one fatty acid, stearic acid. Commonly used in the food industry as a general purpose *emulsifier*.

Glycogen

A *polysaccharide*, similar to *amylopectin*, which is found in animal tissue. Composed of α-glucose units and is broken down in the muscles ultimately to yield energy for muscular activity. On the death of the animal it is converted to *lactic acid* which lowers the pH of the meat.

Glycosides

Substances made up of a molecule to which is attached a sugar molecule; *eg* anthocyanins contain sugars attached to an anthocy-anidin molecule.

Glycosidic links

An oxygen bridge between two sugar molecules. *Maltose* is made of two *glucose* units joined by a glycosidic link between carbon atom one on one molecule, and four on the other. Hence the term α,1–4 glycosidic link'.

Grading

Grading, or quality separation of foods, depends on a number of characteristics, *eg* size, shape, colour and freedom from blemish. Often confused with *sorting* which depends on one characteristic, *eg* size.

Gram stain

A staining technique used to distinguish groups of bacteria. Those which retain the stain (crystal violet) are termed gram positive, *eg Bacillus, Clostridium*. Those which lose the stain are termed gram negative, *eg Salmonella, Pseudomonas*. Gram positive bacteria react often to different antibiotics from gram negatives.

Guar gum

Cost-effective stabiliser used in ice-cream, salad dressings, baked goods and pet foods.

Gums

A wide range of *polysaccharides*, some of complex composition, which absorb large quantities of water and act as *stabilisers* and *emulsifiers*. Examples include *alginates*, gums arabic, tragacanth, guar and xanthan gum. Used in many food applications to prevent water separation and to thicken.

Haemoglobin

Red pigment of blood, composed of an iron containing haem structure joined to a *protein*, globin. Haemoglobin combines with oxygen from the lungs and transports it to the tissues. Iron deficiency (anaemia) results in the inability to produce enough haemoglobin.

Hemicellulose

A group of polysaccharides found in plant cell walls of variable composition. All are soluble in alkali and can be broken down to sugars, which are pentoses (contain five carbon atoms), *eg xyloses*, and some sugar derivatives, *eg uronic acids*.

High-temperature short-time (HTST)

Heat processes such as *pasteurisation* and *sterilisation* of milk using plate heat exchanges. Process allows rapid heating of product with minimal flavour changes but full bactericidal effect of the heat.

High-viscosity juice

Fruit juice that is thicker than normal juices (*low-viscosity juices*) such as lemon juice, and has considerable suspended material thus rendering it opaque, *eg* tomato juice.

Homogenisation

Process applied to milk to break down fat into small stable droplets which do not cream off. Normal method is to use a pressure homogeniser which forces the milk through a small orifice under pressure.

Humectants

The opposite of *anti-caking agents*, since they are used to keep products moist. They release moisture slowly to the product as it dries out. Examples include, *glycerol*, sorbitol, sodium and potassium lactate.

Hydrogen bonds

An electrostatic attraction between oxygen and hydrogen atoms. The oxygen has a slight negative charge and the hydrogen a positive one. Occurs only momentarily but between millions of atoms, so the overall effect is considerable. Involved in binding water to *proteins*, in the *gelatinisation* of *starch* and in most food products.

Hydrogenation

The process by which unsaturated fats or oils are converted to saturated fats. The process involves passing hydrogen gas through the heated fat in the presence of a nickel catalyst. Used extensively in margarine and shortening manufacture.

Hydrolytic rancidity

Fats in the presence of water break down to release *fatty acids* from the *glycerol* in their constituent *triglycerides*. The process is accelerated by lipolytic enzymes (*lipases*) and micro-organisms, especially some moulds. Short-chain fatty acids are only of significance because of their odour.

Hydrostatic retorts

Large, continuous autoclaves used for *canning*. Operate with hot water and steam. The head of water maintains this steam pressure. A moving belt takes the cans through the water pre-heating stage, then to steam heating and finally cooling. High rates of production can be achieved, but high capital outlay is involved.

Hypobaric storage

A method of storing food, particularly fruit and vegetables, that relies on reducing the atmospheric pressure in the store. In fruit it delays *ripening* by lowering the oxygen and ethene (*ethylene*) levels. It is expensive and difficult to maintain. Largely experimental and little used commercially.

Icing

A method of chilling, used particularly for fish. Melting ice is better as latent heat is absorbed, so a greater cooling effect is achieved. Tropical fish keep better by icing than temperate fish.

Immersion freezing

An old method of *freezing* using super-cooled brines. A slow method with little control, rarely used nowadays.

Improvers (for flour)

Chemicals that are used to accelerate the *ageing* of flour and improve its bread-making potential. The *protein* of the flour is affected and *disulphide bridges* produced. Examples: *ascorbic acid, soya flour.*

Individually-quick-frozen (IQF)

Rapid freezing, eg by *fluidised-bed freezing*, of individual foods such as peas. A continuous method giving a higher quality product.

Instantisation

The alteration of a food to make it immediately dispersible and soluble in water. Milk powder is instantised by re-wetting, or not drying completely, so that powder particles stick together to form granules which readily dissolve in water.

Interesterification (of fats)

The process by which the positions of the *fatty acids* attached to *glycerol* in the *triglyceride* of fats are altered. The fat is heated in the presence of a catalyst, sodium ethoxide. Normally used to improve the creaming properties of fats to be blended for shortenings.

Inversion (of sucrose)

The splitting of *sucrose* into its component *monosaccharides*, *glucose* and *fructose*. Sucrose rotates a plane of polarised light clockwise, hence (+); *glucose* and *fructose* together rotate in an anticlockwise direction (−). The change in the sign from (+) to (−) is 'inversion'.

Invert sugar

A mixture of equal amounts of *glucose* and *fructose*. Solutions of sugars rotate a plane of polarised light in a clockwise (+) or anticlockwise (−) direction. As fructose is strongly laevorotatory (anticlockwise) (−) and glucose only slightly dextrorotatory (clockwise) (+) , invert sugar is laevorotatory (−) overall. Similarly, because of the high sweetness of fructose, invert sugar is sweeter than sucrose. Occurs naturally in honey, jams and fruit juices. Produced in or added to confectionery for sweetness and also, because of its high solubility (absorbs water readily), to prevent water being used by sucrose to reform sugar crystals.

Iodine value

A measure of the unsaturation of a fat. A special preparation of iodine (Wij's solution) is used to determine the number of double bonds in fats. Higher iodine values indicate more un-saturation, *eg* butter iv around 29, lard 59, cottonseed oil 110.

ß-ionone ring

The ring structure at the ends of a *carotenoid* structure. An unbroken ring is necessary for a carotenoid to have *pro-vitamin* A activity.

Irradiation

The application of ionising radiations to kill bacteria in foods. Radiations are produced from decaying sources such as cobalt 60 and caesium 137, or by electron accelerators. There is no risk of residual radioactivity. Must not be confused with radioactive contamination or radioactivity.

Iso-electric point (IEP)

Refers to the pH at which a *protein* or *amino* acid has an overall net electrical charge of zero; in other words, all negative charges are balanced by all positive charges. At the IEP the properties of the protein are at a minimum, eg solubility, electrical conductivity and viscosity. The IEP of *casein* is 4·6, hence its precipitation as milk sours.

Isoprenoid derivatives

Compounds built up of isoprene units (C_5H_8). *Monoterpenes* found in *flavours*, such as *essential oils*, are made from two isoprene units. *Carotenoids* are made from eight isoprene units.

Lacquer (in cans)

A resinous coating on the inside of cans which is hardened by heat. The lacquers vary in composition according to function. The main types resist acid attack and others prevent the formation of sulphides from the reaction of sulphur with metal from the can.

Lactic acid

Produced by the *fermentation* of *lactose* in milk giving acidity and the flavour of sour milk. Produced by lactic acid bacteria, *eg Lactobacillus* in pickles. Important in meat, as *glycogen* is converted to lactic acid post mortem, and is responsible for a pH of meat of around 5.4.

Lactose

Only found in milk, at about 4·8%. A *disaccharide* and reducing *sugar*, made from *galactose* and *glucose*. Only about 16% of the sweetness of sucrose.

Laevulose see *Fructose*

Lecithins

Fatty substances belonging to the *phospholipids*. They are made of *glycerol*, *fatty acids* (at least one unsaturated), phosphoric acid and a nitrogenous base, choline. Naturally occurring emulsifying agents found in egg yolk, milk, soya and peanut. Many applications where natural *emulsifiers* are desirable, *eg* chocolate, mayonnaise. Commercially they are produced mainly from soya bean.

Lignin

A complex high molecular weight substance similar to *carbohydrates*. As plants age it is deposited on cell walls to toughen them. Found in old vegetables as a woody texture or as stringiness in runner beans.

Lipases

Enzymes (lipolytic) which break down fats. Usually they release *fatty acids* from their attachment to *glycerol*. Free fatty acids are measured as an indication of lipase activity.

Lipids

General term for fats, waxes and oils. Includes *phospholipids* such as *lecithin*. Most are combinations of *glycerol* and *fatty acids*.

Listeria

A group (genus) of bacteria that can give rise to a number of diseases including meningitis. *L. monocytogenes* has caused concern as it has been found in a number of chilled food products such as soft cheese.

Locust bean gum

Also known as carob gum. Comes from the seeds of the carob tree. High molecular weight polysaccharide used as a stabiliser, thickener and gelling agent (with *xanthan gum*).

Low-viscosity juice

Clear, thin fruit juice with little or usually no suspended matter, *eg* lemon juice, apple juice, grape juice (cf *High-viscosity juices*).

Lycopene

The red *carotenoid pigment* of ripe tomatoes. It does not possess pro-*vitamin A* activity. Unlike most carotenoids, it is synthesised during *ripening* as chlorophyll is degraded.

Maillard reaction

A *browning reaction*, which is *non-enzymic*, resulting from the initial reaction of *reducing sugars* and *amino acids* or *proteins* (amino group). It occurs as the result of heating during cooking and processing, but also takes place slowly in some stored products such as dried milk, if their moisture levels are above a certain level (around 5%). The reaction is accelerated at higher pH and retarded by the addition of acid or sulphur dioxide. In some foods it causes a reduction in nutritive value as essential amino acids can be bound up into complexes. Brown pigments formed are called *melanoidins*. Some intermediate products and melanoidins contribute to flavour and have been used in producing synthetic meat *flavours*.

Malic acid

A common fruit acid found in, for example, apples, plums and tomatoes.

Maltose

A *disaccharide* and *reducing sugar* composed of two *glucose* units. Produced by the malting process from *starch* in barley grains. Its sweetness is about 30% that of *sucrose*.

Melanoidins

Also called *melanins*. A general name for the brown *pigments* produced during *browning reactions*, *eg* the *Maillard reaction*.

Metmyoglobin

The brown pigment of meat when it is old or cooked. The iron of *myoglobin* is changed by oxidation from iron II to iron III. It does not have the capacity to carry oxygen.

Micelles

Small bundles of *casein* molecules that occur in milk. The calcium sensitive(α casein) is protected by the calcium insensitive κ-casein). On coagulation, *eg* in cheese-making, the micelles are modified and cross-linked.

Microwaves

Electromagnetic *radiations* having frequencies in the range of 3-300,000 MHz, although the most commonly used frequencies are between 915 and 2,450 MHz. The microwaves cause molecules to vibrate which generates heat. Only molecules that are irregular and have electrical dipoles (*ie* positive and negative charges) are affected – water is the most important molecule involved. Microwave ovens are still the most common application. Commercial applications include thawing of frozen blocks and *blanching*.

Modified atmosphere

Refers to storage or packaging of products where the atmosphere has been modified in some way, usually by decreasing oxygen and increasing carbon dioxide or nitrogen.

Now used particularly for modified atmosphere packaging where packs are gas flushed. Applications include fish products, fruit and vegetables; spoilage has been reduced and shelf-life increased.

Monoglycerides

Composed of *glycerol* and one *fatty acid*. The remaining part of the glycerol can dissolve in water and the fatty acid chain in fat, thus the monoglyceride is able to act as an emulsifying agent. A common example is *glyceryl monostearate*.

Monosaccharide

Group name for the simplest sugars ranging from three to seven carbon atoms. The most common contain six carbon atoms (hence 'hexose'), eg *glucose*, *fructose* and *galactose*.

Monosodium glutamate (MSG)

A *flavour enhancer*, found naturally in soy sauce, that occurs in many foods. For many years MSG has been added to food products, particularly meats and vegetables. It brings out meat flavour, and tends to round off and suppress undesirable flavours. Excess MSG intake has been shown to cause dizziness and sickness – known as the 'Chinese restaurant syndrome' or 'Kwok's disease'.

Monoterpenes

Derivatives of isoprene (C_5H_8). All monoterpenes are based on two isoprene units ($C_{10}H_{16}$). Many are alcohols, aldehydes and ketones. They are constituents of *essential oils* and are to be found in many naturally occurring *flavours*. Monoterpenes are fairly unstable and can undergo changes in processing which lead to noticeable flavour changes. (See *Terpenoids*.)

Myoglobin

Similar to *haemoglobin* in blood, but only one-quarter of the latter's molecular weight as it contains one haem and not four, as in haemoglobin. Responsible for storage of oxygen in muscles where it is converted to oxymoglobin, the bright red colour of meat.

Myoglobin itself is a duller red and can be oxidised to brown *metmyoglobin* when the iron II atom in the haem part of the molecule is oxidised to iron III.

Naphthoquinone

The main part of vitamin K. There are a number of *vitamins* related to this, called 'substituted naphthoquinones'. They are essential for the working of the blood-clotting system.

Niacin see *Nicotinic acid*

Nickel

A catalyst used in a finely divided state to facilitate the hydrogena-tion of unsaturated oils when converting them to harder fats. Used in margarine and fat manufacture.

Nicotinamide see *Nicotinic acid*

Nicotinic acid

Also known as *niacin* and can exist as *nicotinamide*. A *vitamin* of the B complex. Deficiency leads to *pellagra*, a mental disorder leading to insanity. Found in many foods including meat, cereal germ, yeast and liver. It is added to flour.

Nitrosamine

A carcinogenic substance implicated in cancer of the throat. Formed from nitrite reacting with secondary amines. The former may come from bacon or cured meats. Chances of this occurring are slight.

Nitrosomyoglobin

The name given to the pink derivative of *myoglobin* produced by the action of nitrite during the curing of bacon and similar products.

Non-climacteric fruit

Fruit (and most vegetables) which do *not* show a rise in respiration rate after harvesting. Their *ripening* and respiration is gradual over a long period.

Non-enzymic browning see *Browning*

Novel proteins

Proteins produced by new methods, *eg* mycoprotein from fungi.

Nutritive additives

Vitamins and minerals added to certain foods such as flour, that are convenient carriers to ensure a balanced diet. Margarine, for example, has vitamins A and D added, whilst added to white flour are calcium, iron and the vitamins *thiamin* and *nicotinic acid*.

Oils

Fats which are liquid at room temperature. Usually contain a greater number of unsaturated fatty acids which lower the melting point.

Oleoresins

The non-volatile flavour constituents of spices and herbs. They are normally extracted by solvents such as acetone (propan-2-one). For industrial use oleoresins are mixed with inert carriers, such as *starch*, salt or *dextrose*, to enable easy mixing into foods.

Optical activity (in sugars)
Sugars and some acids have the ability to rotate a plane of polarised light, either clockwise (+) or anti-clockwise (−). Clockwise rotation is referred to as 'dextrorotatory', eg a solution of *glucose*; anticlockwise is 'laevorotatory', *eg* as in a solution of *fructose*. This optical activity can be observed using a polarimeter.

Oxalic acid
An organic *acid* containing two carboxyl (acid) groups. Found in rhubarb leaves, spinach and some chocolate. Toxic in high quantities; can bind iron and other minerals.

Oxidative rancidity
Occurs in unsaturated fats and *oils* and starts adjacent to the double bonds. The reaction is initiated by the presence of metals (particularly copper and iron), ultra-violet light and high temperatures. Highly reactive *free radicals* are involved in the reactions.

Oxidation of the double bonds occurs to produce hydroperoxides which break down to produce the odour of rancid fat. Prevented by the use of *antioxidants*.

Pale soft exudate (PSE)
Refers to the fluid expelled from pork muscle, post mortem, due to a rapid fall in pH. Due mainly to hereditory factors in the species of pig. The pork meat as a result is soft and much paler in colour owing to loss of water-holding capacity and destruction of blood *pigments*.

Panthothenic acid
A *vitamin* needed for the metabolism of fats and *carbohydrates*. Found in many foods, so deficiency should never arise.

Pasteurisation
A heat process intended to kill pathogenic micro-organisms and some spoilage organisms. Generally extends shelf-life but does not achieve any degree of sterility. Milk is pasteurised at 72C for 15 seconds.

Pectin
A complex *polysaccharide* found in plant cell walls and between cells in the middle lamella. Used with sugar and acid to form jam.

Various types:
– Protopectin
  Parent pectic substance; a large macro-molecule found in unripe plant products.

– Pectinic acids (normal *pectin*)
  Made from long chains of *galacturonic acid* and methyl galacturonate – usually more than 50% of the latter. Gels with sugar and acid in preserves.

– Pectic acids
  Found in very ripe fruit. As *pectinic acids* but mainly free of methyl galacturonate. Will not gel with sugar and acid, but will gel with *calcium* and other metal ions.

– Rapid-set pectin
  Pectinic acid with high methyl galacturonate content; sets rapidly, so used to suspend fruit in jam.

– Slow-set pectin
  Used for jams which are pumped or filled into cakes or pastries. Slow setting ensures operation carried out without gelling.

Pelagic fish
Fish living near the surface of the sea. Oily fish with up to 20% oil, eg herring and mackerel.

Pellagra
Deficiency disease caused by the absence of *nicotinic acid* in the diet. Can result in skin problems and mental disorders.

Penicillium
Group of common moulds which spoil many foods. *P. roquefortii* is used to give blue veins and flavour of blue cheeses.

Peptide bond
Link between *amino acids* in forming *dipeptides*, *polypeptides* and *proteins*. Formed from condensation of amino group (NH_2) and carboxyl group (−COOH), hence peptide bond (−CONH−).

Peroxidase test
A test for the efficiency of *blanching*. Peroxidase is a very heat resistant *enzyme* so its *denaturation* by heat can be assumed to have included the denaturation of other enzymes present in the food.

A sample of blanched product is tested by adding a drop of hydrogen peroxide followed by a drop of guaiacol. The peroxidase breaks down the hydrogen peroxide to release oxygen, which turns the guaiacol a brown colour, usually within 30 seconds to a minute. No colour change is observed within this time if the peroxidase is denatured.

Usually performed every 30 minutes after blanching peas, for example, in a freezing or canning plant.

Phage see *Bacteriophage*

Phenolases see *Polyphenolases*

Phenol oxidases see *Polyphenolases*

Pheophytin
A grey-brown substance produced from *chlorophyll* in cooked or processed foods under acidic conditions. Hydrogen ions replace the magnesium atom in the centre of the chlorophyll structure. The formation of pheophytin is prevented by making cooking water slightly alkaline, *eg* by adding sodium hydrogen carbonate (bicarbonate of soda).

Phosphate cross-bonded starch see *Starch*

Phosphatides see *Phospholipids*

Phospholipids
Fatty substances containing glycerol, fatty acids, phosphoric acid and a nitrogeneous base. A common example is *lecithin*, a natural *emulsifier*. Also called *phosphatides*.

Phytic acid
Chemically: *inositol hexaphosphoric* acid. Occurs in the bran of cereals, peas and beans, and has the ability to combine with *calcium* and iron in other foods, hence the addition of calcium carbonate to flour. However, it is not particularly efficient in its binding action.

Phytosterol
A general name given to plant sterols, similar to *cholesterol*, but not implicated in the latter's undesirable effects.

Pigments
Generally refers to naturally occurring colours. Three main groups:

- *chlorophylls* – green
- *carotenoid* – yellow to red
- *benzopyran* derivatives (mainly *anthocyanins*) – red to blue.

Plate freezing see *Freezing*

Polarimeter
An instrument to measure the degree of rotation of polarised light caused by a solution of a sugar, *amino acid* or organic acid.

Polypeptides
Long chains of *amino acids*; combine to form *proteins*.

Polyphenolases
Also known as *phenolases* and *phenol oxidases*. Naturally present *enzymes* in fruit and vegetables which, on damage to the cells, react with diphenols present, in the presence of oxygen, to produce brown *pigments*. This process is known as *enzymic browning*.

Substrates are usually diphenols such as *catechol* in apples. The enzymes react more slowly with monophenols such as tyrosine in potatoes.

Their action is prevented by heat, sulphur dioxide, acids and exclusion of oxygen.

Polysaccharides
Long chains of *monosaccharides* (sugars) joined together by *glycosidic links*. *Starch* is a chain of α-glucose units, *cellulose* is made from β-glucose units. Simple polysaccharides are made from one monosaccharide type, whereas in complex polysaccharides different units are involved.

Pre-gelatinised starches see *Starch*

Preservatives
Substances capable of preventing the spoilage of food by the action of micro-organisms. There is a permitted list for use in foods, the main two being *sulphur dioxide* and *benzoic acid*.

Preserves
A range of food products preserved by the osmotic effect of high sugar concentrations. Main examples are: jams, marmalades, conserves and candied fruit.

Proteins
Essential constituents of all cells, basically composed of carbon, hydrogen, oxygen and nitrogen. They are very large molecules built up of numerous combinations of *amino acids*. Proteins of high biological value contain all the essential amino acids.

Protopectin see *Pectin*

Pro-vitamin A
A *carotenoid* that can be converted in the body to vitamin A. Main examples include α-, β- and γ-carotenes. They must contain an intact *β-ionone ring* at the end(s) of their chain to qualify for pro-vitamin A activity.

Pyridoxine
Vitamin B6, involved in *amino acid* metabolism in most animals. Widely present in foods so deficiency does not usually occur.

Radiations see *Irradiation*

Rancidity
A chemical change in fats and oils brought about by either oxidation or hydrolysis. Leads to the production of odours and flavours (caused by aldehydes and ketones) associated with the deterioration of fat. In the case of *hydrolytic rancidity*, short chain free *fatty acids* produce the odour.
See *Hydrolytic rancidity* and *Oxidative rancidity*.

Rapid dough processes
The traditional dough process is accelerated by the use of mechanical mixing and oxidation. The dough structure is developed and fixed quickly. Little *fermentation* occurs relative to traditional processes. Main example: Chorleywood bread process.

Rapid-set pectin see *Pectin*

Reducing sugars
Sugars which contain a potential aldehyde group (–CHO). Some examples are: *glucose*, *maltose* and *lactose*. Some sugars, such as fructose, contain a ketone group but are still reducing sugars. Tested for by their ability to break down Fehling's solution.

Refrigerated sea water (RSW)

Used in some countries to chill freshly caught fish instead of using ice. Trawlers are equipped with plant to chill the sea water in vats.

Rennet

An extract from a calf's stomach. Can be produced from certain micro-organisms, eg *Mucor meihei* and *M. pusillus*.

Rennet contains mainly the *enzyme* chymosin (rennin) and some *pepsin*. It is responsible for coagulating milk during cheese-making, by breaking down the protective k-casein and allowing *calcium* and phosphate to gel with the *casein* (α_S).

Retinol

The name for vitamin A or more specifically vitamin A alcohol. *Carotenoids*, showing *pro-vitamin* A activity are converted to retinol in the body. An aldehyde version combines with a *protein* to produce visual purple needed for vision in poor light.

Deficiency causes night blindness, growth stunting and skin problems. Main sources are fish liver oils, liver, dairy products and margarine.

Retrogradation (of starch)

The reverse of gelatinisation, in that water is expelled from the gel. The *starch* gradually undergoes a colloidal change and tends to contract with the loss of water. Staling of bread involves retrogradation of starch and in this case can be reversed somewhat by reheating the loaf. Starches are stabilised or cross-linked to reduce retrogradation in processed foods.

Riboflavin

Vitamin B2, which is combined with *proteins* to form part of the enzyme systems essential for oxidation of *carbohydrate* and the release of energy.

Deficiency improves oxidation carried out within the cell, whilst other symptoms include swollen and cracked lips and enlarged tongue. It is found in milk, eggs, liver and pulses. It is also a useful food colour giving attractive yellow shade (E1O1).

Ribonucleotides

Formed from the sugar ribose, phosphoric acid and a base such as guanine or inosine. They are *flavour enhancers* and operate in a similar manner to *MSG*, with which they can be blended.

They are found naturally in yeast, fish and meat. Commercially ribonucleotides are produced by micro-organisms.

Rickets

The disease caused by a deficiency of *vitamin D. Calcium* absorption and bone formation is impaired leading to the bending of bones in the legs and other deformities. Vitamin D is found in fish liver oil and dairy products, and is synthesised in the skin as a result of sunlight.

Rigor mortis

The permanent contraction of animal muscle after death leading to rigidity in the carcass. The muscle *proteins*, actin and myosin, combine to produce actomyosin. The rigidity is lost after several hours due to the action of proteolytic *enzymes* breaking down the actomyosin.

Meat cooked whilst still in *rigor* is tougher and darker than that left until the rigidity has disappeared before cooking.

Ripening of cheese

Changes produced in 'green' cheese by *enzymes*, bacteria and moulds. Three general reactions are involved: fats are hydrolysed by proteolytic enzymes, and *amino acids* and *fatty acids* are released. These changes produce the flavour and texture of cheese; in well-matured cheese the reactions have been allowed to occur over a long period.

Ripening of fruit

Changes that occur after harvesting a mature fruit to produce a product ripe for eating or processing. *Polysaccharides* such as *pectin* and *starch* are broken down to produce sugars, so a softer, sweeter fruit results. *Chlorophyll* is broken down to reveal other *pigments* such as red *carotenoids* or new ones are synthesised. The fruit becomes juicier and acidity is masked by the production of sugars.

Ripeness is a variable term depending on the end-use of the fruit. Fruit for jam-making is usually under-ripe, with a high *pectin* content. Fruit for juice-making is fully ripe with *polysaccharides* such as pectin, well hydrolysed to sugars.

Roller drying see *Drying*

Roughage

A term used to mean dietary fibre, usually supplied as *cellulose*, *hemicellulose* and *pectin*. Basically roughage bulks up food and enables the intestines to function more easily.

Saccharin

An artificial sweetner, 550 times as sweet as *sucrose*. Chemically, *benzoic sulphimide*.

Salmonella

A genus of *gram negative* bacteria which are involved in many food poisoning outbreaks. They are found in many foods particularly poultry, meat and egg products. Typhoid, *S. typhi*, is a member of the genus.

Members of the genus are often given the name of the place where they were first discovered, eg *S. dublin*, *S. london*, *S. montevideo*. Some can survive refrigeration, but all are destroyed by adequate heating.

Screening

A method of size separation or sieving. Used for dry cleaning of foods and *sorting*.

'Sell-by' date

The last date of sale of the food, after which date it must be withdrawn from sale.

'Best before' date is the date up to which the food can normally be expected to retain its freshness.

Sequestrants

Substances which combine with metal ions. Examples include citric acid and EDTA (ethylene diamine tetracetic acid). Traces of metals can initiate *oxidative rancidity* and so the use of a sequestrant will prevent this.

Single cell proteins

Proteins produced by bacteria or fungi growing on, or *fermenting,* suitable substrates such as waste cereals.

Size reduction

A requirement for some processes that food materials be made smaller. Crystalline substances are reduced by rollers or hammer mills. Fibrous materials need to be cut, diced or shredded.

Slow-set pectin see *Pectin*

Smoking

Meat products and fish may be smoked to aid preservation and give flavour. Smoke from burning hardwoods gives the best flavour. The preservative effect comes from *phenols, acids* and aldehydes in the smoke. Smoking also causes surface dehydration of the product. In 'hot smoking' the fish is cooked at the same time as being smoked.

Solvent extraction

Solvents, such as petroleum ether, are used to extract *oils* from vegetable sources, particularly seeds. The solvent is then distilled off to leave a crude oil which needs refining.

Sorting

Separation of food raw materials according to one characteristic such as size, weight or colour. Often confused with *grading* or quality separation.

Spray drying see *Drying*

Stabilisers

Substances, often complex *polysaccharides*, that have the ability to absorb considerable quantities of water. This property makes them good thickening agents, many being able to produce gels. Most can act as *emulsifiers* and prevent fat separation. Examples are *gums, cellulose* derivatives and gelatine.

Star marking (frozen products)

Introduced in 1964 for frozen products and freezers. One star means a temperature of –6C and gives storage of one week. Two stars indicate a temperature of –12C with up to one month of storage. Three stars mean a temperature of –18C and up to three months of storage. Four stars on a freezer indicates an appliance capable of freezing food more rapidly, as well as storing frozen products.

Starch

A *polysaccharide* made from chains of α-glucose. Two forms exist: (a) *amylose* which is a straight chain in the form of a coil and (b) *amylopectin* which is a highly branched form. Starch exists as granules in food products which are unique in appearance and size for each product.

– Phosphate cross-bonded starch
  Starch treated with phosphoric acid to give the amylose fraction the appearance and properties of amylopectin. The result is a stable starch which does not retrograde (see Retrogradation) in canned or frozen products.

– Pre-gelatinised starches
  Starch is mixed with water and heated to produce a gel which is then dried. The dried starch thickens instantly on the addition of cold water or milk. Used extensively in instant products, particularly desserts.

Starter cultures

Special cultures of bacteria incubated under ideal conditions to be added to foods to start *fermentation*, particularly in wines, bread, yoghurt and cheese.
Lactic acid bacteria, *eg Lactococcus* and *Lactobacillus* species are commonly used.

Sterilisation

The achievement, usually by heating, of a complete absence of life (ie, micro-organisms). In reality this is difficult to achieve as a few heat-resistant spores usually survive. The concept of '*commercial stability*' is acceptable to industry where some spores survive but do not usually germinate or grow.

Sucrose

Common sugar, either from beet or cane. A *disaccharide* made from α-glucose and β-fructose. A *non-reducing sugar.*
Crude brown sugar is around 97% sucrose, white sugar is almost pure sucrose at 99.9% Sucrose is usually given a sweetness value of 100 and all other sugars are compared with this.

Sulphur dioxide

A permitted *preservative* use in many products. Usually added as sulphite or metabisulphite. Also protects vitamin C but destroys vitamin B1. Used in fruit products, sausages, wines and campden tablets.

Surfactants

Basically *emulsifiers.* Lower the surface tension (usually of water) between two immiscible liquids in a product, thus aiding emulsification.

Syneresis

Loss of liquid from a gel on standing or as a result of damage.

Tainting

The transfer of odours from one food to another or from packaging materials and diesel fumes. The problem is difficult to trace, particularly in frozen foods during cold storage.

Tannins
Phenolic compounds of very complex structure. Responsible for the astringency of red wines, tea, coffee and apples. They also give body and fullness to the flavour of the product.

Tartar (cream of)
Potassium hydrogen tartrate. A weak acid used with sodium hydrogen carbonate (bicarbonate of soda) in traditional *baking powders*. Can be found as a precipitate in wine barrels after several months or years of storage.

Tartaric acid
An acid containing two acid groups (–COOH), occurring in some plants, particularly grapes. Used to increase acidity of jams, lemonade and desserts.

Tartrazine
A yellow to orange colour of complex structure, an azo dye. It has been implicated in allergic reactions and as a cause of hyperactivity in children. Has been withdrawn from most products, but is still permitted in many countries (E102), and has been replaced with *carotenes*.

Tempering
A process in chocolate manufacture aimed at achieving a proper consistency and hardness in the product. The cocoa butter has to be in a stable, crystal form. The process consists of melting the chocolate, heating it to 49C (120F), and cooling it with agitation down to 24C (84F).

Terpenoids
Isoprenoid derivatives made from two isoprene units (C_5H_8). Found mainly in many naturally occurring *flavours*, particularly *essential oils*.

– Monoterpenoids
  Based on two isoprene units ($C_{10}H_{16}$) and are alcohols, aldehydes and ketones derived from these (see *Monoterpenes*).

– Diterpenoids
  Based on four isoprene units ($C_{20}H_{32}$) (see *Diterpenes*).

Tetrapyrrole derivatives
Composed of four pyrrole rings held together by methane bridges. The basic structure of *haemoglobin, myoglobin* and *chlorophyll*.

Textured vegetable protein (TVP)
Usually refers to soya *protein* which is produced from the soya bean and is defatted. The TVP is either extruded or spun into meat-like cubes. It must then be rehydrated before use. Nutritionally the product is good, but may be deficient in methionine.

Thiamin
Vitamin B1, is needed as part of a coenzyme; deficiency results in the disease *beri-beri*. Symptoms include heart enlargement, cardiac failure, sensory and gastric disorders. The vitamin is found in yeast, eggs, pulses and meat.

Tocopherols
A group of eight compounds which show *vitamin E* activity. Found in many foods, particularly wheat germ and vegetable oils. Deficiency is unusual, leading to blindness and anaemia. Tocopherols are natural *antioxidants*.

Deficiency in rats causes sterility which probably has led to exaggerated claims for the use of vitamin E in humans.

Triglycerides
Made from *glycerol* and three *fatty acids*. Mixed triglycerides contain three different fatty acids, simple triglycerides contain the same fatty acid. Mixed triglycerides are the basic constituents of natural fats.

Trimethylamine
The smell of bad fish. Produced from trimethylamine oxide by bacterial action in fish. Can be used as a measure of fish deterioration.

Ultra-high temperature UHT
High-temperature, short-time *sterilisation* of milk usually carried out in plate heat exchangers. UHT milk is usually called 'long-life' milk.

Uperisation
A sterilisation method employing direct injection of steam under pressure. Extensively used in Europe for producing UHT milk.

Uronic acids
Derivatives of sugars, with a carboxyl group (–COOH) at carbon atom six position. Examples, *galacturonic acid* (from *galactose*) which is a component of *pectin*.

Vitamins
Organic substances required in small quantities but cannot by synthesised by the body. Vitamins absent from, or low in the diet may result in deficiency disease which may be fatal if not remedied.

- Vitamin A see *Retinol*
- Vitamin B1 see *Thiamin*
- Vitamin B2 see *Riboflavin*
- Vitamin B6 see *Pyridoxine*
- Vitamin B12 see *Cyanocobalamin*
- Vitamin C see *Ascorbic acid*
- Vitamin D see *Calciferols*
- Vitamin E see *Tocopherols*
- Vitamin K see *Naphthoquinones*

Votator
A double tubular heat-exchanger consisting of one tube within another. The centre tube is usually chilled by a circulatory chilled brine. Used mainly in margarine manufacture to ensure emulsification and texture development.

Water activity (a_w)
The amount of water in a food can be described in terms of water activity (a_w). Levels of moisture are compared with pure water which has an a_w of 1·0. Preservation methods such as dehydration, concentration, the addition of salt and sugar, rely on lowering the water activity.

At a_w levels of 0·9 and above most bacteria grow readily. At levels of 0·85–0·9 yeasts tend to dominate. Moulds grow in the range 0·80–0·85. Halophilic bacteria (like salt) grow down at 0·75 and osmophilic yeasts (like sugar) at 0·6.

Waxes
Complex fatty materials, usually containing alcohols with long chains of carbon atoms. Found on the surface of some fruits, eg apples.

Wheat proteins
Known collectively as *gluten*. A blend of two main protein types gliadins (40–50%), and glutenins (40–50%) with small amounts of albumin, globulin and proteose. Responsible for the elasticity and extensibility of dough during bread-making.

Whey proteins
Proteins from milk after the removal of *casein*. Mainly comprise of α-lactalbumin and β-lactoglobulin. Can be concentrated or dried and used in foods for their functional properties such as: foaming ability, emulsification and texture modification.

Xanthan gum
High molecular weight natural polysaccharide. Produced by the bacterium *Xanthomonas campestris*. Many useful properties, eg thinning when agitated (thixotropic).

Xanthophylls
Carotenoid pigments that are yellow. They must contain an hydroxyl group (–OH). For example, cryptoxanthin, the chief *pigment* of maize, paprika and mandarin orange.

Xylose
A pentose sugar (five carbon atoms) found in plants, a main constituent of hemicelluloses.

Yeasts
Fungi which are usually involved in fermentation and spoilage of sweetened or salted products.

- *Saccharomyces cerevisiae* – used for bread and beer making
- *S. ellipsoideus* – used in wine making.

Yeasts are useful sources of *protein*, and B *vitamins*. Yeast extracts and hydrolysates are used as savoury flavours of soups and meat products.

Yolk index (of eggs)
An index of freshness for eggs. It is the ratio of the height of yolk to the diameter. The index decreases as the egg ages and deteriorates.

Zwitterion
An *amino acid* at the iso-electric point, the pH at which the net charge on the amino acid is zero. Usually one positive charge on the amino group is balanced by one negative charge on the carboxyl group. The solubility, viscosity and electrical conductivity of the amino acid are at a minimum in this form.

Index

(Page numbers in heavy type indicate the main references to a particular subject)

THE SCIENCE AND TECHNOLOGY OF
FOODS
FOURTH EDITION

EDEXCEL
AQA

Examination
Specification
Analysis
Guide

FORBES PUBLICATIONS

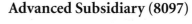

Advanced Subsidiary (8097)

Edexcel Advanced GCE Design and Technology

(Food Technology) (9097)

Information sources for the new specification. All technical food information will be available in the Science and Technology of Foods (Fourth Edition) by R K Proudlove (published by Forbes). Up to the minute social and consumer issues are covered in a number of publications and web sites. This text (publication) is designed to address the theoretical content of the above course. It does not, therefore, address the activities involved.

Subject	Book Reference	
	Section & Chapter	Page
F1 – Products and applications		
(a) Development of range of manufactured products	Section 5	243
(b) Form and function of different products	Section 5	269
(c) Trends, styles, new technical capabilities, and social, political and ethical influences on the design, production and sales of products		
Materials and components		
(a) The range of materials and their potential application		
– basic food materials	Section 1	1-91
– properties and functions	Section 1	1-91
– nutrients	Section 1	1-91
– additives	Section 1	1-91
b)Working characteristics of materials		
– Different hand and commercial methods of preparing, processing manipulating and combining materials to enhance their properties	Section 1	1-47
– Food energy and nutrients	Section 3	171
c)Functional properties		
– carbohydrates	Section 1 / Ch. 2	4-20
– fats (lipids)	Section 1 / Ch. 3	21-35
– proteins	Section 1 / Ch. 4	36-47
– colloidal systems		
– additives	Section 1 / Ch. 9	78-91
Industrial and commercial practice		
(a) Manufacturing systems.	Section 3	171-190
– understand how food products are manufactured		
(b) Stages of production	Section 4	219-226
– understanding stages of production		

Subject	Book Reference	
	Section & Chapter	Page
(c) Detailed manufacturing methods when combining or processing materials – cleaning, peeling, sorting, grading, size reduction, mixing, preservation processes.	Section 3	171-190
– removal of heat	Section 4	191-218
– pasteurisation, sterilisation, canning	Section 4	191-218
– removal of water	Section 4	191-218
– chemical methods	Section 4	191-218
– irradiation	Section 4	216-218
(d) Service to the customer, including legal requirements, availability of resources		
– good manufacturing practice	5	269-273
– risk assessment, HACCP	5	275-279
(e) Use of ICT systems in food manufacture	5	279-282
Quality Quality in terms of the product – quality assurance – specification		
Health and safety (a) The regulatory and legislative framework related to materials and equipment		
– hygiene	2	168-170
basic principles of microbiology	2	160-170
– food labelling requirements	5	230-231
(b) Standard risk assessment procedures in product design and manufacture		
– risk assessment	5	275-279
(c) Safe working practices		
F3 – Materials, components and systems with options **Section A : Classification of materials and equipment** – texture modifiers		
– colours	1	62-69
– flavours	1	70-77
– stabilising agents	1	85-86
– storage-life extenders		
Working properties of materials and components – texture modifiers		
– colours	1	62-69
– flavours	1	70-77
– stabilising agents	1	85-86
– storage-life extenders		
Food manufacture	1	31-33, 62-69, 70-77, 78-92
Testing materials		

Subject	Book Reference	
	Section & Chapter	Page
Section B : Option = Consumer product management	5	232-268
– consumer behaviour	5	233-236
– the consumer and society	5	236-243
– product design and development	5	243-248
– influence of retailers	5	248-255
Section B : Option = Food science		
Chemical aspects		
– carbohydrates	1	4-20
– fats and oils	1	21-35
– proteins	1	36-47
– other constituents	1	48-91
Microbiological considerations	1	160-170
Nutrition	1	160-170
F4 – Further study of materials, components and systems with options		
Section A		
Selection of materials		
New technologies and new materials		
Value issues		
Section B : Option = Consumer product management	5	232 268
– emerging trends	5	255-258
– marketing and market research	5	259-265
– financial aspects	5	265-268
Section B : Option = Food science	2	93-170
Chemical composition:		
– meat and fish	2	110-124
– dairy products	2	94-109
– fruit and vegetables	2	125-135
– cereals	2	136-148
Microbiological aspects	2	160-170

Assessment and Qualification Alliance (AQA)
Design and Technology : Food Technology

The book covers the three main areas of subject content to meet the needs of AS and AZ ;

A   Materials and Components
classification of materials; working properties; manipulation and combining
B   Design and Market Influences
developments in D&T; design in practice; design in the human context
C   Process and Manufacture
product manufacture; industrial practice; system and control

(The following sections give details where in the book the relevant subject details can be found. However, some subjects are found in a number of chapters so please also refer to the index).

Subject	Book Reference	
	Section & Chapter	Page
As section A Materials & Components		
Macro Nutrients:		
– proteins	Section 1 / Ch. 4	36-47
– lipids	Section 1 / Ch. 3	21-35
– carbohydrates	Section 1 / Ch. 2	4-20
Micronutrients:		
– vitamins	Section 1 / Ch. 6	52-61
– minerals	Section 1 / Ch. 5	48-51
Manipulating & combining materials		
– use of raw materials	Section 1 / Ch. 9	78-91
– pre-manufactured components		
– alternative ingredients		
– food additives	Section 1 / Ch. 9	78-91
As in Section B Design & market influences		
Development of Technologies and Design :		
– design sources for new products		
– product analysis	Section 5 / Ch. 1	228-231
– consumer trends	Section 5 / Ch. 2	232-268
– changes in lifestyle	Section 5 / Ch. 2	232-268
– regional & international influences	Section 5 / Ch. 2	232-268
– new processing techniques		
– storage and heat processing equipment	Section 3 / Ch. 1	172-175
(industrial)	Section 4 / Ch. 1	193-200
Role of research and development team	Section 5 / Ch. 2	232-268

Subject	Book Reference	
	Section & Chapter	Page
Design in practice:		
– product life cycles	Section 5 / Ch. 2	232-268
– product analysis	Section 5 / Ch. 1	228-231
– sensory evaluation techniques	Section 1 / Ch. 8	70-77
– qualitative & quantitative tests against quality of standards	Section 5 / Ch. 2	232-268
Stages in food product development		
– market research		
– generation of ideas	Section 5 / Ch. 3	269-282
– design specifications	Section 5 / Ch. 3	269-282
– test marketing	Section 5 / Ch. 3	269-282
– product launch	Section 5 / Ch. 3	269-282
Communication and representation of ideas	Section 5 / Ch. 3	269-282
Design methods	Section 5 / Ch. 3	269-282
Health & safety		
Food safety regulations		
– HACCP	Section 5 / Ch. 3	269-282
Communication methods		
– use of ICT	Section 5 / Ch. 3	269-282
Design in the human context		
– client/consumer groups	Section 5 / Ch. 3	269-282
– social/cultural factors	Section 5 / Ch. 3	269-282
– market trends	Section 5 / Ch. 3	269-282
– social trends & changes in lifestyle		
– nutritional theories	Section 5 / Ch. 3	269-282
– influence of design & technology in society	Section 5 / Ch. 3	269-282
As Section C **Processes & manufacture**		
Industrial & commercial practice		
– eg. size reduction	Section 3 / Ch. 3	171-184
– mixing	&	
– forming	Section 3 / Ch. 4	185-190
– filling		
Effects of micro-organisms and enzymes:	Section 2 / Ch. 7	160-170
– micro-organisms		
– classification		
– functions affecting growth		
– food spoilage		
– food hygiene		
– food storage		
– controlled atmosphere		
– packaging	Section 4 / Ch. 5	219-225